Keep this book. You will need it and use it throughout your career.

About the American Hotel & Lodging Association (AH&LA)

Founded in 1910, AH&LA is the trade association representing the lodging industry in the United States. AH&LA is a federation of state lodging associations throughout the United States with 11,000 lodging properties worldwide as members. The association offers its members assistance with governmental affairs representation, communications, marketing, hospitality operations, training and education, technology issues, and more. For information, call 202-289-3100.

LODGING, the management magazine of AH&LA, is a "living textbook" for hospitality students that provides timely features, industry news, and vital lodging information.

About the American Hotel & Lodging Educational Institute (EI)

An affiliate of AH&LA, the Educational Institute is the world's largest source of quality training and educational materials for the lodging industry. EI develops textbooks and courses that are used in more than 1,200 colleges and universities worldwide, and also offers courses to individuals through its Distance Learning program. Hotels worldwide rely on EI for training resources that focus on every aspect of lodging operations. Industry-tested videos, CD-ROMs, seminars, and skills guides prepare employees at every skill level. EI also offers professional certification for the industry's top performers. For information about EI's products and services, call 800-349-0299 or 407-999-8100.

About the American Hotel & Lodging Educational Foundation (AH&LEF)

An affiliate of AH&LA, the American Hotel & Lodging Educational Foundation provides financial support that enhances the stability, prosperity, and growth of the lodging industry through educational and research programs. AH&LEF has awarded millions of dollars in scholarship funds for students pursuing higher education in hospitality management. AH&LEF has also funded research projects on topics important to the industry, including occupational safety and health, turnover and diversity, and best practices in the U.S. lodging industry. For more information, go to www.ahlef.org.

The LODGING and FOOD SERVICE INDUSTRY

Eighth Edition

Educational Institute Books

UNIFORM SYSTEM OF ACCOUNTS FOR THE LODGING INDUSTRY
Tenth Revised Edition

WORLD OF RESORTS: FROM DEVELOPMENT TO MANAGEMENT
Third Edition
Chuck Yim Gee

PLANNING AND CONTROL FOR FOOD AND BEVERAGE OPERATIONS
Eighth Edition
Jack D. Ninemeier

UNDERSTANDING HOSPITALITY LAW
Fifth Edition
Jack P. Jefferies/Banks Brown

SUPERVISION IN THE HOSPITALITY INDUSTRY
Fifth Edition
Jack D. Ninemeier/Raphael R. Kavanaugh

MANAGEMENT OF FOOD AND BEVERAGE OPERATIONS
Fifth Edition
Jack D. Ninemeier

MANAGING FRONT OFFICE OPERATIONS
Ninth Edition
Michael L. Kasavana

MANAGING SERVICE IN FOOD AND BEVERAGE OPERATIONS
Fourth Edition
Ronald F. Cichy/Philip J. Hickey, Jr.

THE LODGING AND FOOD SERVICE INDUSTRY
Eighth Edition
Gerald W. Lattin/Thomas W. Lattin/James E. Lattin

SECURITY AND LOSS PREVENTION MANAGEMENT
Third Edition
David M. Stipanuk/Raymond C. Ellis, Jr.

HOSPITALITY INDUSTRY MANAGERIAL ACCOUNTING
Seventh Edition
Raymond S. Schmidgall

PURCHASING FOR FOOD SERVICE OPERATIONS
Ronald F. Cichy/Jeffery D Elsworth

MANAGING TECHNOLOGY IN THE HOSPITALITY INDUSTRY
Sixth Edition
Michael L. Kasavana

HOTEL AND RESTAURANT ACCOUNTING
Seventh Edition
Raymond Cote

ACCOUNTING FOR HOSPITALITY MANAGERS
Fifth Edition
Raymond Cote

CONVENTION MANAGEMENT AND SERVICE
Eighth Edition
Milton T. Astroff/James R. Abbey

HOSPITALITY SALES AND MARKETING
Fifth Edition
James R. Abbey

MANAGING HOUSEKEEPING OPERATIONS
Revised Third Edition
Aleta A. Nitschke/William D. Frye

HOSPITALITY TODAY: AN INTRODUCTION
Seventh Edition
Rocco M. Angelo/Andrew N. Vladimir

HOSPITALITY FACILITIES MANAGEMENT AND DESIGN
Third Edition
David M. Stipanuk

MANAGING HOSPITALITY HUMAN RESOURCES
Fifth Edition
Robert H. Woods, Misty M. Johanson, and Michael P. Sciarini

RETAIL MANAGEMENT FOR SPAS

HOSPITALITY INDUSTRY FINANCIAL ACCOUNTING
Third Edition
Raymond S. Schmidgall/James W. Damitio

INTERNATIONAL HOTELS: DEVELOPMENT & MANAGEMENT
Second Edition
Chuck Yim Gee

QUALITY SANITATION MANAGEMENT
Ronald F. Cichy

HOTEL INVESTMENTS: ISSUES & PERSPECTIVES
Fifth Edition
Edited by Lori E. Raleigh and Rachel J. Roginsky

LEADERSHIP AND MANAGEMENT IN THE HOSPITALITY INDUSTRY
Third Edition
Robert H. Woods/Judy Z. King

MARKETING IN THE HOSPITALITY INDUSTRY
Fifth Edition
Ronald A. Nykiel

UNIFORM SYSTEM OF ACCOUNTS FOR THE HEALTH, RACQUET AND SPORTSCLUB INDUSTRY

CONTEMPORARY CLUB MANAGEMENT
Third Edition
Edited by Joe Perdue and Jason Koenigsfeld for the Club Managers Association of America

RESORT CONDOMINIUM AND VACATION OWNERSHIP MANAGEMENT: A HOSPITALITY PERSPECTIVE
Robert A. Gentry/Pedro Mandoki/Jack Rush

ACCOUNTING FOR CLUB OPERATIONS
Raymond S. Schmidgall/James W. Damitio

TRAINING AND DEVELOPMENT FOR THE HOSPITALITY INDUSTRY
Debra F. Cannon/Catherine M. Gustafson

UNIFORM SYSTEM OF FINANCIAL REPORTING FOR CLUBS
Sixth Revised Edition

HOTEL ASSET MANAGEMENT: PRINCIPLES & PRACTICES
Second Edition
Edited by Greg Denton, Lori E. Raleigh, and A. J. Singh

MANAGING BEVERAGE OPERATIONS
Second Edition
Ronald F. Cichy/Lendal H. Kotschevar

FOOD SAFETY: MANAGING WITH THE HACCP SYSTEM
Second Edition
Ronald F. Cichy

UNIFORM SYSTEM OF FINANCIAL REPORTING FOR SPAS

FUNDAMENTALS OF DESTINATION MANAGEMENT AND MARKETING
Edited by Rich Harrill

ETHICS IN THE HOSPITALITY AND TOURISM INDUSTRY
Second Edition
Karen Lieberman/Bruce Nissen

SPA: A COMPREHENSIVE INTRODUCTION
Elizabeth M. Johnson/Bridgette M. Redman

HOSPITALITY 2015: THE FUTURE OF HOSPITALITY AND TRAVEL
Marvin Cetron/Fred DeMicco/Owen Davies

REVENUE MANAGEMENT: MAXIMIZING REVENUE IN HOSPITALITY OPERATIONS
Gabor Forgacs

FINANCIAL MANAGEMENT FOR SPAS
Raymond S. Schmidgall/John R. Korpi

11/13

The LODGING and FOOD SERVICE INDUSTRY

Eighth Edition

Gerald W. Lattin
Thomas W. Lattin
James E. Lattin

American
Hotel & Lodging
Educational Institute

Disclaimer

This publication is designed to provide accurate and authoritative information in regard to the subject matter covered. It is sold with the understanding that the publisher is not engaged in rendering legal, accounting, or other professional service. If legal advice or other expert assistance is required, the services of a competent professional person should be sought.

> —*From the Declaration of Principles jointly adopted by the American Bar Association and a Committee of Publishers and Associations.*

The authors, Gerald W. Lattin, Thomas W. Lattin, and James E. Lattin, are solely responsible for the contents of this publication. All views expressed herein are solely those of the authors and do not necessarily reflect the views of the American Hotel & Lodging Educational Institute (the Institute) or the American Hotel & Lodging Association (AH&LA).

Nothing contained in this publication shall constitute a standard, an endorsement, or a recommendation of the Institute or AH&LA. The Institute and AH&LA disclaim any liability with respect to the use of any information, procedure, or product, or reliance thereon by any member of the hospitality industry.

Editor: Peter Morris

Contents

Preface

THE OBJECTIVES AND PURPOSE of this book are to provide an introduction to the lodging and food service industry, to explain the complex interrelationships involved in the business, and to stress the variety of career opportunities available. People who will benefit from this book include those working in the industry, those entering or thinking of entering the industry, hospitality program educators, career guidance counselors, hospitality industry suppliers, and of course hospitality students.

This eighth edition of *The Lodging and Food Service Industry* updates numerous charts and graphs to keep pace with an industry that often changes rapidly. Similarly, the discussion of many procedures, formulas, key statistics, and sales tools has been updated. Special importance is given to the ever-expanding role of the Internet in hospitality operations and on customer interactions.

We would like to express our special appreciation to renowned hospitality executive Mr. Jim Reed for his insights and to Ms. Alexis Hoey for her assistance in updating the new exhibits. We would also like to thank the staff of the Educational Institute for all of their efforts.

In the spring of 2013, Dr. Lattin passed away at the venerable age of 92. His encouragement and direct assistance on the early stages of this edition were very important and have been incorporated in the text. Your coauthors dedicate this book to our parents, Dr. Gerald and Mrs. Jean Lattin. They both worked very hard, and made many personal sacrifices to ensure that all of their children were well educated and fully instilled with their spiritual beliefs. Through all phases of our careers, they were always there to assist, inspire, and guide us.

Our parents have also served as role models and advisors to countless students of hospitality. The results of their efforts can be seen in the successes of many active and retired hospitality executives. We hope this book will help many more people understand, appreciate, and succeed in their pursuit of a career in hospitality management.

James E. Lattin and Thomas W. Lattin

About the Authors ...

Dr. Gerald W. Lattin

Thomas W. Lattin

James E. Lattin

Dr. Gerald W. Lattin passed away in April 2013 after fifty-plus years of imparting knowledge and wisdom to students and hospitality professionals while serving as a distinguished professor at universities in the United States and overseas. He also offered his expertise to the industry through his consulting firm, Lattin and Associates.

During his long and varied hospitality career, he served as administrator and faculty member at three of the nation's most prestigious hospitality management schools. He was a faculty member and associate dean at Cornell University's School of Hotel Administration for twenty-five years; founding dean of Florida International University's School of Hospitality Management for twelve years; and dean of the Conrad N. Hilton College of Hotel and Restaurant Management, University of Houston, for four years. Noted throughout the industry for combining his practical experience with classroom theory, Dr. Lattin taught many of today's industry leaders.

Among the many honors and awards Dr. Lattin received from both the hospitality industry and the field of education are the H. B. Meek Award, NIFI College of Diplomates; Florida International University Distinguished Service Award; the Stephenson Fletcher Memorial Lifetime Achievement Award; the AH&LA Lamp of Knowledge; and honorary memberships in the Club Managers Association of America and the In-flight Food Service Association.

Dr. Lattin served as President and Chairman of the Council on Hotel, Restaurant and Institutional Education (CHRIE). He wrote three textbooks as well as numerous articles for the trade press. He organized and taught hospitality seminars on every continent of the world except Antarctica, and was the co-founder of the In-flight Food Service Association. He served on the boards of several leading hospitality companies and participated actively in hotel, restaurant, travel, and club management associations.

Thomas W. Lattin currently serves as a Professor at the Conrad N. Hilton College of Hotel and Restaurant Management, University of Houston. He also provides consulting services to the hospitality industry.

Prior to his current positions, Mr. Lattin served as Global Leader—Hospitality Industry for PricewaterhouseCoopers; President and Chief Operating Officer of Patriot American Hospitality, Inc.; Senior Vice President of Paine Webber's REIT Division; Partner in Coopers & Lybrand's National Hospitality Group; National Partner and Chairman of Laventhol & Horwath's International Hotel Group; and President of Mariner Corporation, a hotel management and development company.

Tom holds both Bachelor of Science and Master of Science degrees from the School of Hotel Administration, Cornell University, and is a Certified Public Accountant and General Securities Registered Representative.

Mr. Lattin has lectured at Cornell, Michigan State University, Florida International University, and the Centre Internationale de Glion. He has also spoken at numerous hospitality industry conferences and seminars. He has been a frequent contributor to *Hotel & Motel Management* magazine and *Hotel Executive* magazine, and has published papers in the *Cornell Hotel and Restaurant Administration Quarterly*. He is the coauthor of *Hospitality Financial Management.*

James E. Lattin has enjoyed a wide range of hospitality industry work experience spanning over thirty years. He has held executive positions with Marriott, Doubletree, H.E.I. Hotels, Boykin Management Company, and the Dow Hotel Company. His positions have enabled him to work on four continents.

Mr. Lattin has lectured at major schools of hospitality management in the United States as well as in Switzerland and Guam. He resides in Elmira, New York, where he now assists a number of companies in sales and marketing development.

Mr. Lattin holds a Bachelor of Arts degree from Hamilton College, Clinton, New York, and a Master of Arts degree from Florida Atlantic University in Boca Raton, Florida.

Part I

The World of Hospitality

Chapter 1 Outline

Why People Travel
Where People Travel
Economic and Other Impacts of Tourism
Ecotourism/Adventure Travel
Energy Costs

Competencies

1. Explain why people travel, and identify internal ("push") factors and external ("pull") factors that influence their decisions to travel. (pp. 4–8)

2. Identify where people travel, and describe requirements that destinations must satisfy to support travel and tourism. (pp. 8–9)

3. Describe economic and other factors that affect international, national, and local travel and tourism. (pp. 9–13)

4. Explain what the term "ecotourism" means. (pp. 13–18)

5. Describe how the rising cost of fossil fuels is affecting the travel and tourism industry. (p. 18)

1

The Travel and Tourism Industry in Perspective

IN OUR STUDY of the hospitality industry, we will focus on two of its important segments: lodging and food service operations. But first we need to learn something about the larger enterprise of which hospitality is a part: the travel and tourism industry. What is the travel and tourism industry? What different businesses does it comprise?

The travel and tourism industry includes a vast range of businesses that have one thing in common: providing products and services to travelers. Businesses offering transportation, accommodations, food, drink, shopping, entertainment, recreation, and other hospitality services are all part of the travel and tourism industry.

Many of these businesses also provide products and services to people from the community as well as to travelers. Few food service enterprises could succeed without significant business from community members, while lodging properties usually rely on the traveling public to a greater extent. In this respect, hospitality operations are like retail stores, sporting events, or local festivals—all cater to both the traveling and non-traveling public. They are all "partners" in the travel and tourism industry.

Exhibit 1 is an overview of the travel and tourism industry. Note that the industry is divided into five general categories, according to the services offered. Lodging operations offer sleeping accommodations. Food and beverage operations offer food and beverage service. Transportation services enable tourists to travel to a destination. Retail shops of all sorts, ranging from roadside markets to vast shopping malls with hundreds of stores, offer travelers almost every product imaginable. Finally, a variety of business and entertainment activities are available to the traveling public. There can be considerable overlap in these categories—for example, many lodging operations have food and beverage services, gift shops, and recreational activities on site, and some offer limited transportation services. Likewise, cruise ships and resorts could reasonably be listed under all five categories.

Second in size only to transportation services, the hospitality industry comprises the lodging and food and beverage operations from the categories in Exhibit 1. In addition, there is another segment of food and beverage service typically classified as part of the hospitality industry that does not cater to the traveling public. Institutional (nonprofit) food services are offered in health care and educational facilities, in business offices and industrial plants, in the military, in correctional

Exhibit 1   Overview of the Travel and Tourism Industry

Travel and Tourism Industry				
Lodging Operations	**Food and Beverage Operations**	**Transportation Services**	**Retail Stores**	**Activities**
Hotels	Restaurants	Ships	Gift Shops	Recreation
Motels	Lodging Properties	Airplanes	Souvenir Shops	Business
Resorts	Retail Stores	Autos	Arts/Crafts Shops	Entertainment
Camps	Vending	Buses	Shopping Malls	Meetings
Parks	Catering	Trains	Markets	Study Trips
Pensions	Snack Bars	Bikes	Miscellaneous Stores	Sporting Events
Inns	Cruise Ships	Limousines		Ethnic Festivals
Bed & Breakfasts	Bars/Taverns			Art Festivals
	Food Courts			Cultural Events
				Seasonal Festivals

facilities, in seminaries, and by charitable organizations. These institutional food service operations use the same management principles as those used in their commercial counterparts.

Why People Travel

The travel and tourism industry is growing quickly. Contributing to this growth is the fact that many people have more leisure time available, and they often see traveling as an attractive leisure time activity. People travel more as their average work week decreases, as their amounts of vacation leave and holiday time increase, and as their real income and disposable income levels increase. People working in professional occupations and those over 55 years of age are more likely to travel.

Comfortable, convenient, and fast travel as we know it today has come into being only since the 1940s. However, people have always traveled. Prehistoric nomadic tribes traveled, seeking food or safety. Throughout history, people have traveled in order to fight wars, to spread ideological, religious, or political views, and simply to explore unknown areas. The "modern" era of travel began almost 3,000 years ago when money became a popular medium of exchange. Traders and other businesspeople began to travel in efforts to discover and bring back products to sell in their own lands.

Today, travel is commonplace in the lives of many people, especially Americans. Many businesspeople think nothing of flying from Chicago to New York City for a business meeting and returning the same day. Vacation packages offered by airlines and hotels provide great incentives for businesspeople to mix business travel with pleasure or for families to take annual vacations that would have been "dream" vacations only a few years ago.

Furthermore, pleasure travel is not just for the rich or near-rich anymore. This is due in part to the widespread use and acceptance of credit cards. Credit cards allow people to charge some or all of their vacation—transportation, accommodations, food, even souvenirs—and to pay for it later, either all at once or a little at

Insider Insights

J. T. Kuhlman
President and CEO
One&Only Resorts
Plantation, Florida

Talent, languages, long hours, and a willingness to pack bags often are just some of the ingredients necessary to succeed as a manager in the international hospitality industry. In today's increasingly competitive market, with more people traveling internationally for business and pleasure every year, enthusiasm and old-fashioned hotelier skills are no longer enough. As companies become more global in terms of the people they recruit, the markets in which they operate, and the customers they serve, ambitious employees will need to equip themselves with the business and professional skills necessary to run highly complex, global operations.

Certainly there can be no compromise on the basics—the successful general manager of a hotel should, first and foremost, be a great hotelier. General managers tend to develop their careers by experience, typically following an operational education in, for example, food and beverage, with an apprenticeship building on the educational area. As they rise in the ranks and gain responsibility, a broader business education is usually ad hoc and often dependent on opportunity and personal interest.

The focus in the past has been on delivering a quality product, and service staff and managers were selected primarily on their ability to achieve this objective. The challenge of the future is to maintain all the skills of being a fine hotelier while combining them with the business skills necessary to run a major asset like a hotel.

Today a hotel can be worth several hundred million dollars—large enough to be listed as a separate company on most stock exchanges around the world. To manage such a large asset, a general manager must possess a high level of business skills: the financial skills necessary to manage the assets, the marketing skills required to position and promote the product, and the leadership skills needed to motivate, communicate, and set goals for a large, labor-intensive organization.

Climbing the career ladder often entails making big sacrifices. You must be prepared to uproot yourself and your family every two or three years to move to a different country, not always of your choice. This may require learning a new language or acquiring new skills. You will be expected to work long, often irregular hours, including holidays and weekends. Time spent with your family may be scarce and often subject to last-minute changes. To succeed in this business, you will need perseverance, tolerance, and an ability to think clearly and bounce back in sometimes difficult circumstances.

If you have read this far and are still interested in pursuing a career in the international hotel industry, you are probably the type of go-ahead person this industry needs. The work is certainly challenging, but the rewards can be equally tremendous. With the opportunity to travel extensively and work in many countries around the world, the hotel business offers the chance to experience a wide range of different jobs and acquire an impressive catalog of skills. Compensation

(continued)

Insider Insights *(continued)*

and benefits are highly competitive, and career prospects can offer enormous responsibility at an increasingly early age. As the general manager of a hotel, you will effectively be running your own business — with all the financial and operating problems and rewards that such an entrepreneurial challenge entails — conceivably before you are forty.

After starting work in the international field, I realized that I needed a solid foundation; so, at the age of twenty-seven, I went back to school and graduated from Florida International University in 1975. Over the years, I have had the opportunity to work in many different countries around the world. I have met wonderful people and have become a local citizen of many fascinating cultures.

Despite the usual highs and lows common to the development of all careers, I can honestly say that there has never been a day in my career that I have regretted choosing this challenging and exciting profession. I hope this will be true for all of you.

a time. In addition, credit cards provide an easier way to handle vacation spending. They are more secure from theft than cash and more convenient than traveler's checks. For these reasons, both business and pleasure travel have increased dramatically.

One writer has suggested that there are both internal and external motivating factors that influence the desire to travel.[1]

Internal factors, which motivate one by creating an internal desire to travel, are referred to as "push" elements. For example, some people see travel as a way to maintain or improve their health; spas and health resorts may be destinations for these individuals. People also travel out of curiosity; they wish to experience new people, places, and cultures. Likewise, the desire to participate in or view sports is an important motivator for many. Obviously, some people travel for pleasure. For others, spiritual or religious concerns provide an incentive. Professional and business needs can motivate travel decisions. The desire to visit one's friends, relatives, and/or homeland is another travel incentive. Even prestige — traveling for the purpose of impressing others — is a common reason for travel. When people want to be among the first to visit an exotic destination or to view sights made famous because of current news events, prestige may be a factor in their travel decisions.

External factors, or "pull" elements, attract travelers to specific areas once their desire to travel has been generated. A destination's culture, history, and tradition are attractions to many travelers. Geography, wildlife, entertainment, cuisine, and climate are other major attractions. Some people travel to view architecture. Some people travel to shop. Many destinations are known for certain goods, such as Hong Kong suits, Irish crystal, Mexican leather. Others shop for collectibles as a hobby. Some prefer to travel just for the sake of travel and may "collect" countries in much the same way that others collect postage stamps.

Egypt and the picturesque Nile River are popular destinations for those who like to visit exotic places. Above is the Aswan Oberoi, situated in the winter resort of Aswan on Elephantine Island in the Nile. (Photo courtesy of Oberoi Hotels International)

Some travelers enjoy the travel more than the destination. Cruise ships, first-class air travel, chartered bus trips, and private railcars are examples of travel modes that emphasize pleasurable transportation. Some people travel primarily because they enjoy preparing for a trip (such as learning about a country before visiting it) or because they enjoy the memories of a trip after it has concluded.

There are many other factors affecting where and why people travel. Consider, for example, the increase in travel when airfares decrease or when airlines wage price wars in their competition for business. Pleasure travel is often dominated by cost concerns; more people will travel to places that give them the best value for their vacation dollars. People traveling for business usually do not have this flexibility. They are traveling for business-related purposes and must be at a specific destination at a specific time.

Some attention should be given to reasons people do not travel. There are people who cannot afford to travel. There are people who do not travel for psychological reasons—they feel uncomfortable in strange surroundings and have security-related concerns that reduce their travel interests. Many people avoid all but essential travel during times of international tension, in the aftermath of terrorist attacks, and during actual wars. Some feel they do not have time to travel. Owners and managers of small businesses frequently cite this reason. Others do not travel because of family circumstances. They may, for example, be responsible for a family member who is ill, or they may have small children who make traveling more difficult. People with disabilities may be frustrated with barriers that prevent them from enjoying some travel destinations.

Factors like these can reduce travel, because people facing such obstacles may not realize that many businesses in the travel and tourism industry are willing and able to meet their needs. For example, many lodging operations have weekend packages that allow guests to "escape" without leaving their own community. Campgrounds and mobile homes provide opportunities for people with young children to enjoy a relatively inexpensive family vacation. More and more, tourism operations are working to accommodate the needs of people with disabilities. The Americans with Disabilities Act, first adopted in 1990 and subsequently amended and broadened in 2008, has accelerated the elimination of barriers frustrating people with disabilities.

People travel for a wide variety of reasons. Catering to the wants and needs of such a diverse traveling market requires a significant variety of businesses. For example, some hotels cater to the very rich, while others are marketed to people seeking clean, inexpensive accommodations. Retail shops, transportation companies, and other tourism-related businesses offer products and services that differentiate among tourists based upon the reasons they travel and the needs they have as they travel.

Where People Travel

Where do travelers go? We have stated that pleasure travelers usually have more leeway in making their travel plans than those needing to conduct business. This added discretion means that tourists can reject locations that do not meet specific requirements. Business travelers often cannot do this, though we should note that many businesses decide to locate in areas that are attractive in their own right.

The requirements imposed by tourists on prospective destinations fall into five basic categories.[2]

- Natural resources—A destination must have natural resources available for visitors. Examples of natural resources that may be important to travelers include climate, geography, plants and animals, access to water, beauty of the surrounding area, and other factors that make the natural environment pleasing and hospitable.

- Infrastructure—The **infrastructure** consists of underground or surface construction necessary to service travelers and tourists, as well as the local population. Examples include systems for water, sewage, gas, electricity, and communication. Highways, airports, railroads, parking lots, lighting systems, boat and dock facilities, or any appropriate combination of these services must typically be available (though some travelers may enjoy more exotic destinations that lack these basics).

- Superstructure—The **superstructure** consists of major above-ground facilities that are serviced by the infrastructure and that help make a destination attractive. Hotels, shopping and entertainment centers, museums, and other attractions are examples of superstructure.

- Transportation and related equipment—The physical means for travel, such as automobiles, airplanes, boats, or trains, must be readily accessible.

- Hospitality resources—The cultural wealth of the destination is often important to the success of the tourism industry in that community. The spirit of hospitality shown by the government, businesspeople, and area residents is very important. Cultural resources such as the area's arts, literature, music, and drama frequently contribute to tourism success within a specific area.

Lodging and food and beverage operations are an integral part of a destination. The traveling public needs places to eat and sleep. Most tourists will not go to a destination lacking hospitality facilities. Many tourists specifically want to experience accommodations and cuisine characteristic of an area. For example, thatched-roof huts on a Polynesian island and a temple atmosphere in India may be among expectations of travelers to those destinations. Similarly, travelers may expect fresh seafood in a gulf-coast restaurant and prime steak in a hotel dining room in Omaha or Denver. Decor, table appointments, and employee uniforms also frequently reflect the area within which the hospitality operation is located.

Economic and Other Impacts of Tourism

A conglomerate consisting of many large and varied industries, tourism in its entirety has long been considered the world's largest industry. With sales in the trillions, tourism most certainly is a significant contributor to the world's domestic product and a major provider of jobs throughout the world.[3]

An important factor in international tourism is **globalization**. This refers both to the increasing ease with which people can travel all over the world, and to the trend of major corporations, such as large hotel chains or franchise restaurants, to expand their operations into countries all over the world. Globalization is having a particularly strong impact on developing countries, where new tourism can quickly and significantly affect the local economy.

According to a World Tourism Organization document titled "Tourism Toward 2030," despite decades of shocks and disasters ranging from man-made crises to natural calamities and economic devastations, tourism always seems to rebound and grow. Our desire and need to travel is a powerful force! The document predicts that the number of international travelers will increase by a staggering 43 million per year during the years leading up to 2030.

Of course it is true that the preponderance of international travelers come and go within Europe (with its many countries in close proximity to each other), North America, and the leading economies of North Asia. Nonetheless, the next two decades will see significant growth in travel to less developed destinations in Asia, Latin America, Eastern and Central Europe, and parts of Africa. Tourism has truly become a global phenomenon; by 2010 it represented fully 5 percent of the world's GDP and one in every twelve jobs globally. Exhibit 2 lists the world's top tourist destinations.

Europe can expect to continue to lead as the top international destination, but its overall share of the total should decrease as Asia and the other emerging markets cited above will outpace the growth rates to Europe and North America. This

Exhibit 2   The World's Top Tourist Destinations

2010 Rank	Country	# of Arrivals (Millions) 2009	2010	% Change 2010/2009	% Total 2010
1	France	76.8	76.8	0.0%	8.2%
2	United States	55.0	59.8	8.8%	6.4%
3	China	50.9	55.7	9.4%	5.9%
4	Spain	52.2	52.7	1.0%	5.6%
5	Italy	43.2	43.6	0.9%	4.6%
6	United Kingdom	29.2	28.1	-0.2%	3.0%
7	Turkey	25.5	27.0	5.9%	2.9%
8	Germany	24.2	26.9	10.9%	2.9%
9	Malaysia	23.6	24.6	3.9%	2.6%
10	Mexico	21.5	22.4	4.4%	2.4%
	World Total	**882.0**	**940.0**	**6.6%**	**100.0%**

Source: U.S. Travel Association, *Economic Review of Travel in America: 2010–2011 Edition* (Washington, D.C.: Author, 2011).

is encouraging news for third-world and newly emerging economies as tourism is a proven antidote to poverty. Nations that commit to a strong infrastructure for tourism will see significant growth in jobs.

In terms of outbound travel, by 2030 it is expected that Asia-Pacific will be the region with the largest percentage of growth, especially if the economic juggernaut which is China continues to expand and become more liberal about permitting broad cross-sections of its citizens to freely travel abroad. That being said, Europe will continue to lead in actual numbers of outbound international travel. Air travel is expected to continue its dominance as mode of choice for international travel and may exceed 50 percent of all such travel for the first time by 2030.

Purpose of travel is an interesting category and one travel professionals study keenly to understand what brings visitors to specific destinations. The main categories here are family/religious/health, leisure/holiday, and business/professional. We also learn from "Tourism Toward 2030" that each of these broad categories is expected to increase by 3–4 percent annually through 2030. Leisure/holiday will represent 54 percent, family/religious/health 31 percent, and business/professional 15 percent. Thus countries seeking to bolster inbound travel will be wise to invest in projects that will entice leisure travelers to visit.

Now we will take a look at the impact of travel specifically to the United States. An American Hotel & Lodging Association (AHLA) document titled "2012 Profile Report" shows travel and tourism to be a significant contributor to the economy of nearly every state in the union. In fact in 48 of 50 states tourism is among the top 10 industries. A whopping 1.8 million workers are employed in hotels alone, while fully 7.5 million jobs are directly supported by tourism. Nonetheless, historically the travel and tourism industry has been seemingly unappreciated by state and federal governments. The United States is the only developed country in the world without a national travel office and federal spending to support tourism ranks the country in the bottom 10 percent of industrialized nations. Fortunately, the Internet has made it possible for destinations to promote themselves effectively and affordably. The top ten U.S. cities and states earning international dollars are shown in Exhibit 3. Exhibit 4 shows the top ten state travel budgets.

Exhibit 3   Top U.S. Destinations for International Travelers

Rank	Cities	States/Territories
1	New York City	New York
2	Los Angeles	California
3	Miami	Florida
4	San Francisco	Nevada
5	Las Vegas	Hawaiian Islands
6	Orlando	Massachusetts
7	Washington, DC	Texas
8	Honolulu	Illinois
9	Boston	Guam
10	Chicago	New Jersey

Adapted from U.S. Department of Commerce, Office of Travel and Tourism Industries, "Overseas Visitation Estimates for U.S. States, Cities, and Census Regions: 2011" (Washington, D.C.: Author).

Exhibit 4   Top State Travel Budgets

Rank	State	Budget
1	Hawaii	$74,971,500
2	California	$61,356,500
3	Illinois	$54,618,700
4	Florida	$38,039,740
5	Texas	$35,733,678
6	Michigan	$27,440,000
7	Montana	$17,810,123
8	Virginia	$15,853,763
9	Connecticut	$15,853,763
10	Wisconsin	$15,094,000

Source: U.S. Travel Association, *2011–2012 Survey of U.S. State Tourism Office Budgets* (Washington, D.C.: Author, 2012).

Within the United States, business travel represents 40 percent of all hotel visits, with the balance made up by the family/religious/health and leisure/holiday segments. As the 2012 travel profile demonstrates, there are significant differences between business and non-business travel. For example, 67 percent of business travel is made by males, while other forms of travel are evenly divided between men and women. In addition, business travel generates a $130 per night average room rate, which is more than $20 higher than for non-business travel.

As shown in Exhibit 5, the U.S. remains the world's top tourism earner. Despite such obstacles as economic downturns, natural disasters, and the ever-present threat of terrorism, the United States accounts for 11.3 percent of the world's tourism revenues, which is nearly double the share of its closest competitor (Spain). For many years, the U.S. economy suffered from a **balance of payments** deficit. The balance of payments is the difference between the amount of money that leaves a country and the amount that enters it. When the amount that leaves exceeds the amount that enters a country, it is called a balance of payments deficit. However, since 1989, the United States has enjoyed a positive tourism balance of payments (see Exhibit 6), while the number of international visitors to the U.S. has increased annually since 2002. In 2010, China realized the highest percentage increase in inbound travelers and the AHLA's 2012 travel profile expects this trend to continue.

The AHLA projects that by 2016 spending by international visitors may be as high as 25 percent of all U.S. spending. Of course several factors must always be considered when projecting spending and visitor number increases. In particular, caution must be exercised in light of:

- Currency exchange rates—A relatively weak U.S. dollar is always favorable for international visitors.

Exhibit 5   World's Top Tourism Earners

2010 Rank	Country	Receipts (US $ Billions) 2009	Receipts (US $ Billions) 2010	% Change 2010/2009	% Total 2010
1	United States	$94.2	$103.5	9.9%	11.3%
2	Spain	53.2	52.5	-1.3%	5.7%
3	France	49.4	46.3	-6.3%	5.0%
4	China	39.7	45.9	15.4%	5.0%
5	Italy	40.2	38.8	-3.5%	4.2%
6	Germany	34.7	34.7	0.0%	3.8%
7	United Kingdom	30.1	30.4	1.0%	3.3%
8	Australia	25.4	30.1	19.5%	3.3%
9	Hong Kong (China)	16.5	23.0	39.4%	25.0%
10	Turkey	21.3	20.8	-2.3%	2.3%
	World Total	**851.0**	**940.0**	**6.6%**	**100.0%**

Source: U.S. Travel Association, *Economic Review of Travel in America: 2010–2011 Edition* (Washington, D.C.: Author, 2011).

Exhibit 6   U.S. Tourism Balance of Payments

Year	Travel to U.S. Receipts (billions)	U.S. Travel Abroad (billions)	Balance of Payments (billions)
2010	$919	$103.5	$815.5
2009	851	94.2	756.8
2008	939	110.4	828.6
2007	856	97.4	758.6
2006	743	86.2	656.8
2005	679	82.2	596.8
2000	475	82.9	392.1

Source: U.S. Travel Association, *Economic Review of Travel in America: 2010–2011 Edition* (Washington, D.C.: Author, 2011).

- Terrorism—The terrorist acts of September 11, 2001, significantly slowed the growth of international visits to the United States for several years. Any new instance of such attacks could again be expected to reduce visits and spending.

- Economic conditions—Should the robust economies of China, Russia, and Germany slow down, travel to relatively expensive destinations like the U.S. may likewise decrease.

- Availability and cost of fossil fuels—To date, the steadily increasing cost of petroleum-based fuels has not measurably slowed down the growth of tourism. However, should the cost of jet fuel rise dramatically, then tourism to places like the United States, which depend to a high degree on visits by air, would likely drop.

No discussion of the magnitude of the tourism industry would be complete without a mention of the **ripple effect**. The ripple effect is the economic boost that non-tourism industries receive as a result of the tourism industry. Though economists disagree over the extent of the ripple effect, all agree that the hospitality industry can help other businesses in a geographic area. Some authorities estimate that for every tourist dollar spent in lodging properties, three tourist dollars are spent elsewhere in the community.

Ecotourism/Adventure Travel

It is increasingly apparent that tourism can cause serious environmental consequences to an area, especially a relatively pristine or unusual area that attracts tourism. In his book *Tourism: A Community Approach*, Peter Murphy writes, "A paradox of tourism is that the industry carries within itself the seeds of its own destruction. Successful development can lead to the destruction of those very qualities which attracted visitors in the first place."[4] The result is that the fastest-growing segment of the tourism industry is one characterized by a new approach to tourism that avoids harming or destroying the natural or normal environment.

Insider Insights

Mr. Eric Pfeffer
Chairman and CEO (Retired)
Cendant Hotel Division _____

The wise man who once said, "Time is money," might today be tempted to say, "Time is more valuable than money." Hardly a week passed during my tenure as chairman and chief executive officer of Cendant's Hotel Division that I didn't wish for an extra hour or two—or even just fifteen minutes—and would have been willing to pay for it!

With demands for our time far outstripping supply, the environment hardly is conducive to sacrificing precious minutes and hours. But that's precisely what I believe executives should—and must—do in order to develop the next generation of leaders. There is a popular term for what I am advocating: mentoring.

Mentoring can be defined simply as "sharing." It is the sharing of lessons learned and of insight and wisdom gained from years in the trenches. The tricky part of mentoring is doing it, because the process must be deliberate, thoughtful, and interactive. In other words, mentors must devote time—and lots of it—to be effective.

I believe strongly in mentoring because I benefited firsthand, from teachers and bosses who took the time and made the effort to share their knowledge with me. But my earliest and certainly most influential mentor was my father, who took on that role in a professional sense when I went to work at his restaurant and gained a new appreciation for his work ethic.

My father taught me so well that I was able to horse-trade a bit after I enrolled at the Florida International University School of Hospitality. Having suffered the day-to-day reality of running a restaurant, I was determined to avoid required courses like menu planning and food preparation, which I considered totally redundant to my experience.

So I requested an audience with the then-dean, Gerald Lattin, who courteously welcomed me to his office and listened patiently as I argued my case. To my surprise, Dean Lattin not only accepted my rationale, he encouraged me to take graduate-level courses in lieu of the F&B curriculum.

I selected a graduate-level course in feasibility studies. Neither of us could have realized at the time how incredibly fortuitous this decision would prove to my career. Feasibility studies were an integral part of my responsibilities as a regional manager for the Howard Johnson Company. I wonder whether I would have become CEO of the largest hotel franchise organization in the world without the insights I gained from that graduate-level course.

The important point here is not my good luck in choosing the right course; it is that Dean Lattin, a very busy man, took the time to listen to a twenty-three-year-old freshman and to believe in me, so much so that he was willing to bend the rules on my behalf. Like most ambitious young men, all I needed was a little encouragement.

I was doubly blessed during my years at FIU because another member of the faculty took an interest in me and helped shape my career. Professor Rocco Angelo,

Insider Insights *(continued)*

who currently serves FIU's School of Hospitality and Tourism Management as associate dean and professor of management, helped me make one of the most important decisions in my life.

It was 1977, my senior year, and I was lucky enough to have received two job offers, one from the then–Westin Plaza Hotel in New York City and one from the then–Howard Johnson Hotel in Lake Buena Vista, Florida. I was torn between the Westin's offer of a management training position paying $200 a week and the Howard Johnson's offer of rooms division manager, which paid more, but—in my mind—couldn't match the Plaza Hotel in prestige.

Complicating this decision was the fact that I was newly married and concerned about how my pregnant bride, Carla, and I possibly could survive in New York City on $200 a week. Professor Angelo put the dilemma in perfect perspective for me when he advised, "Don't be influenced by the glamour of the big time; someone has to be president of Howard Johnson!"

How right he was. I was named president and chief executive officer of Howard Johnson International in 1991, after a fifteen-year career with the chain. Cendant Corporation (now Wyndham) purchased the chain in 1990, opening new doors for me, including managing director of the company's Global Services division and Hotel Division president and chief operating officer.

Along that journey, I benefited from the support of another mentor, Michael Anthony Byrne, regional manager of Howard Johnson's company-owned hotels in Florida. Just two years into my Howard Johnson career, he called me into his office to compliment my customer skills and let me know he thought I was a "kid who had a head on his shoulders."

That event set the stage for my upward movement in Howard Johnson, first to area manager, then to regional manager. My relationship with Michael Anthony Byrne proved to me that mentors could be just as significant in the corporate environment as they are in the academic world.

My career has been shaped and blessed by other mentors, notably Al Baerenklau, the man who offered me that first job in Lake Buena Vista. Challenged to rein in my tendency to become a bit overzealous in the pursuit of my responsibilities, Al one day presented me with a plaque inscribed with the definition of tact.

When Prime Hospitality Corp. acquired the Howard Johnson Company in 1985, I gained three more mentors, David Barsky, Curt Bean, and Joe Kane, with whom I have enjoyed a long friendship and professional association. Joe went on to become president & chief executive officer of the Days Inns Worldwide chain.

At Cendant, I was preceded in my position by a master mentor, John Russell, who moved on to inspire an entire generation of hoteliers as chairman of the American Hotel & Lodging Association.

My academic and professional experience proved to me that the influence of a mentor could not be overestimated. I endeavored throughout my career to return the courtesy by mentoring many of my colleagues. I would urge anyone in a position of supervisory authority or leadership to do the same. The return on your investment will be a level of satisfaction that, like time, is worth more than money.

Terms such as adventure travel, sustainable tourism, ethical tourism, green tourism, environmentally friendly travel, and many others are often used as rough equivalents for this movement, though with shades of difference. Most commonly, however, it is known as ecological tourism or **ecotourism**. So what is ecotourism really?

The International Ecotourism Society defines ecotourism as "responsible travel to natural areas that conserves the environment and improves the well-being of local citizens."[5] The Québec Declaration on Ecotourism of 2002 defined it as travel that contributes actively to the conservation of natural and cultural heritage; includes local and indigenous communities in its planning, development, and operation and contributes to their well-being; interprets the natural and cultural heritage of the destination to visitors; and lends itself better to independent travelers, as well as to organized tours for small-size groups.[6]

With regard to the various terms and definitions that exist, one adventure travel website offers a concise guideline:

> Is the environment being cared for? Is there genuine effort to help the local economies? Are resources being left intact for future generations? Is the local culture being honored and valued and not just photographed? These questions will cut through the semantics and allow you to see what is really being offered.[7]

While often used interchangeably, ecotourism and adventure travel are not necessarily synonymous. A 2005 study by the Adventure Travel Trade Association and Michigan State University sought a comprehensive definition of adventure travel. Their conclusion was that the definition had broadened to include a cultural component not recognized in the traditional risk-dominated model of adventure travel.[8] Adventure travel today might mean rappelling off a cliff or bird watching; mountain biking or riding a bicycle built for two.

Modern adventure travel got its start in the 1970s with activities like mountaineering in the Himalayas and rafting on the Nile. The creation of national parks to protect endangered wildlife in Africa led to safari adventures in the 1980s. At the same time, ecotourism was developing as a purposeful alternative to the excesses of traditional travel.

Ecotourism and the adventure travel market took off with the wider public in the 1990s. The period began with a boom. From 1990–1996, ecotourism/adventure travel was characterized by growth rates of 20 percent annually. More than $110 billion was spent each year. Progress continued into the new century when the United Nations designated 2002 the International Year of Ecotourism. In 2004, the World Tourism Organization recognized that ecotourism was growing three times faster than the travel industry as a whole. This was a particularly noteworthy accomplishment in the wake of September 11, 2001. The International Ecotourism Society reports that, as of the end of 2010, tourism represents the principle export for more than thirty developing countries in the world and is the leading export for one-third of the world's twenty poorest nations. Thus it can be seen that the lure of exotic, less-developed destinations can have a significant impact on the countries most needing new sources of hard currency.

Ecotourism owes its success with the traveling public to several factors, none more so than the burgeoning environmental movement. As concerns about global warming increase, more travelers are asking themselves about the impact of their choices on the planet. Air travel—the source of two percent of the world's carbon dioxide emissions—represents the fastest-growing contributor to greenhouse gases. To combat this effect, airlines and travel companies have begun to encourage travelers to purchase carbon offsets for their trip through affiliate companies like TerraPass and Sustainable Travel International. **Carbon offsets** are donations that promote reforestation or solar, wind, and other renewable energy projects in an effort to reduce one's **carbon footprint**.

In this era of heightened environmental awareness and ready access to formerly remote, exotic locales, many countries have begun to actively promote their natural resources as magnets for intrepid travelers. Probably the most identifiable of the world's ecotourism destinations continues to be Costa Rica, where lush rainforests, breathtaking mountains, and abundant beaches have been attracting tourists since the 1980s. The concept of "sustainable development" is readily seen in the many ways Costa Rica has developed its tourism infrastructure, ensuring a careful balance between preservation and promotion to allow for both the long-term health of the ecosystem and tourism economics.

Other Central American nations such as Guatemala and Belize have begun to adopt the Costa Rican formula successfully. Additionally, Australia, New Zealand, and many Pacific Island nations actively promote ecotourism. Sustainable Travel International's creation of a global, comprehensive eco-certification program was inspired by concepts in both the Costa Rican certification and Australian accreditation programs, among others. Certifications are one way in which the tourism industry has been able to quantify its green credentials.

The American Hotel & Lodging Association has partnered with Green Seal—a scientific advisory company that offers independent knowledge to industries seeking green certification—to offer certification to hotels that show environmental leadership. Other eco-conscious certifications that are used by the hotel industry include LEED, Energy Star, Green Globe, and Green Leaf.

A 2011 *Condé Nast Traveler* report on the impacts of ecotourism reported that consumer demand for hotels/resorts to responsibly protect the environment is overwhelming. Ninety-six percent of respondents took this posture and 74.5 percent of the same group said that a hotel's positive environmental policies directly influence their hotel selections. These figures are up from 75 percent and 30 percent respectively from a similar survey taken in 2002.

Some environmental advocates say the risk in not asking a hotel specifically about their environmental policies is that the property may be exaggerating its green credentials, a process known as **greenwashing**, wherein a product or service is heavily advertised as environmentally friendly but contributes little to sustainable practices. TerraChoice—an environmental marketing firm that maintains the Audubon Green Leaf eco-rating program for hotels in the U.S. and Canada—has established objective criteria to help consumers determine whether a product or service is truly green. Their list includes the "seven sins of greenwashing": hidden trade-offs, claims without proof, vagueness, irrelevance, lesser of two evils, worshiping false labels, and fibbing.[9] Consumers are encouraged to ask critical questions using these standards to determine the sustainability of goods and services.

In 2007, the International Tourism Partnership launched its "Going Green" initiative to assist hotels in making sustainable choices for the environment and the communities they serve. This new focus is an outgrowth of the success of ecotourism. One in twelve jobs in the world is in tourism and all but three of the poorest countries in the world rely on earnings from international tourism. Because green is profitable, hoteliers have been able to pursue sustainability. Ecotourism has helped to shape a **triple bottom line** that includes economic, social, and environmental management.

Energy Costs

One clear trend that has emerged in the early twenty-first century which shows no sign of abating is the increasingly high cost of oil as an energy source. The booming new growth economies of Asia have joined Europe and North America as voracious demanders of more and more fossil fuels. What does this mean for tourism?

- Ever-higher fuel costs for airlines translate into reduced numbers of flights, steadily rising ticket prices, and fewer and fewer amenities and in-flight comfort as airlines scrape to maintain viable profit margins. One airline (Delta) has actually purchased an oil refinery to try to stay on top of the situation!

- Destinations with proportionately lower demand will continue to see less service if retained at all by air carriers. Hotels and resorts that depend on air travelers need to keep a wary eye on developments.

- Rising fuel costs also have an impact on automobile travel. Families are looking at vacation destinations closer to home than in previous years. More remote destinations will inevitably feel the pinch as travelers simply may not be able to justify long trips by auto.

- If managed correctly, trains and inter-city buses may reap benefits from increasing fuel costs if infrastructure issues like deteriorating interstate highways/bridges and poorly maintained rails do not stymie potential demand for travel modes less sensitive to fuel costs.

All of these trends will need to be watched closely as the supply of fossil fuels continues to diminish.

Endnotes

1. Lloyd E. Hudman, *Tourism: A Shrinking World* (Columbus, Ohio: Grid, 1980), pp. 35–60.

2. This discussion is loosely based upon Robert W. McIntosh and Charles R. Goeldner, *Tourism: Principles, Practices, Philosophies*, 4th ed. (Columbus, Ohio: Grid, 1984).

3. For more comprehensive coverage, see the U.S. Travel Association at www.ustravel.org or the World Tourism Organization at www.unwto.org.

4. Peter Murphy, *Tourism: A Community Approach* (New York: Cambridge University Press, 1985), p. 32.

5. www.ecotourism.org/webmodules/webarticlesnet/templates/eco_template.aspx? articleid=95&zoneid=2.

6. www.world-tourism.org/sustainable/IYE/quebec/anglais/declaration.html.

7. www.untamedpath.com.

8. www.adventuretravel.biz/research_ati_w06.asp.

9. www.terrachoice.com/Home/Six%20Sins%20of%20Greenwashing.

 **Key Terms**

balance of payments—The balance of payments is the difference between the amount of money that leaves a country and the amount that enters it. When the amount that enters a country exceeds the amount that leaves, it is called a balance of payments surplus. When the amount that leaves exceeds the amount that enters a country, it is called a balance of payments deficit.

carbon footprint—The amount of carbon emitted as the result of a specific activity.

carbon offsets—Donations by environmentally conscious travelers that promote renewable energy projects in an effort to reduce their carbon footprints.

ecotourism—Low-impact tourism that avoids harming or destroying the natural or normal environment; a relatively new approach to promoting enjoyment, as well as protection, of the environment.

globalization—A worldwide perspective; an environment in which people are traveling all over the world with increasing ease, and major corporations, such as large hotel chains or franchise restaurants, are expanding their operations into countries all over the world.

greenwashing—Deceptively advertising a product or service as being environmentally friendly when in fact it is not.

infrastructure—The underground or surface construction necessary to service travelers and tourists, as well as the local population. Examples include systems for water, sewage, gas, electricity, and communication; highways, airports, railroads, parking lots, and lighting systems.

ripple effect—The indirect benefits of tourism that non-tourism parts of the economy receive as a result of direct benefits to the tourism industry.

superstructure—The major above-ground facilities that are serviced by the infrastructure and that help make a destination attractive. Hotels, shopping and entertainment centers, museums, and other attractions are examples.

triple bottom line—An outlook in which social and environmental criteria are considered along with financial ones in evaluating success.

Review Questions

1. In addition to lodging and food service operations, what businesses are part of the travel and tourism industry?

2. What does the term "institutional food service" mean?

3. What role have credit cards played in expanding the travel industry?

4. What is the effect on travel to and from the United States as the U.S. dollar grows stronger or weaker compared to other currencies?

5. What are some arguments that may be used to oppose the expansion of tourism in a community or geographic area?

6. What does the term "infrastructure" mean?

7. What are some common internal factors that cause a desire to travel?

8. What is ecotourism, and how is it likely to affect global tourism?

9. How does the ripple effect work?

10. What section of the world is expected to continue to grow the most in terms of outbound tourists?

11. What new travel and tourism trends have emerged as the result of rising fossil fuel costs?

Internet Sites

For more information, visit the following Internet sites. Remember that Internet addresses can change without notice. If the site is no longer there, you can use a search engine to look for additional sites.

Travel and Tourism

American Hotel & Lodging Association
www.ahla.com

American Society of Travel Agents
www.asta.org

International Hotel & Restaurant
  Association
www.ih-ra.com

National Tour Association
www.ntaonline.com

Smith Travel Research
www.strglobal.com

Travel and Tourism Research
  Association
www.ttra.com

Travel Weekly
www.travelweekly.com

U.S. Travel and Tourism Advisory
  Board
tinet.ita.doc.gov/TTAB/TTAB_home.html

World Tourism Organization
www.unwto.org

Ecotourism/Adventure Travel

Adventure Travel Trade Association
www.adventuretravel.biz

Global Development Resource Center
www.gdrc.org

"Green" Hotels Association
www.greenhotels.com

Green Seal
www.greenseal.org

International Ecotourism Society
www.ecotourism.org

International Tourism Partnership
www.tourismpartnership.org

Québec Declaration on Ecotourism
http://www.gdrc.org/uem/eco-tour/
quebec-declaration.pdf

Sustainable Travel International
www.sustainabletravel.org

TerraPass
www.terrapass.com

Travel Source.com
www.travelsource.com/ecotours

Chapter 2 Outline

Competencies

1. Identify entry-level positions in hospitality businesses and describe the kind of experience, training, and education generally required for those seeking entry-level positions. (pp. 23–25)

2. Identify skilled-level positions in hospitality businesses and describe the kind of experience, training, and education generally required for those seeking skilled-level positions. (p. 25)

3. Identify managerial-level positions in hospitality businesses and describe the kind of experience, training, and education generally required for those seeking managerial-level positions. (pp. 25–27)

4. Describe the advantages and disadvantages typically associated with beginning a career in hospitality with a large or small operation. (pp. 27–29)

5. Describe the diversity of career opportunities available in food service. (pp. 29–33)

6. Describe educational opportunities available for those entering hospitality careers, and identify careers available to those studying hospitality. (pp. 33–36)

7. Describe the nature of hospitality and how it affects the careers available in the hospitality industry. (pp. 36–38)

2

Career Opportunities

THE HOSPITALITY INDUSTRY provides career opportunities for people of almost every age, experience, and education. Like all businesses, it has characteristic advantages and disadvantages that should be carefully considered by anyone contemplating a hospitality career. Its primary advantages are interesting work, good opportunities for advancement, generally excellent working surroundings, social contact, security, and stability of employment. Most positions lack the monotony associated with assembly-line work, offering instead frequent opportunities to meet and serve all segments of the public. For those with managerial, executive, and ownership aspirations, the industry ranks high in opportunity.

Careers in the Lodging Industry

In this chapter, we will use the term "hotel" to represent all types of lodging properties (hotels, motels, motor hotels, resorts, etc.), except when specifically noted otherwise. It is sometimes difficult to distinguish hotels from motels and motels from motor hotels, even though it is generally accepted that they *are* somehow different.

It is difficult to imagine a multi-billion-dollar industry that produces a commodity that is intangible—service to people—but that is an accurate description of the hotel business. The very essence of hotelkeeping is people interacting. Because of this, hotels cannot follow the lead of many other industries and become automated, eliminating the human element wherever possible. True personal service cannot be mechanized or automated. Technologies are being instituted to speed up routine tasks, but the human element remains the determining element of the hospitality business.

Anyone considering a career naturally weighs both its advantages and disadvantages. The frequent interactions with others may seem like an advantage to some people and a disadvantage to others. One type of interaction takes place between different staff members. There may be several separate departments operating in a hotel, requiring frequent communication among staff members to coordinate their activities.

Another type of interaction is between staff members and the guests being served. Of course, not all hotel positions provide guest contact, but those that do bring the employee into contact with people from all walks of life. Guests will include the wealthy and the poor, the famous and the unknown, the engaging and the obnoxious, the cooperative and the difficult. Each guest offers the employee an opportunity to learn more about human nature and presents challenges to provide service that will enhance the guest's stay. Employees not only have direct responsibility for guest service, they also have the benefit of witnessing the guests' satisfaction and of personally receiving approval for a job well done.

From the standpoint of working conditions, a hotel offers a clean, safe, pleasant environment. And when we consider the potential for advancement, hotel managers and division and department heads traditionally have worked their way up through the ranks; the industry is one that lends itself to academic training, but also one in which there is no substitute for experience.

In the short space of one chapter, it would be impossible to list and discuss all the jobs in the lodging industry. Instead, representative jobs on three different skill and training levels will be discussed. The first level comprises the unskilled and semiskilled jobs that require no previous experience or specialized preparation; these are entry-level positions. The second level comprises skilled jobs, which require experience or specialized training. The third level comprises supervisory, executive, and managerial positions, which require the greatest amount of experience, training, and education.

Entry-Level Positions

Individuals with a high school education or less and no hotel or related experience are most likely to start their hotel careers with an entry-level job. Every department has at least one entry-level job classification. Starting here does not hinder one's ability to advance in the organization; a large number of today's hotel managers and executives began at this level. The experience and skills gained can help employees advance to the skilled level of hotel work.

Exhibit 1 lists some representative entry-level jobs. The exact tasks performed by employees in these and related positions will vary according to the specific

Exhibit 1   Representative Entry-Level Positions

Front Office	**Administration**
Bell person	Typist
Telephone operator	File clerk
Lobby attendant	
	Food and Beverage Outlets
Housekeeping	Busser
Room cleaner	Barback
Supply runner	Runner
Linen room attendant	Counter server
Kitchen	**Accounting**
Prep person	Clerk
Dish/pot washer	
	Human Resources
Engineering	Clerk
Maintenance person	
Painter's helper	**Marketing**
Electrician's helper	Clerk
Landscaper	

needs of the property. Some properties, especially small ones, will not require staff for all of these positions.

Skilled-Level Positions

Employees at the second level, the skilled jobs, come from a variety of sources. Some are employees who moved up from entry-level jobs. Others are people who have learned a skilled trade in another industry and sought similar employment in a hotel. Some are graduates of the growing number of technical schools and community colleges that offer hotel training, and others come from business schools or specialized high school training courses.

Let's look more closely at skilled-level positions, the staff members who fill them, and where they come from. A person with a desire to work in food preparation might consider a school that trains cooks, bakers, and other food service personnel; graduates of these programs are in great demand at hotels and other food service operations. People with military training in food service can usually find employment in hotel kitchens. Though their number is declining, some hotels operate apprentice training programs in food preparation, and acceptance into such a program is an excellent start toward a successful career in hotel food preparation.

For those interested in employment as bookkeepers, accounting clerks, secretaries, or accountants, training at a reputable business school is a good start. The skilled-level jobs in the dining and banquet departments depend almost entirely on experience. The usual way to advance is to begin at an entry-level job and move up through the ranks; for example, from busperson to food server to captain to head food server. Mixology, or bartending, is taught at some vocational schools, although many bartenders are former food servers. Likewise, front desk agents and reservation agents might come from the ranks as bellpersons or from technical schools.

Training for some jobs may need to be obtained outside the hotel industry. For example, plumbers, electricians, carpenters, painters, and upholsterers are frequently union members who have completed apprenticeship programs. Anyone seeking employment in these areas should consult either the local unions or contractors employing these trades. Most applicants for such hotel positions attain journeyman status in their trade before seeking hotel work.

Exhibit 2 lists (in no particular order) some representative skilled-level jobs encompassing different levels of responsibility, prestige, and salary.

Managerial-Level Positions

Training, experience, and individual initiative are the keys to attaining managerial-level (executive, managerial, and supervisory) positions. Many of these positions are offered to college-trained people, but opportunities will always be available for qualified employees who have worked their way up through the organization. Many division-head jobs are filled by those who excel in the performance of activities in skilled-level positions.

Young people considering a hospitality management career should give serious consideration to college training. Many colleges and universities now offer a

Exhibit 2   Representative Skilled-Level Positions

Front Office Bell captain Front desk agent Reservations agent	**Administration** Secretary
Housekeeping Head houseman Floor housekeeper (supervisor)	**Food and Beverage Outlets** Server Host/hostess Captain Bartender
Kitchen Baker Garde-manger Saucier Line cook	**Accounting** Payables clerk Receiving clerk General cashier
Engineering Plumber Electrician Painter Carpenter HVAC technician	**Security** Guard **Human Resources** Secretary Supervisor
Marketing Sales representative Lead coordinator	

four-year course in hotel management. While specialized college training is rec-ommended, it is not mandatory; college graduates with a wide variety of majors find hotel employment every year.

Hotel school graduates gain a large amount of technical knowledge and typi-cally receive some practical experience during their college program; however, few are ready for a manager's job upon graduation. A hotel school graduate must go through a **management internship**, or supervised training at a job site, before engaging in actual practice. The length and nature of this training program can vary widely, depending on the size and type of hotel; the training, experience, and interests of the graduate; the graduate's ability; and the availability of opportuni-ties for advancement.

What types of jobs do hotel school graduates find? Large chain operations usually have management training programs for which they recruit college gradu-ates. A trainee may spend up to one year in the program (actual training time var-ies), during which time he or she gains experience in several departments. Some hotels allow a management trainee to specialize in one specific department. Upon completion of the program, the graduate is assigned to a management job in the hotel and begins the climb to increased managerial and executive responsibilities.

Hotels without chain affiliations are also eager to hire hotel school grad-uates. If the hotel does not have a formal training program for managers, the graduate will usually start in a position such as steward, assistant manager, sales representative, food and beverage controller, receiving clerk, accountant, assistant food and beverage manager, or restaurant manager.

Many college graduates, armed with four years of theoretical and technical knowledge, become impatient when told they need experience before assuming high-level positions of responsibility. They do not realize that, though intellectually capable, they generally need more hands-on experience before assuming managerial positions. The crucial management skills of understanding, motivating, and directing people can best be developed through experience. It is vital that graduates understand and accept this situation, or their assets of enthusiasm, ambition, and confidence may gradually be replaced by disillusionment, lethargy, and dissatisfaction.

Some representative managerial-level positions are listed in Exhibit 3. In addition to the usual management positions, multi-unit companies may have area, district, regional, and/or corporate-level management.

Where to Start

People entering the industry frequently wonder whether it is better to begin their careers in a small or large hotel, with an independent or chain operation, or in a particular position. What branch of hotel operation is the best to start in after graduation? Where you start is probably less important than how well you work and whether you make the most of opportunities.

Exhibit 3   Representative Managerial-Level Positions

Front Office Manager	**Security** Loss prevention/safety manager
Housekeeping Executive housekeeper	**Food and Beverage** Director Outlets manager Banquet maître d'
Kitchen Sous chef Executive chef	
Human Resources Director	**Other** Resident manager Night manager General manager
Accounting Controller Credit manager Purchaser	**Typical Multi-Unit Positions** Director of training Vice president, finance Vice president, real estate Director of franchising Regional director of rooms Regional director of food and beverage Regional director of accounting Regional director of human resources Regional director of sales/marketing
Engineering Chief engineer	
Marketing Sales manager Revenue manager Director of sales Marketing manager Catering manager	

Early on, it is important to learn something about all phases of hotel operation. You may prefer to work first in those departments you know least about. Then, with some exposure to all areas, you can begin to focus on your areas of interest.

You should not worry about starting in a different department or in a different type of hotel from someone else. People have risen to the top from virtually every position in a hotel. Initiative is what counts in the end. You should get on the job and give it the best you have. While doing so, evaluate your present work, consider your past experiences, develop a new job goal, and begin working to attain it.

Security, independence, a comfortable home life, respect, dignity, and the sense of accomplishment that comes from a job well done—you can attain all these running any size property in any location. What's important is to work hard at all aspects of your job, take advantage of opportunities that arise, and develop and adhere to a career management plan.

Nonetheless, there are some differences between a large and small property you should consider when you seek your first position. Typically, you can learn the basics of all phases of operation through hands-on experience more quickly in a small operation. This is because a staff member in a small hotel is likely to perform a variety of tasks that would be divided among several staff people in a large property. A manager with unit-wide responsibilities must be a generalist, so a broad range of experience may be gained more quickly in a small property.

Cooperation among all levels of staff is important to achieving success in the hotel business. An important difference between small and large properties relates to coordination of activities. In both cases, the staff must work as a team. But in a small property, the hotel manager can personally supervise each employee. In a larger operation, the hotel manager may oversee several levels of supervisors, who each direct a group of staff members, who may in turn supervise other staff.

In a large hotel, there are more divisions or departments, and the operations within them are more complex than in a small hotel. Thus, graduates have a chance to observe a wider variety of activities, a more structured system of communication among divisions, and a greater reliance on technology. In addition, the staff of a large hotel typically fills a wider range of jobs than are found in a small hotel, and staff members are able to become very skilled and experienced in their defined job duties. The opportunity to work with highly skilled people in a wide range of jobs is one of the major advantages of training in large hotels.

A successful hotel manager must have self-confidence. Many potentially fine executives, when placed in high-level positions too quickly, ruin their careers in the process. In a large property, advancement typically comes when a staff member is ready for it. By contrast, a smaller property may need to expand the job duties of its relatively few staff members more quickly. This is an advantage to the individual who is ready to take on more responsibilities, but it can be a serious problem for those who are less prepared.

Managers encounter a tremendous variety of problems in a large hotel. The challenge of resolving these problems is considered an advantage by some people and a disadvantage by others. The following conditions are associated with working in a large hotel:

- One must learn to manage large groups of employees.

- Communications among the staff are complicated by the larger size of the organization.

- A manager can become "lost" in a large company.

- The pace of activities is faster; there is more demand on personal energies in a large property.

- Participation in community activities is not possible as soon, nor as completely, as in a smaller organization.

For those aspiring to own their own business, there are advantages to both large and small hotels. In a small property, you can advance more quickly through the organization. You will be able to make decisions—and see their results—without having to deal with an elaborate bureaucracy. At a large property, you can interact with more managers and learn from their insights and experiences, and you gain exposure to more sophisticated systems and procedures.

Careers in the Food Service Industry

As mentioned earlier, both hotelkeeping and food service provide career opportunities for people of almost every age, experience, and education. Like hotelkeeping, food service offers interesting work, excellent chances for advancement, social contact, stable employment, good working conditions, and average or better earnings.

Employment in the food service industry also offers excellent opportunities to use initiative, express ideas, and earn the satisfaction that comes from serving other people.

Jobs in the food service industry can also be classified as entry-level (unskilled and semiskilled) positions, skilled-level positions, and managerial-level positions. Preparation and training for these levels is very similar to that already discussed for the job levels found in the hotel industry. Examples of jobs at each level in the food service industry are included in Exhibits 1, 2, and 3.

As is true in the hotel business, training, experience, and individual initiative are the keys to success in executive and managerial positions. Many of these jobs are filled with graduates of college hotel and restaurant management programs. However, there are many people today with little or no formal education who hold responsible high-level positions. Food service operations are similar to hotel properties in that some managerial positions are filled by the promotion of successful skilled-level staff. Still, people considering management careers in the food service industry should think about college training, since it can give them a competitive edge.

College graduates entering the food service industry have the same ambitions, skills, knowledge, and impatience as those entering the hotel industry. They also must be willing to gain the hands-on experience necessary to move into executive-level positions and should not expect to step directly into a top-level job.

Insider Insights

Jorgen H. Hansen, CHA
Senior Vice President, South Region (Retired)
Hilton Hotels International _____

Since my very first day in the hospitality industry, I can never recall having regrets about going to work. I can only attribute this to the always-changing conditions, the ever-present challenge, and the many varied experiences which each day contains. During my years working back of the house, I was amazed by the international staff I had the opportunity to work with—the creative and artistic performance by chefs, cooks, and pastry chefs, and the ever-changing pace. In the front of the house, what intrigued me was the constant change of guests and the multitude of their needs, tastes, backgrounds, and attitudes. Here I experienced firsthand the reward of satisfying a guest.

As I moved into a management position, the industry took on a new dimension for me. Besides service and food preparation, I now had to focus on budgets, compliance with statutes under which the hotel industry operates, preparation of forecasts, and performance of administrative functions to ensure that the hotel, besides being a hostelry known for its services and quality of operation, also made economic sense for its owners.

Being successful in the hotel industry does not necessarily mean becoming a general manager, but rather working in the capacity that gives the greatest personal satisfaction day in and day out. The many young people who have entered our industry in hotels in which I was involved were always advised that they should become involved in departments in which they thought they had the most strength and could best contribute; that they should concentrate on their day-to-day achievements and not on future career moves, and should strive to build a solid background of expertise in at least two areas of our industry. Furthermore, they should realize that the world doesn't stand still and neither does our industry; continuing education is necessary to keep abreast of new developments. Most important, they should have a good attitude toward other people, have respect for each job position, associate with people willing to share their expertise and knowledge, and make it their own.

The last few decades have seen many new developments in our industry, not only in the way hotel reservations are transmitted, in computer applications to front office operation, in energy conservation, and in strategic planning of sales and marketing functions, but also in the guests' growing awareness of quality.

Increasingly competitive market conditions will continue to demand better and more sophisticated services of each hotel to attract its fair market share. In contrast to yesteryears, we are no longer competing to serve the guest who travels the highways and routes on which our hostelry may be located. We are competing for business as a destination, whether it be for leisure, cultural, or business travelers; and competing not only with other national destinations, but often with the world at large.

With more leisure time, longer vacations, increased competition, and growing world commerce, the future of the hotel industry is bright and challenging, and offers a wealth of opportunities for people who like people.

Insider Insights

Hans Weishaupt, CHA
A retired Hilton International general manager
living in Switzerland _____

Throughout my forty years in the international hotel business, I have always
played on what I call my "Swiss advantage," which embraces the qualities I gained
while growing up in Switzerland.

A big advantage is the social standing that hotel work carries in Switzerland. To
work in a hotel is a respected endeavor. It is an officially certified trade that must be
acquired through a regulated apprenticeship, whether it is in the area of service, the
kitchen, or the front office. It is considered a career choice, not something one does
while waiting for something better to come along. A hotel manager is treated with
great respect, since the hotel industry is recognized as an important contributor to
the economy of Switzerland.

Another advantage is growing up with a close exposure to several languages
and cultures. No one who lives in tiny Switzerland can avoid meeting people who
speak another language or come from another cultural background. Swiss people
learn early on to understand and respect these differences. To be comfortable and
confident with people from a variety of linguistic and cultural backgrounds is a big
advantage in international hotels.

Growing up in Switzerland also teaches one a respect for the pecking order,
a sense of loyalty, pride in a job well done, and a desire to strive to exceed people's
expectations—all qualities that employers really appreciate!

Someone with these qualities in his or her rucksack has a certain advantage in
climbing the rocky cliffs of employment in the international hotel business. However,
while these qualities make for a good follower, a dependable doer, and a desirable
employee, they do not make for a pioneering mover and shaker, a visionary innovator, or an entrepreneurial spirit.

I find it amusing when accolades are showered on the Swiss for our standard-
setting, pioneering role in the international hotel business. Americans are especially
generous in appraising us this way. As someone who has the "Swiss advantage"
and also has had the viewpoints of academia, operations, and the executive suite, I
have a different perspective.

Looking at how hotelkeeping on an international scale came about, I find that
we Swiss were supporting players. It was in the United States that Ellsworth Statler
lifted hotelkeeping from a local, individually operated enterprise to a structured,
nationwide business operation. Statler introduced concepts of management,
control, human relations, and sales that permitted the operation of a chain of large,
multi-unit hotels. Sadly, even in the United States, this pioneer and innovator who
shaped hotelkeeping into a major industry has never been properly recognized for
his genius and achievement. It was another American who had the courage and
foresight to apply Statler's concepts as the basis for hotel expansion abroad.
Conrad Hilton launched and set the standards for the international hotel industry
with his hotel chain, which ultimately spanned the world.

(continued)

Insider Insights *(continued)*

It was also in the United States that the business principles and skills needed for the successful operation of these large operations were fully recognized. Americans were the first to establish courses in hotel administration at institutes of higher education—courses which culminate in academic degrees.

While I am not eager to give up the Swiss advantage and the accolades that come with it, I do feel that recognition should be given to those who really formed the principles of international hotelkeeping—those whose ideas lifted simple inn-keeping to a complex industry that spans and bonds the world.

Diverse Opportunities

Too often, applicants consider food service jobs only in hotels and restaurants. This is unfortunate. There are many different segments in the food service industry worth considering. Excellent opportunities exist for staff at all job levels in department store food service; school, college, and university food service; hospitals and nursing homes; city and country clubs; business and industry; parks and recreation; and the military services (which employ civilians to manage clubs and other food and lodging functions). And then there is the **quick-service** industry, which includes commercial establishments that offer drive-through and/or counter service to customers.

Quick-Service. If there is a mystery in the food services, it has to concern the quick-service or fast-food industry. Quick-service is the single largest segment of the food service industry. The quick-service industry has lots of job opportunities available at every level. However, few students consider these jobs, and even fewer educators and educational institutions address this segment in their classes. Why is this?

Some students, believing that quick-service operations lack status, prefer positions in hotels and expensive restaurants. Others say that quick-service operations do not provide significant challenges. Still others maintain that the quick-service industry offers little opportunity to use the technical skills and procedures they have learned in college.

In truth, responsibility comes quickly to new employees in quick-service who demonstrate interest and ability, and that responsibility is increased as rapidly as each employee can handle it. It is not uncommon for a recent graduate to become a unit manager within six to nine months after joining a company, responsible for a small business averaging sales of $750,000 or more per year. Graduates who perform well will typically move beyond the unit manager level within 12 to 14 months. In no other area of the hospitality industry does responsibility come so quickly or in such large proportions.

Perhaps those students who sense a lack of status in quick-service careers perceive quick-service corporate headquarters as somehow less sophisticated or less professional than other corporations. Nothing could be further from the truth. Their methods, practices, and procedures typically make use of the very latest technology; they are often far more sophisticated and advanced than similar offices in other hospitality industry corporations.

Do quick-service salaries compare favorably with salaries in other areas of the hospitality industry? Indeed they do! As one proceeds from unit manager and enters the corporate ranks, one's salary will invariably exceed the average for similar positions throughout the industry. People aspiring to careers in food service should consider all segments of the industry. Quick-service is an exciting and growing element that provides challenges and opportunities for people who are willing to consider this "forgotten" segment of a vast industry.

In a recent interview, the chairman of a large quick-service company expressed the following points: quick-service has excellent career potential for young men and women. Hospitality school graduates entering the field will probably surpass both retail and banking employees in salary earned.

Contract Food Management Companies. Like quick-service operations, **contract management companies** often suffer from long-standing, misguided prejudice. These companies often contract their services to **institutional food service** operations, which provide meals in a closed, non-commercial environment, such as a hospital, school, or correctional institution. Beliefs persist that institutional not-for-profit operations are low paying and don't make use of new technology. However, the truth is that institutional food service operations—with menu, purchasing, and marketing systems—are as sophisticated as any operations in the commercial segment. Unfortunately, most hotel and restaurant school graduates have limited exposure to this segment because few of their teachers have any background with a contract food management company.

Employment with a management company offers excellent hours, a high degree of responsibility very quickly, a good salary, and excellent opportunities for advancement. Since management company personnel use the same basic management principles practiced by effective officials in any type of food service operation, people with experience in these companies can freely move to other segments of the industry. Employment opportunities in contract management present an excellent career choice.

Education for Hospitality Management Careers

A great many changes in the ways people prepare for careers in food service have occurred over the years. It used to be most typical for people to start in entry-level positions, work their way up to skilled positions, and then move up to management positions. Future cooks and chefs entered apprenticeship programs and moved up to higher positions as they gained experience. Cooks moved to different organizations in order to learn specific skills from a particular executive chef. Food servers became captains, maîtres d', and restaurant managers. Some chefs and restaurant managers even joined the entrepreneurial ranks and opened food service operations of their own.

Over the years, formal education has played an increasingly prominent role in preparing people for careers in food service. Apprenticeship programs and opportunities have generally decreased in number, although the American Culinary Federation, a professional association of chefs, has developed an apprenticeship program for its members. Just when industry leaders were expressing grave concern over the shortage of trained cooks, bakers, and chefs, a new form of training came to the rescue. The Culinary Institute of America began a program to prepare people for careers in the culinary arts. When the Institute moved into its present facilities in Hyde Park, New York, education in the area of food preparation came into its own. More recently, Johnson & Wales University initiated its culinary program. Both institutions found themselves with many more applicants than spaces available. Today, these institutions have developed branches in other states, and new culinary schools have opened in Florida, Colorado, and California. Community colleges offering hotel and food service programs have begun to proliferate across the country. These programs prepare students for technical positions in food production and middle management positions in other areas of the industry.

There has also been a significant increase in the number of four-year colleges and universities that offer programs in hospitality industry management. A continuing demand for trained personnel means readily available employment opportunities for graduates of these programs.[1]

Many post-secondary schools now offer degree programs in travel and tourism, leading to employment in travel agencies. The most common entry-level position in the travel agency business is that of travel counselor, who works directly with travelers and travel planners. The position requires the computer skills necessary for using sophisticated electronic reservations systems to book airlines, hotels, cruises, and rental cars, and of course considerable knowledge of attractions, facilities, and transportation options in destinations all over the world. The perks of this position may include deeply discounted travel opportunities in the form of familiarization trips. Tourism entities offer these trips, hoping to benefit from the increased knowledge travel counselors acquire about their destination and specific products. Many airlines, hotels, resorts, and tourism boards are eager to show their offerings to travel counselors.

Not all of the education for industry positions takes place in formal classrooms. Some employees in the hospitality industry have the necessary intelligence and ability to move up in the industry, but, for a variety of reasons, cannot attend an institute or college. Fortunately for them, the American Hotel & Lodging Educational Institute offers educational packages that may be completed while the employee continues to work full-time. The Educational Institute, a non-profit educational foundation, is the largest educational resource center for the hospitality industry in the world. Besides producing textbooks, videotapes, seminars, and other resources for use in schools and on the job, the Institute offers individual courses and certification programs to those who meet educational and experience requirements. The highest certification is the Certified Hotel Administrator (CHA). The Institute also offers programs resulting in the following designations: Certified Food and Beverage Executive (CFBE), Certified Rooms Division Executive (CRDE), Certified Hospitality Facilities Executive (CHFE), Certified Hospitality Housekeeping Executive (CHHE), Certified Hospitality Supervisor (CHS), and Certified Master Hotel Supplier (CMHS).

Other Career Paths to Consider

Every graduate of hotel programs, whether two-year or four-year, has many career paths to consider. A number of these opportunities are only indirectly related to hotels and restaurants, but can offer rewarding careers. For example, some graduates over the years have enjoyed success in convention and trade-show management, while others have taken a related path to convention and visitors bureau executive positions. Another area well worth considering is meeting planning, in which a graduate can use a large portion of his or her hospitality training.

Those interested in accounting have opportunities within both individual and corporate hotels as well as restaurants, but are not limited to those areas. Hotel accounting firms actively recruit graduates for both their audit and consulting divisions. Industry consulting is not limited to accounting firms. Firms such as PKF Consulting employ many hospitality graduates. Hotel consultants now can join their own professional society. Additionally, many graduates of hospitality programs now can work for hotel owners as asset managers who oversee the performance of hotels managed by chains or third-party operators.

A cruise ship is essentially a "floating hotel" and offers a variety of positions both at sea and in corporate headquarters, for which hotel graduates have the required technical and administrative skills. However, because most cruise ships sail under a foreign flag, seagoing positions are somewhat limited.

A relatively new, rapidly expanding area is senior services management. Senior services organizations resemble resort operations combined with assisted living and nursing services. A number of university-level hotel schools are developing either a major or a concentration in this area. Career opportunities within this field are multiplying rapidly and will continue to do so.

Another possibility is that of educator. A graduate needs to gain a sound background of industry experience and knowledge before entering this field. Early in his or her career, a hospitality graduate could undertake the necessary graduate training to qualify academically, and could pursue advanced education while teaching. It is true that many hotel educators have entered the field of education full-time only after a very successful industry career. However, many of them served as lecturers, adjunct professors, and guest speakers during their hotel careers.

An area often overlooked but ripe with opportunity is that of private ownership. Hotel executives have often expressed a wish to retire and own a small hotel or inn just to keep them from becoming bored and restless. However, one need not wait for his or her retirement years to enjoy the personal satisfactions and independence of ownership. Many young graduates select ownership as their primary goal while still in college. Placement directors tell us that graduates are seeking ownership opportunities to a greater degree than at any other time. For those doubting Thomases who say that private ownership for young people is nothing but a pipe dream, consider the following two examples provided by Harris Rosen and Jeremy Wladis.

Even as an undergraduate at Cornell's School of Hotel Management, Harris Rosen aspired to become a hotel owner. He realized, however, that he needed management experience and time to check out his approach to successful hotel operation. Following graduation in 1961, he served in executive positions with major hotel corporations. By 1970, he knew he was ready to own and successfully operate hotels.

Rosen Hotels and Resorts was born June 24, 1974, with the purchase of the Quality Inn International in Orlando, Florida. Its original 256 rooms have grown to 728 rooms. Just six months later, Rosen purchased the Rodeway Inn International. In 1984, Quality Inn Plaza became the first Rosen hotel planned from blueprint to full construction. Today, with 1,020 rooms, it is the world's largest Quality Inn. The company has continued to grow. With the opening of its seventh hotel, the Rosen Shingle Creek, Rosen Hotels and Resorts earned a position among the ten largest privately held hotel companies in the United States. This impressive portfolio now numbers over 6,300 rooms in total.

The authors salute Harris Rosen for his success. He endowed the Hotel Management Program at the University of Central Florida with a multi-million-dollar gift, and was the driving force behind the University's Rosen College of Hospitality Management.

As stated, our second example is that of Jeremy Wladis. Upon graduation from University of Houston Hilton College, Jeremy honed his management skills for several years in the food service industry. Opting to gamble on a private ownership career, he opened his first restaurant, a French-American bistro, in New York City. Success followed. Today, with his company, the Restaurant Group, he owns and manages two New York City restaurants and a small chain of pizzerias. Jeremy admits that the challenges are great, but are far outweighed by the satisfactions and joy of doing it his way.

The Nature of Hospitality

People interested in careers in the hospitality industry must take a close look at the nature of hotel and food service work. To enjoy a hospitality career, an employee must possess technical knowledge and skills, a friendly personality, and a commitment to providing quality customer service.

Communication

Because the hospitality industry requires frequent interactions with people, job candidates must demonstrate solid communication skills. Employees at every level need to communicate well; the ability to handle difficult guests or to direct staff while maintaining good employee relations requires effective, tactful communication.

Getting a job interview usually requires applicants to "sell" themselves in a well-written **résumé** and concise **cover letter**. A résumé is a formal written presentation of an individual's work experience, skills, and education. A cover letter explains the specific job sought and reiterates the applicant's relevant experience for the job. Job candidates should think of their résumés and cover letters as sales tools to get them interviews, where they will have the opportunity to complete the sale by persuading the employer to hire them. It is vital that these sales tools be as well-written and persuasive as possible. Industry executives agree unanimously that the great majority of applicants do not effectively promote themselves in their résumés and cover letters. These applicants often fail to get interviews and therefore lose employment opportunities. A great number of books on résumé and cover letter writing are available to help job candidates today.

The interview itself is another place where good communication skills are important. The main purpose of a résumé is to get an interview; the main purpose of an interview is to get a job offer. Applicants should demonstrate an ability to understand and answer questions articulately while displaying a friendly, helpful demeanor. Applicants should also discuss their skills, education, and experience that make them especially suited to a job. Finally, job candidates can display their skills in communication and courtesy—another trait essential for successful hospitality employees—by sending a brief thank-you note to the interviewer following the interview.

Turnover

As is the case in many professional fields, the turnover rate of new graduates entering the hospitality industry is significant. One reason for this seems to be that many people are attracted to the hospitality field without really knowing what they are getting into. Once employed, they discover that the job is not what they expected. They dislike the long hours, low pay rates, and physical labor associated with beginning jobs. They recognize too late that they must work weekends, evenings, holidays, and at other times when most people are not required to work.

Partly to alleviate this turnover problem, most college and university hospitality programs now require **student internships** in the industry prior to graduation. By giving students on-the-job experience before they graduate, student internships help students gain an understanding of the industry and its job requirements and demands. They learn what to expect in their first post-graduation jobs. If their internship work experiences are unsatisfactory, they may realize, before committing themselves to several years of study, that the hospitality industry is not for them. In addition, some of the turnover could be avoided if students were better informed about the range of opportunities available in some of the other, less visible segments of the industry.

Demands and Rewards

Hours of work have changed in hotels and restaurants. The forty-hour work week is now in effect throughout much of the industry; the days of extremely long hours and split shifts are history. But work hours may be non-standard or unusual, especially in hotels, which must keep their doors open twenty-four hours daily. The work may be during the evening and night, and it often includes holidays and weekends. Occasionally, a little extra time may be called for to ensure complete service to the guests. The employee who moves up into the managerial ranks will likely put in some extra hours. Anyone aspiring to management positions cannot be a clock watcher.

While many entry-level jobs in hotels and restaurants pay only minimum wage, advancement may come rapidly. The pay rate for skilled- and managerial-level jobs in lodging and food service is competitive with those in other industries.[2] The U.S. Bureau of Labor Statistics notes that wages for skilled- and managerial-level positions in the hospitality industry vary greatly depending upon the size of the establishment, previous work experience, educational background, and job duties. Labor unions, region of the country, and chain affiliation (if any) may also influence wages and benefit programs.

A hotel and restaurant work shift varies dramatically from hour to hour. It has peaks and valleys, changing from quiet to busy in a matter of minutes. Hospitality is never a routine business. Every day brings new problems to be solved and new excitement. Anyone who enjoys a lack of routine will find the business fascinating. Those who prefer a more orderly routine may find the industry too unpredictable. It is not that hotels and restaurants are disorganized operations; it is simply the nature of the business that it is impossible to harness the ups and downs to produce a crisis-free routine.

Since the advent of mass production in American industry, opportunities for workers to take pride in what they produce have been greatly reduced. In the personal service field, however, this opportunity still exists. The chef creates his or her own culinary masterpiece and views it with personal pride and satisfaction. The same is true for the baker, the pastry chef, the pantry personnel, and many others. For many hospitality employees, the product—service—is intangible, but the recipient expresses thanks and satisfaction directly, allowing the employee to know that the work is appreciated and to have a feeling of accomplishment.

Hotels and restaurants are sensitive to changes in the national economy. Both types of businesses typically offer stable employment. For those who possess the interest, technical skills, emotional makeup, and motivation, the hospitality industry offers some of the most fascinating, rewarding careers available anywhere.

Endnotes

1. The Council on Hotel, Restaurant, and Institutional Education, located at 2810 N. Parham Rd., Ste. 230, Richmond, VA 23294 and online at www.chrie.org, can provide names and addresses of educational institutions with hospitality management programs.

2. For the latest Bureau of Labor Statistics report on wages and salaries in the hospitality industry, contact the Bureau of Labor Statistics, Postal Square Building, 2 Massachusetts Ave., N.E., Washington, D.C. 20212-0001. The American Hotel & Lodging Association and the National Restaurant Association can also provide information on the employment outlook, salaries, and benefits in the lodging and food service industries.

Key Terms

contract management company—Businesses that contract their management services to food service operations, often in an institutional setting.

cover letter—In a job-seeking situation, a concise written message that states what specific job is being sought and relates the applicant's relevant experience for the job.

institutional food service—Operations that provide meals in non-commercial, closed environments, such as hospitals, schools, or correctional institutions.

management internship—Supervised training that hotel school graduates must have before engaging in actual management; takes place at a job site.

quick-service—The single largest segment of the food service industry; composed of commercial establishments that offer drive-through and/or counter service to customers. Also known as fast-food.

résumé—A formal, written presentation of an individual's work experience, skills, and education. Job applicants use résumés to obtain job interviews.

student internship—On-the-job experience for hospitality students required by most college and university hospitality programs; internships help students gain an understanding of the industry and its job requirements and demands.

 Review Questions

1. Why has automation developed relatively slowly in the hospitality industry?
2. What is a management internship?
3. Where can unskilled workers gain skills for skilled-level positions in hotels?
4. What are some of the advantages of starting a hotel career in a small hotel?
5. What are some of the advantages of starting a hotel career in a large hotel?
6. Other than hotels and restaurants, what types of places offer food service employment?
7. What are some pros and cons of a career in the quick-service field?
8. Why is a résumé important for a job candidate?
9. Why is the turnover rate so high among entrants to hospitality management?
10. What are some pros and cons of a career with a food-service management company?

 Internet Sites

For more information visit the following Internet sites. Remember that Internet addresses can change without notice. If the site is no longer there, you can use a search engine to look for additional sites.

Associations

American Culinary Federation
www.acfchefs.org

American Hotel & Lodging
 Association
www.ahla.com

American Hotel & Lodging
 Educational Institute
www.ahlei.org

Club Managers Association of America
www.cmaa.org

Council on Hotel, Restaurant and
  Institutional Education (CHRIE)
www.chrie.org

Destination Marketing Association
  International
www.destinationmarketing.org

Educational Foundation of NRA
www.nraef.org

Hospitality Financial and Technology
  Professionals
www.hftp.org

Hospitality Sales and Marketing
  Association International
www.hsmai.org

International Association of Conference
  Centers
www.iacconline.com

International Hotel & Restaurant
  Association
www.ih-ra.com

National Restaurant Association
www.restaurant.org

University Internship Services
www.internsearch.com

Publications—Online and Printed

Bon Appétit
www.epicurious.com/bonappetit

CuisineNet Cafe
www.cuisinenet.com/cafe/index.html

Global Gourmet
www.globalgourmet.com

Food Management
http://food-management.com

Food Network
www.foodnetwork.com

Internet Food Channel
www.foodchannel.com

Lodging Magazine
www.lodgingmagazine.com

Nation's Restaurant News
www.nrn.com

Restaurant Hospitality
http://restaurant-hospitality.com

Wine Business Monthly
http://winebusiness.com/

Part II

The Lodging Industry

Chapter 3 Outline

Competencies

1. Trace the origins of the European lodging industry and describe the roles of the grand tour, professional hoteliers, and early hotel schools. (pp. 43–45)

2. Characterize the transit, vacation, and grand hotel types that were produced in the first move toward "market segmentation" in Europe. (pp. 45–46)

3. Outline the history of U.S. hotels from the colonial period to the early 1960s, and identify developments that significantly affected the lodging industry. (pp. 46–53)

4. Identify characteristics that distinguish independent hotels from chain-affiliated hotels. (pp. 53–61)

5. Describe referral associations and consortia, and identify their purposes. (p. 61)

6. Identify key differences between resorts and other types of hotels and cite reasons for the expansion of the resort into a full-time business. (pp. 62–63)

3

The Early History of Lodging in Europe and America

A COMPLETE HISTORY of the lodging industry would take us back some 12,000 years; however, from a practical standpoint, innkeeping as we know it today was not possible until the adoption of a standardized medium of exchange. With the establishment of money during the sixth century B.C.E. came the first real opportunities for people to trade and travel. As travelers' areas of movement widened, their need for lodging became greater. Early inns were nothing more than space within private dwellings. Typically, the inns provided only the basic necessities, paid little attention to service or hospitality, were rarely clean, and, more often than not, were run by disreputable and unprogressive landlords.

In spite of these hardships, travel activity has continued to increase right up to the present. Comparable evolutionary processes for eating and rooming establishments have taken place in many different parts of the world. Many countries have produced their own native form of **hostelry**, such as the ryokan in Japan, the parador in Spain, and the pousada in Portugal. As much as any others, however, the European hotels have come to impress their particular style and characteristics upon the industry as it is today. Therefore, it is appropriate to focus initially on the history and evolution of European hotels.

The Origins of the European Lodging Industry

Aside from the traditionally nomadic peoples, early Europeans began moving from place to place for very specific utilitarian reasons. Pleasure travel and sightseeing as we know them today were unknown. There were few categories of typical travelers. Mercenaries moved from their homes to their assigned military units and back. Pilgrims and clergymen sought out their places of worship or the seats of their religious orders. A few itinerant merchants provided an early system of distribution for goods and services.

The first innkeepers exercised their hospitality chores on a part-time basis. They were clergymen, mountain guides, coachmen, or farmers who began by taking in short-term boarders. Accommodations were rarely comfortable, but always frugal. In time the pioneer innkeepers began to introduce what they believed to be some of the comforts of home. Design, building materials, the right fabrics, a good down pillow, and wholesome food and drink began playing an increasingly important role.

Innkeepers began transferring their businesses from father to son. A surprising number of the earliest inns and guest houses have remained intact, and continue to be operated as hostelries to this day. Their names evoke the coats of arms of their most illustrious guests: Three Kings, Golden Lion, Cardinal's Hat, Black Eagle, Two Swords, and many more.

From 1750 to 1825, English inns gained the reputation of being the finest in the world. Their early development began in London where innkeepers increased services, maintained standards of cleanliness, and, at least to some extent, catered to guests. As roads improved, new ideas that originated in the metropolitan area were adopted by the countryside inns. The inns of England reached their peak of development from 1780 to 1825.

Voyagers passed along information to each other about the best places to stay and eat. One of the earliest guidebooks was *The Pilgrim's Guide,* dating back to the thirteenth century. Guidebooks at first were not thought of as guidebooks in the usual sense of this term. Rather, they were chance accounts of travel from diaries, letters, or ad hoc remarks intended to inform and offer advice. In the early days they were often written in Latin. Sir Francis Bacon produced an essay entitled "Of Travel," which is probably one of the earliest records of travel advice in the modern sense.

The Grand Tour

In reviewing the great historic travel patterns, mention must be made of the **grand tour**, often referred to as "the golden age of travel," whose heyday occurred in the second half of the eighteenth century, prior to the French Revolution and the advent of the railways. A grand tour of the European continent was an indispensable element in the education of the young offspring of Britain's most powerful and wealthy families. The tours often lasted up to several years. In response to this fast developing demand, inhabitants of the tour destinations in France, Italy, Austria, Switzerland, and Germany began establishing lodging and tourist services. Thus it is clear that European expertise in hotel matters did not develop out of an innate predisposition. Rather, the entrepreneurs of the time evolved their skills in reaction to the requirements of the marketplace.

Increasing expertise brought increasingly elaborate services and accommodations. Hotels such as the Dolder Grand in Zurich, the Imperial in Vienna, the Vier Jahreszeiten in Hamburg, and the Des Bergues in Geneva were the result. Hotels emerged wherever fashion dictated.

The Professional Hotelier

Professional hoteliers began to make their mark in the mid-1800s. The first to become well known on a national level were the scions of pioneering hotel families. Later, personalities such as César Ritz, teaming up with famous chefs (in Ritz's case, Georges Auguste Escoffier), became famous beyond their own nation's boundaries. The Ritz hotels in Paris, London, Madrid, and Lisbon constituted the first hotel management chain.

Early Hotel Schools

The first hotel training schools were established at the end of the nineteenth century and early in the twentieth century as a consequence of ever-larger hotels, increased technology, and increasingly complex administrative problems. The traditional methods of on-the-job training supervised by guilds were replaced or complemented by more formal and scientific educational methods. Formal apprentice programs were established. Part of the apprentice's time was spent on the job and part of it in a school-like environment. Those who sought jobs at the managerial level were required to spend more time in school than other hotel students. Being selected for training by one of the great hotels was a noteworthy distinction; it provided a professional reference that often meant more money in terms of future earnings. Work certificates from grand hotels were cherished like some precious scroll. Often, parents of aspiring hotel workers were required to pay the hotel for the privilege of having their youngster train there. Apprentices were obligated to work very hard; they received poor treatment and next to no pay. In some instances, these policies prevailed well into the 1950s and 1960s.

New Era—New Markets

As new modes of transportation developed, access to remote but picturesque resorts became possible. **Funiculars** (cable railways) began serving hotels in the mountains. Bürgenstock, Territet-Glion, and Giessbach are a few examples of Swiss hotels that rapidly developed thanks to funicular train service to their areas. Both Alpine and seaside resorts became quite the rage. While many of the transportation lines were established by English companies, the hotels were developed by the local people. With the discovery of winter sports, European royalty began frequenting the winter resorts in Montreux, Switzerland, and other relatively snow-free towns situated in close proximity to higher-lying ski runs.

Three Types of Hotels. The first move toward what today we call **market segmentation** produced three types of hotels: transit, vacation, and grand.

Transit hotels were the descendants of the early inns. (The term "transit" is a European label and does not describe the same property as the "transient" label often used in the United States.) They continued to provide economical, efficient, and clean overnight accommodations at major crossroads. Thus, they were the European equivalent of a much later development in America—the motel.

Transit hotels were geared to rapid turnover, because their guests typically needed these accommodations only for short stays. Services in transit hotels tended to be modest and uniform.

Vacation hotels have been a part of Europe since ancient times when the Romans enjoyed the healthful properties of their mineral springs. These waters—and the resorts and towns located near them—came to be known as **spas** (after Spa, a watering place in eastern Belgium). Gradually the pursuit of health led Europeans to the simultaneous pursuit of pleasure. Spas at Marienbad, Vichy, Wiesbaden, Ragaz, and Loeche-les-Bains became centers of social activity. Entertainment, costume balls, concerts, and dancing contributed to the well-being of guests who were "taking the waters." Gambling was added to the attractions and, little by little, the curative side of spas decreased in importance.

The French Riviera resort region was first frequented for health reasons. The region also enjoyed ample sunshine and a mild winter climate. A visit there by Queen Victoria in 1899 was later followed by a multitude of celebrities, members of royal families, statesmen, artists, and financiers, many of whose names became permanently associated with the region. Other vacation hotels were developed at spots of scenic beauty. Zermatt and St. Moritz in the Alps are good examples.

Grand hotels were (and are) establishments which, over the years, afforded their guests an ideal mixture of unique architecture, luxurious interiors, impeccable and truly personal service, a well-trained staff, exquisite food, and style and ambience beyond comparison. Qualification as a grand hotel is earned over a long period of time. It cannot be gained arbitrarily or through luxurious accommodations alone. A very limited number of hotels throughout the world deserve this distinction, and they have to work constantly at preserving it. A true grand hotel enjoys an undisputed international reputation by achieving a delicate balance among luxury, elegance, and good taste.

Decades of Difficulties

The 1930s were rather negative years for hotels across the continent because of the international tensions leading up to World War II.

The 1940s were dominated by World War II, which brought massive destruction and social upheaval to many European countries.

The 1950s could be characterized as years of steady but slow growth. This decade was the first to allow growth and progress unencumbered by the vestiges of a wartime economy. On the other hand, there were still numerous travel complications engendered by pre-war bureaucratic methods. Personal and vehicular traffic between countries was complicated. In spite of these drawbacks, modest hotel growth and development did occur, but it was confined to national boundaries.

The European hotel industry became truly international with the advent of jet travel in 1959.

The Early History of Hotels in the United States

The Colonial Period

In the American colonies, inns were located in seaports. Colonial innkeepers patterned their establishments after inns in England, but while English landlords were conservative and slow to change, their American counterparts demonstrated no such inhibitions. American innkeepers were aggressive expansionists who took chances. Within a few years after the American Revolution, inns in the United States were well on their way to offering the finest services available anywhere. Admittedly, by today's standards these services would be totally inadequate, but for their time they were the best. By 1800, it was evident that the United States was assuming world leadership in the development of the lodging industry.

In addition to the pioneering spirit of the American innkeeper, several other factors influenced the rapid rise of the lodging industry in the United States. While European hotels operated on the premise that only the aristocracy was entitled to luxury and comfort, American hotels were run for more universal enjoyment. Anyone with enough money could take advantage of the services of a hotel, and the rates were within the means of almost everyone. In fact, some Americans chose to reside permanently in hotels.

Probably the most important factor in the growth of U.S. innkeeping was that the average American traveled considerably more than typical residents of other countries. In fact, the habit of extensive travel enjoyed by many Americans was—and continues to be—a considerable benefit to the worldwide hospitality industry.

1794–1900

It was in 1794 that the City Hotel—the first building in America erected specifically for hotel purposes—opened in New York City. Until this time, innkeepers had merely converted their own or someone else's home into an inn. The City Hotel was actually an overgrown inn, but with seventy-three rooms it was generally considered an immense establishment. It quickly became the social center of New York, which at that time was a booming town of 30,000.

Boston, Baltimore, and Philadelphia, not to be outdone by New York City, quickly opened similar establishments. In Boston it was the Exchange Coffee House, in Baltimore the City Hotel, and in Philadelphia the Mansion House. Each of these landmark hotels became a fashionable meeting place. (It is interesting to note that New York's first skyscraper was the Adelphi Hotel—a building of six stories.) Within thirty-five years of the opening of New York's City Hotel, the stage was set for a golden age of hotels in the United States.

The Original First-Class Hotel. In 1829, the first-class hotel was born in Boston. The Tremont House richly deserved the title "the Adam and Eve of the modern hotel industry"; it was something absolutely new in the history of hotelkeeping, and it surpassed its contemporaries, both in America and in Europe. With 170 rooms, the Tremont was the largest and costliest building that had ever been erected in America. Its architect, Isaiah Rogers, became the leading authority on hotel construction, and he strongly influenced hotel architecture for the next fifty years. It is generally acknowledged (although some may disagree) that the opening of the Tremont House established America's supremacy in the science of hotel management.

In addition to its size, cost, and luxury, the Tremont offered many innovations that made it a favorite topic of conversation among all who stayed there. The typical inn of the day consisted of one or two large rooms containing from three to ten beds. The beds were large enough to accommodate several people at one time, and an innkeeper never considered it a profitable night unless each bed was occupied by at least two guests. The Tremont was the first hotel to feature private single and double rooms; for those who valued privacy, this must have seemed like a dream come true. Not only were there private rooms, but each door had a lock. Two other innovations were considered extreme luxuries: every room was equipped with a bowl and a pitcher, and every room was supplied with free soap. Under the management of the Boyden family, a complete staff was hired, trained, and instructed to treat hotel guests with dignity and respect. French cuisine was offered for the first time in a hotel; the Tremont had the first bellboys; and the annunciator—the forerunner of the room telephone—was introduced there.

Ironically, while the Tremont initiated up-to-date hotel development, it soon fell victim to the trend it had started. Other cities took up the challenge of building finer hotels, and within twenty years the Tremont had to close for modernizing. With the fast pace of hotel improvements, the life span of the Tremont was sixty-five years, but during the last twenty it was a second-class hotel.

A Boom in Hotel Building. Throughout most of the nineteenth century, the contest among hoteliers to build better, larger, and more luxurious hotels continued. Every city in the nation wanted a hotel as good as the Tremont had been, in spite of the fact that often there was insufficient business to warrant such an operation. The theory seemed to be that no city amounted to much if it did not have at least one hotel that could impress upon visitors the greatness and hospitality of the community.

The hotel boom followed the westward movement. The excitement and competition of hotel building, which was at its peak between 1830 and 1850 in the East, went on all the way to the Pacific Coast. Chicago had the Grand Pacific, the Palmer House, and the Sherman House; the Planters was the pride of St. Louis; and Omaha extolled the virtues first of the doomed Grand Central Hotel and later of the Paxton. San Francisco built the Palace, the most ornate and expensive hotel of its day. The original Palace was built in 1875, cost $5 million (a tremendous sum in those days), occupied 2.5 acres in the heart of San Francisco, and had 800 rooms. The Palace never made money, but in appearance, structure, equipment, and lavishness, it was a real triumph.

Near the end of the nineteenth century, the hotel boom slowed; many people believed that every possible convenience, service, and new idea had been incorporated in the country's modern hotels. Little did they realize that within a few years the world's greatest hotelier would be building a hotel so new that it would be called an invention and would set the standards for twentieth-century hotel construction and management.

The intense competition among both cities and hoteliers to build the biggest and best hotel resulted in considerable deviation from the American tradition of hotels designed for everyone. At the close of the nineteenth century, there were many elegant, luxurious establishments, typified by New York's old Waldorf Astoria, Denver's Brown Palace, and San Francisco's Palace. At the other extreme were the small hotels built close to railroad stations; these were little more than overgrown rooming houses, and, because of their inadequacies, travelers often found them undesirable. Many people of modest means found the luxury hotels too expensive and the small hotels lacking in basic standards of service and cleanliness. Forced to choose one of two extremes, they were seldom content, whatever their choice.

New Developments

The turn of the century saw two new developments in the United States that were to significantly influence the future of the lodging industry. First, as the country's economy expanded, the commercial traveler became increasingly prominent in the business world. As the **commercial travel** group grew in number, there developed an increasing need for suitable lodging accommodations and conveniences to serve this new market. Second, improvements in roads, railroads, and water transportation made travel easier and less expensive. In a society seemingly ever restless and eager to be on the move, such a development immediately led to a tremendous upsurge in the number of travelers. Once the middle class of American society could afford to travel, it became an entirely new and vast population desiring lodging services.

1900–1930

At the very beginning of the twentieth century, the hotel industry was confronted with the challenge of serving a new traveling population. It had to face such questions as: What types of accommodations did the traveling salesperson need? Were new services necessary? Would these accommodations and services appeal to the middle-class traveler also, or was an entirely different type of operation necessary to meet these demands? What room rates would attract business and still provide a fair profit? Answers to these questions were not immediately available. Fortunately for the industry, Ellsworth M. Statler had foreseen the development of this situation and was ready to meet the challenge himself; while leaders in the field were discussing the alternatives, he was drawing plans for his first hotel. By 1907, construction was under way in Buffalo on the Statler Hotel.

The First Commercial Hotel. The opening of the Buffalo Statler on January 18, 1908, marked a new age in the American hotel industry; this was the birth of the modern commercial hotel. This "invention" (for as truly as Henry Ford invented the modern automobile, Ellsworth Statler invented the modern hotel) embodied all the known techniques of the day plus a lifetime of Statler's own experiences and ideas, which he had carefully recorded. Many services and conveniences that are taken for granted today were first introduced in this hotel. Fire doors protected the two main stairways. Keyholes for door locks were placed above the knob, so they could be easily located in a dark hall. A light switch just inside the door eliminated groping through the room in the dark. Rooms featured a private bath, a full-length mirror, and circulating ice water. A free morning newspaper was provided for each guest. Besides those specialties designed to increase guest comfort, the hotel contained many new structural and engineering designs, and, because of them, the Statler Hotel became the model for modern hotel construction for the next forty years. Truly, here was a hotel that provided comfort, service, and cleanliness for the average traveler at an affordable price. The hotel's advertising slogan was "A Room and a Bath for a Dollar and a Half." Immediate public acclaim ensured the success of the Statler Hotel and promoted the development of the Statler Hotel Company.

Following the excitement generated by the first Statler Hotel, the industry remained relatively inactive; this was caused in part by World War I. But the period from 1910 to 1920 turned out to be only the calm before the storm, for the prosperous Roaring Twenties were a boom period for hotel construction. Just as Wall Street thought there was no limit to the nation's prosperity, hoteliers considered the demand for hotel services and space limitless. During this decade, many of today's most famous hotels were built. New York's Hotel Pennsylvania (now the Penta) was the world's largest when it opened. Only a few years later, Ralph Hitz's Hotel New Yorker surpassed the Pennsylvania as New York's largest hotel. But in 1927 the giant of them all—the Stevens Hotel—opened in Chicago. With its 3,000 rooms, the Stevens (now the 1,600-room Chicago Hilton & Towers) took over the title "The World's Largest Hotel," a distinction it held until the completion in 1967 of the 3,500-room Hotel Rossiya in Moscow. Two luxury hotels that also were opened during this era were the present Waldorf Astoria and the Pierre, both in New York.

But large cities and name hotels had no monopoly on the building fever of the 1920s. Cities and towns everywhere were acquiring new hotels. Some were financed by communities, some by corporations, and some by private individuals, but the enthusiasm was shared by all.

The 1930s: The Depression

Then, just as bigger and better plans were being readied, the bubble burst, and hotels dropped into the unhappiest period of their history. In 1930, when the country plunged into the Great Depression, hotel rooms emptied, and business sank to an all-time low. Rate wars were commonplace, but even reductions in price did not attract business. So severe were the effects of the Depression that 85 percent of the nation's hotels went either into receivership or through some form of liquidation. Many hotels were purchased for almost nothing by entrepreneurs who would later refurbish them for operation or sell them as part of elaborate real estate deals. Properties worth millions could be bought for a few cents on the dollar. Many financial experts openly expressed the opinion that the hotel industry would never recover. Even later, when the general economy showed definite signs of improvement, investors thought the supply of hotel rooms was too great for any future demand and were unwilling to invest in them. Credit must be given to the hotel operators of this period. Many lost their savings and their businesses, but the majority of them never lost faith and remained to guide the hotel industry through its darkest hour.

The 1940s: World War II and Its Aftermath

By 1940, the industry was slowly stabilizing at a level which, although considerably below that of the 1920s, brought mild optimism about the future to a few hoteliers. However, no one envisioned the tremendous upswing that was to occur only two years later. The outbreak of World War II set into motion the greatest mass movement of people the United States has ever experienced. Millions of Americans went into the armed services. Millions more moved to areas around defense plants. Thousands of others—those coordinating the defense program—also found it necessary to travel. With this activity in full force, the demand for hotel rooms and services reached an all-time peak, and it became common to see people sleeping in hotel lobbies because there just were not enough rooms available. The hotel world had never experienced nor expected such a situation.

Undoubtedly, the war years presented the greatest single challenge the lodging industry ever faced. Hotels operated at capacity every day of the week, in spite of the fact that they had often lost half of their trained professional staff to the armed services. Since most hotels were understaffed, managers were forced to employ large numbers of people with no hotel experience. Standards of service necessarily suffered, but the fact that service was even maintained is amazing considering the handicaps under which hotels had to operate. Although the hospitality industry was not classified by the U.S. government as an essential industry as it is today, hoteliers could feel justly proud of their contribution to the nation's war effort.

The 1950s and Early 1960s

The prosperity of the war years continued through 1947, with hotel occupancy rates running above 90 percent. In 1948, a downward business trend began that set the scene for hotels for the 1950s.

Unlike the decade following World War I, the 1950s did not give rise to a boom in the building of major hotels. The Los Angeles Statler Hilton, which opened on October 27, 1952, was thought to be a trendsetter in hotel construction. One complete wing of the building was devoted to leasable office space; the theory was that rental income from office leasing would stabilize the hotel's financial structure by carrying fixed costs of operation during the slack periods of the year. While the theory appears valid, few, if any, later hotels followed the pattern.

Noted as a period of many new developments, the 1950s will best be recalled as the period when the motel and the motor hotel really came of age. In retrospect, it is easy to explain the phenomenal growth and success of this segment of the hospitality industry. More and more American families were traveling as a unit, and the prevailing mode of transportation was the automobile. The habits, tastes, and desires of the motoring public had undergone a considerable change. A new note of informality had entered the American way of life. Motels and motor hotels provided a way to eliminate formal dress, lobby parades, tipping, and parking problems. The rooms were new and featured modern furniture, wall-to-wall carpeting, and television. A swimming pool was often an added attraction.

At first, many hoteliers had difficulty deciding just what role motels would play in the industry. To many, they were a novelty that would soon wear out and fade away. To others, they were a new kind of competition and had to be beaten. The more farsighted hoteliers recognized that motels represented progress and quickly adopted the theory, "If you can't beat them, join them." Slowly but surely, established hotel companies moved into the motel business.

Unfortunately, members of the lodging industry spent much time between 1950 and 1960 arguing over the relative merits of hotels and motels. At times, an observer might well have believed that the two proponents were archenemies whose interests were completely incompatible. Slowly, however, the truth of the situation became obvious—motels and motor hotels were not a new and different industry at all. They merely represented a new concept in the art of innkeeping and were very much an integral part of the vast hospitality industry. Some alert individuals had recognized a need and had developed a product to meet it. As more and more professionals in all segments of the industry recognized this fact, suspicion and opposition turned to cooperation and understanding. A significant

Motels offered the casual comfort that the new traveling public wanted. There were no lobby parades, tipping, or parking problems. The rooms were new and featured modern furniture and wall-to-wall carpeting. (Photo courtesy of State Archives of Michigan)

event occurred in 1962 when the American Hotel Association changed its name to the American Hotel & Motel Association (AH&MA). Today there is a very positive, cooperative atmosphere throughout the Association (now named the American Hotel & Lodging Association [AH&LA]) and the dynamic and exciting industry it represents.

The Motel and Motor Hotel Boom. Once the motel boom got underway, it took off like a rocket. When looking at this segment of the lodging industry today, it is hard to believe that its origin was in the little roadside cabins and motels that were occasional dots on the landscape. From 1939 to 1962, 36,000 new motels were built in the United States. Although the early motels were small and frequently operated by a husband and wife team, a change took place in the 1950s. Motels grew in size (number of units) and in plushness and service. With increased size came many additional duties and managerial responsibilities. Professional management became not only desirable, but, often, essential.

In the early 1950s, a fifty-room motel was a real giant; within a few years, it was not even average. That is how rapidly the increase in size occurred. Most new motels built in the late 1950s and early 1960s contained a minimum of eighty rooms; the average was close to 100 rooms. In fact, the size explosion created a problem of terminology or classification. Soon the large motels were being called motor hotels, and it became difficult to differentiate between a motel and a hotel or between either of them and a motor hotel.

Initially, it was said that a motel was single-storied and a hotel multi-storied; furthermore, the hotel offered a much more complete variety of services. Soon motels became multi-storied, and then the larger motels instituted all of the usual hotel services. A new definition became necessary. In reality, the only difference between the traditional hotel and a motel or motor hotel is that parking is always available at motels and motor hotels. Also, since motel guests more frequently travel by auto than their motor hotel counterparts, the number of parking spaces per room is likely to be greater in a motel. Perhaps the safest conclusion is that motels are becoming more and more like hotels, while hotels are becoming more and more like motels.

Within any given area, motor hotels first grew up along the highway outside the city and slowly formed a ring around the city. The outskirts were considered the ideal location, and very few experts believed that motor hotels located in the center of town could succeed. As if to emphasize the rapidly changing nature of the hospitality industry, motor hotels began to appear within many downtown areas. The success of these downtown locations is evidenced by their continued growth. Because of the high cost of land in the city, these downtown motor hotels are usually large, high-rise constructions.

Earlier in this chapter, we noted the decline in hotel occupancy rates throughout the 1950s. This decline occurred in spite of a rapidly increasing incidence of travel and number of people needing lodging accommodations. Obviously, these people found rooms, and where they found them, of course, was in motels and motor hotels. Here, then, is the principal reason for the hotelier's concern about the mushrooming motel industry. Rooms business is by far the most profitable aspect of hotel management, and hotels suddenly found this profitable business declining at a rapid rate. Hotels in smaller cities were the first to receive the full brunt of the motel competition, and the attrition rate among them shot up alarmingly. Within a few years, many of these hotels closed or converted to non-hotel uses. Some disappeared completely and were replaced by parking lots.

Independents and Chains

One approach to classifying the lodging industry is to see it as being composed of two basic segments: independents and chains. The term **independent** refers to an operator owning one or more properties that have no chain relationship. By contrast, a **chain** refers to properties that are affiliated with others. Chain properties may be: (1) owned and operated by a chain company; (2) privately owned, but managed by a chain company; or (3) privately owned, but managed by a third-party management company (franchise). Many people incorrectly believe that a franchise and a chain operation are the same. They are not. While a franchise property is part of a chain, a chain property is not necessarily a franchise.

The Growth of Chain Operations

Chain operation is not new to the hotel industry. The operation of several hotels by one organization has been a common practice for over fifty years. Initially, the number of hotels under chain control represented only a small part of the total industry.

The tremendous growth of chains started during the last years of World War II and immediately afterward when the three major chains—Statler, Hilton, and Sheraton—began to grow rapidly. The conservative Statler group built the Washington and Los Angeles Statlers and started construction in Dallas and Hartford. Hilton and Sheraton decided a quicker method of growth was to purchase existing hotels. Both groups bought and sold properties so rapidly that a scorecard was necessary to keep up with the transactions. Both Hilton and Sheraton were referred to as real estate brokers rather than hotel operators. Whether the charges were justified or not is now of no consequence, since both groups have long since proved that they are in the business to operate first-class properties.

Today, chains dominate the industry, and the largest of these chains own or operate hundreds of properties around the world, as shown in Exhibits 1, 2, and 3. A quick glance at industry statistics should be enough to convince even the most stubborn independent fan that chain operations overshadow independents in today's hospitality industry. In 1987, chains owned 62 percent of all the hotel rooms in the United States. Today the figure is well over 80 percent.

Why are chains growing so quickly? The best one-word answer would be efficiency. When faced with stiff competition from efficient chain operations, an independent hotel operator traditionally has three alternatives. First, he or she might try to compensate for the decline in business by cutting down maintenance expenditures and forcing up room rates. This approach has been popular but is frequently suicidal. Second, if the independent has or can obtain capital, he or she can gamble and invest in improvements, modernization, and promotion. This approach can be sound and has kept many hotels independent. The third recourse is to sell in hopes of making some profit before it is too late; this is the reason that

Exhibit 1   World's Largest International Chains by Number of Properties

Hotel Chain		Number of Properties
1.	Wyndham Hotel Group	7,205
2.	Choice Hotels International Inc.	6,178
3.	InterContinental Hotels Group	4,480
4.	Accor	4,426
5.	Best Western International	4,086
6.	Hilton Worldwide	3,843
7.	Marriott International Inc.	3,718
8.	Magnuson Hotels	1,804
9.	Home Inns & Hotels Management	1,426
10.	Shanghai Jin Jiang International Hotels	1,243
11.	Starwood Hotels & Resorts Worldwide Inc.	1,090
12.	Carlson Rezidor Hotel Group	1,076
13.	Louvre Hotels Group	1,075
14.	Vantage Hospitality Group	1,045
15.	7 Days Group	944

Adapted from "Special Report: Hotels' 325," *Hotels* 46 (July/August 2012): 24.

Exhibit 2   Largest International Chains by Number of Rooms

Hotel Chain		Number of Rooms
1.	InterContinental Hotels Group	658,348
2.	Marriott International Inc.	643,196
3.	Hilton Worldwide	633,238
4.	Wyndham Hotel Group	613,126
5.	Accor	531,714
6.	Choice Hotels International Inc.	497,205
7.	Starwood Hotels & Resorts Worldwide Inc.	321,552
8.	Best Western International	311,894
9.	Shanghai Jin Jiang International Hotels	193,334
10.	Home Inns & Hotels Management	176,824
11.	Carlson Rezidor Hotel Group	165,663
12.	Magnuson Hotels	140,700
13.	Hyatt Hotels Corp.	132,727
14.	Westmont Hospitality Group	98,404
15.	7 Days Group	94,684

Adapted from "Special Report: Hotels' 325," *Hotels* 46 (July/August 2012): 24.

Exhibit 3   Major U.S. Hotel Chains

1. Marriott International Inc.	6. Best Western International
2. Hilton Worldwide	7. Carlson Rezidor Hotel Group
3. Wyndham Hotel Group	8. Magnuson Hotels
4. Choice Hotels International Inc.	9. Hyatt Hotels Corp.
5. Starwood Hotels & Resorts Worldwide Inc.	10. Westmont Hospitality Group

Adapted from "Special Report: Hotels' 325," *Hotels* 46 (July/August 2012): 26.

chain operators have been able to expand without engaging in a great deal of new construction.

Some of the advantages of chain operations include:

- Purchasing—Buying anything in bulk reduces costs. Because chains own a number of properties, they can buy everything from room furniture to telephone equipment to catsup in large quantities at lower prices.

- Human resources—By spreading the expense over their properties, chains can hire experts in every area of hotel operations, something few independents can afford to do.

- Promotion—National advertising campaigns in magazines, newspapers, radio, and television cost too much for independent hotels. However, chains can divide advertising costs among their properties so that each receives the benefits of widespread promotion at a small portion of the total expense. A recognized brand name often attracts guests more readily.

- Reservations—Centralized reservations can direct substantial business from one property within the chain to another. A large number of reservations that might otherwise go to other properties are made this way.

- Financing—Groups can raise money more easily than individuals, and thus chains can raise capital for improvement or expansion more efficiently.

- Centralized accounting, research and development, and real estate development—Personnel in these areas can serve all the hotels in a chain at a lower cost per unit than in an independent operation.

- Loyalty programs—Only with the economies of scale afforded by large chains can hotels afford to offer substantive frequent traveler rewards programs.

- Distribution systems—The complex set of mainly Internet-based reservations makers is best handled within the support structure of a hotel chain.

Although the world's first hotel chain was created by César Ritz, chain growth and development is most frequently associated with the American hotel industry. However, national hotel chains today operate in many countries of the world. Examples are: Steigenberger (Germany), Oberoi (India), Accor (France), Dusit Thani (Thailand), Mandarin Oriental, New World, Shangri-La (Hong Kong), Ciga (Italy), Othon (Brazil), and InterContinental Hotels Group (England). Exhibits 4–8 show the largest chains in major segments of the world.

Because of competitive pressure from chains, the independent operator faces great challenges. However, independent hoteliers can cite many advantages of independent ownership/management which, for some operators, make the competitive efforts worth the time and expense.

Paul Handlery, chairman and CEO of Handlery Hotels, Inc., wrote: "Owner/operators must realize that they also have a competitive edge. In most cases, they are entrepreneurs. This alone should enable them to do a better job of managing and operating a hotel property. Because of their vested interest (not to mention blood, sweat, and tears), they have the upper hand on a paid manager of a chain operation. More important, they can accomplish things more quickly and easily

Exhibit 4   Africa's Largest Chains

Hotel Chain	Headquarters
1. Tsogo Sun Holdings	Bryanston, South Africa
2. Jaz Hotels, Resorts & Cruises	Giza, Egypt
3. Protea Hospitality Group	Sea Point, South Africa
4. City Lodge Hotels	Cramerview, South Africa

Adapted from "Special Report: Hotels' 325," *Hotels* 46 (July/August 2012): 26–38.

Exhibit 5   Asia's Largest Chains

Hotel Chain	Headquarters
1. Shanghai Jin Jiang International Hotels	Shanghai, China
2. Home Inns & Hotels Management	Shanghai, China
3. 7 Days Group	Guangzhou, China
4. China Lodging Group	Shanghai, China
5. Toyoko Inn Co.	Tokyo, Japan
6. GreenTree Inns Hotel Management Group Inc.	Shanghai, China
7. Shangri-La Hotels and Resorts	Hong Kong, China
8. HK CTS Hotels Co.	Beijing, China
9. Okura Hotels & Resorts	Tokyo, Japan
10. BTG-Jianguo Hotels & Resorts	Beijing, China
11. The Prince Hotels	Tokyo, Japan

Adapted from "Special Report: Hotels' 325," *Hotels* 46 (July/August 2012): 26.

Exhibit 6   Mexico & Latin America's Largest Chains

Hotel Chain	Headquarters
1. Groupo Posadas	Mexico City, Mexico
2. Groupo Cubanacán	Havana, Cuba
3. Groupo de Turismo Gaviota	Havana, Cuba
4. Atlantica Hotels International	São Paulo, Brazil
5. Hoteles Islazul	Havana, Cuba

Adapted from "Special Report: Hotels' 325," *Hotels* 46 (July/August 2012): 30–32.

Exhibit 7   Europe's Largest Chains

Hotel Chain	Headquarters
1. InterContinental Hotels Group	Denham, England
2. Accor	Paris, France
3. Meliá Hotels International	Palma de Mallorca, Spain
4. Louvre Hotels Group	Paris, France
5. NH Hotels	Madrid, Spain
6. Whitbread	Dunstable, England
7. Barceló Hotels & Resorts	Palma de Mallorca, Spain
8. Riu Hotels & Resorts	Playa de Palma, Spain
9. Travelodge Hotels	Thame, England
10. Scandic Hotels	Stockholm, Sweden
11. Millennium & Copthorne Hotels	London, England
12. Iberostar Hotels & Resorts	Palma de Mallorca, Spain
13. Nordic Choice Hotels	Oslo, Norway
14. Pandox	Stockholm, Sweden
15. Club Méditerranée	Paris, France
16. Barony Hotels & Resorts Worldwide	London, England

Adapted from "Special Report: Hotels' 325," *Hotels* 46 (July/August 2012): 26.

Exhibit 8   North America's Largest Chains

Hotel Chain	Headquarters
1. Marriott International Inc.	Bethesda, Maryland
2. Hilton Worldwide	McLean, Virginia
3. Wyndham Hotel Group	Parsippany, New Jersey
4. Choice Hotels International Inc.	Silver Spring, Maryland
5. Starwood Hotels & Resorts Worldwide Inc.	Stamford, Connecticut
6. Best Western International	Phoenix, Arizona

Adapted from "Special Report: Hotels' 325," *Hotels* 46 (July/August 2012): 26.

than chain operation managers can. [Independent operators] can do so because they are the decision-makers and have no layers of upper management to go through for approvals. Having permanence in one's property gives stability in, and connection to, the social and business community."[1] Gary Saunders of the Boston Park Plaza put it another way when he said, "Some data say that 74 percent of travelers prefer chain hotels. That means 26 percent don't. I am glad to be fighting along with other independents for one quarter of the market ."[2]

It is important to note that, in contrast to the United States, less than 30 percent of the hotel rooms in Asia, Europe, and Latin America are chain affiliated.

Historically, small community hotels faced a double challenge—the efficiency of chain operations and the competition of the motel industry, which had already made heavy inroads into the rooms business. Caught in this crossfire, and with survival directly dependent upon their ability to adjust to this new situation, independent hoteliers were forced to change their mode of operation. To remain in business, many attempted to increase food and beverage revenue to counteract the decline in room revenue. This strategy worked in some instances, though many independent properties have closed.

The largest first-class independent hotels counterattacked the chains. Protective of their independence and rightfully proud of their reputation for fine service, they sought various means to gain certain advantages of chain operation without sacrificing autonomy. The Distinguished Hotels group exemplified this attitude. (Today, the industry has Preferred Hotels, an expansion and refinement of the original concept.) The Robert Warner Agency persuaded several famous independent hotels to pool their resources for advertising, promotion, and reservation services. Working as a group, the hotels were able to match the efficiency of chain operation in these three areas, but they were careful to point out that they were not a chain.

What will happen to the chains in the future? They are likely to expand and to represent an even larger percentage of the hotel room inventory. Not too many years ago, one could point to The Essex House in New York, The Brown Palace in Denver, and The Mark Hopkins and The Fairmont in San Francisco as examples of top-quality independent hotels. Today, however, each of them is a member of a chain operation. The independent fan can still point to a group of real stars—The Cloister on Sea Island, Georgia; Grand Hotel on Mackinac Island, Michigan; the Alameda Plaza in Kansas City, Missouri; and the Boston Park Plaza, which, with

Insider Insights

John Norlander
Retired CEO
Carlson Hospitality Worldwide
Minneapolis, Minnesota

While I was serving as its president, the Radisson Hotel Corporation was a relative newcomer to the international hospitality market, but it made some dramatic inroads in a very short period of time. We accomplished this by creating a long-term strategy of where we wanted to be ten years out. We started our international planning in the mid-1980s when it was easy to see that the results of overbuilding in the United States would put a damper on the growth rates we had set for ourselves (i.e., one hotel every ten days until the year 2000). So we set our focus on the global market. We determined that, to achieve our growth goals, we could find only half our goal in the domestic market and would have to look outside the U.S. for the other half. And, because of overbuilding, we would look to "conversions" rather than "new builds" for the domestic growth.

We were also aware that we would have to find new ways to handle our international development. Those companies that had started their growth right after World War II had a different set of opportunities. At that time, every city needed hotel facilities, and the American was the key target market. By the 1990s, that was no longer the case. The globalization of commerce makes the American business-person/tourist just one of many target markets. And Europe, although not over-built, didn't have the same need for new facilities that it had had forty years earlier. On the other hand, we perceived that Eastern Europe was almost in the same position in the late '80s and early '90s that Western Europe had been right after the war. Perhaps the one difference was that the people of Europe in the '40s and '50s knew that they had years of hard work ahead of them to reach a strong economic and political comfort level. The people of Eastern Europe in the '90s didn't have the same desire. The political confusion and economic conditions that engendered are unique in history due to the Communist system that held sway for more than forty years (and more than seventy in Russia).

Radisson looked at this set of conditions and decided that Eastern Europe was an excellent bet for the long run. We were very interested in putting our brand on hotels in the key cities in this emerging market. We wanted to do this early while the market was still in its development stages. We felt that those that came in early would be better positioned when the markets began to mature.

That is why we set up a joint venture in the USSR with the Intourist organization to manage the 630-room Slavjanskaya Hotel that was already in the construction phase. We created a partnership with an American business center operator to make it a 430-room hotel with 200 business center units, both of which were badly needed by the western business community trying to establish itself in Moscow.

Of course we expected to have problems on entering this new market. And we weren't disappointed! We got all the problems we anticipated plus the August 1991 aborted coup, and then the disintegration of the USSR and the shaky affiliation of the Commonwealth of Independent States. Our cup runneth over with problems!

(continued)

Insider Insights *(continued)*

But the good news was that our hotel was full! Wouldn't every hotel operator like to have that problem? So we were working every day to keep current with the changes in the banking regulations in the new Russia, which were "Byzantine" in comparison to most western countries. And the banking problems were compounded by the uncertainty of the ability of first Mr. Yeltsin (and now Mr. Putin) to make the ruble a convertible currency. All of this was mixed into the stew of the daily changing political situation. Russia was then experiencing a "war of laws" with new laws being passed almost daily to set the rules for working under a market economy, but the old laws of the managed economy were never voided. This created a golden opportunity for every type of problem to arise from the "Russian Mafiya" to the most basic "con schemes." And all of this occurred in the background of conditions that were somewhere between forty and seventy years behind the western democracies in everything from transportation to women's rights. It was an exciting time. But it was also dangerous. Our American partner, the CEO of our business center business, was murdered in broad daylight in the center of Moscow. His murderers were never found.

But we were committed and had jumped in with both feet. Not only did we open in Moscow with the only American-managed hotel, but opened in Sochi on the Black Sea, then Poland, followed by Latvia. While we were negotiating to build or manage hotels in a variety of other Eastern European locations, we hadn't forgotten Western Europe. We entered into an agreement with the SAS hotel group for them to develop Radisson-SAS hotels in Europe and the Middle East. At the time, our combined number of operations in the area was about twenty-eight. Today that number is over 100. This wouldn't have happened had we not been ready with our long-range plan to move outside the United States for some of our growth.

After the agreement with SAS, Radisson was able to shift a bit of focus to the Far East and Australia, where the company now operates in more than thirty locations.

Radisson's plan was to grow around the world by working with strong local partners in each area. In this regard, we developed a variety of joint ventures and partnerships in Canada, Mexico, Australia, the United Kingdom, Germany, and Jamaica.

The training of staff to the level required to service the western clientele's expectations has been a unique challenge. Our "Yes I Can" philosophy of service does not come naturally to those raised under the Communist regimes, but we have had great success in developing excellent service-oriented people. Given the chance to smile (along with the "smile instructions") and an opportunity to receive "incentives" (to help them smile!), the people respond.

Long-term planning was the key. A leadership position in the technology of hospitality marketing helped us find the right partners in each part of the globe, and a structured training plan that could be carried around the world was the glue that still holds it together.

its 977 rooms, is the largest independently owned and operated hotel in the United States. Around the world, the independent fan can still point with pride to the Vier Jahreszeiten (Four Seasons), Hamburg, Germany; the Ritz in Paris; Claridge's in London; the Dolder of Zurich; the Imperial, Vienna; Raffles Hotel, Singapore; the

Hassler in Rome; the Ritz, Madrid; the Bayerischer Hof in Munich; Grand Hotel, Stockholm; the D'Angleterre, Copenhagen; and the Imperial, Tokyo. (This listing is simply representative of the independent hotels of the world; there are many hotels of equal stature around the world.)

Referral Organizations

As lodging chains grew, independent operators found themselves in a tough competitive position. Generally, brand names and symbols have attracted American travelers. The chains, of course, had ready-made brand names and symbols that they promoted with great success. A chain operation was easily recognized by its facilities, the rather standardized architectural patterns, sometimes the color and decor, or possibly the road sign or the symbols used in its advertising. Chain properties could and did refer business to one another. They had advance registration and guaranteed reservation plans. In many cases, they enjoyed nationwide advertising and sales promotion campaigns.

In order to service the independent operator, a number of referral organizations grew up in the United States. Several achieved great growth and success. **Referral associations**, which are organized on a non-profit basis, are owned and controlled by the members. Through these organizations (similar to the Distinguished Hotels concept discussed earlier), the independent operator could obtain sales promotion benefits similar to those enjoyed by a chain operation without sacrificing individual control of his or her business. In addition, by belonging to a well-known referral organization, an independent had the brand-name image that could help marketing efforts.

Several of the largest referral associations in the United States were Quality Courts, Best Western, Best Eastern, and Master Hosts. Most of these have now evolved into full-service membership associations that are barely distinguishable from franchise companies.

Today there is a wide spectrum of marketing associations designed to publicize hotels regionally and globally. Both independent hotels and national chains join these marketing groups to expand the reach of their name or niche. These organizations were usually classified as voluntary chains/associations, but are now known as consortia. The five largest organizations in this category are shown in Exhibit 9. Today, they represent over 2.8 million rooms in 17,000 hotels around the world.

Utell/Unirez, based in the United States, has some 8,000 member hotels, both chains and independents, in 150 countries. The organization has some fifty reservation offices and interacts with eighty-five major airlines.

SynXis Corporation is the world's second largest consortium. When combined with Utell/Unirez, they represent 76.4 percent of the rooms served by consortia worldwide. Supranational Hotels includes numerous chains among its members. Leading Hotels of the World has five-star deluxe hotel members in sixty countries around the world. Deluxe chain members include Okura, Taj, Oberoi, and Regent.

As global competition heats up, the prognosis for consortia is for continued growth.

Exhibit 9   World's Largest Consortia

Organization	Headquarters
1. Utell Hotels & Resorts	Dallas, Texas
2. Hotusa Hotels	Barcelona, Spain
3. Great Hotels of the World	London, England
4. Best Eurasian Hotels	Moscow, Russia
5. Preferred Hotel Group	Chicago, Illinois
6. Keytel	Barcelona, Spain
7. Associated Luxury Hotels International	Orlando, Florida
8. WorldHotels	Frankfurt am Main, Germany
9. Supernational Hotels	London, England
10. Global Hotel Alliance	Geneva, Switzerland

Adapted from "Special Report: Hotels' 325," *Hotels* 46 (July/August 2012): 44.

Resorts

Resorts differ from traditional hotels mainly in the purpose of visit and the number and type of physical amenities they offer. Unlike other types of hotels, which place a strong emphasis on business travelers, resorts have a heavy bias toward leisure travelers. By definition, resorts feature more recreational amenities to cater to the leisure traveler, including such common amenities as lap pools, full-service spas, and extensive exercise facilities. Depending on the location and type of resort, the traveler may also find tennis courts, golf courses, waterparks, marinas, or ski slopes—all features designed for the enjoyment of travelers seeking a break from the work-a-day grind.

In the decades immediately following the American Civil War, luxury resorts began to show up around natural springs, making it possible for families to escape the heat of summer and enjoy "the cure." Trendsetters in this genre included Saratoga Springs, New York, White Sulphur Springs, West Virginia, and Warm Springs, Georgia. As transportation to remote locales improved, more resorts sprung up in cool mountain climes like the Adirondacks, the Poconos, and the Allegheny mountain ranges. All of these locales were in relatively easy reach of the major east coast metropolises from Boston to Washington, D.C. Similarly, ocean-side resorts began showing up in Maine, Cape Cod, the Jersey Shore, and as far down the coast as Ocean City, Maryland. Soon after World War I, winter-oriented resorts that featured skiing, skating, and other cold-weather activities began to appear. Sun Valley, Idaho, and Squaw Valley, California, were among the first ski resorts to enjoy widespread popularity.

Through most of the twentieth century, resorts tended to be seasonal in nature, often closing for the months that did not fit their orientation. Economic conditions and increased competition later dictated that resorts do two important things in order to remain in business. First, resorts began catering to companies and associations to offset the dwindling numbers of individual couples and families (who more frequently were availing themselves of second homes in resort locales or

Spring House, original site of the "healing waters" that first brought fame to The Greenbrier, White Sulphur Springs, West Virginia. (Photo courtesy of The Greenbrier)

joining timeshare organizations). In order to appeal to this new market, resorts began building extensive ballrooms and conference facilities to attract meetings and conventions. Secondly, resorts began finding ways to "stretch" their seasons to as close to year-round as possible by broadening their offerings to include special events and festivals that would attract visitors in months they previously had ignored. Today, most resorts have found ways to remain open year-round.

The resort business is very competitive and it faces many new challenges in the twenty-first century. Ease of travel to overseas destinations has broadened the options for vacationers. Long-haul air routes and jumbo jets mean that affluent travelers from all developed countries of the world can choose from an almost endless selection of countries and regions with resorts and special destination hotels. Resorts in Asia, Oceania, India, the Middle East, and South America now compete with the longer-established resort locales in Europe, North America, the Caribbean, and Hawaii. Cruise ships have even made Antarctica a vacation destination, so that it can now be said that leisure travel exists on all seven continents.

The Grand Hotel on Michigan's Mackinac Island—an early summer resort that is still world-famous today. (Photo courtesy of Grand Hotel)

Endnotes

1. Paul Handlery, *Arizona Hospitality Trends,* School of Hotel and Restaurant Management, Northern Arizona University, Spring 1992, p. 3.

2. Gary Saunders, personal conversation, AH&LA conference, late 1996.

Key Terms

chain—Properties that are affiliated with others. Chain properties may be: (1) owned and operated by a chain company; (2) privately owned, but managed by a chain company; or (3) privately owned, but managed by a third-party management company (franchise). A franchise and a chain operation are not the same; while a franchise property is part of a chain, a chain property is not necessarily a franchise.

commercial travel—Travel for business purposes, not for pleasure.

funicular—A cable railway that carried pleasure travelers to remote vacation hotels, such as the Alpine resorts.

grand tour—An extended trip across the European continent that served as part of the education of young British aristocrats; its popularity peaked in the eighteenth century.

hostelry—A lodging operation.

Las Brisas Hotel, Acapulco, Mexico—a famed year-round resort. (Photo courtesy of Las Brisas)

independent—A word referring to an operator who owns one or more properties that have no chain relationship. Contrast with *chain.*

market segmentation—The consideration of sources of business differently according to their purposes and needs. For example, in the lodging industry, business can be divided according to the guests' purposes for visiting: attending conventions, conducting company business, or traveling for pleasure. Hotels can be segmented or grouped according to their level of services also—for example, full-service, limited-service, or all-suite hotels.

referral associations—Associations that provide service to independent hotel owners. They are organized on a non-profit basis and are owned and controlled by the members. Through these organizations, the independent operator can obtain sales promotion benefits similar to those enjoyed by a chain operation without sacrificing individual control of his or her business.

spa—A mineral spring, or a locality or resort hotel near such a spring, to which people resorted for cures (from Spa, a watering place in eastern Belgium). Today, the word *spa* is used more loosely to refer to any fashionable resort locality or hotel.

Review Questions ⎯⎯⎯⎯⎯⎯⎯⎯⎯⎯⎯⎯⎯⎯⎯⎯⎯⎯⎯⎯

1. What types of people took the grand tour?

2. What factors brought about the establishment of early hotel training schools?

3. What types of hotels were produced by the first move toward market segmentation, and what were their distinguishing characteristics?

4. What characteristics defined the Tremont as the first first-class hotel?

5. Why was the Statler Hotel in Buffalo considered an "invention"?

6. What factors influenced the development of motels in the 1950s?

7. What is the primary difference between motels and hotels?

8. How, throughout history, has the hotel industry been affected by the principal mode of transportation of the time?

9. What is the primary difference between chain and independent lodging operations? How have independent operations been affected by the growth of chains?

10. What two strategic decisions helped resorts become year-round businesses?

11. What new challenges does the resort industry face in the twenty-first century?

 Internet Sites ⎯⎯⎯⎯⎯⎯⎯⎯⎯⎯⎯⎯⎯⎯⎯⎯⎯⎯⎯⎯⎯⎯⎯⎯⎯

For more information, visit the following Internet sites. Remember that Internet addresses can change without notice. If the site is no longer there, you can use a search engine to look for additional sites.

Lodging Associations

American Hotel & Lodging
 Association
www.ahla.com

American Hotel & Lodging
 Educational Institute
www.ahlei.org

Hospitality Financial & Technology
 Professionals
www.hftp.org

Hospitality Sales and Marketing
 Association International
www.hsmai.org

International Council on Hotel,
 Restaurant and Institutional
 Education
www.chrie.org

International Hotel & Restaurant
 Association
www.ih-ra.com

Lodging Companies

Best Western International, Inc.
www.bestwestern.com

Choice Hotels International, Inc.
www.choicehotels.com

Gaylord Opryland Resort &
  Convention Center
www.gaylordhotels.com/
gaylordopryland

Hilton Hotels Corp.
www.hilton.com

InterContinental Hotels Group
www.ichotelsgroup.com

Ritz-Carlton
www.ritzcarlton.com

Walt Disney World Resorts
http://disneyworld.disney.go.com/
wdw/index

Travel and Lodging Search Sites

HotelsOnline
www.hotelsonline.com

InfoHub Specialty Travel Guide
www.infohub.com

Priceline
www.priceline.com

Resorts Online
www.resortsonline.com

Travelocity
www.travelocity.com

Chapter 4 Outline

The Three-Party Structure
Hotel Franchising
    How Does Franchising Work?
    Franchise Fees
    Franchisor-Franchisee Relations
    International Franchise Companies
Hotel Management Contracts
    What Is a Hotel Management
        Company?
    Benefits of Management Contracts to
        Hotel Chains
    The *Woodley Road* Lawsuit
    Independent Hotel Management
        Companies
    Competition Among Hotel
        Management Companies
Brand Conversions
Market Segmentation
    Smith Travel Research
Consolidation
    Major U.S. Hotel Brands
    Pros and Cons of Consolidation
Globalization
    Europe
    Hawaii
    Asia and the Pacific Rim
    Mexico
    Central and South America
    The Middle East and Africa

Competencies

1. Explain the "three-party" hotel structure as it exists today. (p. 69)

2. Describe a hotel franchise agreement and the benefits of franchising to both the franchisee and the franchisor. (pp. 69–72)

3. Describe a hotel management contract plus its benefits to the hotel owner and manager. (pp. 73–76)

4. Identify the market conditions that make brand conversions popular. (p. 76)

5. Explain the impact that market segmentation and consolidation have had on the lodging industry. (pp. 76–80)

6. Describe the lodging industry as it exists in various locations around the world. (pp. 80–89)

4

The Birth of the Modern Lodging Industry

THIS CHAPTER EXAMINES the structure of the modern lodging industry and explores how that structure developed. The chapter begins with an explanation of the three-party lodging structure (i.e., the owner, the manager, and the brand). It then moves on to a discussion of how this structure came about and how hotel companies have developed growth strategies in order to expand throughout the United States and the world. The chapter also reviews franchising, management contracts, hotel brand conversions, and market segmentation before concluding with a look at industry consolidation and globalization.

The Three-Party Structure

In the early years of the U.S. lodging industry, most hotels were small independent properties. As late as 1950, there were only two major chains—Hilton and Sheraton—offering about 38,000 rooms or roughly 2 percent of the total number of rooms available in the United States. In those days, Hilton and Sheraton owned and managed their hotels. Today, there are a plethora of other hotel brands, but it is rare to find a hotel chain that owns and operates many of the hotels that fly their flags. Instead, most hotels are owned by a large real estate company or wealthy investment group, but are corporately managed by a hotel chain or independent management company and are branded by a hotel franchise company. This three-party structure enables real estate companies to own hotels while having them managed and branded by hotel professionals. This structure also makes it possible for hotel management companies and brands to grow rapidly and generate significant profits without the financial risks associated with hotel ownership. In other words, the hotel operator and brand are essentially guaranteed a profit since they receive a percentage of the "top line" on the income statement—revenues—as their fees. Meanwhile, the owner of the hotel assumes the risk that there will be a "bottom-line" operating profit at the end of the year large enough to pay all of the hotel's financial obligations and provide a favorable return on the equity investment.

Hotel Franchising

A primary reason for today's three-party approach is franchising. Hotel franchising became popular during the 1950s as the U.S. interstate highway system was constructed. New hotel franchise companies were formed with the goal of opening hotels under their brand names at each exit of the new interstate highway system. Companies like Holiday Inn, Howard Johnson, and Ramada Inn were the first hotel franchise companies, each with the same goal—to add new hotels to their chain and establish a nationwide reputation for quality and value. Franchising proved to be an excellent growth strategy for these chains, as they successfully created nationally recognized brands. As a result, the 1960s are often referred to as the "Golden Age of Franchising" in the lodging industry.

Today, the number of major chains has grown to include Marriott, Hilton, Starwood, Hyatt, InterContinental, Carlson, Wyndham, and many more. Most chains, however, actually manage only a small percentage of the hotels that fly their flags and own even fewer. These companies have been transformed from hotel real estate/operating companies into primarily hotel franchise companies. There is even a major hotel company that franchises multiple brands but neither owns nor operates a single property—Choice Hotels International. Exhibit 1 presents a list of today's largest hotel franchise companies and shows each company's number total hotels and franchised hotels.

How Does Franchising Work?

Franchising works this way: a hotel developer plans, finances, and builds a hotel and enters into a **franchise** agreement with a hotel brand. Under the terms of the agreement, the franchisee pays fees to use the franchisor's brand name and other brand services. The franchisee also agrees to comply with the franchisor's rules, regulations, and quality standards. In return, the franchisee receives the substantial benefits of chain affiliation, which include:

- The image and reputation of the brand.

- The brand's central reservation system.

Exhibit 1   Companies that Franchise the Most Hotels

Rank	Company	Hotels Franchised	Total Hotels
1.	Wyndham Hotel Group	7192	7205
2.	Choice Hotels International Inc.	6178	6178
3.	InterContinental Hotels Group PLC	3832	4480
4.	Hilton Worldwide	3205	3843
5.	Marriott International Inc.	2467	3718
6.	Accor SA	1678	4426
7.	Vantage Hospitality Group Inc.	1045	1045
8.	Carlson Rezidor Hotel Group	1030	1076
9.	Home Inns & Hotels Management Inc.	728	1426
10.	Shanghai Jin Jiang International Hotel Group Co. Ltd.	536	1243

Adapted from "Special Report: Hotels' 325," *Hotels 46* (July/August 2012): 40.

- New technology advancements.

- More easily obtainable financing.

- Access to the brand's international sales offices and marketing programs.

- The chain's guest loyalty program.

- Assistance in areas such as purchasing, interior design, and architectural planning.

- Pre-opening training of property-level staffs.

Franchise Fees

There are three types of fees charged to a franchisee: an initial franchise fee, an ongoing royalty fee, and fees for "chain services." Chain services include national/international advertising programs, guest loyalty programs, central reservation systems, regional sales offices, technology systems, and centralized purchasing programs. Chains charge an initial franchise fee of between $50,000 and $100,000 based on the size of the hotel. The ongoing royalty fee is usually between 3 percent and 5 percent of room revenue. The cost of chain services is allocated to all the hotels in the chain, either as a percentage of room revenue or on a per-available-room or per-occupied-room basis.

While franchising has many benefits to the brand, it can pose risks to a franchisor's name and reputation since the franchisor cannot exercise the same level of control over the operation of its franchised hotels as it does over the hotels that it manages. However, these risks are offset by the fact that franchises provide an inexpensive way for hotel companies to grow because the franchisee develops the hotel with his or her own money and is responsible for all hotel operating costs.

It would be difficult to overstate the tremendous influence that franchising has had on the lodging industry. Excluding properties under twenty-five rooms and strictly seasonal inns, today about 75 percent of all U.S. hotels are franchised.

Franchisor-Franchisee Relations

Not surprisingly, franchisor-franchisee relations are not always calm, smooth, and friendly. Every major franchisor has a franchisee advisory council comprising selected franchisees that is designed to promote cooperation between the two parties by reducing dissension and distrust. During the early part of the twenty-first century, conflict between franchisors and franchisees garnered a lot of press coverage. The Asian American Hotel Owners Association (AAHOA) publicly and emphatically stated its opinion that franchisors dominated and took advantage of franchisees. See Exhibit 2 for AAHOA's "12 Points of Fair Franchising." The war of words was loud and bitter and resulted in the withdrawal of support for AAHOA by a major franchise company. Major issues were the perceived negative economic impact that new hotels of the same brand were having on existing franchise properties, the difficulty of transferring franchises to a new owner when a hotel was sold, franchise termination rights, renewal options, and arbitration.

Exhibit 2   AAHOA 12 Points of Fair Franchising

1. Performance—a hotel brand should perform at a minimum percentage of occupancy or the franchisee can exit the agreement without liquidated damages.

2. Impact /Encroachment/Cross Brand Protection—there should be a fair formula established to protect a franchisee's assets.

3. Buyout /Voluntary termination—at present, average liquidated damages are a very unreasonable $2,000 a room; instead, liquidated damages should be negotiated on a reasonable period of time to replace the property.

4. Vendor exclusivity—franchisees should be free to buy from any vendor, not just those mandated by the franchisor.

5. Dispute resolution—an independent and fair process should be established for arbitration and mediation of disputes.

6. Venue—in the event of a dispute, the proceedings should take place in the country and state where the property is located.

7. Transferability—minimize transfer fees.

8. Database information—it should not be used for crossbrand selling by the franchisor; also, add a clause that grants the franchisee shared proprietary rights to the database.

9. Sale of franchise company—if a franchisor sells the brand to another entity, and that new owner wants to change system requirements, the franchisee should have the option of leaving the system or remaining and making the requested changes.

10. Disclosure—there must be greater franchisor accountability for marketing and reservation fees.

11. Quality assurance inspection—franchisors should permit an independent quality inspection in the event of a dispute.

12. Franchise sales ethics/practices—franchisors should mandate "good faith and fair dealing" practices among their sales agents.

Source: Asian American Hotel Owners Association (AAHOA), 2004.

International Franchise Companies

While U.S.-based hotel brands have expanded rapidly overseas in recent years, particularly in China, India, and Latin America, internationally based franchisors have been few in number. The French hotel company Accor and the Asian hotel company Shanghai Jin Jiang International are the only two international hotel companies to make the top ten list of hotel franchisors. European reservation and referral systems have been quicker to attain international status than franchisors. Today, some operators, such as Swiss-based Mövenpick, use a combination formula of franchising, management, and ownership. The French group Novotel comes closer to a pure franchising system. Its budget hotels are developed and operated by local contractors in accordance with Novotel guidelines under the Novotel concept of a low room rate and minimal food and beverage service.

Hotel Management Contracts

The 1970s witnessed the emergence of another growth strategy that also contributed to the creation of today's three-party hotel structure—the hotel **management contract**. Major hotel companies such as Marriott, Hilton, Sheraton, and Hyatt developed a strategy designed to increase the profitability of their companies and generate additional cash flow for their shareholders. This approach called for selling the hotels they owned and operated to major financial institutions, but retaining the right to manage the hotels on behalf of the new owner. This strategy benefited these hotel chains because they were able to eliminate depreciation expense from their income statements, while also generating huge sums of cash for their shareholders through the sale of the hotels. Life insurance companies such as Prudential, Travelers, Aetna, and Equitable purchased many of these full-service branded hotels and became the largest owners of hotels in the United States. Hotel companies changed from being primarily real estate/operating companies to being management/franchise companies. When the chains sold their properties, they negotiated management contracts with the new owners. If the 1960s was the Golden Age of Franchising, the 1970s ushered in the Golden Age of the Management Company.

What Is a Hotel Management Company?

Hotel management companies are firms that are hired by a property's owners to manage the hotel for them. The management contract gives full and complete control of the hotel to the management company, which is paid a fee for managing the property. The average base management fee for a full-service hotel is around 3 percent of total revenue. The operator often can also earn an incentive fee of 10 to 20 percent of gross operating profit under clearly established guidelines. For a limited-service hotel, the average management fee is around 5 percent of total revenue plus an incentive fee based on the hotel's profitability.

Benefits of Management Contracts to Hotel Chains

A chain's use of a management contract achieves many of the same goals achieved by franchising, but there is one major difference. Under a management contract, the chain has complete control over the day-to-day operations of the hotel, including quality standards, service levels, pricing, and the hiring and firing of staff members. Franchising does not provide this control.

Management contracts are thus another means by which chain operators can expand and gain market share without having to construct and own the hotels that fly their flags. The management contract arrangement permits chains to increase the number of properties they manage with little or no financial risk or equity investment. The operating losses often associated with the first few years of operation are also funded by the owner, not the operator. In addition, the management contract arrangement allows the operator to avoid the financial risks of market changes, overbuilding, recessions, and construction cost overruns.

The *Woodley Road* Lawsuit

During their early years, management contracts usually favored the hotel operator. In 1999, however, the pendulum swung to favor the hotel owner (at least in the United States) as the result of the *2660 Woodley Road Joint Venture* v. *ITT Sheraton Corporation* lawsuit. In this case, a jury awarded $51.8 million in damages against Sheraton. The jury also decided that the owner of the Woodley Road property was entitled to terminate Sheraton's management contract, which had more than thirty years remaining, without cost or penalty. *Woodley Road* established the hotel operator to be an agent of the owner with a "fiduciary obligation" to manage the hotel in the best interest of the owner rather than in the best interest of the hotel chain.

This case brought to light the practice of hotel management companies selecting for their managed hotels telephone companies, insurance companies, and other vendors based on rebates or payments from those vendors that the management companies did not disclose to the owners. Believing that they had an arm's-length relationship with the hotel owner, hotel operators felt no obligation to disclose these rebates to the owner and assumed that they were free to keep the full amounts of the rebates or payments. As fiduciaries, however, full disclosure and scrupulous accounting for the owner's benefit are now required.

The amount of damages was greatly reduced on appeal, and some elements of the decision were overturned, but other elements were affirmed. The case is quite complex and has left some confusion in its wake, but it seems that most states have accepted the argument that management companies have, at least in some respects, fiduciary relationships with hotel owners. The case has significantly affected how new management contracts are drafted and negotiated. Hotel operators now know that a failure to act in the best interests of the hotel owner may result in the payment of substantial damages and possibly even the termination of a long-term management contract. It is easier and cheaper to add disclosure requirements to a contract than to litigate such issues later.

Independent Hotel Management Companies

Not all hotel management companies are branded hotel chains. Today, in the United States alone, there are several hundred independent companies offering hotel management services. These companies manage both franchised hotels and independent properties. During the recession of the 1970s, a large number of lenders foreclosed on lodging properties and then needed someone to manage the properties until the hotels could be resold. Independent management companies were formed to meet this need, which led to a major shift in the industry. Today's largest independent and branded hotel management companies are listed in Exhibit 3 and Exhibit 4.

Competition Among Hotel Management Companies

Over the years, competition between branded and independent hotel management companies has become keen. This has brought about other changes in management contracts and has shifted considerable risk from the owner to the operator. Operator equity contributions are now more the rule than the exception. These contributions

Exhibit 3   Top 10 Independent Management Companies

Rank	Company	# Rooms Managed
1.	Interstate Hotels & Resorts	62,948
2.	White Lodging Services	23,849
3.	Pillar Hotels & Resorts	21,300
4.	GF Management	21,006
5.	TPG Hospitality	17,103
6.	Pyramid Hotel Group	16,900
7.	Aimbridge Hospitality	16,625
8.	Crescent Hotels & Resorts	15,396
9.	Remington	14,196
10.	Davidson Hotels & Resorts	13,215

Source: http://lhonline.com/hotel-development-resources/top_hotel_management_companies_signup/index.html.

Exhibit 4   Companies that Manage the Most Hotels

Rank	Company	Hotels Managed	Total Hotels
1.	Marriott International Inc.	1021	3718
2.	Home Inns & Hotels Management Inc.	698	1426
3.	Extended Stay Hotels	685	685
4.	Accor SA	671	4426
5.	Westmont Hospitality Group	655	659
6.	InterContinental Hotels Group PLC	637	4480
7.	7 Days Group Holdings Ltd.	533	944
8.	Starwood Hotels & Resorts Worldwide Inc.	517	1090
9.	Shanghai Jin Jiang International Hotel Group Co. Ltd.	464	1243
10.	Hilton Worldwide	439	3843

Adapted from "Special Report: Hotels' 325," *Hotels 46* (July/August 2012): 26, 40.

may take the form of providing working capital, funding pre-opening expenses, purchasing furniture, fixtures, and equipment; and even contributing equity for a minority ownership position. Today, most management contracts also include a performance clause requiring the operator to achieve certain levels of occupancy, average daily rate, and profitability. Operators who fail to comply risk termination by the owner with no penalty.

During the early 1980s, management contracts averaged twenty to twenty-five years in length with renewals at the option of the operator. During the 1990s, management contracts for full-service hotels averaged closer to ten years in length, while those for limited-service hotels averaged about five years. Today, management contracts are often even shorter in length and are performance-driven.

Brand Conversions

By the 1990s, the flood of new construction that began during the 1960s had slowed to a mere trickle, with financing for new construction almost non-existent. The chains therefore turned to brand conversions to grow their distribution systems and market shares. A **conversion** takes place when (1) an independent hotel property joins a chain, (2) a branded hotel changes from one brand to another (for example, a Holiday Inn becomes a Days Inn), or (3) a branded hotel becomes independent.

Hospitality Franchise Systems (which later became Cendant and then Wyndham) and Choice International Hotels were the fastest-growing franchise chains during this period. HFS's franchising strategy was nearly 100 percent conversion-driven, with half the growth coming from independents and half from other competitive brands. Choice International's growth in the United States was about 90 percent from conversions, while its European growth was nearly 75 percent from conversions. The use of conversions for growth was the primary strategy for many other chains as well. By the mid-1990s, however, new construction began to increase again as the economy was booming and financing became available. As a result, conversions were no longer the only key to growth. During the latest economic downturn, which began in 2007, new hotel construction once again slowed and since then has been essentially limited to locally financed select-service, limited-service, and budget hotels, and publicly financed large convention center properties.

Market Segmentation

Until the 1980s, the lodging industry was categorized into four types of properties, each with a rather general market: there were luxury hotels, commercial hotels, resort hotels, and motor hotels. All that changed when the creation of carefully targeted lodging packages led to greater market segmentation. As early as the 1970s, hoteliers had begun using market research, including focus groups, to assess the wants and needs of lodging consumers and to target potential lodging customers whose interests were not being met by existing hotels. Then major brands such as Marriott, Hilton, Starwood, and InterContinental created brands within brands such as Courtyard by Marriott, Fairfield Inn, Hilton Garden Inn, Four Points by Sheraton, Hampton Inn, Embassy Suites, Residence Inn, and Holiday Inn Express. Later, other niche brands such as Starwood's Hotel W and Aloft, InterContinental's Hotel Indigo, and Hyatt's Hyatt Place entered the crowded marketplace.

Smith Travel Research

Soon after Smith Travel Research began reporting statistics on the hotel industry, its data came to be regarded as the most accurate and reliable in the industry. Exhibit 5 shows its market segmentation categories by brands. Smith Travel

Exhibit 5   Market Segments with Representative Brands Listed

Luxury Segment	Upper Upscale	Upscale
Conrad	Club Quarters	Aloft Hotel
Fairmont	Embassy Suites	Courtyard
Four Seasons	Gaylord	Crowne Plaza
Grand Hyatt	Hilton	Doubletree
InterContinental	Hyatt	Four Points
JW Marriott	Joie DeVivre	Hilton Garden Inn
Loews	Kimpton	Homewood Suites
Mandarin Oriental	Marriott	Hotel Indigo
Ritz-Carlton	Mikko	Hyatt Place
St. Regis	Omni	Novotel
Trump Hotel Collection	Renaissance	Radisson
W Hotel	Sheraton Hotel	Residence Inn
Waldorf-Astoria	Swissôtel	Sonesta Hotel
	Warwick Hotels	Springhill Suites
	Westin	Staybridge Suites
	Wyndham	

Upper Midscale	Midscale	Economy
Comfort Inn	America's Best Suites	America's Best Inn
Drury Inn	Baymont Inn & Suites	Budget Suites of America
Fairfield Inn	Best Western	Days Inn
Hampton Inn	Candlewood Suites	Econo Lodge
Holiday Inn	Hawthorn Suites by	Extended Stay America
Home2 Suites by Hilton	Wyndham	InTown Suites
Isle of Capri	Howard Johnson	Knights Inn
Lexington	La Quinta Inn & Suites	Microtel Inn
Ramada Plaza	Quality Inn	Motel 6
Sunspree Resorts	Ramada	Red Roof Inn
TownePlace Suites	Sleep Inn	Scottish Inn
Wyndham Garden Hotel		Super 8
		Travelodge
		Value Place

Source: Smith Travel Research.

reports statistics on 187 brands, but, for illustrative purposes, the exhibit includes only representative brands in each segment. Nearly every major hotel chain has successfully developed a "family" of brands within its primary brand as a strategy to expand market presence and penetration.

In addition to satisfying the lodging needs of special market segments, segmentation has also provided another huge advantage to franchisors. Today it is not unusual to find a Marriott Hotel, a Courtyard by Marriott, a Fairfield Inn, and a Residence Inn in the same market, all within a few miles from one another. All of these brands are owned by Marriott and share the same reservation system and loyalty program. Thus, market segmentation has provided major hotel brands with the ability to significantly increase their market penetration and profitability.

Consolidation

Another major development in the lodging industry was a trend toward **consolidation**, which began around 1980. Throughout the 1980s, newspapers were filled with stories of large corporate mergers, acquisitions, and takeovers. No hostile takeovers occurred in the hotel industry, but changes in ownership were so numerous that it often seemed as though hotel brands were playing a game of musical chairs. Consolidation took place both nationally and internationally, with the end result being a dramatic reduction in the number of hotel brands being placed into fewer and fewer ownership companies. When the 1980s opened, the industry comprised thirty-eight individual chains, as listed in Exhibit 6. By midway through the 1990s, thirty-two of those thirty-eight chains had been sold or merged at least one time.

This trend accelerated in 1998 when twenty-five mergers and acquisitions took place, the largest number of transactions in hotel history. The total value of

Exhibit 6   Once-Independent Hotel Chains

Hilton Hotels	Ciga Hotels
Sheraton Hotels	Knights Inns
InterContinental Hotels	United Inns
Howard Johnson Motor Lodges	Super 8 Motels
Marriott Hotels	Red Lion Hotels
Western International Hotels	Regent Hotels
Ramada Inns	Microtel
Holiday Inns	Hawthorn Suites
Rodeway Inns	Ritz-Carlton Hotels
Doubletree Hotels	Registry Hotels
Guest Quarters Hotels	H.E.I. Hotels
Days Inns	Carefree Resorts
Radisson Hotels	Travelodge
Stouffer Hotels	Kempinski Hotels
Dunfey Hotels	The Bally Company
Omni Hotels	Red Roof Inns
Méridien Hotels	Hospitality Franchise Systems
Forte Hotels	Choice International Hotels
Bass plc	Accor

those deals was $32.9 billion. Consolidation activity continued during the first decade of the twenty-first century as several major transactions occurred:

- InterContinental Hotels purchased Candlewood Suites

- MeriStar Hotels & Resorts and Interstate Hotels Corporation merged to form Interstate Hotels & Resorts

- MGM Mirage purchased Mandalay Resort Group

- Harrah's purchased Caesars

- Choice Hotels purchased Suburban Franchise Systems

- The long-expected reunification of Hilton Hotels Corp. and Hilton International occurred

- The biggest newsmaker was the Blackstone Group, a private equity firm, that:

  - Purchased La Quinta

  - Sold Baymont Inns to Cendant

  - Sold AmeriSuites to Global Hyatt Hotels, which renamed it Hyatt Place.

  - Purchased Wyndham Hotels and resold it to Cendant, now Wyndham Hotel Group.

  - Purchased Hilton Hotels Corporation for a record-setting price of $26 billion.

Marriott also made headlines in 2012 by adding another brand to its already large stable of brands. Gaylord Entertainment agreed to sell the Gaylord Hotels brand and management rights to its four hotels to Marriott. Gaylord will continue to own the hotels and other businesses and will reorganize in a real estate investment trust (REIT).

Major U.S. Hotel Brands

Today, seven companies dominate the U.S. lodging landscape: Accor, Choice, Hilton, InterContinental, Marriott, Starwood, and Wyndham. Together they account for about two-thirds of the branded properties and guest rooms in each of five lodging segments.

Pros and Cons of Consolidation

Consolidation has had its proponents and its critics. Advocates state that consolidation is inevitable. Proponents believe that consolidation is the only way a hotel company can achieve the resources necessary to compete globally. Critics of consolidation have raised the following questions:

1. Is the industry following in the footsteps of the airline industry, so that eventually five or six major companies will own every hotel brand?

2. Is consolidation good for the industry, or is it good for chain executives who make millions of dollars from acquisitions and mergers?

3. Will individual brands lose integrity and independence under mega-chain control?

4. Do the top corporate lodging executives worry about individual franchisees?

5. Will consolidation put thousands of people out of work?

6. Is big really better?

The critics of consolidation have called it an ominous trend. They contend that chains are growing not by satisfying customers and franchisees, but through balance sheet tricks and other manipulations—including taking stocks public, taking them private, and buying and selling corporate interests at a rapid rate that has little to do with the management of hotels and hotel brands. Now that consolidation appears to have slowed somewhat, at least for the time being, the next few years could tell us who is correct—the proponents or the critics.

Globalization

Today, in business circles around the world, the word heard most often is "globalization." Every major hotel chain places a great emphasis on international expansion. Exhibit 7 lists the world's most global chains today. Exhibit 8 lists foreign chains with a U.S. presence.

Europe

It is pointless to try to describe the European hotel industry as a whole. The structure of the industry in each country is different, and there is no consistent approach to quantifying or rating the hotels from one country to another. The common denominator is the predominance of independently owned and operated hotels. There are large chains based in each of the European countries, often with operations in two or more other countries in Europe. Of the European nations, France's lodging industry most closely resembles that of the United States. It has the most chain-affiliated hotels, the most chains, the most segmentation and branding, and the most hotels affiliated in other European countries. The French hotel industry is dominated by Accor, which has about 40 percent of all chain-affiliated hotels in France. Even so, chain-affiliated hotels in France account for only about 20 percent of the country's lodging industry. Chain-affiliated hotels in the United Kingdom account for about 15 percent of that country's industry. About 10 percent of Germany's hotels are chain-affiliated, and many of them are French and British.

In Europe, the lower midscale and midscale (moderately priced) segments are the least organized and least dominated by major hotel chains, except in France by Accor. The budget and luxury segments are expanding and are increasingly becoming dominated by well-established European and U.S. chains.

The United Kingdom, France, Germany, and the Benelux countries (Belgium, the Netherlands, and Luxembourg) are the most advanced economically, have the largest gross national products (GNPs), and generate and receive the most business travelers. These countries are equivalent to 13 percent of the geographical area of the United States, but have a population equal to 85 percent of the U.S. population. The cultures of these countries are still distinct, but they are increasingly

Exhibit 7   Lodging Companies in the Most Countries

Rank	Company	# of Countries
1.	Carlson Hotels	150
2.	InterContinental Hotels Group	100
3.	Starwood Hotels and Resorts	93
4.	Accor Hotels	90
5.	Hilton Worldwide	81
6.	Best Western International	80
7.	Marriott International, Inc.	67
8.	Wyndham Hotel Group	66
9.	Hyatt Hotels	51
10.	Choice Hotels International	35

Source: Salem Nuri, "The Top Ten Hotel Companies." Available at www.ehow.com/list_6853821_top-ten-hotel-companies.html.

Exhibit 8   Foreign Chains in the U.S.

- Accor
- Four Seasons
- Fairmont Raffles Hotels International
- Taj Hotels Resorts and Palaces
- Nikko Hotel International
- Group Hotusa
- Grupo Posadas
- Louvre Hotel Group (headquartered in Paris, but owned by Starwood)
- Van der Valk Hotels, Restaurants en Vergaderzalen
- Pestana Hotels & Resorts
- Mandarin Oriental Hotel Group

integrated economically. It has also become much easier to travel within Europe since the advent of the European Union, which is creating an excellent opportunity for Pan-European hotel systems.

Most global brand players are active in the European market, where they compete with strong national brands: Whitbread and Thistle in England, Dorint in Germany, Sol Meliá in Spain, Golden Tulip in the Netherlands, and Scandic in the Nordic regions. Seven countries host 75 percent of Europe's hotel rooms: Austria, England, France, Germany, Greece, Italy, and Spain.

Among Europeans traveling within Europe, heavy business/commercial trade tends to move among the United Kingdom, France, Germany, and Scandinavia. The United Kingdom is the leading outbound business travel market, while Germany is the major international business travel destination for Europeans. European leisure travel is focused primarily on the warmer-weather countries such as Spain, Portugal, Italy, southern France, and Greece. Business travelers represent only 15 percent of total European travelers, but that percentage converts to 25 million trips per year. Leisure travelers are very seasonal and generally are very cost-conscious. When they stay at hotels (which many avoid), they tend to stay at inexpensive ones.

Hawaii

Hawaii is one of the most successful visitor destinations in the world. While its first great surge of popularity was the result of romantic Hollywood movies that depicted an exotic Polynesian paradise, its enduring popularity is due to its ideal climate, tropical setting, and a unique blend of Polynesian, Asian, and American cultures.

The biggest single impact on the tourism market and the economy of Hawaii occurred when the value of the Japanese yen doubled against the U.S. dollar between 1985 and 1988. The Japanese government began encouraging travel and investment abroad, and Hawaii was the logical destination. There was a corresponding tidal wave of Japanese investments in Hawaiian real estate, primarily "trophy" hotels, resorts, golf courses, and commercial buildings.

Those years brought rapid growth in outer island luxury hotels, with Japanese investors fronting much of the capital. Unfortunately, many of these hotels were built at a cost in excess of $500,000 per room, meaning that even during prosperous times it was difficult to realize any reasonable rate of return on investment. By the mid-1990s, the number of expensive deluxe rooms had increased from 4,000 to 14,000, but the demand for such accommodations was falling drastically. Many of these hotels went into bankruptcy or were sold at bargain-basement rates. For example, the $180 million Ritz-Carlton was sold for $75 million; the $350 million Kahala Hilton brought only $50 million; four hotel properties with a combined value of $129 million sold for $41.1 million; and ANA Hotels closed the doors of their Sheraton Makaha. By 1997, Japanese losses in Hawaii totaled over $1 billion. The Japanese began to divest their trophy hotels even faster than they had acquired them. As a result, Japanese ownership of hotels in Hawaii today is insignificant.

Tourism is extremely important to Hawaii, so it is not surprising that the state undertook an aggressive marketing campaign to reverse the decline in tourism visitors and income. The campaign landed Hawaii among the three states having the highest travel budgets. Hawaii's tourism business has always had a peak-and-valley nature due to external factors, such as national and international economies, wars, and terrorism threats. Yet as long as demand remains strong to visit these beautiful tropical islands, especially from mainland Americans and travelers from the strong Pacific Rim countries, tourism will continue to flourish in Hawaii and remain the staple of the Aloha State's economy.

Asia and the Pacific Rim

The 1980s in Asia were dominated by the buoyant and incredibly aggressive Japanese economy. Japanese developers, spurred by very favorable credit terms from their lenders, undertook to acquire existing hotels and to build new ones in virtually every corner of Asia. This spending spree was accompanied by an ever-increasing flow of Japanese travelers, a trend inspired by the Japanese government's strategy of encouraging workers to take more time away from their jobs. Major Japanese investment in foreign lands also meant an accelerated pace of foreign business travel. As a result, Japanese-owned (and frequently Japanese-managed) hotels can now be seen along the Western Pacific Basin from Australia and New Zealand to the south all the way to Taiwan and South Korea in the north.

Toward the end of the 1980s, a near mirror-image set of developments occurred with South Korea, whose foreign travel restrictions were greatly liberalized after the 1984 Seoul Olympics. South Korean investment in hotels and resorts has accelerated each year of the twenty-first century. This trend is expected to continue.

Some of the key areas that have seen major tourism development in recent years include: Guam and Saipan; Okinawa; Korean Highlands; Cheju Island; Cebu, the Philippines; Phuket, Thailand; Bali, Indonesia; and Queensland, Australia.

As the economies of Asian countries—most notably Taiwan, Hong Kong, Singapore, Thailand, and Malaysia—continue to grow, more investment in tourism, both within their borders and internationally, can be expected. Their citizens will increasingly demand to partake of the fruits of economic success by enjoying leisure travel.

Hotel companies with extensive Asian experience are enjoying success in securing management contracts for this new wave of Asian resorts and hotels. Obtaining these contracts often involves some investment on the part of the hotel companies. Among the companies most active in the area are Hilton, Hyatt, Shangri-La, Four Seasons, Regent, Swissôtel, and Sheraton. Most recently, Marriott has entered the picture with commitments in Australia, Japan, and Indonesia to supplement its presence in Hong Kong.

Without a doubt, the most explosive growth in new hotels and tourism infrastructure during the first decade of the twenty-first century has occurred in China. This growth has paralleled the overall quantum growth in China's economy. A further stimulus to the growth of four- and five-star hotels came with the 2008 Olympic Games in Beijing. This growth has represented a major portion of international development among the world's largest hotel companies. Hilton, for instance, now has more than fifty properties in China under its umbrella of brands. By comparison, Hilton had only six hotels in China in 2006. InterContinental is by far the biggest hotel presence in China, Hong Kong, Taiwan, and Macau; it has grown from 125 to 250 hotels in this region between 2007 and 2012. Similarly aggressive expansion is being undertaken by Marriott and Hyatt. Even U.S.-based economy brands are taking hold in China. For example, Wyndham-owned Super 8 initiated a master franchise agreement with a Chinese company to open one hundred units.

If China continues its economic growth and the liberalization of its trade policies with foreign countries, then more new hotel opportunities can be expected. The whole realm of leisure-oriented hotels, golf courses, theme parks, beach resorts, and other diversions will grow immensely as the Chinese people clamor for recreational options.

Following closely behind China in its meteoric rise to a world economic power has been India. Although its tourism infrastructure is not as well established as China's, many international companies have made major commitments to an Indian presence since the start of the twenty-first century. The enormous

Insider Insights

David Jones
Vice President
Shangri-La Hotels
Hong Kong ———————————————————————————————————

A great deal has been said about how growth in the Pacific Rim will make Asia the focal point of the new century. While there is little question of the growing economic impact of the region, few North Americans understand or appreciate the contrasts within Asia.

An understanding of the differences in cultures from one Asian country to another, and also of the differences in how business is done in Asia versus North America and even Europe, will be essential in working with Asia and within it. The most common mistake North Americans make is assuming that all Asians are alike and basing their expectations on one stereotype. Nothing could be more offensive to the Asian businessperson with whom you are dealing.

So much has been made of Japanese success that it is common to depict theirs as the typical Asian culture. However, the fact is that, even within Asia, the Japanese are treated differently. Hotels throughout the rest of Asia do as much as they can to separate Japanese travelers from all others, at the request of the Japanese. This includes supplying special Japanese menus, having Japanese restaurants run by Japanese in hotels, employing Japanese nationals as sales staff purely to secure Japanese business, and employing as many Japanese-speaking staff as possible in guest contact areas. The influence of the Japanese is evident in all of Asia, but not the integration; Japan remains separate.

The future of Asia in this century will be shaped by a number of other key players, including the "four dragons" (Hong Kong, Korea, Taiwan, and Singapore) and China, the giant neighbor to the north. Each of these countries has tremendous economic potential and will be factors in the hospitality industry as destinations and as outbound markets for business and leisure travel. Therefore, North Americans will have to become more aware of how the cultures and business practices of these countries differ from Japan's as well as from one another's. It is important to note that North America has been very influential in the development of Korea and Taiwan, while the United Kingdom has greatly influenced Hong Kong and Singapore. Taiwan, in fact, has the largest surplus of U.S. dollars of any country in the world, including Japan. American cars are commonplace in Korea and Taiwan, yet far less of the population can speak English than in either Hong Kong or Singapore.

China is an incredible sleeping giant that makes up one-third of the world's population. Although China remained isolated from the rest of the world during the Cultural Revolution, its spread of influence in all of Asia is immense. The Chinese population outside of China is a major factor in every other Asian country, particularly in the business community. Those whose families left China generations ago still feel strong ancestral ties to China. This has been especially evident in recent years with the re-opening of relations between countries such as Taiwan, Singapore, Malaysia, and Indonesia, which has resulted in a major increase in outbound travel back to China. The continued economic success and increased level of higher education within the four dragons has raised incomes and also the cost of

Insider Insights *(continued)*

labor, which has made China an extremely important source of workers for labor-intensive industries. This, combined with the more open attitude of government to capitalistic ways and the incorporation of Hong Kong into China in 1997, puts all the ingredients for China's success into place. These points are crucial for North Americans to understand, because the Chinese are very different from the Japanese in culture and business practice.

Understanding the diversity of each of these countries is essential because each has a strong sense of national pride. However, many customs that have been influenced by the Chinese and Japanese carry throughout the region. These customs determine how business is done and are vastly different from all of the Western world. Probably the most significant is the intense work ethic. It can best be summarized as "work before self." Most North Americans understand the attitude of work before pleasure, but this is much different: it is an unconditional commitment to work success and the personal rewards that go with it. It's probably most noticeable in Japan and the four dragons, but carries throughout the region where Chinese ethics have influence. An important driving force in this work ethic is a materialistic view of success: "The one with the most toys wins." This has led many Japanese businesspeople to purchase hotels and other real estate at far more than they are worth. On the other hand, the Chinese prefer to negotiate and always compare how well one did in getting a bargain than another. This is another important difference to understand when doing business with a Japanese versus a Chinese.

A second important ideological concept that differentiates Asian business ethics from those in the Western world is that of "face." In a nutshell, it simply means you can never directly tell an Asian that he or she is wrong, or you risk giving him or her a major loss of "face," which in turn will make you the loser. North Americans, on the whole, are very self-critical and are receptive to constructive criticism. They are also accustomed to personal evaluations and individual performance goals. These tools do not easily adapt to the Asian "face" ideology. Therefore, to accomplish the same objectives, you must approach management issues from an entirely different direction. This is particularly important in directing employees and motivating them to achieve a targeted result.

The third custom that differentiates Asian business practices from those of North America is that of "respect for the elders." The concept applies not only to the senior person in chronological terms, but also in terms of status on the corporate ladder. It is simply not acceptable to go against the wishes of the elders, as they are seen to know best; whether you personally agree is irrelevant. This is very different from the North American approach that challenges senior staff members to listen to and involve others in the decision-making process. It also makes the sales-approach method of asking for the business much more difficult, because it is viewed as improper to question the decisions of others. Modifying the sales effort to a more public relations–oriented approach where the customer's status level is nurtured is important.

North Americans have always viewed Asia as very mysterious, largely because of a lack of understanding of important differences in some of the basic principles of doing business and a lack of education about the region's culture and

(continued)

Insider Insights *(continued)*

geography. The globalization of the hospitality industry through the increased international ownership of hotels and hotel companies, especially by Asians, has made the entire world smaller. Therefore, it is imperative that we all do more to adapt to and understand the contrasts in Asia instead of imposing our own ideological concepts and stereotypes.

---

demand for hotels by business travelers tapping into India's growing economy far exceeds the supply. This has resulted in huge increases in average daily rates for international-class hotels.

The list of hotel companies scrambling to meet the growth in the Indian economy is similar to those vying in China, and run the gamut from economy to luxury. One factor that may limit the growth of hotels in India is the extremely high price of land in India's major cities. This problem may be alleviated if the Indian government changes its laws limiting the amount of land for sale. It can be expected that, with the continued growth of multinational companies doing business in India, ways will be found to provide lodging for business travelers.

When Great Britain returned Hong Kong to the Chinese in 1997, there was uncertainty as to how this significant political change would affect Hong Kong's booming free-trade economy. Such concerns proved to be unfounded, as tourism and commerce have proceeded. Lack of building space and the expense of land are bigger deterrents to Hong Kong's growth than is Chinese rule.

Mexico

Mexico's beautiful white beaches, clear blue waters, and sunny, warm climate have long been favorites of vacationers from the United States, Canada, and Europe. In addition, there has been an increasing interest among cultural tourists in the pre-Columbian archaeological sites. The great sport fishing areas along the Pacific coast of the Baja California Peninsula also are very popular. Small hotels have been built along the 1,000 miles of beautiful seashore from Tijuana to Cabo San Lucas, including a large number of first-class hotels in Cabo. Recent gang-related drug violence, however, has had a negative impact on the number of international tourists visiting Mexico.

Relaxing in Mexico was always easy; doing business in Mexico has historically been difficult. Things, however, have begun to change because Mexico is now actively promoting foreign investment. As a result, international business in Mexico is increasing, and so is the number of business travelers. Mexico's large commercial and industrial cities—Mexico City, Queretaro, Guadalajara, Monterrey, and Leon—along with the petroleum areas of Tampico and Tabasco, are welcoming more travelers every day. One of the biggest changes has been the opening up of many Mexican industries to 100 percent foreign ownership. Foreign companies can now own more than 50 percent of Mexican companies and can also own land in Mexico. International hotel companies were among the first to take advantage of this new economic climate. Mexico's largest hotel chain, Grupo Posadas, has been joined by a wide assortment of hotel companies (see Exhibit 9).

Mexico uses a "Stars and Diamonds" rating system similar to the one used in the United States. However, there are differences that make comparisons with U.S. properties difficult and sometimes misleading.[1] For example, a five-star hotel in Mexico is equivalent to a four-star property in the United States. The Mexican government completed a study of the rating system with an eye to developing an official government rating system. Currently, the 400,000-plus hotel rooms in Mexico fall into the following categories:

Unclassified	33.3%
1 Star	10.1%
2 Star	13.5%
3 Star	13.9%
4 Star	13.9%
5 Star	15.4%

The future for the Mexican hotel industry appears somewhat uncertain. Stability of government, the curtailment of gang violence, and the strength of the oil industry will dictate Mexico's future success.

Exhibit 9   Hotel Brands Operating in Mexico

Best Western	Holiday Inn	ONE
Camino Real Hotels	Holiday Inn Express	Quality Inn
City Express	Howard Johnson Hotels	Radisson Hotels
Comfort Inn	Hyatt Place	Raintree Resorts
Courtyard	Hyatt Regency	Ramada
Crowne Plaza Hotels	Ibis Hotels	The Ritz-Carlton
Days Inn	InterContinental Hotels	Riu Hotels & Resorts
DoubleTree	JW Marriott	The Royal Resorts
Econo Lodge	Krystal Hotels	Royal Solaris Resorts
Embassy Suites	La Quinta Hotels	Secrets Resorts & Spas
Fairfield Inn	Live Aqua	Sheraton Hotels & Resorts
Fiesta Americana	Marriott	Sleep Inn
Fiesta Inn	Meliá Hotels & Resorts	Staybridge Suites
Four Seasons Hotels	Motel 6	Super 8
Hampton Inn	NH Hotels	W Hotels
Hilton	Novotel	Westin Hotels & Resorts
Hilton Garden Inn	Omni Hotels	Wyndham Hotels

Central and South America

Extensive, sustained growth of tourism in Central and South America has been deterred by a number of factors. First, there is the considerable distance between this region and both North America and Europe, which are the top generators of tourist volume. The second factor is the common perception of unstable political conditions. Tourists like stability and serenity. Similarly, several countries must deal with reputations of lawlessness due to drug trafficking. Also, these regions suffer from a lack of well-known natural attractions to draw tourists. Major exceptions include Peru's Machu Picchu and the beaches of Rio de Janeiro and Punta del Este. This problem is magnified by the reality that most Central and South American countries lack the financial resources to mount major awareness campaigns to the wealthy people of the Northern Hemisphere.

However, several recent developments may boost tourism in this region. One of these is the increasing popularity of ecotourism, which has brought many travelers to places such as Costa Rica and Panama, countries blessed with virgin rain forests and tropical mountain regions. In addition, several Central American countries, including Honduras and Guyana, have developed successful entrepreneurial tourism with scuba diving establishments. Finally, as trade barriers have diminished between the United States and Central and South American countries, multinational hotels have emerged to cater to business travelers tapping into the improved business climate.

The Middle East and Africa

The seemingly endless cycle of wars and terrorist acts has made tourism in many parts of the Middle East a very difficult challenge. This is not to say that the lodging industry is not thriving and growing in many Middle Eastern countries. The strategic oil reserves in this part of the world have enabled countries with this precious resource to build impressive economies. Business travel to Saudi Arabia and the Arab Emirates has continued virtually unabated despite the strife in the overall region.

It is predicted that some $3 trillion will be invested in tourism and infrastructure improvements in the Middle East by 2030. Significant among these projects is the creation of an extensive resort complex in Dubai to rival any in the world. Dubai and Bahrain have created havens of leisure for travelers from inside and outside the Arab world. But they are not alone, as resorts with world-class golf courses and spas have opened or are in development in Qatar, Abu Dhabi, Luxor, and Amman.

Countries in the Middle East are expected to find new ways to diversify their economies and reduce their dependence on oil in the coming years. This bodes well for the hotel and resort industry.

This optimism cannot be found in the Middle Eastern areas of persistent terrorist activity and war, such as Israel, Lebanon, and Iraq. International tourism to these locales lags well behind levels seen in the 1980s and early 1990s. Political stability will be necessary to reestablish a healthy tourism sector in these economies. To a lesser extent this is also true of Egypt, although the established tourism venues of Luxor, the Pyramids and Sphinx, and Red Sea resorts continue to attract foreign visitors except at times of heightened insecurity.

It is very difficult to generalize about conditions on the mammoth and diverse continent of Africa. Tourism exists to varying degrees in parts of the continent, from the ancient cultures of Morocco in the north to the modern, vibrant new world of South Africa. Photo safaris and ecotourism boost the Kenyan economy in the east central region, and, as mentioned above, the heritage and culture of Egypt continue to draw international travelers. But, by and large, the rest of the continent sees very little tourism. The emerging oil markets along the west coast of Africa are attracting mainly business travelers seeking to capitalize on the potential oil profits. Abject poverty, civil strife, and political instability are the norm in many of Africa's young nations, and, obviously, tourism cannot flourish under such conditions.

Endnote

1. http://www.frommers.com/destinations/mexico/0231027613.html#ixzz2FLUhXONz.

Key Terms

consolidation—Process by which the number of owning companies of brand hotels decreases due to purchases, mergers, and other ownership transfers.

conversion—The activity that takes place when an independent joins a chain or when a property changes from one corporate flag to another (for example, a Holiday Inn becomes a Days Inn or a Ramada becomes a Comfort Inn) or a chain property becomes independent.

franchise—Refers to (1) the authorization given by one company to another to sell its products and services; or (2) the name of the business format or product being franchised.

management contract—A contract that authorizes a chain to exercise complete control over the standards and quality of each property and is responsible for day-to-day operations; franchising does not provide this control. Of course, with franchising, the chain does not need a large professional operating staff; with a management contract, it does.

Review Questions

1. What is a franchise hotel?

2. Discuss similarities and differences between a chain managed hotel and a franchised managed hotel.

3. What key factors lead to antagonism between hotel franchisors and franchisees?

4. What are independent management companies?

5. How has market segmentation diversified the lodging industry?

6. What factors led to globalization of hotel companies?

7. Name ten or more of the major international hotel chains.

8. What factors led to today's high rate of lodging industry development in Asia and the Pacific Rim?

 ## Internet Sites

For more information, visit the following Internet sites. Remember that Internet addresses can change without notice. If the site is no longer there, you can use a search engine to look for additional sites.

Hotels and Hotel Companies

Best Western
www.bestwestern.com

Fairmont Hotels & Resorts
www.fairmont.com

Hyatt Corporation
www.hyatt.com

InterContinental Hotels Group
www.ichotelsgroup.com

Marriott International, Inc.
www.marriott.com

Radisson Hotels & Resorts
www.radisson.com

Ritz-Carlton Hotel Company
www.ritzcarlton.com

Sheraton Corporation
www.starwoodhotels.com/sheraton

Smith Travel Research
www.strglobal.com

Westin Hotels & Resorts
www.starwoodhotels.com/westin

Chapter 5 Outline

Size and Scope of the Industry
American Hotel Classifications
    Commercial Hotels/Full Service
    Airport Hotels
    Conference Centers
    Economy Properties/Limited Service
    Suite or All-Suite Hotels
    Extended-Stay Hotels
    Convention Hotels
    Residential Hotels
    Casino Hotels
    Resort Hotels
    Bed and Breakfast Hotels
    Boutique Hotels
European Hotel Market Segments and
    Hotel Types
Organization of American Hotels
    The Rooms Division
    The Food and Beverage Division
    The Engineering and Maintenance
        Division
    The Marketing and Sales Division
    The Accounting Division
    The Human Resources Division
    The Security Division
Organization of European Hotels
The Importance of Cooperation

Competencies

1. Describe the size and scope of the lodging industry. (pp. 93–95)

2. Identify American hotel classifications and the primary market segments they attract. (pp. 95–101)

3. Describe European hotel market segments and hotel types. (pp. 101–102)

4. Describe the typical organization of an American hotel. (pp. 102–103)

5. Explain the primary responsibilities of the major divisions and departments within a hotel. (pp. 103–108)

6. Describe the organization of European hotels. (p. 108)

7. Explain the importance of cooperation among hotel divisions and departments in relation to guests, suppliers, the community, and government agencies. (pp. 108–111)

5

The Organization and Structure of Lodging Operations

THE PROFESSION OF HOTEL MANAGEMENT is one of the most challenging and, at the same time, least understood in the American economy. Although most communities have one or more lodging properties, and although the average citizen has had some contact with them, few people realize the diversified knowledge, variety of skills, and creativity demanded of the successful hotel manager.

Size and Scope of the Industry

Hotels are found in every country and city of the world. It is no wonder that hotel-keeping ranks high among the largest worldwide industries. The World Tourism Organization estimates that there are nearly 12 million hotel rooms worldwide, with more than 50 percent of the rooms in Europe, and about 33 percent in North America.

In Europe, most hotels are smaller than their overseas counterparts. A hotel with more than 100 rooms is considered large, and one with more than 300 rooms is considered extremely large. Individually owned and managed properties are far more common than chain-operated properties. However, every year more and more hotels become members of chains or associations. This trend will probably gain momentum because of the many advantages of affiliation. Independent hotels will continue to play a significant role for those guests who dislike what they perceive as the uniform quality of chain hotels. Independent hotels may join marketing or referral associations to gain some chain-like benefits without giving up their individuality.

In America, hotelkeeping ranks third among service industries, following public transportation and restaurant management. According to the American Hotel & Lodging Association, there are approximately 52,500 hotels in the United States with a total of 4.9 million rooms. U.S. hotel revenue amounts to $155.2 billion, and the U.S. lodging industry employs 1.8 million people.

When we hear or read about a hotel, it is usually a famous hotel in a large city—New York's Plaza or Waldorf Astoria, Atlanta's Marriott Marquis, the Excalibur in Las Vegas, Tokyo's Imperial, or the Oriental in Bangkok. However, even though large and famous hotels play an important role in lodging, they are not typical of the lodging industry in the United States or in the world. Less than 5 percent of all hotels worldwide have over 300 rooms. In the United States, 87 percent of hotels have 150 or fewer rooms. Exhibit 1 shows a breakdown of United States hotels by type (or location), Exhibit 2 shows United States hotels by size, and Exhibit 3 shows United States hotels by rate.

Traditionally, hotels were small enough for individuals to own and operate. In recent years, however, skyrocketing costs have resulted in a trend toward corporate ownership, which has produced a new class of hoteliers—college-trained

Exhibit 1   U.S. Hotels by Type

By Location	Properties	Rooms
Urban	4,853	760,709
Suburban	17,593	1,750,855
Airport	2,216	305,429
Interstate	7,379	500,623
Resort	3,840	601,508
Small Metro/Town	16,333	955,713

Source: 2012 Lodging Industry Profile (www.ahla.com).

Exhibit 2   U.S. Hotels by Size

By Size	Properties	Rooms
Under 75	28,977	1,238,936
75–149	17,147	1,801,069
150–299	4,410	882,000
300–500	1,143	425,327
over 500	537	527,505

Source: 2012 Lodging Industry Profile (www.ahla.com).

Exhibit 3   U.S. Hotels by Rate

By Rate	Properties	Rooms
Under $30	410	41,514
$30–$44.99	4,727	339,579
$45–$59.99	14,637	874,545
$60–$85	15,300	1,254,804
Over $85	17,140	2,364,395

Source: 2012 Lodging Industry Profile (www.ahla.com).

The Willard InterContinental in Washington, D.C.

people who have chosen hotel management as a profession. In addition, absentee ownership has created a maze of sophisticated management, financial, and operating systems, the intricacies and complexities of which can be understood and handled only by someone with extensive training. Because of this, corporate ownership of hotels has been one of the primary forces in the development of college-level training in the field of hotel management.

American Hotel Classifications

Classifying hotels is not always an easy task. Because of the industry's diversity, many hotels do not fit into one, or only one, well-defined category. Nonetheless, there are several useful general classifications.[1]

Commercial Hotels/Full Service vs. Economy Properties/Limited Service

An obvious way to classify hotels is to distinguish based upon the amount of services provided. Commercial or full-service hotels make up the largest group of lodging facilities. Most of the clientele are business travelers, so these hotels tend to be located in close proximity to downtown areas, business parks, and corporate office buildings. Commercial hotels commonly feature room service, uniformed service, one-day laundry/dry cleaning, one or more restaurants and lounges, and a gift shop. Guestrooms likely include a variety of bath amenities, high-speed Internet access, a coffeemaker, and satellite TV and pay-per-view movies.

By contrast, economy or limited-service properties eliminate most of the services and amenities offered at full-service properties, enabling these facilities to remain profitable while offering considerably lower room rates. Limited-service properties appeal to traveling families, government employees, budget-conscious business travelers, and motor coach tours.

Airport Hotels

Several categories of lodging establishments reflect the locations where they are typically found and/or the guest needs that they attempt to serve. Airport hotels are an example. This group encompasses both full- and limited-service facilities. The defining element is the facility's proximity to airports. The vast majority of airport hotels offer complimentary airport shuttle and flexible check-in/check-out hours, as dictated by airline schedules.

Convention Hotels

Full-service convention hotel properties are commonly located very close to free-standing convention centers. These hotel properties feature a large variety of meeting and function rooms, from vast ballrooms and exhibit halls to smaller conference rooms and boardrooms. Convention hotels cater to trade and professional associations, fraternal and hobby organizations, and corporate meetings and trade shows. In recent years, large resort hotels have increasingly begun to offer convention facilities to boost off-peak business levels.

Conference Centers

Conference centers are similar in concept to convention hotels, but generally cater to smaller, more intense conferences and training programs. Conference centers offer state-of-the-art audiovisual and electronic amenities, ergonomically designed chairs, and excellent lighting.

Suite or All-Suite Hotels

Suite or all-suite hotels are one of the fastest-growing segments of the lodging industry. Accommodations feature separate bedrooms and living rooms, or at least clearly defined areas within one room. Hotel suites sometimes also contain a kitchenette, a refrigerator, and a wet bar. These hotels are typically located outside the

Insider Insights

Humberto "Burt" Cabañas
President & CEO
Benchmark Hospitality, Inc.
The Woodlands, Texas _____

Conferences and meetings have been an integral part of companies', corporations', and associations' efforts to maintain internal and external communications. As organizations have grown in size and complexity, an increasing demand has evolved for facilities at which to hold their conferences.

Some corporations and associations have included conference rooms in their headquarters. Such in-house meeting facilities are typically convenient and comfortable. However, subtle considerations often make the corporate conference room less desirable than expected.

It is the demand for more appropriate facilities that resulted in the development of the conference center concept. Conference centers avoid the problems that accompany multi-market-oriented hospitality facilities and in-house corporate meeting rooms by concentrating full time on the off-premise small meetings market of fewer than fifty persons per conference.

The primary purpose of conference centers is to satisfy and accommodate conference groups by offering a self-contained learning environment. Maximum results are achieved when a balance among *living, learning, and leisure* is achieved.

The term *conference center* has taken on several definitions as its popularity as a concept for meetings has grown. Executive and resort centers closely resemble full-service hotels and feature sophisticated audiovisual offerings, extensive exercise facilities, and a wide variety of assembly halls and smaller meeting rooms. A dedicated staff of conference coordinators is available. The resort type of center will also include a greater variety of recreational facilities, often including golf courses and tennis courts.

Proprietary and *not-for-profit* centers usually feature less luxurious sleeping rooms than the above categories and are so defined because they commonly restrict usage. Proprietary centers are designed for a company's needs, and not-for-profit centers usually are restricted to technically oriented academic and college groups.

Non-residential centers resemble the above types but do not include overnight accommodations.

The final type is called an *ancillary conference center*. These facilities are merely add-on complexes to other buildings (such as hotels and resorts). They will normally include similar meeting rooms and dedicated staff as in the executive/resort type center.

Conference centers have proven to be invaluable to organizations seeking a quiet, flexible training meeting and executive level meetings.

city center. Businesspeople find suite hotels particularly attractive, since they offer a place to work and entertain separate from the bedroom. Suite hotels may also provide temporary quarters for people who are relocating or for vacationing families.

Extended-Stay Hotels

Extended-stay hotels are lodging facilities that resemble apartment buildings. The guestrooms feature full kitchens, living areas, and bedrooms. They cater to travelers who need to stay in an area for an extended period (usually defined as more than seven days) and thus do not experience the weekend occupancy declines that affect most commercial hotels. These properties also benefit from operating efficiencies resulting from the lower rate of turnover. In recent years, extended-stay has been the industry's fastest-growing segment.

Residential Hotels

No longer as popular as they once were, residential hotels offer principally long-term accommodations, though they may accommodate short-term guests as well. The residential hotel usually offers housekeeping service, a dining room, room meal service, and possibly a cocktail lounge. Rooms may resemble suites in layout and design. The food and beverage division is usually small and exists more as a convenience for the residents than as a true source of income; sometimes outside catering firms provide food service. Residential hotels range from the luxurious, offering full suites for families, to the moderate, offering single rooms for individuals.

Casino Hotels

In casino hotels, the rooms and food and beverage operations may function primarily to support the gambling facilities (though they are expected to contribute their own profit). These hotels may be quite luxurious. They frequently offer top-name entertainment, extravagant shows, specialty restaurants, and charter flights for high rollers in order to attract gaming revenues. In the United States, this segment will likely grow as more states legalize casino gaming and/or more Native American tribes become involved in these enterprises.

Resort Hotels

Unlike some other lodging properties, the resort hotel is the planned destination of guests, usually vacationers. This is because resorts are located in some particularly scenic area, such as the seashore or mountains, or because they offer spa or health club facilities. Generally, resorts are situated away from the clamor of large cities, but can be reached easily by plane, train, or automobile.

Resorts often provide special activities for guests—dancing, golf, tennis, horseback riding, nature hikes, and so forth—and the resort may employ an activities director or even an entire recreational staff. Because guests expect to be entertained wholly on the premises, the contact between guests and management is much greater than at other hotels.

Although many guests spend from one week to an entire season at a resort, a resort hotel's weekend business often represents the difference between profit and loss for the operator.

There are many types of resorts. Some are classified according to property type, such as condominium resorts. Resorts are also categorized on a seasonal basis, such as summer resorts, year-round resorts, cold winter resorts, and warm winter resorts. In addition, there are other defining characteristics. The following types are especially noteworthy in the Caribbean, but they exist elsewhere as well and often overlap with other classifications. They include:

- Modern resort hotels, which feature a variety of restaurants, extensive meeting and conference space, possibly a casino, pools, golf course(s), a tennis center, retail space, and an ocean beach. They cater to a variety of guests from upscale to economy, depending on their overall level of quality and intended market position. Within this group are the Hyatt Cerromar, Puerto Rico; The Wyndham, Jamaica; Frenchman's Reef, St. Thomas.

- Mixed-use destination resorts. These hybrid resorts are typically anchored by a modern resort hotel, but also include a number of real estate units. The residential real estate is composed of attached or detached villas, apartment-style condominiums, interval-ownership units, and building lots. Since these resorts boast hundreds, even thousands, of acres, the open layout of the facilities evokes a greater feeling of freedom and leisure than do the resort hotels themselves. Caribbean examples include Casa de Campo, Dominican Republic; Palmas del Mar, Puerto Rico; and Carambola, St. Croix.

- Urban resorts, typified by the Condado Plaza and the Caribe Hilton, Puerto Rico; the Jaragua, Dominican Republic; and the Caribbean, Curaçao. These hotels are located in or near urban areas proximate to government agencies, business centers, and airports and have relatively outdated designs. They cater more directly to commercial travelers and certain group meeting participants than do the modern resort hotels. Given the nature of the Caribbean market, however, none of these hotels can afford to neglect the leisure traveler.

- Casino resorts. Although many newly constructed hotels have small casinos as part of their entertainment offering, they do not earn a significant portion of their revenues from them. The casino resort depends on gaming operations for a significant percentage of its revenues. Representative are the Paradise Island Resort and Casino and Carnival's Crystal Palace in the Bahamas; the El San Juan Hotel and Casino, Puerto Rico; and the Hyatt Regency, Aruba.

- All-inclusive resorts. Pioneered by SuperClubs in Jamaica, the all-inclusive resort is growing in popularity throughout the Caribbean. The all-inclusive resort offers unlimited use of its product (including unlimited food and beverages, sports equipment and facilities, and entertainment) for a set pre-paid price. Guests need no money unless they wish to participate in off-property excursions and buy gifts. Most all-inclusive packages are sold through wholesale travel agents and usually include airfare and ground transfers. While this type of resort traditionally catered to the cost-conscious guest, upscale all-inclusive properties are now being developed. One example is the Grand Lido in Negril, Jamaica.

- Boutique resorts. These exclusive resorts cater to very wealthy guests by offering the finest accommodations, five-star food and beverage service, an intimate and secluded environment, and the highest level of personal attention. The Cap Juluca and the Malliouhana on Anguilla and the Guanahani on St. Barts exemplify this category.

Insider Insights

Richard L. Erb, CHA
General Manager
Stein Eriksen Lodge
Park City, Utah ————————————————————————————————

One of the latest types of special-purpose hotels is the resort hotel community, or condominium resort. These properties usually emerge through one of two ways: Existing facilities, such as many of the hotels at ski resort areas in Vermont and Colorado, may be sold as condominium hotel investments; or, totally new resort communities may be developed. An example is the Grand Traverse Resort in northern Michigan, where I formerly served as chief operating officer.

Many years ago, I decided to learn about resort development community management, as it appeared that virtually all new resorts would emerge under this umbrella, while most existing ones would be wise to consider real estate projects in conjunction with their resort property. When we opened the Mauna Kea Beach Resort Hotel in Hawaii more than forty years ago, I saw the value of the barren, lava-covered land around the hotel skyrocket overnight. I've never forgotten that.

At Grand Traverse Resort Village, we built a quality resort to bring guests who would become interested in purchasing a condominium or a second home. The resort development community product is usually a condominium. There are many types of lodging condominiums, from a single room in a hotel to luxurious villas with complete kitchens, bars, fireplaces, and garages.

Resort condominiums may be purchased by individuals and then rented out as hotel or resort rooms by a management firm whenever the owners do not need to use them.

Condominium hotels and resorts often operate within a larger plan for total area development. One common version is the resort development community, which offers various real estate and hotel products through a complex marketing plan mix. The market research must identify the potential resort/hotel guest and then go on to qualify the guest as a potential condominium or real estate buyer.

Initially, existing resorts sold home lots around their golf courses or ski slopes to their guests. Now, new resorts exist primarily as a tool for selling the real estate product. They try to attract resort customers who are potential buyers as well.

AAA has recognized condominium rooms as a subclassification for AAA tour books, beginning with the 1993 editions. This made full-service condo accommodations available to thousands of AAA travel agents and millions of their members.

Marketing resort condominiums presents a challenge, since the product is still perceived as something other than a hotel room. Now, however, with national affiliations emerging for central reservations and chains showing a sincere interest, the tremendous growth of condominium resorts will continue.

- Guesthouses and inns. These accommodations are small, provide a relatively high level of personal service, and cater to the individual traveler. Perhaps the best known are the paradores in Puerto Rico.

- Budget hotels, which are often non-chain-affiliated and cater almost exclusively to commercial travelers. They are located in the largest cities of the Caribbean, offer limited amenities and facilities, and maintain a high price-value relationship.

Bed and Breakfast Hotels

Bed and breakfast hotels—or B&Bs—derive their name from the fact that they provide sleeping accommodations and breakfast to guests. These properties come in a variety of forms—sometimes a private home with a few guestrooms, at other times a small building with twenty to thirty rooms. The owner usually lives on the premises and is responsible for serving breakfast to guests. This meal may range from a simple continental breakfast to a full-course meal. There are thousands of B&Bs in operation today. They are popular because of their intimate, personal service.

Boutique Hotels

Boutique hotels have a relatively high average daily rate. They range in size from 100 to 400 rooms; most boutique hotels have 150 to 200 rooms. These hotels stress a home-like atmosphere and offer highly personalized service and a distinctive style with generous amenities and available, easy access to the Internet. There are currently about 170 properties in this classification. Boutique hotels are located in major metropolitan areas.

European Hotel Market Segments and Hotel Types

In some respects, market segmentation in Europe has followed the same patterns as in the United States. In others, Europe has made its own patterns.

Some hotels primarily cater to certain guest segments that are common in Europe. Nationality hotels are organized to serve visitors of a specific nationality. Another prevalent tourist group is the sun worshippers—inhabitants of northern countries who like to vacation near the Mediterranean to prolong their short summers. Sports fans are another large guest segment that hotels may be designed to serve. Cultural tourists favor cultural events, festivals, exhibitions, and visits to historic sites. Some hotels do a strong summer business with visitors from Asia, the United States, and Latin America. Ethnic travelers are overseas visitors with European roots making trips to their countries of origin. While not all these groups warrant hotels designed specifically for them, each does represent a significant segment of travelers in Europe.

The typical European classifications are fairly self-descriptive and include:

- Grand or deluxe hotels.
- Four-star business hotels.
- Economy business hotels.
- Mountain, sea, lake, and spa resorts.
- Airport hotels.

- Country inns.
- Grand tour operators' hotels.

Many hotels offer a combination of these characteristics. All-suite hotels are noticeably absent from this list, as they have not found a market in Europe.

Some uniquely European hotel types include:

- Relais et Châteaux, an association of independently owned and operated small inns that offer their guests character, calm, comfort, cuisine, and courtesy. Originally European, the association now comprises about 360 hotels in thirty-five countries.

- Relais du Silence, an association started in 1968 by a group of French hoteliers. Its member properties focus on peaceful, natural surroundings providing calm and tranquility, comfort, character, authenticity, owner presence, hospitality, and gastronomy.

- Palace hotels, which are large, individualistic, often historic hotels. Most of them date back to the late nineteenth or very early twentieth century, and they enjoy a unique market position. Most of these hotels have remained independent of chain affiliation. Typical palace hotels include Hotel Frankfurter Hof, Frankfurt; Hotel Ritz, Paris; Palace Hotel, St. Moritz; Hotel Imperial, Vienna; and Grand Hotel, Rome.

- Pensions, which are either table d'hôte-type American plan or modified American plan boarding houses, designed for longer average stays. In some respects, they resemble American B&B operations. Some are seasonal and serve as a peak season extension of the rooms business generated by the traditional hotels. For example, Alpine farmers often turn their homes into pensions for the winter season to supplement their incomes.

European restaurants that have a few guestrooms and are famous for their culinary offerings are meccas for gourmets. Owned and operated by famous chefs, they enjoy a local, regional, and even international clientele. They are prominently featured in the guides of Michelin or Gault et Millau. Restaurants with three stars in the *Guide Michelin* are world-famous; these include establishments operated by Paul Bocuse, Frédy Girardet, and the Troisgros brothers.

Organization of American Hotels

A model or standard organization plan that describes how all hotels *should* be organized does not and cannot exist. The plan for any particular hotel depends on a wide range of variables, such as property location, clientele served, services offered, structural layout, type of ownership, and the background, personalities, abilities, and training of management staff. For the purposes of discussion, however, we can make some general statements about how hotels are organized.

The use of the terms "department" and "division" is not standardized in the industry. Some properties call their various main functional areas (rooms, food and beverage, accounting, and so forth) departments; the smaller functional areas within departments (for example, catering and room service within the food and beverage department) may then be called sub-departments, functions, or some other term. Other properties (typically larger ones) call their main functional areas divisions; the various units within divisions are then usually called departments. Neither option is better than the other. For consistency, we will call the main functional areas divisions and smaller areas departments.

An **organization chart** is a drawing that shows the relationship between departments or divisions and specific positions within an organization. Exhibit 4 offers an organization chart for a small property. The organization is relatively "flat"—there are only two layers. Nonetheless, small properties perform the same activities that large properties do. Tasks assigned to specialized positions in large properties are combined into more generalized jobs in small hotels. For example, in a large property, different employees may be assigned to guest registration, reservations, and telephone switchboard duties. In a small property, one employee (the front desk agent) may be responsible for all these duties.

For many years, the terms **front of the house** and **back of the house** have been used to classify the various operational areas within a hotel. Front-of-the-house areas are those in which employees have extensive guest contact. Examples include the food and beverage and rooms divisions (including the front office and reservations departments). Back-of-the-house areas are those in which personnel have very little direct guest contact; examples include the engineering, accounting, and human resources divisions.

Another type of classification is financial. Divisions and sometimes departments within divisions are classified as **revenue centers** or **support centers**. Revenue centers are those areas that directly bring in revenue to the hotel, such as the front office department, the food and beverage division, and any other function that sells goods or services to guests. Support centers do not directly bring in revenue, but are necessary to the functioning of the revenue centers. These include housekeeping, accounting, engineering and maintenance, and human resources. This chapter offers a brief outline of each of these areas.[2]

The Rooms Division

The rooms division comprises those departments most involved in providing hotel services directly to guests. It includes the front office, housekeeping, uniformed

Exhibit 4   Sample Organization Chart for a Small Property

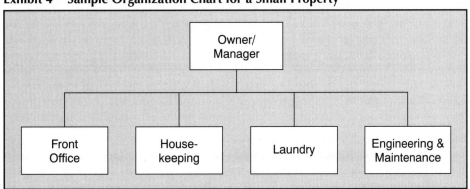

service, reservations, and telecommunications departments. (The reservations and telecommunications functions are sometimes part of the front office.) Hotels with garages or other parking facilities often place responsibility for this function with the rooms division. This division, a revenue center, usually earns the most money for the hotel.

The Front Office. The most visible area in a property, with the greatest amount of guest contact, is the front office. The front desk itself is the focal point of activity in the front office because it is where the guest is registered, assigned to a room, and checked out.

The mail and information section of the front office department was once a very prominent section of most properties. In recent years, however, the responsibility for providing guests with information and messages has been divided among the desk agents, PBX (private branch exchange—the term used for the switchboard equipment) operators, and cashiers, so a single full-time employee is usually not required for these duties.

Cashiers receive payments and post charges to guest accounts. Point-of-sale terminals (electronic cash registers) help reduce the manual posting of charges. The busiest time for the cashier occurs when guests check out of the property.

Recently, some American hotels have added **concierge** services to their front office functions. Concierge services are special services provided to hotel guests, such as making theater reservations and obtaining tickets; organizing special functions, such as VIP cocktail parties; and arranging for secretarial services for guests. In a sense, the concierge section is simply an extension of the front office that specializes in guest service. Concierges are often found in European hotels.

Telecommunications. The telecommunications section of the rooms division centers on a switchboard, as it does in any large company. A dedicated staff may be employed to handle calls and perform other telecommunications functions, or the front desk staff may be responsible for doing so. Telecom industry technical advances now make it possible for most lodging establishments to use equipment that can efficiently route long-distance calls to the least expensive option, automatically mark up prices and post charges to guest accounts, provide voice mail messaging, and place automated wake-up calls. Since many guests now travel with cell phones, it is becoming increasingly difficult for hotels to earn a profit from their telecommunications sections. Therefore, costs must be closely monitored.

Reservations. The reservations section of the rooms division is responsible for receiving, accepting, and making reservations for guests of the hotel. In addition, this department must keep exact records regarding the status of guestrooms and make sure that future dates are not overbooked. Reservations staff members work closely with sales and marketing personnel. With the increasing frequency of guest booking options via the Internet, it is becoming a very important function of the reservations section to monitor reservations volume from numerous sources.

Uniformed Service. Parking attendants, door attendants, porters, limousine drivers, and bell staff make up the uniformed service staff. They meet, greet, and help guests to the front desk and to their rooms. At the end of the stay, they may help guests to their transportation.

Housekeeping. This department's staff cleans vacant rooms to make them ready for occupancy, cleans occupied rooms, and helps the front office keep the status of every room current. In addition, housekeeping has the responsibility to maintain cleanliness in all public areas of the hotel, including lobbies, corridors, and restrooms. An executive housekeeper heads the department and may be assisted by inspectors, room attendants, a laundry manager, housepersons, and, if the department is large enough, an assistant housekeeper. Some large properties may employ people to monitor the housekeeping inventory and people to do sewing repairs.

Housekeepers, also called room attendants, are assigned to specific sections of the hotel. The quota of rooms per attendant may range from fifteen to twenty per day, depending on the level of service expected, the room size, the tasks required, and the degree of assistance given to the housekeeper.

Some hotels have their own laundries. In larger properties, the laundry equipment can be quite complicated. It may include folding and ironing machinery in addition to commercial washers and dryers.

The Food and Beverage Division

The food and beverage division is another important revenue center of the hotel. This division is often second only to the rooms division in the amount of revenue it earns.

In properties operating their own food and beverage facilities, a food and beverage director manages the activities of the division. Other positions depend upon the nature of the property's food and beverage operations.

There are many varieties of hotel food and beverage operations—for example, gourmet and specialty restaurants, coffee shops (which may offer 24-hour service), lounges or dining rooms in which live music or shows are performed, room service, and combined banquet and meeting room facilities. Food service in hospitality suites or employee food service may be additional operations. Some chains attempt to standardize their restaurants so that all the properties within the chain are alike.

The sale and service of alcoholic beverages is usually a distinct operation, purposely separated from food sales and service. The beverage section has separate storerooms, servers, sales areas, and preparation people (bartenders); its hours of operation may extend well past the hours of the food service operations.

Banquets and catered meals are sometimes handled by food and beverage staff or specially designated personnel. While revenues from banquets are included in the total food and beverage sales, the banquets themselves usually take place in special function rooms or areas of the property. Both banquet and catering services may contribute a significant portion of the revenues earned by the food and beverage division.

The Engineering and Maintenance Division

The engineering and maintenance division maintains the appearance of both the interior and exterior of the property and keeps all equipment operational. A chief engineer or director of property operations directs the division in larger properties. He or she usually reports to the property's general manager.

This division's work can be divided into five main activities—regular maintenance, emergency work, preventive maintenance, energy conservation, and special project assignments. The staff members of this division are often skilled in carpentry, plumbing, and electrical work. Maintenance staff perform such tasks as painting, minor carpet repairs, furniture refinishing, and preventive equipment maintenance. However, major problems or projects may require outside specialists. For example, full-scale refurbishing of public areas and guestrooms is usually contracted to specialists in interior decorating, and elevator maintenance and repair are usually contracted out to elevator specialists.

This division handles indoor and outdoor swimming pool cleaning and outdoor sanitation. It also does landscaping, which entails cutting the grass, planting flowers, caring for shrubs and trees, watering plants, and keeping the property's grounds in good condition.

Guest satisfaction depends upon well-maintained rooms. As a result, the engineering and maintenance division must stay in close contact with the front office and housekeeping, handling guest complaints and problems that room attendants identify quickly. If a room cannot be rented because repairs are necessary, the engineer must notify front office staff to take the room out of service.

The Marketing and Sales Division

Although some hotels do not have formal marketing divisions, every hospitality enterprise conducts marketing activities. The primary activities of marketing and sales operations are sales, convention services, advertising, and public relations. The late marketing and sales expert C. DeWitt Coffman wrote:

> What all this boils down to is that it makes sense to find out, methodically and scientifically, who your best sources of business are, what they want and need, what your competition is doing, what you can do better than your competition; and then plan how, exactly, to get maximum revenue for your operation from those sources.[3]

It is now common in full-service hotels to incorporate the function of yield management in the marketing and sales division, often with a high-level manager leading the function. Yield management is the implementation of strategies to maximize room revenue by manipulating occupancy and rates based on information gained from various reservation sources. Offering or restricting discounts and instituting or lifting minimum-length stays are examples of yield management strategies.

The size of the marketing and sales division in a hotel can vary from just one person, usually the manager spending only part of his or her time handling this function, up to a staff of fifteen or twenty full-time employees. Coordination with and knowledge of all other departments and divisions in the hotel is essential for smooth functioning in the marketing and sales division.

The Accounting Division

The accounting division, headed by a controller (sometimes called a comptroller), handles the financial activities of the operation. A hotel's accounting division must work very closely with the front office's cashiering and guest accounting functions. The number of people on the accounting staff varies, depending partly upon whether most of the accounting is done off the property or on-site.

If the accounting is done off-site, the local property's accounting staff simply collects and sends out the data without computing the operating results. For example, time sheets are forwarded to corporate offices where payroll checks are drawn and mailed back to the properties. Operating figures may be sent out daily, weekly, or at some other regular interval. Income statements are then computed and transmitted from the corporate office to the local property.

If all accounting functions are performed within the hotel, the accounting staff has many more responsibilities and is therefore larger. These responsibilities include paying all bills (accounts payable), sending out statements and receiving payments (accounts receivable), computing payroll information and writing payroll checks, accumulating operating data (revenue and expenses), and compiling the monthly income statement, balance sheet, and general ledger. In addition, the accounting staff makes bank deposits, secures cash, and performs any other control and monitoring functions required by the hotel's ownership or management.

The Human Resources Division

The human resources division assists other divisions in recruiting and selecting the most qualified job applicants. It also administers insurance and other benefit programs, handles personnel-related complaints, ensures compliance with labor laws, is involved with labor union matters (when applicable), and administers the property's compensation program. In properties that are not large enough to justify the creation of a separate office or position, the general manager may handle the human resources functions.

The scope of the human resources division has changed in recent years. New legislation, the shrinking labor market, and increasing competition among properties have led hotels to place more importance on human resource management. As this division has expanded in size and importance, so have its responsibilities and influence.

The Security Division

Security procedures are generally developed on an individual property basis, because every property has different security needs. National security standards are not feasible for such a varied industry.[4] The security division usually reports directly to the general manager or the manager-on-duty. The staff might be made up of in-house personnel, contract security officers, or personnel with police experience. Some local police departments allow their officers to hold off-duty jobs, and their trained personnel may be hired to work in security at a hotel.

However a hotel's security program is structured, the safety and security of guests, visitors, and employees requires the participation of all staff. For example, front desk staff should issue room keys only to registered guests and make sure all keys are returned at check-out. Housekeeping staff should note any damage to locks, doors, or windows, and the engineering and maintenance division should repair these promptly. All employees should report suspicious activities anywhere on the property to the appropriate security personnel.

The security staff is responsible for helping guests and employees stay safe and secure at the hotel. Specific duties may include patrolling the property or monitoring any television surveillance cameras. The division may also develop and implement procedures for emergencies such as fires, bomb threats, and natural disasters. The security division should maintain a good working relationship with local police and fire departments, since their cooperation and assistance is critical to the security division's effectiveness.

Organization of European Hotels

European hotels have traditionally been owned and managed by an individual or a family. Under the proprietor or manager were three individuals with near-absolute powers that occasionally even exceeded those of the manager. These three were:

- A *chef de reception*, who had responsibilities similar to today's front office manager.

- A *maître d'hôtel*, who had responsibilities similar to today's director of the food and beverage division, but had no authority over the chef de cuisine.

- A *chef de cuisine*, who had total authority in the kitchen.

These three people were present at all hours of the day and were personally known to each guest. They gave special, personal treatment to every guest—they were the current public relations and guest history departments personified. If the hotel was owned by a family, the wife was traditionally responsible for housekeeping, storerooms, and maintenance. She usually carried the title of *gouvernante générale* and acted as the co-manager. In cases where the manager was a single person, the services of an *aide du patron*, or a boss's helper, were retained. This was usually someone who had just completed studies at a hotel school, but who lacked practical experience. The job did not usually pay well, but it offered excellent opportunities for acquiring practical skills, and it was sometimes a stepping stone to becoming a manager.

Since the 1960s, there have been some changes to the traditional model, even though owner-managed hotels remain common. Exhibit 5 depicts a typical European hotel organization as it would appear today. European hotels are usually much smaller than their overseas counterparts, which accounts for this rather simple organizational structure in owner-managed properties. The larger and newer European hotels, particularly the chain-operated and big-city ones, are structured more like American hotels.

The Importance of Cooperation

All employees have a role to play in maintaining the property's reputation for value in service and products. Practically every service offered requires the cooperative efforts of two or more departments or divisions. To get an incoming guest from the lobby to a freshly cleaned room involves the front office, uniformed service,

Exhibit 5 Owner-Managed European Hotel Organization

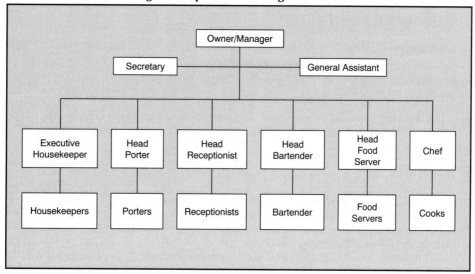

and housekeeping. Suppose a hotel sales representative sells a local business manager a special function room for a sales meeting and arranges for a luncheon and an evening banquet in the ballroom. The sales representative makes the arrangements, but the actual setup of the rooms, the preparation and service of the meals, and the general decorative arrangements are handled by departments over which the sales representative has no control. Failure on the part of any one department or any one person in a department can mean unsatisfactory service and a dissatisfied guest. Whether a hotel is serving a single meal in the coffee shop or handling a large convention, the joint efforts of several departments must be coordinated to ensure successful and satisfactory service to the guest.

Close interaction among the property's owners, management staff, and all employees is necessary. In addition, there are several groups of people external to the property with whom the hotel staff interacts. These groups include guests, suppliers, the community, and government agencies.

Guests. Guests are interested in having their accommodation wants and needs satisfied to the maximum extent possible. The wants and needs of hotel guests are influenced by such factors as:

- The object of the visit (a social occasion or a business trip).
- The guest's concept of value (price relative to quality).
- Absolute price (the price that the customer will not go beyond even if the service or product being purchased is deemed to be of value).
- Social/economic factors.
- The guest's age, sex, and marital status.
- Ethnic or religious background.

Insider Insights

Karl-Heinz Hatzfeld
Retired Senior Vice President Operations
Europe and Israel
Sheraton Hotels _____

When asked, "What is the most important factor in determining the success of a hotel?" E. M. Statler's well-known reply was, "Location, location, location!" I fully agree with him, especially if someone is planning to build a new site.

However, once the hotel goes into operation, the focus shifts. At that point, my answer to the above question would be service, service, service! Fortunately, most hotel operators have realized this, having seen the success of other service-oriented industries and having created their own service-oriented programs. Good service takes commitment, not just by the guest-contact staff, but by the entire hotel staff, led by the general manager. If the general manager is not committed to quality service, the whole program will fail.

I recently retired after thirty-two years from the Sheraton Corporation as its director of operations, Europe and Israel. In that position, I supervised as many as thirty hotel general managers at a time. I can tell you from personal experience that those managers who moved about the hotel and were visible and available to guests and to staff always ran a better hotel than those managers who sat in their offices and made guests and staff battle their way past one or two secretaries to get to see them.

This commitment to service must be led by the general manager, and must be seen in every employee. It must be honestly felt, and presented in a cheerful, friendly manner. Therefore, I will rephrase my answer to the opening question. The most important criteria in managing a hotel successfully are commitment to service, honest service, friendly service!

Guests choose destinations based in part on the destination's ability to satisfy their needs and wants. Historically, the steamship lines, the railroads, and, most recently, the airlines have recognized the need for suitable food and lodging along their routes and at their destinations to better satisfy their guests. As a result, many of the finest hotels and restaurants were owned and operated by transportation companies. However, this type of ownership is not prevalent today.

Suppliers. Companies that supply products and services to the hotel are another group with special concerns. As business operators, suppliers want to make a profit. Hoteliers should guard against having an "I win—you lose" attitude in negotiations with suppliers. This approach is, at best, shortsighted. Fairness and mutual satisfaction provide the best basis for a relationship between hoteliers and suppliers. Remember that suppliers and their employees may also be prospective guests of the hotel. As residents of the community, suppliers also have numerous opportunities to discuss good and bad aspects of a property with other prospective guests.

The Community. The community is another group that influences the hotel. Since early colonial days, the growth of American hotels has directly paralleled the growth of American cities and towns. In fact, the size and comfort of a city's hotels have long been considered an indicator of a city's prestige.

In recent years, cities have become more keenly aware of the business to be gained from travelers. Large cities often form **convention bureaus**, agencies created to attract regional and national conventions and other large gatherings or meetings. The success of these bureaus depends upon their ability to offer visitors sufficient and comfortable accommodations. Small communities also have recognized the advantages of having a good hotel. In many smaller cities, businesspeople conduct fundraising campaigns to finance a community hotel. These people earn much smaller returns than they could receive by investing their money in other areas, but they feel that the presence of a hotel will add prestige to the community and indirectly boost all local business.

Other factors promote the close relationship between a hotel and its community. For example, homes have become smaller, and few people employ servants. This means that large dinner parties, small dances, wedding receptions, and other group gatherings which used to be held in homes are now often held outside the home. Hotels are equipped to handle these functions and to assume all the chores of planning, decorating, and serving. The declining use of domestic help has also contributed to the growing number of people dining out. It is common today to see an entire family enjoying a meal in the local hotel coffee shop or dining room.

Government Agencies. Hotels must also interact with government agencies. These organizations regulate lodging properties, imposing limitations within which hotels must operate, and collect taxes and other fees as required. These agencies have an interest in the success of the hotel because of the tax revenue a viable operation generates. Government agencies sometimes offer tax incentives to encourage hotels to locate in a particular community.

Endnotes

1. Parts of this discussion are taken from Michael L. Kasavana, *Managing Front Office Operations,* 9th ed. (Lansing, Mich.: American Hotel & Lodging Educational Institute, 2013).

2. This discussion is adapted from Kasavana.

3. C. DeWitt Coffman, *Hospitality for Sale* (Lansing, Mich.: American Hotel & Lodging Educational Institute, 1980), p. 16.

4. For further information, see David M. Stipanuk and Raymond C. Ellis, Jr., *Security and Loss Prevention Management,* 3rd ed. (Lansing, Mich.: American Hotel & Lodging Educational Institute, 2013).

Key Terms

back of the house—Areas of a lodging operation in which personnel have very little direct guest contact; examples include the engineering, accounting, and human resources divisions.

concierge—A section of the hotel that provides special services to hotel guests, such as making theater reservations and obtaining tickets; organizing special functions, such as VIP cocktail parties; and arranging for secretarial services for guests. In a sense, the concierge section is simply an extension of the front office that specializes in guest service.

convention bureaus—Agencies in large cities created to attract regional and national conventions and other large gatherings or meetings.

front of the house—The areas of a lodging operation in which employees have extensive guest contact. Examples include the food and beverage and rooms divisions (including the front office and reservations departments).

organization chart—A drawing that shows the relationship between departments or divisions and specific positions within an organization.

revenue centers—Those areas that directly bring in revenue to the hotel, such as the front office department, the food and beverage division, and any other function that sells goods or services to guests.

support centers—Areas of the hotel that do not directly bring in revenue, but are necessary to the functioning of the revenue centers. These include housekeeping, accounting, engineering and maintenance, and human resources.

 Review Questions

1. What is the essential difference between front-of-the-house and back-of-the-house employees? Give examples.

2. What is the essential difference between revenue center departments and support center departments? Give examples.

3. What functions does a concierge perform?

4. In what types of operations might hotel food and beverage employees work?

5. What are three functions of the engineering and maintenance division?

6. What other department does the accounting department work most closely with?

7. What three external factors have increased the importance of the human resources department?

8. What security functions do hotel staff other than security personnel typically perform?

9. Which four groups outside a hotel organization play an important role in the hotel's business?

10. In what ways does government become involved in a hotel's business?

11. What features does a typical boutique hotel possess?

Internet Sites

For more information, visit the following Internet sites. Remember that Internet addresses can change without notice. If the site is no longer there, you can use a search engine to look for additional sites.

Hotels and Hotel Companies

Best Western International, Inc.
www.bestwestern.com

Fairmont Hotels & Resorts
www.fairmont.com

Hyatt Corporation
www.hyatt.com

InterContinental Hotels Group
www.ichotelsgroup.com

Marriott International, Inc.
www.marriott.com

Sheraton Hotels & Resorts
www.starwoodhotels.com/sheraton/

Casino Hotels

Bally's Casinos
www.harrahs.com/brands/ballys/
hotel-casinos/ballys-brand.shtml

Harrah's Casino Hotels
www.harrahs.com

Trump Entertainment Resorts
www.trumpmarina.com

Chapter 6 Outline

Competencies

1. Describe the primary responsibilities of the front office department. (pp. 115–116)

2. Summarize the functions of the rooming section of the front office department. (p. 117)

3. Describe the cashiering functions performed by the front office department, and explain the function of a night audit. (pp. 117–121)

4. Summarize the functions of the mail and information section of the front office department. (pp. 121–122)

5. Describe the primary responsibilities of the reservations department. (pp. 122–124)

6. Describe the responsibilities of the telecommunications department. (pp. 124–125)

7. Summarize the functions of the uniformed service department. (pp. 125–126)

8. Explain the primary responsibilities of the housekeeping department and describe some of the ways that the "green movement" has affected the department. (pp. 126–129)

6

The Rooms Division

THE ROOMS DIVISION is likely to have the largest staff in a hotel. Five departments are often classified as part of the rooms division. These are:

- Front office
- Reservations
- Telecommunications
- Uniformed service
- Housekeeping

Sometimes the responsibility for parking facilities is also assigned to this division. A sample organization chart for the rooms division of a large hotel is shown in Exhibit 1. Though we will not treat them as such in this chapter, many properties regard reservations, the switchboard, and uniformed service as sub-departments of the front office.

Small lodging operations are not likely to have specialized departments for each of the functions listed in Exhibit 1. In a large property, many staff members may have duties involving only the front office. In a small operation, one or two employees may perform front office duties, provide telephone service, offer guest information, and handle reservations.

The Front Office Department

The front office department represents the single largest profit center for the hotel, which is room sales. The front office is the hotel's nerve center and the liaison between the guest and the property. Front desk agents often handle incoming and intra-hotel calls as well. It is often said that, to the guest, the front office *is* the hotel. During the guest's stay, the front office is the focus of requests for information and services. Check-in and check-out activities are usually the guest's first and last impressions of the property, its staff, and its philosophy of guest service.

First impressions are very important. If a guest begins a visit in a pleasant frame of mind because of front office courtesy and service, chances are good that he or she will view other hotel services favorably as well. However, let the front office err, delay, or be indifferent, and the guest's dissatisfaction may spread to all aspects of his or her stay. Similarly, the front desk is also where guests turn when they have questions or problems. If those issues are handled with compassion and thoroughness, the mood of a potentially disgruntled guest can be transformed into respect for the professionalism of the staff member and the property.

Exhibit 1   Organization Chart for the Rooms Division of a Large Hotel

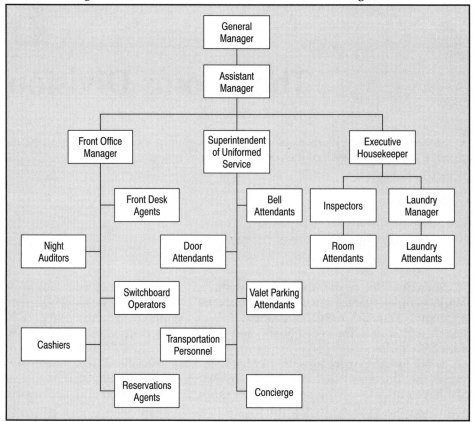

Adapted from Michael L. Kasavana, *Managing Front Office Operations,* 9th ed. (Lansing, Mich.: American Hotel & Lodging Educational Institute, 2013), p. 65.

The three main functions of the front office are: (1) to sell rooms, which includes registering guests and assigning rooms; (2) to keep accounts, determine credit, render bills, receive payments, and provide for proper financial and credit accommodations; and (3) to provide services such as handling mail, fax, and messages for guests, and furnishing information about the hotel, the community, and any special attractions or events.

Although the physical size and layout of front office facilities will differ, every front desk will have three distinct functional spaces corresponding to the three main functions, each sized to the specific needs of the operation. These three main areas are the rooming section, the cashier section, and the mail and information section. In large hotels, each of these areas may be staffed by a number of clerks in order to handle the numerous transactions involved. In smaller operations, efficient use of space may make it possible for one or two workers to handle all functions in a compact area.

The Rooming Section

Guest registration is the main function of the front office. Here rooms are sold and assigned, and here the guest's registration record is created. A guest's registration record contains information about the guest, including his or her home address and phone number, arrival and expected departure dates, and method of payment. The registration record helps the front office meet special guest needs, forecast room occupancies, and settle guest accounts properly. A guest's registration record may be kept in a guest registration book, on a registration card, or in a computer file.

Front desk agents use some form of a rooms inventory system to keep track of the status of all guestrooms. Hotels with computerized rooms divisions include this within the property management system, which ties in directly to the housekeeping department to provide up-to-the-minute status of occupied and vacant rooms. Front desk agents often try to fill one floor or wing of the hotel at a time to cut down on the amount of traveling a housekeeper or engineer must do to get to his or her assigned rooms.

The Cashier Section

The cashier section of the front office in larger operations is staffed by billing agents and cashiers, and, in smaller facilities, by personnel who provide all the services of front desk agent, information agent, billing agent, and cashier. This section keeps each guest's account up to date, cashes checks for guests (if the hotel offers this service), verifies the outstanding accounts receivable, renders the daily reports to management, and collects payment from the guests.

The primary tool of the cashier is the **guest folio** (see Exhibit 2), a record of the guest's charges associated with the current visit. Because there are so many charges, most large operations use computers to post these charges to guests' accounts. **Point-of-sale terminals**, which are electronic cash registers that enter a sales transaction into a hotel-wide computer system, are used in parts of the hotel where items can be charged. For example, charges for a meal at a restaurant in the hotel may be entered into a point-of-sale terminal in the restaurant and instantly transferred to the guest folio at the front desk.

Point-of-sale systems may be found in all areas of the hospitality industry. In hotels, they are in the food and beverage outlets, the gift shops, the salons—just about any location where a guest might make a purchase. Point-of-sale systems save tremendous amounts of paperwork and employee time. They also provide greater accuracy on guest checks and charges. Compare this with the traditional method—still used in a few small properties—that requires hand-carrying charge slips to the front desk for manual addition to a guest's account. The number of missed breakfast charges at morning check-out is certainly reduced when electronic systems are used.

Properties offering guest credit must have specific policies regarding acceptable guest identification, credit limits, procedures to follow when credit limits are reached, and all other credit-related concerns. Large properties may have credit managers in the cashier's department to administer guest credit services. By contrast, some smaller properties, which offer either limited services or none at all

Exhibit 2   Sample Guest Folio

ROOM	(LAST) NAME (FIRST) (INITIAL)	RATE	FOLIO NUMBER	403131

STREET ADDRESS	OUT	PHONE READING	OUT	
CITY, STATE & ZIP	IN	FROM FOLIO	IN	
NO. PARTY	CREDIT CARD	CLERK	TO FOLIO	

DATE	REFERENCE	CHARGES	CREDITS	BALANCE	PREVIOUS BALANCE PICKUP
Jul 27 A RESTR 103		** 14.25		* 14.25	A* 14.25
Jul 27 A ROOM 103		** 60.00		* 74.25	A* 74.25
Jul 27 A LDIST 103		** 6.38		* 80.63	A* 80.63
Jul 27 A MISCCR 103			** 18.38	* 62.25	A* 62.25
Jul 27 A PAID 103			** 62.25	* .00	
				Last Balance Amount Due	

beyond rooming, may ask guests to pay in advance for the rooms upon registration; in this case, no other guest accounting is necessary.

All but the smallest and simplest hotel operations have become fully computerized with property management systems that detail all phases of a guest's stay, especially regarding charges and billing details. This has dramatically reduced the amount of time front desk agents spend posting charges to room accounts and has made these procedures significantly more accurate than in the past. The accounting or electronic data machines in the cashier section are used to validate vouchers sent from the charging department, post charges to the guest's account, and calculate up-to-the-minute balances on each guest folio. They maintain daily balances of all transactions posted through them and are used to verify the accuracy of the accounts receivable outstanding balance and the charge-sales records of each operating department.

The electronic register at the front desk maintains a continuous record of cash transactions. Exhibit 3 is an example of a cash report that is usually made at each cashier shift change. *Paid* and *paid out* are keys on the electronic register. When

Exhibit 3   Sample Cash Report

CASH REPORT						
CLASSIFICATION	DATE	TRANS. SYMBOLS	NET TOTALS	CORRECTIONS	MACH. TOTALS	
PAID						
CLOSING						
OPENING						
CASH RECEIVED						
PAID OUT						
CLOSING						
OPENING						
CASH PAID OUT						
NET CASH						

ON DUTY _____

OFF DUTY _____

CASHIER

_____

N C R   B-6760—114YY

a cashier begins a shift, he or she subtotals these keys, and machine totals are printed out and recorded on the cash report under the machine totals column. The opening machine totals for paid and paid out must be exactly the same figures that appear on the previous shift's cash report as the closing machine totals for paid and paid out.

At the close of a shift, the cashier subtotals these keys again and records closing figures in the machine totals column. If, during the shift, the cashier accidentally miskeys any transactions, adjustments to the machine totals are made in the corrections column of the cash report and corrected figures are entered in the net totals column. The difference between the closing and opening figures in the net totals column of the paid section should yield the exact amount of cash received during the cashier's shift. Similarly, the difference between the closing and opening figures in the net totals column of the paid out sections should yield the exact amount of cash paid out during the cashier's shift.

The difference between cash received and cash paid out yields the net cash sum for the cashier's shift. Usually, the cashier extracts this sum from the cash drawer and, along with a supervisor, secures the money in the hotel safe until it can be deposited in a bank. Once the net cash has been secured, the cash drawer should contain exactly the same amount it contained when the cashier opened his or her shift. Both the outgoing and incoming cashiers count the contents of the cash drawer and verify the beginning "bank" for the new shift. If cash overages or shortages are discovered, the outgoing cashier must recheck the cash report and search through transaction records for possible miskeyed entries.

With certain exceptions (to be discussed in the next section), transactions that affect the guest's folio must have confirming vouchers to support the posting of charges. The posting of room charges is one exception; this is done by the night auditor.

The Night Audit. All accounts are balanced at the end of each day. Because the task is very important and needs to be done after all of the hotel's sales outlets are closed (to be sure that all charges are included), the audit is usually performed during the third shift in the early morning hours (even though computerization has made it much easier to perform the audit at any time). This is called the **night audit** (or sometimes the front office audit). In larger hotels, there may be more than one night auditor, while in smaller operations the night audit may be undertaken by a staff member serving as a front desk agent or information agent as well.

The first step in the audit is to post any charges that have not yet been included on the guest's account. Then, the totals of all accounts carried in the accounting machines or computer system are compared with the sales reports of the various operating departments to ensure that all charges have been properly accounted for. Any errors or problems must be rectified and resolved by a complete search of folios, vouchers, and departmental sales records.

After the totals are balanced and room occupancy is verified, room and tax charges are posted to each guest account, and a final balance is recorded on each folio. Finally, a report summarizing the up-to-date amounts owed to the hotel in both the guest ledger (the accounts for those currently registered in the hotel) and the city ledger (the accounts of former guests and non-guest accounts) is generated and balanced.

Most hotels now use electronic data-processing equipment to maintain guest accounts, to make the necessary verifications, and to create reports. When a guest registers, guest information is entered into the computer, which prepares a folio automatically. Subsequent charges to the guest are entered into computer terminals and added to the folio. The daily transcript of accounts receivable, completed by the night auditor, is both a verification of departmental totals and a complete printout of each guest's bill. This daily transcript enables cashiers to check out guests early in the morning without calling up their folios for a printout. Display boards are also provided at the cashier's area where guests can review any charges or payments made to their accounts.

Some hotels also offer guests a chance to preview their accounts in their guestrooms through an automated system. Guests can select a designated channel on the room's television and view any charges made to their accounts in the comfort and privacy of their rooms. Any discrepancies or disagreements can be handled before actual check-out time, thus avoiding an annoying delay at the cashier's window during check-out.

Sometimes charges are made to guests' accounts without a back-up voucher. For example, guests may use a room key instead of money in vending machines located in guestrooms to purchase liquor, foods, ice, or sundries. The charges for these sales are then recorded in the front office area or directly in the computer for inclusion in folios. Likewise, charges for in-room movies are sometimes automatically tallied and added to the guest folio.

The most often used form of no-voucher charging is the automatic telephone counter. Located in the front office area, this device keeps track of the number of local calls made from any room phone. Differences between registration counts and check-out counts (maintained on folios) tell cashiers how many calls to charge to a guest without having to maintain traffic sheets or to make vouchers for each call through a central switchboard. Long-distance calls may be accounted for on vouchers from the telephone company by means of a direct-dial system keyed to the individual room phone for accounting purposes. Automated telephone systems will be discussed in more detail later in the chapter.

Most hotels now provide an express check-out service whereby the night audit staff prints up-to-date folios for guests due to depart the following morning. Some overnight staff members, commonly a security officer or bellperson, will deliver these bills under the guestroom door of all check-out rooms. This service eliminates a considerable amount of time and effort at the front desk each morning, and saves the guest valuable time.

The Mail and Information Section

The mail and information section is the area where services are performed that do not involve registration, check-out, or financial procedures. Services provided in this section may include distributing keys or key cards, holding keys while guests are out, handling messages and mail for guests, and answering guest questions about available tours, local points of interest, hours of banking, and the community in general. This function has become easier since the advent of searches on computers. Front desk agents in this area also must know about the services and hours of operation of all in-house departments, such as restaurants, lounges, and room service. In many hotels, front desk agents are fluent in more than one language.

Handling guest mail, packages, and messages is an important function. Often very valuable information and items are entrusted to the hotel personnel involved. Nowadays, most properties are sufficiently automated that incoming messages can be passed directly into voice mail and can be tracked within the property management system as backup. If mail or other packages are held at the front desk, employees can notify guests via a message light on the guestroom telephone. Documentation of time of receipt and location of material can be noted in the property management system.

Some hotels assign those guest information duties concerning the local area and entertainment to the bell captain's desk. Other (usually upscale) properties increasingly use concierge services—which may be provided by an individual or an entire staff—to handle these information requests.

Concierges were popular in European and Asian hotels long before they were common in the United States. The concierge is the information center of the hotel. Even the general manager may rely on the concierge for information about the city, transportation, entertainment, and local news and events. A concierge can also assist guests in re-confirming travel plans and making changes in travel itineraries. Conveniently located in the lobby, the concierge provides special attention to the guests and, at the same time, frees front desk agents for registration, check-out, and other responsibilities.

Information racks with brochures promoting area attractions may supplement or replace concierge services in some hotels. Tourist centers and chambers of commerce usually provide printed booklets and brochures that outline an area's major points of interest, the schedule of cultural events, and the hours of operation of major transportation systems, businesses, and governmental centers. Front offices may place these brochures in a convenient place for guests.

The Reservations Department

Probably no department in a hotel has experienced as major a change in staffing levels and overall functioning as the reservations department. In years past, the bulk of reservations were handled in-house with two or more staff members handling the phones to talk with prospective guests. This would be supplemented by reservations made at off-site call centers and transferred to the hotel periodically.

Hotels can no longer rely simply on bookings from chain and local toll-free number sources and calls guests make directly to the hotel. Today, global distribution systems (GDSs) link real-time room inventories to the booking computers of thousands of travel planners worldwide. Even more dramatic is the growth and importance of third-party web wholesalers, who have developed sophisticated Internet sites that feature virtually the same room inventories and availability that travel agents and hotel reservation agents can see.

As these booking sources become ever more popular with a public increasingly comfortable with booking travel plans online, hotels have (often reluctantly) become compelled to offer rates and wide availability to the third-party sources. Hotel companies have reacted to this phenomenon by enhancing their own websites and offering attractive discounts to electronic bookers in an effort to regain control over the booking of inventories of rooms. These actions have become a paramount priority for hotel chains. It is critically important to control room offerings through third-party providers, because poorly managed discount reservations can significantly erode profitability.

While electronic interfaces link directly to the hotel property management system and create control problems, the proliferation of online and mobile third-party reservation sources has also reduced the need for hotels to have their own reservation staffs. Indeed, these interfaces are so secure and well-established that it is now common for individual hotels to significantly reduce the staff on hand to handle reservation calls.

As the function of making hotel reservations continues to move away from the individual hotels, the oversight of the room inventories has also changed. Nowadays, the abundance of electronic sources available to the prospective guest means that enormous changes can occur in the volume of reservations. As a result, oversight of room inventories must include carefully monitoring the flow of reservation demand against expectations. Careful revenue management has become increasingly important to a hotel's success in managing its most profitable offering:

the guestroom. A revenue manager must make frequent changes in rate and availability based on specific demand for given dates in the future, how the competition appears to be strategizing dates, and the pickup of group rooms in comparison to what has been reserved for them. It's a complicated, ever-changing dynamic that requires the revenue manager to get input and research from the sales department, the general manager, and executives from the front office. Mistakes can backfire spectacularly—often in a matter of minutes!

Types of Reservations

There are several different kinds of reservations, and a single reservation may fit more than one category.

Guaranteed Reservations. With a guaranteed reservation, the hotel assures the guest that a room will be held until the guest's arrival or until check-out time the next day—whichever occurs first. In return, the guest guarantees payment for the room, even if it is not used, unless the guest cancels the reservation in accordance with the hotel's required cancellation procedures. Some of the types of guaranteed reservations are:

- Payment card—Major payment card companies have developed systems by which participating properties can be guaranteed payment for reserved rooms that were left empty by no-shows. (A person with a reservation who does not use a room or cancel the reservation is called a **no-show**.) Virtually all reservations made electronically are guaranteed reservations that the guest secures by providing a payment card number.

- Advance deposit—An advance deposit guarantee (or partial prepayment) requires the guest to remit to the property a specified amount prior to the guest's stay. The prepayment may be for one night's lodging, plus taxes, or for the entire stay.

- Corporate—Under a corporate guarantee, a corporation or business agrees to accept financial responsibility for any no-shows. This procedure is often set up in advance when the corporation signs a contract with the hotel.

Non-Guaranteed Reservations. The hotel agrees to hold a room for the guest until a stated cutoff time. If the guest does not arrive by that time, the hotel may sell the room to a **walk-in** guest (a guest arriving without a reservation) if additional space is not available. Of course, if the guest arrives after the cutoff hour and rooms are still available, the hotel will accommodate the guest.

Confirmed Reservations. The confirmed reservation details the intent of both parties and includes the material points of the agreement—i.e., dates, rate, type of accommodations, number of guests. If it is made early enough, the property may mail the guest a written confirmation, which the guest may be asked to produce at registration. Many properties now send confirmations by e-mail as well. An oral confirmation that includes the material points is also a binding agreement between both parties. Confirmed reservations may be either guaranteed or non-guaranteed.

Hotel-Specific Reservations. Hotels may also establish other types of reservations for their own use, based on criteria such as type of guest or source of reservation. Examples include VIP reservations, convention delegate reservations, travel agent reservations, and paid-in-advance reservations.

Special Concerns

A casual observer might think that handling hotel reservations is a rather simple, mechanical, routine job. However, the job is not as simple as it first appears. The ideal situation, of course, is to have every room booked and every reservation honored. No hotel can hope to have all of its rooms filled every night of the year, but, when the business is available, it is uneconomical to have any rooms vacant. It is often said that there is no commodity more perishable than a hotel room. If the room is not sold on a specific night, that sale is lost forever.

On any given day, when all available rooms are reserved, a hotel is 100 percent booked. Experience tells us, however, that invariably there are last-minute cancellations, no-shows, and early check-outs. How does a hotel protect itself from being left with vacant rooms for which a demand existed? The usual answer is to consider the number of rooms *likely* to be available for sale based on previous records and reliable estimates. The more accurately a hotel can estimate the number of rooms *actually* available for sale, the less likely it will be that service problems will occur.

For example, suppose a hotel knows that, on the average, it has about 5 percent no-shows, about 8 percent cancellations, and an overstay rate of about 5 percent (5 percent of current guests will decide to stay longer than the agreed-upon check-out date). During a period of full occupancy, the hotel may choose to accept reservations in excess of actual rooms by 8 percent (5 percent no-shows + 8 percent cancellations − 5 percent overstays).

If these percentages were always accurate, problems would seldom arise. But there are times when things go wrong; no one cancels, or all room reservations are honored, or inclement weather grounds all outgoing planes, greatly increasing the number of overstays. In such a situation, every room may be occupied, and other guests with reservations may be asking for rooms that simply are not available.

When this occurs, all the front desk agent can do is handle the guest in the most courteous manner and assist him or her in finding accommodations elsewhere. This is called **walking a guest**. Unfortunately, all the guest really understands is that, even with a reservation, no room was available. These situations can easily lose customers for a hotel.

With increased emphasis on consumer protection, several U.S. states have enacted legislation prohibiting the practice of overbooking. Hoteliers who carelessly overbook invite additional restrictive legislation for the hospitality industry. The hotel industry is attempting to develop new solutions to the no-show problem.

The Telecommunications Department

The telecommunications department is a vital part of guest service. Although an operator rarely sees the guest, his or her voice and telephone manner can influence a guest's opinion of the hotel and its service. A switchboard or PBX supervisor (who may or may not occupy a switchboard position) heads this group, which handles in-house, local, and long-distance calls.

Starting in the 1980s, call accounting machines made it possible for guests to place calls directly, without an operator intervening to request the room number. These machines also allowed hotels to add surcharges to calls made by guests, thus making the telecommunications department a revenue center. These and other technological advances have decreased the responsibilities and workload of the telecommunications department considerably.

For example, in most new hotels, computers make wake-up calls automatically. In the past, many guest complaints and more than a few lawsuits centered on wake-up calls, or, more accurately, the lateness or absence of a requested wake-up call. With the hotel's computer system now often linked to the telephone system, a guest may enter wake-up call data directly. This has nearly eliminated the missed or late wake-up call.

Telephone systems now frequently include a voice mail option whereby guests can hear actual recordings of callers' messages. This option alleviates a great deal of time for the hotel operator in processing messages and also gives the guest a better level of service and personalization.

The telecommunications department plays a vital role in the hotel's security program. Operators protect guests' privacy by not divulging room numbers, and the department acts as a communications center in the case of accidents and other emergencies.

Internet-savvy travelers increasingly expect hotels to provide access for their laptop computers via a dedicated data line or wireless network. Also, more and more travelers look for the high-speed access they enjoy in their homes and offices. All varieties of lodging establishments offer this technology as a necessary amenity in guestrooms and function rooms as a means of remaining competitive. Regrettably, this technology does not directly enhance profitability; instead, it can represent a major expense for many establishments. In addition, a large proportion of today's travelers use their own cellular phones, thereby making the telecommunications department nearly irrelevant regarding local and long-distance calls. With all the advances in telecommunications technology, the size and influence of a dedicated department has been diminished to the point where many hotels are eliminating the telephone operator positions and relying on front desk agents to handle all phone calls.

The Uniformed Service Department

This department is aptly named, since its only product is service. Staff members perform their duties in front of the guest. None of the jobs are complex, but their functions are important, since members of the uniformed service department are often the first and last hotel employees to interact with guests.

Uniformed service includes door attendants and bellpersons. Lobby porters may be included in this department, but they are usually assigned to the housekeeping department. In large hotels, a superintendent of service directs the uniformed service staff. In small hotels, the bell captain supervises other staff and is, in turn, directed by the assistant manager or the executive assistant manager.

The door attendant serves as the hotel's greeter. Stationed at the main lobby entrance, he or she meets all arriving guests, helps them unload their luggage, guards the luggage of arriving and departing guests, assists the bellperson in handling baggage, summons taxis for guests, and may supervise the parking of guest automobiles. Door attendants should be well informed on local points of interest because guests will often ask for such information.

The bellperson's principal duty is rooming guests. When a guest has completed registration, the bellperson is called to the desk to receive the rooming slip and the key/key card. (The guest rooming slip includes such information as the guest's name and address, room rate, and check-out time, and may also include information advertising hotel activities and services, such as lounge entertainment, meal specials, and concierge services.) The bellperson checks to see if the guest has any mail or messages, carries the baggage, and escorts the guest to the guestroom. A good bellperson will check the room for orderliness and properly functioning lights, television, and other equipment, and will explain services to the guest, answer any questions, and leave the key and guest rooming slip in the room. The bellperson's courtesy, tact, and efficiency can solidify the feeling of welcome already generated by the desk agent.

In their frequent trips to all parts of the hotel, bellpersons serve as the eyes and ears of the hotel; it is their duty to report anything out of the ordinary. Other duties include assisting the departing guest with luggage, running errands and handling messages, paging guests, and carrying baggage on room changes. At various times, bellpersons may be called upon to show rooms to patrons or to conduct group tours through the hotel. Because of their direct contact with the guest (who frequently asks for information), bellpersons can be excellent salespeople for the restaurants, lounges, and other services of the hotel.

The Housekeeping Department

The housekeeping department is one of the busiest in the hotel. Housekeeping employees are responsible for the neatness and cleanliness of all the guestrooms and maintenance of most public areas. The executive housekeeper manages the housekeeping department. Since the department is a back-of-the-house operation, few guests understand the full scope of housekeeping or see the executive housekeeper unless they have complaints about the department. However, the work of the housekeeping department greatly influences guests' opinions of the hotel.

In a small hotel, the executive housekeeper may be the only supervisor and the housekeepers may be the only staff in this department. (Housekeepers are also called room attendants.) In larger properties, there are often additional supervisors called room inspectors. These inspectors ensure the proper cleanliness and maintenance of the rooms. Usually there is one inspector for every 80 to 100 rooms. Housepersons maintain the public areas and guestroom corridors and may assist the housekeepers with certain duties. Housepersons are frequently under the supervision of a head houseperson. In many hotels, the head houseperson is also responsible for distributing cleaning and guestroom supplies. Again, depending on the size of the hotel, there may be one or more assistant head housepersons.

The headquarters of the housekeeping department may be the linen room or some other place close to housekeeping supplies. A supervisor coordinates all activities and daily work assignments from these headquarters.

Communication between the front office and housekeeping is vital to ensuring the smooth flow of departures and new arrivals. The ready communication of which guestrooms are vacant and ready to clean, and which are clean and available for check-in, streamlines this process in well-managed hotels.

Many hotels are now sufficiently automated to have a system whereby the housekeeper can key in a code for guestrooms that have been cleaned. This information is transmitted into the property management system and is available on terminals located in the housekeeping office and at the front desk. The information tells the housekeeping supervisor or inspector which rooms are ready for inspection. Hotels with these systems also use specific codes that housekeepers punch into guestroom telephones to notify housekeeping and the front desk when rooms are vacant and ready to re-sell.

Of course, all the same information can be communicated orally between departments, albeit in a much slower, less efficient manner.

A double-check of all rooms occurs at least once each day to ensure that the listed room status is correct. This is called *checking the rack* and is a room-by-room comparison of the room status shown at the front desk with that shown on the report made by housekeeping staff. In those hotels with computerized systems, this check occurs automatically. Any discrepancies in the status listed by the two departments must be physically checked by a housekeeper.

The primary responsibility of the day shift in housekeeping (8:00 A.M. to 5:00 P.M.) is to clean all guestrooms. In most hotels, the evening shift (4:00 P.M. to midnight) will be responsible for cleaning any rooms that request late service. The evening shift also performs any special VIP service, such as turndown service. It is also the responsibility of evening shift personnel to clean offices and public areas.

The housekeeping department frequently maintains the lost and found storage area for the hotel. Typically, all articles found in the hotel by employees or guests are sent directly to housekeeping, where they are labeled, logged, and stored by date. State law may dictate procedures for the storage and eventual disposal of such items.

It takes a large volume of sheets, pillowcases, towels, and table linens to operate a hotel. Large hotels usually operate in-house laundries. There is continuing debate in the industry regarding whether an in-house system is practical and profitable. If a hotel uses a commercial laundry, the housekeeping department is responsible for keeping an accurate inventory of linens. All linen must be checked daily for quality. Most large hotels with in-house laundries have a separate laundry department to perform cleaning, ironing, and ongoing quality control checks. They may also have a sewing room where linens are repaired. It is usually the housepersons' responsibility to keep each floor's linen storage closet stocked with the necessary types of linen.

The greatest number of employees in the housekeeping department serve as housekeepers and housepersons. When coming on duty, they report directly to the housekeeping office, sign out keys, and receive the daily report. This report will indicate the status of assigned rooms. Normally, early-service requests and check-out rooms are cleaned first.

The housekeeper's first responsibility upon reaching the assigned floor is to take a "house count" to physically verify the status on the report. Any discrepancies are reported immediately to the housekeeping office and the front desk. Periodically through the shift, an inspector will visit the rooms and report the progress to the housekeeping office. Before going off duty at the end of the shift, the housekeeper will repack the linen cart and replenish supplies for the following shift. Any rooms that refused service or requested later service are reported to the supervisor of the next shift so that the task of cleaning those rooms can be reassigned.

The houseperson works in close cooperation with the housekeepers. A typical hotel staffing pattern suggests one houseperson for each five to eight housekeepers. The houseperson regularly cleans all hallway carpets and maintains the general cleanliness of public areas and service corridors. Heavy cleaning jobs within guestrooms may be assigned to the houseperson on a regular schedule. These duties include carpet cleaning with heavy-duty vacuum cleaners and shampooers/steamers; cleaning walls, baseboards, and windows; moving furniture for more thorough cleaning; and turning mattresses. Large properties may have personnel with specialized duties who, for example, shampoo carpets on a full-time basis.

The heavy usage and wear in hotel rooms creates a need for frequent maintenance and refurbishing. It is an important responsibility of supervisors and inspectors to keep a close and constant check on the guestrooms for items requiring replacement and repair. Most hotels use a multi-part **work order** form that the housekeeping staff fills out to request specific repairs or maintenance work. One part of the form is sent to the engineering division to indicate requests. These orders are logged and dated. Upon completion of the order, the engineering copy of the form is returned to the housekeeping department and logged accordingly. Requests that are minor and do not require immediate attention may be held by engineering until a slack period of occupancy, at which time they will be completed.

The housekeeping department is also responsible for purchasing all guest-room and cleaning supplies for the hotel. Accurate perpetual inventories of all supplies must be maintained.

The Green Movement

It is now common for hotels to give guests the option of less-than-daily cleaning and replacement of towels and linens to further support energy savings. Some hotels indicate as high as 40 percent acceptance of this procedure. Undoubtedly, it will become more prevalent as it saves on water and chemicals and extends the life span of these laundered goods.

One of the high-impact waste removal issues confronting hotels is the issue of what to do with worn-out mattresses. A typical hotel mattress occupies 23 cubic feet of space. Imagine how many mattresses must be discarded every year from hotels. *Green Lodging News* reports this pile of discarded mattresses would in the United States alone reach over 600 miles high every year! Sadly, most of these mattresses end up in landfills, creating quite a heap of waste metal, wood, and foam.

In a response to this environmental challenge, bedding vendors are beginning to offer mattress systems with replaceable parts, so that the entire unit need not be discarded. Replaceable tops and pads can greatly increase the life span of a hotel mattress. As such modular units become more prevalent, many hotels will be able to save money on replacement costs, while also slowing down the rate of usage at the nation's landfills.

Another way the housekeeping department is becoming more green-oriented is by using biodegradable cleaning chemicals and guestroom soaps and shampoos. Non-toxic supplies keep local water systems cleaner by reducing the levels of fat, oil, and grease going into sewage systems.

For several years, J.D. Power and Associates has been surveying hotel guests on their awareness of and participation in green practice conservation programs. The percentage of guest awareness has increased steadily from 71 percent in 2007 all the way up to 94 percent in 2011. The percentage of guests who reported that they participate in such programs has likewise increased in the same timeframe from 73 percent to 77 percent.

Key Terms

guest folio—A file (electronic or paper) containing all of a guest's charges during the guest's stay at a lodging property.

night audit—An accounting task in which guest charges are posted and totals of all accounts are compared with sales reports of operating departments; usually performed after all of a hotel's sales outlets are closed. Also called a front office audit.

no-show—Someone who made a room reservation but did not register or cancel.

point-of-sale terminal—An electronic cash register that transfers a guest's charges from a hotel sales outlet to the guest folio at the front desk.

walk-in guest—A guest who arrives at a hotel without a reservation.

walking a guest—A situation in which a hotel is unable to honor a guest's reservation and helps the guest find accommodations elsewhere.

work order—A document used to initiate requests for maintenance services.

Review Questions

1. What three distinct areas does the front desk in the typical hotel comprise?

2. What key function does a concierge perform?

3. Where might you find point-of-sale terminals in a typical hotel?

4. How is a guest ledger different from a city ledger?

5. What is a no-voucher guest charge? Provide two or more examples of them.

6. Why might a hotel oversell on a given night?

7. What department is usually the guest's first and last contact with the hotel?

8. In a typical hotel, what department is responsible for the lost and found function?

Internet Sites

For more information, visit the following Internet sites. Remember that Internet addresses can change without notice. If the site is no longer there, you can use a search engine to look for additional sites.

Hotel and Hotel Companies

Best Western International, Inc.
www.bestwestern.com

Four Seasons Hotels and Resorts
www.fourseasons.com

Hyatt Corporation
www.hyatt.com

InterContinental Hotels Group
www.ichotelsgroup.com

Loews Hotels
www.loewshotels.com

Marriott International, Inc.
www.marriott.com

National Trust for Historic Preservation
www.preservationnation.org

Preferred Hotels & Resorts
www.preferredhotels.com

Sheraton Hotels & Resorts
www.starwoodhotels.com/sheraton

Smith Travel Research
www.strglobal.com

Front Office Technology

Agilysys InfoGenesis
www.agilysys.com/home/Hospitality/
Solutions/infogenesis_pos.htm

CSS (front office systems)
www.csshotelsystems.com

Hospitality Industry Technology
Exposition and Conference
www.hftp.org/HITEC

Hospitality Net
www.hospitalitynet.org

MICROS Systems, Inc.
www.micros.com

Newmarket International
www.newmarketinc.com

RoomKey
www.roomkeypms.com

Travel and Lodging Search Sites

HotelsOnline
www.hotelsonline.com

InfoHub Specialty Travel Guide
www.infohub.com

Priceline
www.priceline.com

Travelocity
www.travelocity.com

Part III

The Food Service Industry

Chapter 7 Outline

Food Service in America
    The Colonial Inn and Tavern
    French Cuisine in the United States
    Delmonico's
    The 1800s
    The Cafeteria
    Employee, School, and Hospital Food
        Service
Food Service in Europe
Modern Food Service in America
    Prohibition
    The Roaring '20s and the Great
        Depression
    World War II and the 1950s
    The 1960s
    The 1970s
    Nouvelle Cuisine
    Food Festivals
    American Wine
    The 1980s
    The 1990s and Forward
Modern Food Service in Europe
    Europe Versus the United States
    Guest Expectations and Behavior
    The Work Force
    Employee Remuneration
    Government Regulation
    Regional Cuisine
    Physical Facilities
    Menu Prices
Franchising Developments in Food Service
    The 1980s, 1990s, and the Twenty-First
        Century
    Increasing Unit Sales
    Consistency Is Important
    Franchise Agreements and
        Relationships
    Quick-Service Restaurant Employees
    Franchising Problems
Management Companies in Institutional
    Food Service
    Management Company Operations

Competencies

1. Describe the early development of food service in Europe and the United States, and distinguish à la carte menus from the table d'hôte menus used in early European food service establishments. (pp. 133–137)

2. Describe the development of modern food service operations in America and Europe. (pp. 138–146)

3. Trace the development of franchising in the food service industry, identify characteristics of successful franchise operations, and discuss franchising problems. (pp. 146–152)

4. Identify the role of management companies in various segments of the food service industry. (pp. 152–155)

7

The Growth and Development of Food Service

Evidence suggests that tribes in Denmark cooked food in large kitchens and ate together in large groups as much as 12,000 years ago. The first cabarets (shops selling wines and liquors) were established around 4000 B.C.E. Cabarets flourished during the Roman and Byzantine empires. Rome also offered *thermopolia*, forerunners of the modern restaurant, which provided hot food and drink. Most of these operations were located in cities near temples or government houses. During the Middle Ages, the cities declined, and the feudal manor became the important center of economic activity. It was in the manors, where kings and lords had to feed courts or households totaling as many as 30,000 people, that cooking first developed a bit of institutional character.

About the year 1200, public cook shops that offered the customer pre-cooked food to take home opened in London. Another 200 years passed before refinements such as table linen, crystal glasses, and eating instruments that resembled forks and knives as we know them appeared. Instead of merely piling the food on platters, the cooks began to arrange it artistically and in smaller quantities.

When Catherine de Médicis married King Henry II of France in the sixteenth century, she brought with her from Italy the very finest chefs, who added new refinements to royal cookery and prepared some very artistic banquets. As the years passed, new items were added to the menu. Jacques Coeur, for example, brought turkey to France. Olivier de Serres demonstrated how vegetables could enhance a menu and a diet. He is reputed to be the first Frenchman to praise the potato and strongly influenced culinary practices. Serres took his suggestions to King Louis XIV (1638–1715) and his culinary staff. Many of the suggestions were accepted and influenced the training and development of excellent chefs and expert kitchen masters. Thus was born the French reputation for fine food.

The influence of the royal kitchens eventually filtered down to the inns and taverns that served the travelers of the time. Appropriately, the word restaurant is derived from the French word *restaurer*, meaning to restore.

Food Service in America

The stage had been set for many food service ideas and practices to travel to America. Samuel Cole opened the first American tavern in 1634. In 1656, Massachusetts passed a law that required every town in the colony to have a tavern or be subject to a fine. The first coffeehouse in Boston was established in 1670.

The American population began to demand more inns and would soon be demanding hotels and restaurants. As inns grew in number, cooks borrowed culinary ideas and recipes from European chefs, slowly modified them, and initiated the first stage of what we know today as American cuisine.

The Colonial Inn and Tavern

American food service really began its growth and development in the colonial tavern or inn. Located near the center of activity, the tavern provided an informal meeting place, a chance to talk politics with good food and ale to accompany the conversations. The tavern was owned and presided over by a personable innkeeper who was knowledgeable about local events. When there was business in the tavern, he was on the floor with the customers. Saturdays were military training days in the colonies. After marching and drilling, both the officers and men headed for the tavern to relax and sample the innkeeper's food and drink.

About 1740, the first stagecoaches began to roll out of Boston and provided new customers for the inn or tavern. The roadside inn became famous in America and was the birthplace of the American hotel industry. The heyday of the roadside inn lasted until the American Revolution. Until this time, colonists patterned their eating habits after the English, although with a few frontier modifications.

French Cuisine in the United States

Following the American Revolution, French cuisine became quite popular, particularly in government and society circles, in part because the English were out of favor in America. American and foreign diplomatic corps were served in the French manner. Presidents Washington and Jefferson served French cuisine at social as well as political dinners. Refugees from the French Revolution brought with them both a taste for and culinary expertise in their national dishes, which further promoted American interest in French food.

It was during this period that the roadside inn or tavern began to diminish in importance as the principal gathering place for the people. Even the most famous—The King's Arms and The Blue Anchor Tavern—felt the competition from the newest European import, the restaurant. Historians disagree over which establishment deserves to be designated the first American restaurant—the Sans Souci, Niblo's Garden, or Delmonico's. All three opened in the 1820s in New York and soon became the most fashionable eating places in the city. The Sans Souci and Niblo's Garden both served French cuisine, while Delmonico's brought the Swiss influence into American food service.

Delmonico's

Delmonico's deserves special recognition because it was more than just a famous restaurant; it became a symbol of American fine dining. The Delmonico brothers opened the first of many eating establishments in 1827, a cake and wine shop on William Street in New York City. Four years later, the Delmonico brothers brought their nineteen-year-old nephew Lorenzo from Switzerland to the United States. It was Lorenzo Delmonico who, for over fifty years, cultivated the excellent taste in food, decor, and clientele that was so important in New York society circles. Delmonico's closed in 1923, a victim of Prohibition.

Virtually every nation's cooking has been influenced by the French. (Photo courtesy of Le Palais Restaurant, Resorts International Casino Hotel)

The 1800s

A number of significant events occurred during the 1800s that directly affected the growth and refinement of American food service:

- The first ice refrigerator went into use in 1803.

- In 1815, Robert Owen established a large eating room for workers and their families, and industrial food service began in America.

- 1825 marked the first recorded use of a gas stove.

- Harvey Parker of Boston offered the first à la carte menu in his restaurant around 1855.

- In the 1860s:

  - the dishwashing machine was invented.

  - the first martini was made in San Francisco's Occidental Hotel.

  - George M. Pullman developed railroad dining cars.

  - H. J. Heinz opened his food business.

- Late in the century, Antoine Feuchtwanger introduced America to the hot dog in St. Louis, Missouri. He sold hot "franks" along with cotton gloves to hold the hot sausage.

- Harry M. Stevens really popularized these franks when he sold them at New York's Polo Grounds as "Red Hots."

The Cafeteria

Following the birth of the American restaurant, the next important milestone in commercial food service was the development of the cafeteria. Credit for developing the cafeteria belongs to John Krueger. Inspired by the **smorgasbord** that he had seen served in Sweden, Krueger designed a similar commercial food service system. The cafeteria made its first appearance in California during the famous Gold Rush days. On the East Coast, the cafeteria arrived around 1890 when the Exchange Buffet opened near the Stock Exchange in New York City. The cafeteria has also found great popularity in Europe.

Employee, School, and Hospital Food Service

Although its birth goes back to 1815, employee food service did not really begin to grow extensively until around the turn of the twentieth century. In 1902, Illinois Bell began a form of in-plant food service. By 1906, when Sears Roebuck opened the Seroco Restaurant to provide food service for its employees in Chicago, employee food service had become big business. Yet, as impressive as the Seroco Restaurant was (it prepared as many as 12,500 meals daily), employee food service was only in its infancy and would grow and develop even more, particularly after World War II.

Two other aspects of American food service that have their roots in Europe include school food service and hospital food service. School lunch programs go back to 1849 when canteens for schoolchildren first appeared in France. Writer and social commentator Victor Hugo started school food service in England in 1865 by providing warm meals in his home for children from a nearby school. In the United States, the first food service in a school was provided by The Children's Aid Society of New York in 1853. By 1910, "penny lunch programs" had become quite widespread in elementary schools.

While hospital food service can be traced back several centuries in one form or another, it was rather primitive until Florence Nightingale made her contribution. It was during the Crimean War in 1854 that Nightingale, reformer of the nursing profession and the first hospital dietitian, assumed charge of the nurses in the English Military Hospital at Scutari, Turkey. From her emphasis on the role of a proper diet in a patient's recovery came the development of a more scientific approach to patient care and food service.

Food Service in Europe

Food and food service as we know them today have always played an important role in Europe. Perhaps it was through the advent of the celebrated gourmets and party hosts, such as Jean-Jacques Régis de Cambacérès, archchancellor under Napoleon, and Jean Anthelme Brillat-Savarin, frequent dinner guest of Foreign Minister Charles-Maurice de Talleyrand-Périgord and author of the legendary *La Physiologie du Gout*, that French cuisine gained its reputation as the cradle of culinary art. Or perhaps it was only through the legendary chefs Marie-Antoine Carême, Prosper Montagné, and Georges Auguste Escoffier and writers like Curnonsky that the world at large became aware of the overwhelming influence the French have had on modern cooking. While all countries of the world have their own culinary traditions, it is also true that every nation's cooking has been influenced by one or both of two cultures of gastronomy: the French and the Chinese.

Along with the culinary art, the service of food and beverage was also raised from simple delivery to a highly ritualistic and artful ballet. The basic score for this ballet has always been the bill of fare or menu. There have always been two basic types of menu:

- The **à la carte menu:** a complete list of all food items served

- The **table d'hôte** or **prix fixe menu:** a complete breakfast, lunch, or dinner menu sold at a fixed price

Until the end of the nineteenth century, the classical menu structure of at least 12 courses was followed for the service of formal banquets. Exhibit 1 shows this classical structure. At the beginning of the twentieth century, these menus were greatly reduced. A menu of six to eight courses became the standard. Today, a menu of three or four dishes is the rule rather than the exception.

Food and beverage service also reflects the trend toward greater simplicity and informality. Just as menu structures were very formal, so too were special service styles. When Ueli Prager, founder of Mövenpick Restaurants, replaced tablecloths in his restaurants with American-style place mats, it was considered a very courageous innovation. Today, place mats and informal plate service are more the rule.

Exhibit 1   Pre-1900 Formal Banquet Menu Structure

Hors d'oeuvre froid (Cold appetizer)
Potage (Soup)
Hors d'oeuvre chaud (Hot appetizer)
Poisson (Fish)
Pièce de résistance (Main dish)
Entrée chaude (Hot entrée)
Entrée froide (Cold entrée)
Sorbet (Sherbet)
Rôti, salade (Roast, salad)
Légume (Vegetable)
Entremet de douceur chaude (Hot sweet)
Entremet de douceur froide (Cold sweet)
Dessert (Dessert)
Fromage (Cheese)

Modern Food Service in America

Although American food service history goes back hundreds of years, it was during the twentieth century that growth, development, change, and innovation accelerated at an almost unbelievable pace. Several noteworthy events occurred in the early part of the century:

- The hamburger was served for the first time in 1904 at the St. Louis World's Fair.

- In 1919, the National Restaurant Association was founded.

- Also in 1919 Roy Allen and Frank Wright opened a root beer stand—the first of what would become over 2,500 A&W Root Beer units. Most of these properties were franchised, so Allen and Wright became the men who pioneered the franchise concept in the food service industry.

While franchising has played a part in the growth of the food industry since the 1920s, the amazing growth of franchise operations was still fifty years in the future.

Prohibition

In 1920, the advent of Prohibition wrought major changes in the American food service industry. Suddenly unable to serve liquor, the nation's hotels and restaurants found it difficult to change their patrons' habit of having wine and liquor with a fine meal. To the hotel and restaurant owners' dismay, those patrons began to frequent illegal **speakeasies,** where they could still purchase alcoholic beverages. Food inevitably became part of the offerings of these establishments—after starting with sandwiches, speakeasies were soon serving full meals to their customers. Both hotel dining rooms and regular restaurants were forced to close for lack of business.

After the repeal of Prohibition in 1933, many speakeasies developed into successful restaurants, among them the famous Club 21, Lindy's, and El Morocco. Many guests who had formerly eaten in hotel dining rooms never returned. As a result, Prohibition shifted the dining habits of Americans toward restaurants and away from hotels.

The Roaring '20s and the Great Depression

The 1920s are often referred to as the Roaring Twenties because of great economic growth in many industries and the atmosphere of optimism and enthusiasm. However, restaurants did not experience the same growth that occurred in many other industries, including hotels. When the Wall Street Crash of 1929 sent the nation spiraling into the Great Depression, the food service industry was devastated. During the 1930s, more than the usual number of restaurants went out of business, and both gross sales and gross profits suffered severe blows in those properties that remained open.

The 1930s were not, however, an entirely dismal period for the food service industry. In 1932, the National Restaurant Association selected Chicago as its permanent headquarters. Attendance at the NRA convention exceeded 10,000 in 1937, establishing a record to that time. (That record would be broken many times in the future—well over 100,000 people attend the convention today.) Prohibition was repealed in 1933, providing another boost to the restaurant industry. In addition, during the Great Depression, the school lunch program grew dramatically. Massive government aid was channeled into the program at this time, and significant subsidies were granted under the Federal School Lunch Program and related programs established in the 1940s.

World War II and the 1950s

In 1941, the United States entered World War II. Wartime restrictions were placed on travel, but the war accelerated the demand for restaurant meals. The demand went from the pre-war level of 20 million meals a day to more than 60 million meals after war was declared. Restaurant operators found rationing, price controls, labor shortages, and the incredible burden of reports and government red tape extremely frustrating. However, they survived and actually prospered. The close of World War II brought on a period of great prosperity for the United States, and the food service industry shared in this prosperity. By 1951, the industry became the third largest in the United States. Growth continued throughout the 1950s, and, by 1960, the American food service industry accounted for yearly sales of $18 billion.

The 1960s

The 1960s were eventful times for the food service industry. In 1964, a U.S. Supreme Court ruling strengthened the prohibition against racial discrimination in hotels and restaurants. The first tentative efforts to use computers to streamline food services were made. The nation's minimum wage law was revised and expanded so as to apply to an increasing number of hotels and restaurants. While all this was transpiring, food service sales continued to grow. During this ten-year period, yearly sales more than doubled from $18 billion to $45 billion.

The 1960s saw a significant increase in the development of convenience foods. The efforts of university personnel and the research and development departments of supply companies were enlisted. Their goal was to develop prepackaged food that could be prepared quickly by relatively unskilled workers and still offer quality to diners.

An approach that appeared to have merit was to develop manufacturing centers where food could be produced and then transported to retail outlets for final preparation and service. A number of companies had **commissary** operations where this process had been used to a limited degree. After preparation and with proper presentation, food could be transported to various locations or inventoried in a single large operation. Once the food arrived at the individual property, it needed only to be prepared for serving.

As early as 1925, Clarence Birdseye had developed a method of freezing certain foods that would preserve them for long periods and then permit thawing and cooking without quality deterioration. Many scientists worked to develop ways to freeze entrées and other menu items while maintaining the same quality achieved in conventional food preparation.

By the 1950s, a number of large companies entered the frozen food business. Stouffer's and Armour were two of the largest manufacturers to produce complete lines of frozen entrées. Kaiser Hospitals in California began to use frozen meals, which were simply transported to the hospital and stored there. At mealtime, personnel reconstituted the platters and served them to the patients. Kaiser Hospitals received tremendous publicity for their "kitchenless kitchens." During the same period, Philip Parrott introduced a similar idea with his "kitchenless kitchen" at Continental Airlines. Frozen entrées were reconstituted by either the boil-in-the-bag method on a range top or in microwave ovens. Either system could be handled by flight attendants with limited culinary skills. In spite of the tremendous amount of research and attention given to convenience foods, industry experts never felt that convenience food quality quite measured up to freshly prepared quality.

As the country approached the end of the 1960s, young Americans began to develop keen interest in the culinary arts as a profession. The Culinary Institute of America in New York had more applicants than it could handle. Other fine professional cooking schools developed around the country and began to produce qualified graduates. Suddenly, the predicted shortage of culinarians was less of a problem. This fact, along with general skepticism about the quality of reconstituted convenience foods, blunted the development of convenience foods. Nonetheless, convenience food technology has had great applications in items that are sold in supermarkets for home consumption.

The 1970s

As the industry entered the 1970s, a great sense of optimism was evident. Public interest in food and wine was reaching new highs, sales were accelerating, and the industry was on a firm financial footing. Most important, franchising and chain operations climbed to new sales records. In spite of two recessionary periods, yearly food service sales grew from $45 billion in 1970 to $118 billion in 1980.

During this period, individual entrepreneurs began to sell out to chains, and whole chains were acquired by conglomerates. Space does not permit the detailing of all these events, but one example will demonstrate the trend:

- Kentucky Fried Chicken was acquired by Heublein, a major distilling company.
- Del Monte acquired Service Systems Corporation (a food management company) and other operations.
- Then R. J. Reynolds acquired both the Heublein and Del Monte companies.

The largest fast-food franchising chains—McDonald's, Wendy's, Burger King, Kentucky Fried Chicken, and others—had their greatest growth period, both in sales and unit expansion, during the 1970s. It was only toward the close of the decade that sales began to slow down.

An important factor influencing this phenomenal growth was the American public's greatly increased interest in food, wine, and cooking. Many television stations regularly featured gourmet chefs who taught the novice how to prepare even ordinary foods in more interesting ways. Thousands enrolled in private cooking schools operated by chefs or cooking experts.

Nouvelle Cuisine

The creation of the so-called *nouvelle* (new) *cuisine* in France led to a great deal of journalistic comment. The new cuisine recognized that Americans and Europeans alike need to eat smaller amounts of lighter foods and more fresh fruits and vegetables. Indeed, the eating habits of the American public have changed dramatically in the last thirty-five years. The American restaurant patron is eating simpler foods and is staying away from sauces, fatty foods, and fancy cookery. Dessert consumption has decreased, and the typical diner is selecting fewer items. There is no question that the interest in dieting and weight control has had a lot to do with this. Less complicated foods are being consumed at home, and guests also desire such foods when they go out to eat.

Food Festivals

Another development has been the growth of food festivals. Festivals held in major cities around the United States have drawn millions of people. Many of these festivals are now annual affairs, and the number continues to grow every year. Guests gain exposure to an area's restaurants and hotel food and beverage operations, and to many new food items as well. Also, many culinary arts shows are held annually in many cities. Through such events, the industry advertises and promotes its products and services and, in doing so, builds business.

American Wine

Appreciation for American wine has been an area of phenomenal growth. Just forty years ago, few Americans drank wine with their meals, and those who did rarely considered a domestic product. Today, however, all of this has changed. Europe's fine wines are very expensive, and wine connoisseurs in the United States now speak glowingly of many domestic wines, particularly those from California and New York. As a matter of fact, even Europeans admit that the best American wines compare favorably with their European counterparts. Young adults in particular have learned to enjoy wine with their meals, and, consequently, wine sales have exploded as never before. Today, even supermarkets carry a large assortment of wines.

The 1980s

Dollar sales in the food service industry continued to increase in the 1980s, but real growth slowed considerably, usually fluctuating between 2.5 and 3 percent annually. However, compared with other industries, the food service field did well. In fact, certain areas of the industry enjoyed excellent prosperity. Hamburger and pizza chains did well, as did Mexican and down-home properties such as Grandy's. However, because of federal budget cutbacks, the school food service program declined significantly.

In the mid-1980s, midscale restaurant chains showed greater growth than the quick-service segment. This was especially true in operations like Chi-Chi's, Bennigan's, and T.G.I. Friday's. Many of these units did a volume of $2 million yearly due to large-volume alcoholic beverage sales and a high check average. However, in the late 1980s, sales for this segment leveled off quickly. A principal reason was the strong public campaign to de-emphasize alcohol consumption, led by Mothers Against Drunk Driving (MADD) and other organizations.

The acquisition and divestiture activity that marked the 1970s continued through the 1980s and into the 1990s at a rapid pace. International companies continued to invest in the American food service industry:

- Kyotaru, a Japanese restaurant company, purchased Restaurant Associates (however, Nick Valenti, president of Restaurant Associates, orchestrated a management-led buyout of it from Kyotaru).

- Another Japanese chain, Skylark, bought Red Robin.

- Allied Domecq, a British firm, acquired Baskin-Robbins, Dunkin' Donuts, and Mr. Donut.

- Grand Metropolitan, also British, purchased the Pillsbury Company and sold off Steak & Ale and Bennigan's, but kept Burger King and added Wimpy's, Pizzaland, and Perfect Pizza to its holdings.

The 1990s and Forward

The mid-1990s were relatively calm in the merger, sale, and acquisition arena. However, consolidation activity accelerated as the new century approached and has continued in the twenty-first century at a fairly steady pace:

- Long John Silver's was purchased out of bankruptcy by Yorkshire Global Restaurants, which then dual-branded it with A&W.

- Tricon changed its name to Yum! Brands and added Long John Silver's and A&W Restaurants to its portfolio.

- Flagstar became Advantica and divested all its other concepts to concentrate on Denny's. It then changed its name to Denny's Corporation.

- Diageo sold Burger King to a Texas investment group.

- Outback Steakhouse acquired Carrabba's.

- McDonald's took over Boston Market and purchased a share of Café Express.

- Tillman Fertitta, chairman of Landry's, took the company private and added several restaurant brands to its growing portfolio including:

    - Babin's Seafood House
    - Bubba Gump
    - Chart House
    - Grotto
    - McCormick & Schmick's
    - Vic & Anthony's

Modern Food Service in Europe

The food service industry in Europe is very diversified, as it is in the United States. Virtually every category of food service is represented in various dimensions and volumes. However, there are notable differences between the industry in the United States and Europe due to cultural, historical, and socioeconomic factors.

Europe Versus the United States

Traditionally, Europeans are accustomed to more involved, varied cooking at home, especially in the southern regions. The traditional role of the homemaker has changed little over the centuries, and cooking and its related activities play a major role in the homemaker's life. Dining at home is also more formal than it is in the United States. A dining table is set with a variety of dishes and the entire family is expected to be present every day at a set time for the main meal. The type and time of this meal varies from country to country. In northern Europe, the noontime meal tends to consist of a cold sandwich or similar fare, and the evening meal, taken around 6:00 P.M., is a full hot supper. British working classes actually call this meal "tea," but it is very similar to an American dinner. Further to the south in Europe, the midday meal becomes more extensive and lasts longer, and in the Mediterranean countries is often followed by a siesta. The time for the evening meal varies from 8:00 P.M. in northern France to 10:00 P.M. or later in southern Italy and Spain.

The result of these cultural differences is quite evident in the food service industry. In those countries where the noon meal is more elaborate, many companies offer rather extensive dining facilities where the employees take a full hour for a three- or four-course meal, some even accompanied by a glass of wine or beer. Institutional catering is a vast industry, particularly in France, which has some of the world's largest companies in this field. Employers may subsidize up to 50 percent of the total cost of the meal, or may require employees to pay for the food products at cost while the employer covers the fixed and operating expenses. Also very popular in these countries is a restaurant luncheon voucher offered by small employers that do not have an employee dining facility. In other countries, people often take their lunch to work, though more and more companies have restaurants that are operated by outside catering companies, a rapidly growing segment of the industry.

Guest Expectations and Behavior

Due to the high quality and variety of home-cooked meals, guest expectations when dining out are much higher. Restaurant meals are more involved and extensive. Because of this and the higher social emphasis on eating, guests tend to spend much more time eating dinner in a restaurant. Two hours is the norm, but dinner can be an all-night affair lasting up to four hours, especially in larger groups. Full-service restaurants generally do not expect to turn their tables and must be satisfied with a one-seating evening.

There are exceptions, however. The brasseries in Paris are notorious for their lively environment with servers running large platters from the kitchen to the tightly spaced tables filled with guests from 7:00 P.M. to 1:00 A.M. daily. Three to four table turns are common in these restaurants.

Two major factors affecting European guest behavior are a generally lower discretionary income and relatively higher restaurant prices. The result is a dining-out frequency that is a mere one-tenth of that found in the United States. Businesses entertain less frequently due to more restrictive and lower deductibility rules in many European countries. Thus, dining out becomes a much more special occasion. It is safe to say that the European restaurateur has to live up to much higher guest expectations than does his or her American colleague.

On the other hand, younger people tend to visit a restaurant more often and eat more rapidly, but they frequent lower-priced restaurants. In the Netherlands, the "choose-your-own" menu is more popular than a fixed, rather low-priced menu.

The Work Force

The food service industry work force in Europe is also significantly different from the food service work force in the United States. Some of these differences are based on culture and history; others are influenced from the outside due to government regulations and union contracts.

Technical qualifications are required both in the front and the back of the house. Traditionally, an apprentice system is used in both service and kitchen areas, with boys and girls starting as young as fourteen to sixteen years of age, working several days a week and being schooled in mostly technical aspects on the remaining days. A strict system of different levels of qualifications, each with clearly defined tasks, must be mastered one step at a time. A good example is the French restaurant hierarchy, which has as many as seven levels from assistant busperson to maître d'. The emphasis on technical qualifications contrasts with the emphasis on friendliness found in the United States. European visitors never cease to comment on the outgoing, accommodating demeanor of the American restaurant service employees, and find that it more than overcomes any lack of technical qualifications.

Whereas in the United States many restaurant workers are students or others who view their jobs as only temporary, in Europe, many service workers view their careers as lifelong ones. This is beginning to change, however—as the number of restaurants in Europe rises and younger people increasingly live on their own, more and more part-time students work in the food service industry for just a few years.

Employee Remuneration

Remuneration is also quite different. In most European countries, the gratuity is included with the meal and then either distributed in a trunk system to the servers or kept by the operation, which pays the staff a fixed salary. The concept of tip credit is non-existent, and labor costs make up a significantly larger portion of the profit and loss statement. While labor costs in a typical U.S. restaurant run about 30 percent, these expenses reach up to 50 percent of sales in Europe. A portion of this difference is caused by the social charges and benefits, which are much higher in Europe. Tips are given and, though highly appreciated by the servers, are not an official part of the salary. The usual tip amounts to about 5 percent of the total bill.

Government Regulation

In most European countries, industries are subject to a series of strict government regulations and union rules. Employees tend to have contracts specifying their exact positions and the number of hours worked per week. Interestingly enough, much of this regulation and its restrictive effects are avoided in many of the small-scale food service environments. In many European countries, beating the system has become a national sport.

Regional Cuisines

From a culinary standpoint, the variety found in Europe is striking. Distinctive regional cuisines are abundant. The major metropolitan areas boast a bountiful selection of restaurants from Europe and around the world. Smaller towns have at least one Chinese restaurant and an Italian pizzeria. The United States has also contributed a vast array of hamburger chains, fried chicken, and American-style bistros like T.G.I. Friday's. Many international hotel chains offer an American-style restaurant and European restaurateurs are discovering "California cuisine."

Some typical differences exist. In addition to their stateside menu, the popular American hamburger chains offer some items not offered in the United States. For example, mayonnaise is served with french fries more often than catsup is. The portion size and plate composition differ in that the meat portions are considerably smaller and the vegetable selections more extensive. Also, the dinner salad offered as a starter or separate course in an American restaurant is virtually non-existent. Luncheon salads are common, but, at dinnertime, salad is offered only as an accompaniment with some dishes and, rarely, as a course after the main course in a French restaurant.

Physical Facilities

Physically, European restaurants differ little from their American counterparts. Anything can be found from a "hole in the wall" to large-capacity restaurants. The use of place mats rather than tablecloths is more limited, and Europeans tend to offer a wider variety of cutlery with specific implements for different food products, such as the use of fish cutlery and up to three different sizes of regular cutlery. The spacing of tables is generally tighter, with the French leaving barely an inch between adjacent tables. Outdoor terraces are popular and abundant even in northern countries, and are used for afternoon coffees, drinks, and light meals. In the south with late dining in warm climates, many restaurants offer strictly outdoor seating.

Menu Prices

Due to the higher labor costs, low table turnover, and sometimes extensive preparations, restaurant prices are considerably higher than in the United States. In addition, most of Europe has embraced the value added tax (VAT) system with a tax on restaurant meals of about 18 percent. Next, a 12 percent to 15 percent service charge is included in the menu price, resulting in prices almost double those in the United States.

With an understanding of the differences and similarities between the industries on these two continents, a restaurateur can succeed in either. Such an understanding also helps in catering to the needs and expectations of the European visitor.

Well-known American chains are finding their way in Europe, but are learning that success may vary from country to country. For example, McDonald's is successful in the Netherlands, but attempts to introduce Burger King and KFC were not. T.G.I. Friday's is a success in England but not on the continent.

In 1993, the European Union became a fact. The ensuing years have led to increased interchange among the European countries, people, and cultures. People have become more used to foreign differences and more open to other habits, trends, and tastes. Both chain and individually owned restaurants have benefited from this interchange.

Franchising Developments in Food Service

Perhaps more than any other force, franchising has shaped the development of the food service industry. Franchising in the food service industry has developed along two traditional lines. Early in the twentieth century, product franchising was undertaken by A&W Root Beer of Los Angeles. Later, the Coca-Cola Company of Atlanta, Georgia, built its business by franchising its products through independent bottlers. After this initial phase, no great strides were made in franchising in the food service business until the early 1950s, when business operations rather than products began to be franchised.

In 1954, James McLamore and David Edgerton franchised their first Burger King restaurants. They were just barely under way when super-salesman Ray Kroc received permission from the McDonald brothers of California to franchise the now well-known Golden Arches. Few people remember that Beverly Osborne of Oklahoma City preceded both of these pioneer organizations with his chicken-in-a-basket operation.

These organizations operate under what is called a *business format* franchise. This kind of franchise seeks to establish a fully integrated relationship that includes product, operating and service standards, trademarks, marketing and strategic planning, quality control, and a communication system that assists in the flow of information through the organization.

The 1980s, 1990s, and the Twenty-First Century

In the 1980s, American food chains began expanding internationally. This expansion continued in the 1990s at an accelerated pace. Today, American chains operate on every continent except Antarctica. The following profiles some of the largest international franchise food service companies:

KFC (www.kfcfranchise.com)

- In more than 109 countries and territories around the world

- 80% franchised units
- 5,200 restaurants in the United States
- 15,000 units in 109 countries around the world

McDonald's (www.aboutmcdonalds.com)

- 160,000 locations in America
- 34,000 worldwide
- Operates in 119 countries

Dunkin' Donuts

- 10,100 franchised units (http://www.franchisedirect.com/foodfranchises/dunkin-donuts-franchise-07676/ufoc/)
- Operates in thirty-six U.S. states (www.dunkindonuts.com)
- 3,068 international shops in thirty-two countries (www.dunkindonuts.com)
- 100 percent franchised company (www.dunkindonuts.com)

Subway

- An estimated 37,335 units worldwide (http://www.franchisedirect.com/directory/subway/ufoc/915/)
- Operates in ninety-nine countries (www.subway.com)

Burger King

- Approximately 12,300 units (http://www.franchisedirect.com/foodfranchises/burger-king-franchise-07118/ufoc/)
- In all fifty states and in seventy-three countries and U.S. territories worldwide (www.bk.com)

Pizza Hut

- Approximately 13,430 units (http://www.franchisedirect.com/foodfranchises/pizza-hut-franchise-07054/ufoc/)
- Approximately 6,000 restaurants in the United States (http://www.pizzahutfranchise.com/about-best-pizza-franchise.php)
- More than 5,000 restaurants in ninety-four other countries and territories around the world (http://www.pizzahutfranchise.com/about-best-pizza-franchise.php)

Domino's

- 9,750 units (http://www.franchisedirect.com/foodfranchises/dominos-pizza-franchise-07460/ufoc/)
- 1,100 independent franchise owners in the U.S. (www.dominosbiz.com)
- 10,040 stores in more than seventy countries around the world (www.dominosbiz.com)

Taco Bell

- 5900 units (http://www.franchisedirect.com/foodfranchises/taco-bell-franchise-07099/ufoc/)

Wendy's

- 6500 units (http://www.franchisedirect.com/foodfranchises/wendys-franchise-08373/ufoc/)

- Owns or franchises more than 6,500 restaurants in twenty-six countries and territories (www.aboutwendys.com)

One of the most interesting events in restaurant history was the 1990 opening of the first McDonald's in Moscow. By far the largest McDonald's in the world, it was a smash hit from the day it opened. One reporter wrote that the new McDonald's had replaced Lenin's Tomb as Moscow's number-one tourist attraction. During the first year of operation, the unit served 40,000–50,000 customers per day, 15 million for the year. More than 4 million Big Macs and 5 million soft drinks were purchased by customers who regularly waited in line 20–90 minutes. The newest market is Eastern Europe, and many American chains are already there. A number of them, including both McDonald's and Burger King, operated with mobile units until they could establish permanent stores.

As is the case with hotels, franchisors typically operate some company-owned stores in addition to offering franchises. (Exhibit 2 shows the ratio of company-owned to franchised units for some of the major franchise companies.) This approach enables multi-unit chains to expand quickly. Given this expansion,

Exhibit 2   Ratio of Company-Owned and Franchised Units in Major Food Service Companies

Chain	% franchised	% owned
Subway	100	none
McDonald's	81	19
KFC	84	16
Burger King	90	10
Dunkin' Donuts	99.8	0.2
Baskin Robbins	100	none
Domino's	95	5
Taco Bell	75	25
Wendy's	77	23

Source: worldfranchising.com and brand websites.

the need to operate under strict franchise agreement terms becomes obvious; all units—company stores and franchises—must offer a consistent product and level of service to attract and retain customers (who will not know whether they are eating at company-operated or franchised units).

Increasing Unit Sales

For a number of years, the principal growth of franchise restaurants came from the addition of new units to the chain. Gradually, prime locations became fewer in number and, to at least some extent, expansion in the number of new units slowed; the average sales per unit also flattened or decreased. Eager to maintain or exceed the yearly growth figures they had achieved, companies began to look for other ways to increase sales. Their approach has focused on building unit sales.

Companies have spent large sums on advertising, hoping to boost their share of the market. During the late 1970s and early 1980s, these organizations concentrated on expanding their menus. Some augmented their menus by introducing breakfasts or by adding new breakfast items. Still others experimented with salad bars or introduced new sandwich accompaniments or dessert items. These efforts have increased unit sales dramatically for many properties. Today, there are many franchised units with sales greater than $1 million annually.

Sales in franchised units have been built primarily on four or five best-selling items. Hamburgers are the largest-selling products in franchised operations. Hamburgers, steak, pizza, chicken, pancakes, and waffles account for 75 percent or more of food service sales in franchised restaurants. Today, there is a trend toward increased sales of Mexican food, seafood, and various specialty sandwiches such as those made with croissants. The future of ethnic foods, particularly Mexican and Chinese foods, looks excellent. The sale of seafood has been growing at a steady, sometimes spectacular rate.

The three dominant operations in the pizza field are Pizza Hut, Domino's, and Papa John's. Pizza Hut ranks first in dine-in sales. Domino's is the leader in delivery service.

A new twist in the franchising field was introduced by Marriott, which developed fast-food complexes at Travel Plazas on tollways and at its Host airport terminal operations. Marriott has become a franchisee of Sbarro, Nathan's, Dunkin' Donuts, Roy Rogers, Popeye's, Mrs. Field's Cookies, Bob's Big Boy, TCBY, and Burger King, and operates several of these franchises at each complex.

While the listing of successful franchised operations could continue, one such operation draws particular attention to itself. In many respects, the McDonald's story is almost a fairy tale, an unbelievable success story of a franchise organization that continues to improve its performance year after year. Over the last fifty years, this organization, built around a concept originally put together by the McDonald brothers in California, has grown from a single roadside restaurant located in Des Plaines, Illinois, to more than 30,000 units located throughout the world. In some respects, the McDonald's organization can be compared to Du Pont or Coca-Cola. Like these two industrial giants, it has not only produced leadership for itself but also for a score of other companies.

Consistency Is Important

Franchising's first great strength was (and is) its consistency. Consumers quickly learned to expect similar products and services at every store in the chain. Standardization was the hidden persuader that caused people to return again and again. Achieving such operational consistency has traditionally been one of the most difficult goals for fast-food franchisors to accomplish. Inattention to the small details often accounts for restaurant failures. All successful franchises have certain things in common:

- Quality—Franchises consistently produce a good, standard product.

- Service—Franchises consistently provide fast service.

- Cleanliness—Franchise units are consistently cleaner than most of their independent competitors.

- Value—Franchises consistently offer good-quality products for the consumer's money.

Much of the success of fast-food franchises lies in the fact that unit buildings are engineered and built with ease of maintenance and constant cleanliness in mind. In addition to these concerns, the design of the units emphasizes ease of construction, flexibility for future expansion, and economical use of labor.

The interiors of most franchised operations are masterpieces of planning that make it possible for each unit to consistently deliver its type of food service to thousands of customers with maximum efficiency. In this respect, fast-food franchisors are far ahead of most of their counterparts in the restaurant field. They deliberately build for high volume and fast service. High sales per square foot and greater levels of productivity per employee are keys to the kind of profitability that fast-food franchising can deliver.

Franchise Agreements and Relationships

As in every other kind of business organization, relationships between a parent company and its franchisees are important. There are sometimes stresses and strains between partners, which may intensify as the nature of food franchising continues to be redefined or as franchise contracts move closer to their expiration date. As a result of the inevitable disagreements between franchisors and franchisees, just about every successful company has a franchise council, sometimes operated at arm's length between the two organizations.

Franchisees are concerned about the terms of the renewal of their franchise contract. The major franchising organizations know that their basic ideas and programs have made millionaires out of their franchisees. In addition, franchisors know that one poorly run, dirty unit with ineffective employees can affect the reputation of many other operations in an entire area. Therefore, they insist on checking the prescribed standards imposed by the contracts. To further protect themselves, they include in their contracts the right to cancel a license with a franchisee when there is good cause.

A standard contract usually requires the franchisee to use the franchisor's trademarks, company insignia, and standard packaging. At one time, many franchisors insisted that franchisees also purchase all or many of their supplies from a central source controlled by the franchisor. In the past, McDonald's franchisees even operated on leased land and in company-owned buildings. In recent years, however, the courts have generally ruled that franchisors may not require such tie-ins as a part of their contract with the franchisee. Nonetheless, many franchisees believe that franchisors are primarily interested in satisfying their own stockholders or the company that owns them. They say that franchisors often violate their own agreements and "invade" territory that has been set aside for the exclusive development of franchisees. Says one franchisee, "It is unfortunate that some franchisors refuse to accept their franchisees as their business partners." Some franchisees complain that franchisors continually underestimate the intelligence and the ability of their franchisees and fail to acknowledge and use their expertise.

Under the best of circumstances, the franchisor-franchisee arrangement results in imprecise definitions and differing perceptions of the nature of the relationship. There is simply no way that everything that might occur can be covered in a contract. Franchisors refer to their franchisees as independent businesspeople. However, many franchisees feel that the control exercised by the franchisor and the latter's ability to terminate contracts keep them feeling quite dependent on the franchisors.

But even with a long history of strained relationships, difficulty in agreeing on business methods, and other problems that arise from the peculiar compact between unequal partners, the necessity for maintaining standards and uniformity in operating procedures is proven again and again by the success stories of huge organizations that even operate internationally. There can be no denying the power and strength that reside in the franchising concept. Nor can anyone who knows the history of the small independent restaurant business deny that franchising has been the vehicle that has made this segment a strong and viable one.

Quick-Service Restaurant Employees

Franchised quick-service units employ thousands of people. The quick-service industry offers employment opportunities with good salaries and benefits to those who have the education and experience to move up to the corporate level. The majority of these employees come to the company without any previous background or training in food service. It has, therefore, been necessary to institute complete training and development programs for all franchisees. Training and human resource development is a necessary part of corporate and regional planning and development. Some franchisors such as McDonald's, Burger King, Long John Silver's, Shoney's, and others operate their own training schools, using classroom instruction, audiovisual aids, and participatory situations. They also offer programs in advanced restaurant operations, multi-unit management, regional general management, local marketing, and small business management. In addition, they develop and coordinate training programs at regional centers located throughout the country. Instructors in the training programs have all had experience in running a quick-service restaurant and thus are well equipped to answer questions.

All franchises have difficulty motivating hourly workers who must do repetitive tasks. These hourly workers have, until fairly recently, been drawn almost entirely from high school students and others who have had little interest in staying on the job long and therefore little commitment to an operation. But the work force is slowly changing as more and more adults apply for positions in quick-service restaurants. The typical assistant manager is in his or her middle or late twenties. Today there are many more mature people who want part-time employment in these restaurants. Unlike high school students, these people want to know how they as employees fit into the company's plans and where the company is heading.

Franchising Problems

Franchising as a system has proven to be a highly effective way of expanding the food service industry by means of a standard formula. However, franchising has potential problems. There have been notable failures along with successes.

A classic case was the demise of Sambo's. While there were a number of factors that led to the failure of Sambo's, one of the most significant occurred when the U.S. government ordered the company to end a fringe benefit plan the company called "a piece of the action." This plan allowed each manager to buy a minority interest in his or her own restaurant as well as others being built. This program had been so successful that the Sambo's chain grew quickly during the early 1970s, with over 800 new units being built all across the country. When the federal government ordered Sambo's officials to end its unique program, the company offered a less lucrative substitute program to its managers without many of the benefits of the original package. The result was management resignations on a wholesale basis; the organization that had been built upon a liberal benefits program collapsed as a "piece of the action" ended.

Lum's of Miami is another franchising organization that had a history of financial problems. Even ownership by Friedrich Jahn, one of Europe's most successful restaurateurs, failed to solve the problems, and Lum's went into bankruptcy. Minnie Pearl Country Dairy Stores, designed especially for small towns, hardly got off the ground before it too was in serious trouble. No trace remains of the original organization, and the few units that do remain are independent restaurants. Famous names (including Joe Namath, Al Hirt, and Mickey Mantle) were not enough to save a number of other franchises, either.

Even these well-publicized failures or near-failures often do not discourage people in the industry from trying to build a successful new concept. Nonetheless, all of these examples of instability and failure point out that franchising has not always proven to be a cure-all. There are far more promoters and restaurateurs who think that their ideas are good enough to franchise than there are success stories.

Management Companies in Institutional Food Service ———

Just as franchising has greatly affected the development of commercial food service, management companies have influenced the development of institutional food service. Exhibit 3 lists the leading management companies based on worldwide sales. Two of the companies have headquarters outside the United States, but now have a significant presence in the U.S. as the result of purchases of or mergers

Exhibit 3   Leading Food Service Management Companies

1. Compass Group North America
2. Aramark Corp.
3. Sodexo, Inc.
4. Delaware North Companies
5. Centerplate
6. Thompson Hospitality
7. Guckenheimer Enterprises, Inc.
8. Guest Services, Inc.
9. Ovations Food Services
10. Valley Services, Inc.

Excerpted from Mike Buzalka, "FM's 2011 Top 50 Management Companies," Food-Management.com (Sept. 1, 2011). Available at http://food-management.com/business-amp-industry/fms-2011-top-50-management-companies.

with American companies. Using only North American sales figures, Compass takes first place, closely followed by ARAMARK and Sodexo.

Management companies in Europe operate in areas similar to their American counterparts. Companies active internationally in the institutional, airline, and shipboard food service fields include Belgavia (Belgium), Servair and Wagon Lits (France), SAS Service Partners (Scandinavia), LSG Lufthansa Services (Germany), Cunard (England), Holland America Line (Holland), Gate Gourmet (Switzerland), Saudi Catering (Saudi Arabia), Abela Corporation (France), and Cara (Canada).

Management Company Operations

Management companies operate in the food service segments of recreational food service, employee food service, health care food service, and educational food service.

Recreational Food Service. Unlike health care, educational food service, and, to some extent, employee food service, recreational food service is primarily a for-profit segment of the industry. The trend is for increased participation by management companies, especially in recreation and sports centers. Currently, management companies account for nearly 50 percent of the $8.5 billion in annual sales generated at these centers.

Employee Food Service. For years, manufacturing plants and other business organizations operated their own employee cafeterias. Today, the majority of employee food service operations are run by management companies. Employee food service is a major segment of the industry, with annual sales over $6 billion. Many changes have occurred in this segment. Gone is the institutional image of old—unimaginative fare such as meat loaf and gravy served up on stainless steel and plastic tableware. The management companies call this segment *business and industry food management* and run it virtually like a commercial restaurant enterprise. Operations range far beyond cafeteria service into executive dining rooms, catering operations, and semipublic restaurants.

With more and more business organizations viewing employee food service as a key tool for improving employee productivity, management companies, according to ARA Services' Michael Cronk, are becoming more commercial, especially in the sense that they have the same sales and marketing and merchandising drive as a restaurant. Operations are designed to be more efficient and cost effective with fully computerized food production, inventory, and accounting systems.

Health Care Food Service. The health care segment of the industry involves the three principal markets of (a) acute care hospitals, (b) long-term care facilities, and (c) retirement communities. Many industry experts state that this segment has the greatest short- and long-term growth potential in the food service industry. With current sales of over $18 billion, it is readily understandable why nearly every major contract management company is involved in the health care field, along with many smaller, specialized firms.

Health care facilities have traditionally operated their own food service departments to emphasize health and nutrition rather than financial considerations. In many instances, this is still the case. However, reduced income and pressures for cost containment create a need for managers to run health food service operations as professional businesses. Consequently, a growing number of health care facilities are turning to management companies.

Those in favor of management companies in the health care setting cite the following advantages:

- Organizational resources of large nationwide companies can focus on solving specific problems in the individual units with expertise, automation, and savings brought about by effective negotiations with food suppliers.

- Contract management companies can often operate dietary programs at a lower cost than their self-operated counterparts.

- Reduced internal direction by staff administrators may be another plus. Facility administrators, trained in areas other than food service operations, can delegate responsibilities for making decisions to professional food service managers.

Opponents of management companies cite the following disadvantages:

- Loss of internal control means that management companies may have too much discretion in matters that affect the institution's public image, long-range operating plans, and other important issues.

- Questions about the propriety of involving a profit-making business in a health care food service program are often raised.

- Miscellaneous operational problems include concerns that the company will decrease quality or take other contractual shortcuts.

- The health care food service operation may depend too much on the management company. What will the operation do if the management company wants to discontinue the contract? How long will it take the operation to implement its own program or find another management company?

- Higher operating costs are also possible when management companies are used. How is it possible to use a management company to *reduce* costs when now we are suggesting that operating costs might *increase*?

The answer to whether management contract companies belong in health care food service depends on the specific management company and on the food service operation. Minimizing costs while retaining quality is at the heart of the food management company controversy.

Educational Food Service. This segment includes food service at primary and secondary schools, colleges, and universities. As is the case with health care facilities, the majority of educational institutions operate their own food service. However, the trend is toward increased management company participation. Currently, management companies account for approximately 25 percent of the sales at colleges and universities and 40 percent of the sales at primary and secondary schools. The advantages and disadvantages of management companies for health care facilities also apply to educational food service.

 ## Key Terms

à la carte menu—A menu in which food and beverages are listed and priced separately.

commissary—A central food production area from which food is transported to individual outlets for final preparation and service.

prix fixe menu—A menu that offers a specific meal consisting of several courses at a fixed price; also called a *table d'hôte* menu.

smorgasbord—A variety of foods presented in a buffet-type arrangement.

speakeasy—During Prohibition in the United States, a type of establishment that served alcoholic beverages illegally. Starting with sandwiches, the speakeasy was soon serving full meals to its customers. After the repeal of Prohibition in 1933, many speakeasies developed into successful restaurants.

table d'hôte menu—A menu that offers a specific meal consisting of several courses at a fixed price; also called a *prix fixe* menu.

 ## Review Questions

1. What establishments began offering food service in colonial America?

2. What important developments or inventions of the 1800s led to the growth of food service in America?

3. What two events contributed to the deep decline in restaurant sales during the 1920s? How did they affect sales?

4. What challenges did World War II create for the food service industry?

5. What does the term "kitchenless kitchen" mean?

6. What factors encouraged the development of convenience food? What factors worked against its acceptance?

7. Why does *nouvelle cuisine* appeal to restaurant patrons?

8. How did franchising begin in the food service industry? Describe and discuss franchising's early days and the pioneers in the field.

9. What phases or steps does a food service franchise company go through as it seeks annual growth in sales?

10. Why would a franchisor create its own training center?

11. What are the pros and cons of management companies operating in the health care setting?

 Internet Sites ——————————————————————————————

For more information, visit the following Internet sites. Remember that Internet addresses can change without notice. If the site is no longer there, you can use a search engine to look for additional sites.

Food Service and Related Associations

Academy of Nutrition and Dietetics (formerly American Dietetic Association)
www.eatright.org

American Culinary Federation
www.acfchefs.org

American Hotel & Lodging Educational Institute
www.ahlei.org

Association of Nutrition & Foodservice Professionals (formerly Dietary Managers Association)
www.anfponline.org

Hospitality Financial & Technology Professionals
www.hftp.org

International Association of Culinary Professionals
www.iacp.com

International Food Service Executives Association
www.ifsea.com

International Franchise Association
www.franchise.org

International Hotel & Restaurant Association
www.ih-ra.com

National Association of College & University Food Services
www.nacufs.org

National Restaurant Association
www.restaurant.org

School Nutrition Association (formerly American School Food Service Association)
www.schoolnutrition.org

Society for Foodservice Management
www.sfm-online.org

Restaurants and Restaurant Companies

AFC Enterprises
www.afce.com

Macayo's Mexican Kitchen
www.macayo.com

Bittersweet Bistro
www.bittersweetbistro.com

McDonald's Restaurants
www.mcdonalds.com

Burger King Brands, Inc.
www.bk.com

Perkins Restaurant & Bakery
www.perkinsrestaurants.com

Hard Rock Cafe
www.hardrock.com

Pizza Hut, Inc.
www.pizzahut.com

Hemispheres Restaurant & Bistro
www.metropolitan.com/hemis

Taco Bell Corp.
www.tacobell.com

KFC Corporation
www.kfc.com

Food Service Search Sites

Chef2Chef Culinary Portal
http://chef2chef.net

eATNET.TV
www.eatnet.com

DineSite
http://dinesite.com

Waiter.com
www.waiter.com

Chapter 8 Outline

Competencies

1. Describe the composition and size of the food service industry, and differentiate commercial from institutional and military food service operations. (pp. 159–160)

2. Identify food service operations within major market classifications. (pp. 160–167)

3. Discuss the development of food service in hotels and identify the functions of the five primary departments of a large hotel food and beverage division. (pp. 167–169)

4. Contrast the organizational structures of large and small restaurants. (pp. 169–171)

The Organization and Structure of the Food Service Industry

THIS CHAPTER EXAMINES the segments of the food service industry and illustrates that food service operations are not at all limited to fast-food restaurants, conventional restaurants, or hotel dining rooms.

Composition and Size of the Food Service Industry

The food service industry may be classified in many different ways. One way is to categorize it according to various markets. These major categories are shown in Exhibit 1 and provide the basis for most of the discussion in this chapter.

Food service operations may also be classified according to the economic objectives of the operation. There are three main categories of food service operations under this type of classification: commercial, institutional (or noncommercial), and military. Exhibit 2 lists these main categories and their subcategories.

Commercial, institutional, and military food services each have different economic objectives. Commercial food service operations, for example, exist primarily to make a profit on the sale of food and/or beverage products. These operations attempt to maximize or at least to emphasize profits. In institutional food service operations, the main economic objective is to minimize expenses. The military's main objective is to stay within the budget. Food and beverage operations in restaurants and lodging properties are typical examples of commercial food and beverage programs. Food services operated by schools and health care facilities are examples of institutional programs (although some institutional food service programs are now operated by for-profit management companies and might be classified as commercial operations).

Exhibit 3 shows the approximate share of sales each of these categories commands in the total food service industry. It should be noted, however, that sales figures tend to underrepresent the relative size of the commercial, institutional, and military categories of the industry because commercial restaurants sell food at prices needed to make a profit, while institutional food services typically charge only enough to meet expenses.

159

Exhibit 1   Major Classifications of Food Service Markets

```
                        ┌──────────────────┐
                        │   Food Service   │
                        │     Industry     │
                        └──────────────────┘

┌──────────────┐  ┌──────────────┐  ┌──────────────┐  ┌──────────────┐
│   Separate   │  │Transportation│  │    Retail    │  │   Student    │
│Eating/Drinking│  │    Market    │  │    Market    │  │    Market    │
│    Places    │  │              │  │              │  │              │
└──────────────┘  └──────────────┘  └──────────────┘  └──────────────┘

     ┌──────────────┐  ┌──────────────┐  ┌──────────────┐  ┌──────────────┐
     │    Hotel     │  │   Leisure    │  │  Business/   │  │ Health Care  │
     │    Market    │  │    Market    │  │  Industrial  │  │    Market    │
     │              │  │              │  │    Market    │  │              │
     └──────────────┘  └──────────────┘  └──────────────┘  └──────────────┘
```

Suggested by *Restaurant Business.*

Scope of the Food Service Industry

Whether the food service industry is classified by markets or by economic objectives, its scope is massive. A few statistics will detail the size and illustrate the importance of this major industry. The U.S. food service industry's annual sales now top $660 billion. Given estimates that each dollar spent in the industry generates two dollars in other industries, the total economic impact of the industry is estimated at $1.8 trillion. Sales constitute 4 percent of the U.S. gross domestic product. More than 980,000 restaurant locations nationwide employ 13 million employees.[1] Exhibit 4 details how sales have grown since 1970.

While the food service industry is growing, there is a difference between dollar volume (or *nominal*) growth and what the industry designates as *real* growth. Real growth comes from selling more food and from increasing customer counts. **Nominal growth** may result merely from raising food prices. In a period of high inflation, it is quite possible to have increased dollar sales growth (because of increases in selling price) and negative real growth (because of decreased customer counts).

A general description of some of the major market segments composing the food service industry points out the industry's diversity.[2]

Eating and Drinking Places

This market can be divided into six categories (each category can include single- or multi-unit companies):

- *Full-menu restaurants and lunchrooms* offer a wide variety of menu items and table service. They may serve only one meal or stay open twenty-four hours a

Exhibit 2   Food Service Classifications by Economic Objectives

Group 1 Commercial Food Service
  Eating and Drinking Places
      Restaurants and lunchrooms
      Limited-menu restaurants and refreshment places
      Commercial cafeterias
      Social caterers
      Ice cream, frozen custard, and frozen yogurt stands
      Bars and taverns
  Food Contractors
      Manufacturing and industrial plants
      Commercial and office buildings
      Hospitals and nursing homes
      Colleges and universities
      Primary and secondary schools
      In-transit food service (e.g., airlines)
      Recreation and sports centers
  Lodging Places
      Hotel restaurants
      Motor hotel restaurants
  Other
      Retail host restaurants
      Recreation and sports
      Mobile caterers
      Vending and non-store retailers

Group 2 Institutional Food Service—Business, Educational, and Government Organizations Operating Their Own Food Service
  Employee food service
  Elementary and secondary schools
  Colleges and universities
  Transportation
  Hospitals
  Nursing homes
  Clubs, sporting, and recreational camps
  Community centers

Group 3 Military Food Service
  Officers and non-commissioned officers clubs (open mess)
  Food service—military exchanges

Adapted from *Restaurants USA,* National Restaurant Association.

day. Some offer a California-style menu on which items that are usually served for breakfast, lunch, or dinner are offered at all times. Full-menu restaurants and lunchrooms generally have indoor seating and may serve alcoholic beverages.

Exhibit 3   Projected 2013 Food Service Industry Sales by Segment Type

Commercial Food Services		$602.5 billion
Eating places*	$441.9 billion	
Bars and taverns	19.5 billion	
Managed services	45.6 billion	
Lodging places	33.1 billion	
Retail, vending, recreation, mobile	62.4 billion	
Noncommercial Food Services		55.5 billion
Military Food Services		2.5 billion
Total		$660.5 billion

* Includes full-service and quick-service restaurants, cafeterias and buffets, social caterers, and snack and non-alcoholic beverage bars.

Source: National Restaurant Association, *2013 Restaurant Industry Forecast.*

Exhibit 4   Growth of Food Service Sales

Year	Sales (in billions)
1970	$42.8
1980	$119.6
1990	$239.3
2000	$379.0
2013*	$660.5

* projected

Source: National Restaurant Association website (www.restaurant.org).

- *Limited-menu restaurants* offer only a few items (for example, only or primarily pizza or hamburgers). Typically, the customer walks to a service counter or drives up to a service window and orders food. Then the customer carries the food to a table, if there is inside seating, or consumes the food off the premises. Some limited-menu properties offer table service.

- *Public cafeterias* are often similar to full-menu restaurants and lunchrooms because they offer a wide variety of menu items, but table service is usually limited. Their markets include families and, as the check average increases, businesspeople and adults without children.

- *Social caterers* prepare meals for large or small banquets and may provide food service in off-site locations.

- *Ice cream, frozen yogurt, and frozen custard stands* offer primarily frozen dairy and related products, sometimes with indoor seating.

- *Bars and taverns* serve alcoholic beverages and offer only limited food service.

Hotel Operations

Food and beverage sales generate about 31 percent of the total sales dollars earned by the U.S. lodging industry. This figure suggests that food and beverage divisions are much more than casual operations offered for the convenience of guests. In fact, many hoteliers and management personnel realize that food and beverage operations usually cannot generate required profits from in-house sales alone; extensive patronage by the community is necessary for food and beverage operations to realize their economic goals.

Food Services for the Transportation Market

Food services offered on planes, trains, in terminals, on interstate highways, and aboard passenger and cargo ships are included in this segment. These services may be provided by a for-profit management company, or they may be operated by the transportation company itself. Services can range from vending operations to sandwich and short-order preparation to extravagant, expensive food service. As the American public travels more, this market segment will expand. Leading food service providers for the transportation market include Gate Gourmet, Servair, Flying Food Group, Cara Operations, SATS Catering, dnata, and Chelsea Food Services.

Food Services for the Leisure Market

This segment comprises food service in theme parks and for sporting events in arenas, stadiums, and racing tracks. Also included are food service operations in drive-in movie theaters, bowling lanes, summer camps, and hunting facilities. These programs may be self-operated or operated by management contract companies. An increase in the public's leisure time will increase sales in this market segment. Leading food service providers for the leisure market include Accor, Best Western International, Choice Hotels International, InterContinental Hotels Group, Hilton Worldwide, Marriott International, Starwood Hotels & Resorts Worldwide, and Wyndham Hotel Group.

Retail Food Services

Retail food service may range from simple lunch counter or cafeteria service to formal, high-check-average table service. Examples include:

- Department stores that have employee and public dining facilities.

- Variety and general merchandise stores that have food service operations for employees—even if only vended services are provided.

- Drug and proprietary stores that have public dining outlets and/or vended services for employees.

- Convenience food stores that offer sandwiches, snacks, and beverages. Some stores even have booths and tables for in-store consumption.

- Other specialized retail stores—grocery stores, gasoline stations, and a variety of other properties—that sell food items for on- or off-premises consumption.

Business/Industrial Food Services

Business and industrial food services include the following categories:

- Contract food service—Outside, for-profit companies provide food service in plants and business offices.

- Internal food service—Plants and business offices provide self-operated food service.

- Food service to waterborne employees—This category includes food service to employees on ships, oil rigs, and so forth.

- Mobile on-street catering—"Meals on wheels" programs involve **canteen** operations that visit construction sites and factories, and street vendors who sell a variety of products.

- Food vending machines—Foods from snacks to complete meals are offered for customers and/or employees.

- Food service to military personnel—Meals consumed by members of the armed forces make up this category.

- Food furnished to food service employees—One way of again stressing the immense size of the food service industry is to note that the cost of food purchased merely to feed food service employees runs over $9.15 billion per year, about 5 percent of the total purchases for commercial and institutional food services.

Student Food Services

Food service in the student market includes self-operated and management company-operated programs in public and parochial elementary and secondary schools, and in colleges and universities. Elementary and secondary schools may participate in the federally subsidized National School Lunch Program and related Child Nutrition Program. Some programs, such as those in large cities, may serve hundreds of thousands of meals daily. School food service programs may include breakfast, milk, supplemental foods, and senior citizen meals in addition to traditional lunches.

The college and university food service market is enormous. There are more than 3,000 accredited post-secondary schools in the United States. There are another 3,000 or more trade schools which, while they do not offer extensive food service operations, may have vending machines or snack bars. Perhaps 1,500 of the post-secondary schools arrange for food service through a for-profit management company. Of the remaining schools, an estimated 500 offer only vending machines or buffet food services; 1,000 schools are large enough to have extensive food service programs for boarding students and others attending classes.

Health Care Food Services

Hospitals and nursing homes of all types make up a primary segment of the health care food service market. Some of these facilities are privately owned; others are run by the government. Besides traditional acute-care hospitals and nursing homes that provide permanent residences for patients, there are also homes for orphans and mentally and physically handicapped people. Programs that are self-operated and managed by for-profit companies are included in this category.

As is true with many types of institutional food service operations, nutrition is emphasized. In many of these operations, the patients and residents receive all their food at the sites, so nutrition plays an important role in protecting their health and well-being. In other facilities, nutrition is important because of its recuperative effects. Dietitians are often retained on a full-time or consulting basis, and, in some cases, might actually manage the food service operation. In other cases, they provide specialized assistance to managers in areas involving clinical and therapeutic dietetics.

Club Food Services

Although clubs are not mentioned in Exhibit 1, they form an important segment of the hospitality industry. The service of food and beverages is one of the prime functions of most clubs.

Clubs existed in ancient Greece and the Roman Empire; during the nineteenth century, they became a major part of American culture. The Olympic Club in San Francisco and the Union League Club in Philadelphia were both founded during the 1860s. The Country Club in Brookline, Massachusetts, founded in 1882, is considered the oldest country club in the United States.

There are many different types of clubs and even subtypes within types. The principal kinds are country, city, yacht, fraternal, military, development, specialty, and health clubs/spas:

- *Country clubs* have a clubhouse with lounges, food and beverage facilities, and recreational outlets. Country club activities usually center on the golf course(s), but swimming and tennis are also very common. The larger clubs may offer a much wider variety of athletic accommodations. There are more than 4,000 private country clubs in the United States.[3]

- *City clubs* serve the needs of people who work in an urban area. In addition to the food and beverage function, this type of club may offer athletic facilities, a library or reading room, and overnight accommodations. There are approximately 1,600 city clubs in the United States.

- *Yacht clubs* are similar to country clubs except for location and the fact that activities center on boating rather than golf.

- *Fraternal clubs* are social organizations like the Elks, Knights of Columbus, Eagles, or American Legion. Typically, a restaurant, bar, lounge, billiard room, and card room are found in these clubs.

- *Military clubs* were developed to provide recreation areas for the officers and enlisted personnel. These clubs resemble country clubs without golf courses. Each branch of the armed services operates its own clubs. Traditionally, they were divided into officers' clubs, non-commissioned officers' clubs, and enlisted clubs, but in recent years, there has been a shift toward clubs that welcome military men and women of all ranks.

- *Development clubs* are really country clubs built as integral parts of real estate development projects. The existence of a club is often an incentive for a customer to purchase or rent property in the development.

- *Specialty clubs* center on one particular activity (for example, tennis, swimming, racquetball) and usually do not have a clubhouse but do need a manager. Snack bar food service is often available.

- *Health clubs/spas* typically offer various types of exercise equipment, organized fitness activities, and massage, salon, and/or various other health and wellness services.

Clubs are either member-owned or proprietary. Most of the older private clubs are owned by the members and governed by a board of directors elected by the members. The members are considered shareholders, and normally each member has one vote. Member-owned clubs may be tax exempt, but must meet certain criteria established by the Internal Revenue Service.

An outside individual or a corporation owns a proprietary club. The members have no equity interest in the club and, in many cases, little effective control over its policies or operation. Development clubs are the prime example of this type of ownership. The club is a for-profit operation that is subject to corporate income taxes.

Whether member-owned or proprietary, a club needs management. In most clubs, the top executive who controls all phases of the operation is the manager. The word *control* may be misleading when one is speaking of a member-owned club, however, because various member committees exercise most of the control. Thus it may be more accurate to say that the manager coordinates activities as directed by the committees.

Country clubs and development clubs have a more extensive organizational hierarchy because of their diversification. There will be a clubhouse manager whose responsibilities cover every aspect of operations within the building. Primary among these responsibilities is the food and beverage function; clubs are noted for providing the very finest in food and service for the members. The clubhouse manager usually has no authority over most of the recreational activities. The golf pro manages the golf course, the tennis pro runs the tennis facility, and the greenskeeper maintains the golf course. Each of these administrators typically reports to a committee of club members. In some cases, such clubs also employ a general manager who is in charge of the total club operation. If so, the managers previously mentioned report to the general manager.

For many years, the person who operated the club was called the steward and really was more of a glorified maître d'hôtel than a manager. Then, in 1927, the Club Managers Association of America was formed. This fine organization has been most successful and effective in increasing the level of expertise of its members and in enhancing the role and image of the club manager. Today, the position carries the same professional status as hotel or restaurant manager. The great majority of club managers are college graduates, and courses in club management are taught in the major hospitality schools of the country.

Segmentation by Menu

Another way to describe the restaurant portion of the industry is to classify by type of menu. Exhibit 5 shows some of the leading segments along with the top sales producers in each segment.

Other Food Services

Other food service operations include programs operated by correctional institutions, religious seminaries and convents, and government-sponsored programs. Communities may have athletic facilities, libraries, and reading rooms that provide some form of food service.

One point should be clear by now: the food service industry is enormous. It includes any type of operation that prepares meals for people away from home—and sometimes even at home, in the case of caterers.

The Organization of Hotel and Restaurant Food Service ——

Since hotel food service in particular has changed greatly in the past fifty years, our discussion of hotel food and beverage divisions will begin by placing current developments in their historical context.

Hotel Food and Beverage Divisions

Through most of the first half of the twentieth century, food and beverage service occupied a position of minor importance in the minds of many hotel operators. In some cases, it was treated as a necessary evil—a service available strictly for the guests' convenience. From an economic standpoint, it was important to break even or to lose as little as possible, a feat made more difficult by the fact that the food

Exhibit 5   Restaurant Segments and Their Sales Leaders

Segment	Share	Leaders
Bakery/café concepts	24%	Panera Bread, Corner Bakery, Au Bon Pain, Einstein's Bagels
Mexican/Southwestern	22%	Taco Bell, Del Taco, Taco Cabana
Specialty/healthy	20%	Saladworks, Souper!Salad!, Freshii Fresh Food Custom Built
Sandwich	13%	Subway, Arby's, Panera Bread, Quiznos
Chicken	11%	KFC, Popeye's, Chick-fil-A, Church's
Burger	10%	McDonald's, Burger King, Wendy's, Sonic

Source: National Restaurant Association, 2012.

and service offered were often of very high quality. Room sales, where the profit was to be made, were expected to make up the difference. As long as one could fill the guestrooms, the profit or loss figures on food and beverages were relatively unimportant.

During the 1950s, this whole concept changed radically. Perhaps the most important factor was the growth and expansion of motels and motor hotels. As motel occupancy rates grew, hotel occupancies declined, and income decreased. At the same time, operating costs increased. The financial pinch was on. Managers had to seriously re-evaluate the entire operation. They could no longer afford to operate the food and beverage division at break-even or loss levels. Small hotel operators were in the most serious position because of their competition with motels. Much of their rooms business was gone. If they were to continue operation, it would be necessary to develop other sources of sales and profit.

Clearly, there were profits to be made in food and beverage sales. After all, restaurants had made money for years. But it was just as obvious that hotels needed a change of image. The average citizen considered hotel dining too expensive and too formal.

Hotels have worked hard to change this image and, fortunately, have succeeded. They recognized that the traditional formal hotel dining room was largely obsolete, or at least insufficient in itself. Guests demand a variety of dining alternatives: a rapid-service coffee shop, a snack bar, a cocktail lounge with a distinctive atmosphere, a specialty theme restaurant. Today, the coffee shop is standard in hotels, and **specialty restaurants** are thriving. Specialty steak houses and seafood restaurants are common in hotels today.

It is interesting to note that almost every hotel restaurant has a street entrance. In many cases, the guest may not even realize that the restaurant is part of the hotel. The street entrance symbolizes the hotel restaurant's growing importance as a revenue center in its own right. No longer is the food and beverage business simply a necessary evil; it is promoted, merchandised, and sold through creative planning.

Hotels have made tremendous strides in increasing food and beverage sales, though they would be the first to admit that there is still room for improvement. For example, studies reveal that a majority of hotel guests eat breakfast in the hotel, but that fewer have dinner there, and that the smallest number eat lunch in the property. Hotels would like to change these figures because dinner frequently offers the greatest **contribution margin** (income minus direct costs) while breakfast offers the smallest contribution margin.

Changing the image of hotels and attracting new business was a start in making hotel food service more profitable. However, if food service suffered a loss, increasing the number of patrons merely increased the loss. Food and beverage divisions had to be put on a profit-making basis, and this meant a major revision of standards and procedures in many lodging operations. The chain properties were the pioneers. Every aspect of an operation was analyzed; every procedure was scrutinized. Most important, new ideas and methods were instituted. Purchasing and receiving standards and specifications were developed, sophisticated pre-cost and pre-control systems were adopted, yield tests were conducted, forecasting became a management tool, and staffing guides were created and followed. The result has been an increase in food and beverage profits.

Consumers today have many options for all three meal periods, and hotel owners and operators have had to break away from the past to develop new and more restaurants within their hotels. Some hotels are doing this by leasing their restaurant space to a well-known operator, partnering with a successful restaurant, or buying a well-known restaurant franchise that includes recipes, operating manuals, and anything else needed for success. The trend known as branding allows the restaurant within a hotel to gain immediate recognition. This kind of recognition typically does *not* occur when the hotel operator creates a new concept that must then be marketed against all the well-known restaurant brands.

Many operators have found that restaurant operators who do nothing but operate successful restaurants can do a better job. This approach also gives the hotel a source of guaranteed income from the lease or partnership while offering visibility in the community.

Even when using this approach, though, an owner or operator usually keeps control of and operates the catering department and room service. Kitchens are separate from the leased restaurant. Catering generally provides a high profit margin because attendance is guaranteed; the catering department supports the hotel's ability to sell conferences, conventions, and other groups. Hotels prefer to operate room service as a means of personalizing their service offerings and to control who is in the guestroom corridors by using only hotel-supervised employees whose references the hotel operator has thoroughly checked.

Any manager will acknowledge that making a profit on food is difficult and requires modern operating procedures and experience that is not acquired quickly or easily. Today, there is a tremendous demand for qualified food and beverage managers. Salaries are excellent. In addition, the path to top-level hotel management is wide open for executives with a sound food and beverage background.

Though figures still show room sales as the number-one source of revenue, many hotels produce more food and beverage revenue than rooms revenue. The importance of the food and beverage division to the overall success of the lodging property is clear.

The five primary departments in large hotel food and beverage divisions are:

- Catering—responsible for banquets and special functions

- Culinary operations—responsible for food production

- Stewarding—responsible for warewashing, clean-up, and (in some operations) purchasing

- Beverage—responsible for production and service of alcoholic beverages

- Restaurant operations—responsible for food service in all outlets, including room service

The Organizational Structure of Restaurants

For the most part, restaurants have not faced the type of problems hotels have had to face in the last fifty years. Still, it is true that, like hotels, restaurants have had to face a tightening budget and have therefore had to improve their methods of planning and control.

Exhibits 6 and 7 provide sample organizational structures of large and small restaurants. In the larger organization, the restaurant manager immediately supervises two positions: the controller (who is responsible for cashiers and a clerk) and the assistant manager (who is responsible for four department heads). The department head positions involve food production (chef/head cook), purchasing and sanitation (chief steward), beverage production (head bartender), and the front of the house (dining room manager). Each of these department heads also supervises employees. In some cases, fourth-level personnel (**sous chef**/assistant cook) supervise food service workers. Again, while each of the functions must also be performed in the smaller property, the number of required organizational levels and personnel in each position can be reduced.

Exhibit 6   Sample Organization Chart for a Large Restaurant

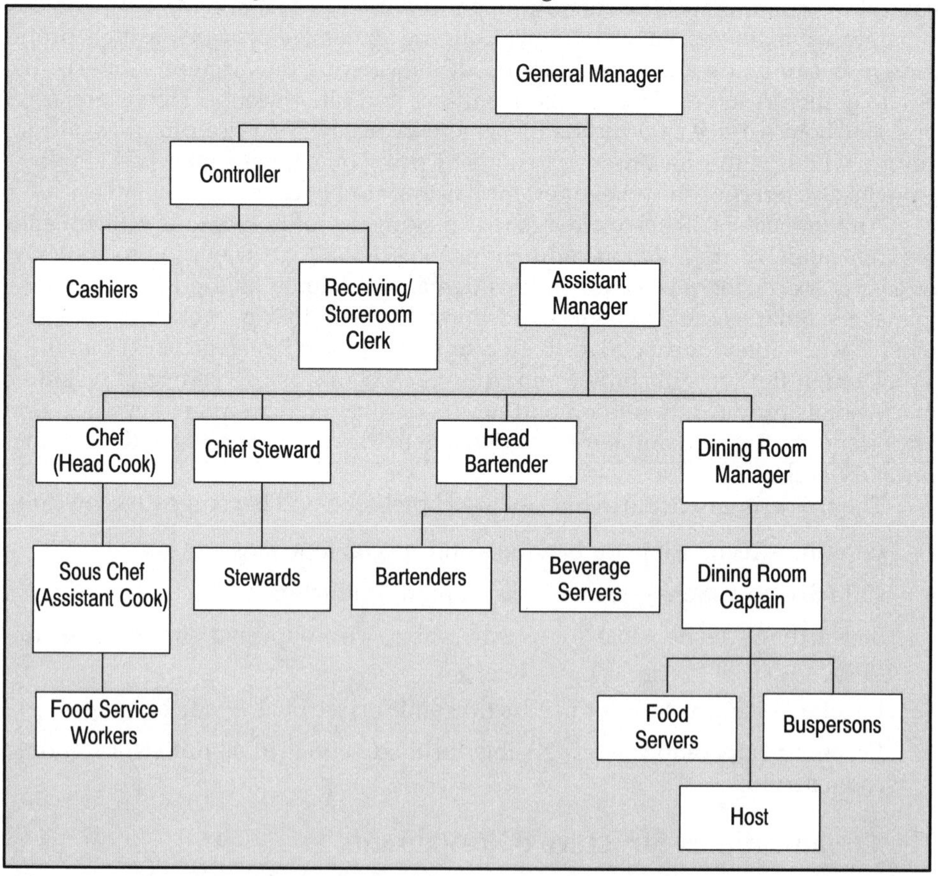

Source: Jack D. Ninemeier, *Management of Food and Beverage Operations,* 5th ed. (Lansing, Mich.: American Hotel & Lodging Educational Institute, 2010), p. 37.

Exhibit 7   Sample Organization Chart for a Small Restaurant

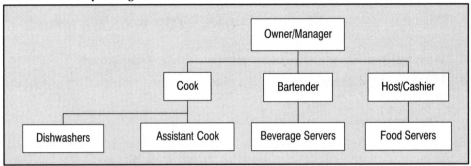

Source: Jack D. Ninemeier, *Management of Food and Beverage Operations,* 5th ed. (Lansing, Mich.: American Hotel & Lodging Educational Institute, 2010), p. 36.

These organization charts illustrate at least two important facts: (1) While the terminology may differ, the work to be done and the basic positions required do not vary significantly among operations of different sizes; and (2) a great deal of interaction and cooperation is needed to make things work in food service. Food service managers at all levels have heard the phrase, "Food service is a people business." It is, and the people include employees as well as guests. Food service managers must understand and constantly apply skills in interpersonal relations. The ability to do this separates the good managers from the bad.

Endnotes

1. National Restaurant Association (http://www.restaurant.org/Industry-Impact/Employing-America/Economic-Engine).

2. This discussion is adapted from Jack D. Ninemeier, *Management of Food and Beverage Operations,* 5th ed. (Lansing, Mich.: American Hotel & Lodging Educational Institute, 2010).

3. John Paul Newport, "Country Clubs Fight an Exodus," *Wall Street Journal,* November 29, 2008 (http://online.wsj.com/article/SB122791013395165349.html).

Key Terms

canteen—A portable or mobile food service operation.

contribution margin—A food or beverage item's selling price minus direct costs of preparing the item.

nominal growth—An increase in revenue that results merely from raising prices, as opposed to the real growth that occurs when business volume increases.

sous chef—An assistant chef or cook.

specialty restaurant—A theme restaurant that features certain types of food.

Review Questions

1. What three markets does the food service industry serve? How does each of these markets compare to the others?

2. What is the difference between nominal growth and real growth?

3. What are the differences between a member-owned club and a proprietary club?

4. What are several categories or types of clubs?

5. In the 1950s, hotels placed greatly increased importance on the food and beverage department. What caused this change in emphasis?

6. What new dining alternatives did hotels begin to offer in the second half of the twentieth century?

7. The chain properties were the pioneers in putting hotel food and beverage divisions on a profit-making basis. How did they do so?

8. What reasons do hotels have for preferring to operate their own catering department and room service?

 Internet Sites

For more information, visit the following Internet sites. Remember that Internet addresses can change without notice. If the site is no longer there, you can use a search engine to look for additional sites.

Food Service and Related Associations

Academy of Nutrition and Dietetics (formerly American Dietetic Association)
www.eatright.org

American Culinary Federation
www.acfchefs.org

American Hotel & Lodging Educational Institute
www.ahlei.org

Association of Nutrition & Foodservice Professionals (formerly Dietary Managers Association)
www.anfponline.org

Educational Foundation of NRA
www.nraef.org

Hospitality Financial & Technology Professionals
www.hftp.org

International Association of Culinary Professionals
www.iacp.com

International Food Service Executives Association
www.ifsea.com

International Franchise Association
www.franchise.org

International Hotel & Restaurant Association
www.ih-ra.com

National Association of College &
  University Food Services
www.nacufs.org

National Restaurant Association
www.restaurant.org

School Nutrition Association
  (formerly American School Food
  Service Association)
www.schoolnutrition.org

Society for Foodservice Management
www.sfm-online.org

Chapter 9 Outline

The Role of the Hotel Food and Beverage
   Division
Some Misconceptions About Food Service
A Recipe for Success in Food Service
   Excellent Environment
   Excellent Service
   Excellent Food and Beverage Products
   Excellent Value
   Excellent Management Controls
Food Service Subsystems
   Menu Planning
   Purchasing
   Receiving
   Storing and Issuing
   Food Production (Cooking and
     Holding)
   Serving
   Catering
The Beverage Department
   Beverage Sales and Promotions
Food and Beverage Control
   Production Forecasting
   Calculating Food and Beverage Costs
   Payroll Costs and Controls

Competencies

1. Explain the role of the hotel food and beverage division, discuss some misconceptions about food service, and describe the key elements of success in food service operations. (pp. 175–179)

2. Identify critical features of a food service operation that involve the menu planning control point. (pp. 179–181)

3. Identify critical features of a food service operation that involve the purchasing, receiving, storing, and issuing control points. (pp. 181–184)

4. Identify critical features of a food service operation that involve the food producing and serving control points. (pp. 184–187)

5. Describe the hotel catering function. (p. 187)

6. Describe operational procedures of a well-run beverage department. (pp. 188–190)

7. Identify features of an effective food and beverage control system. (pp. 190–196)

The Management and Operation of Food Services

ANY COMMUNITY BENEFITS from a good food and beverage establishment, whether in a restaurant or in a hotel, since a good (and therefore busy) operation provides employment for more people. In the end, the good operation returns a better investment to the owner, and this, of course, is what the free enterprise system is all about.

Effective food service operations are vital to the financial goals of restaurants, many hotels, and a wide range of institutional facilities. Unfortunately, various factors (many of which cannot be controlled by management) cause food and beverage profits to fluctuate tremendously—often going from a profit to a severe loss from month to month or from one season to another. Food costs can be affected by weather, a turn of political events, labor unrest, crop failure, or any number of occurrences. While the volume of business can vary unexpectedly from day to day, many expenses are fixed and will not fluctuate with sales levels.

This chapter focuses on restaurant and hotel food service, but many of the points made in the discussion apply to food service operations in any setting. Although this chapter treats hotel and restaurant operations together, any significant differences are noted.

The Role of the Hotel Food and Beverage Division

The food and beverage division occupies an important position in the lodging industry. For example, about one-third of the revenue in an average hotel comes from food and beverage sales. However, because of the division's complex operation, it contributes less than one-fourth of the property's actual profit.

A food and beverage operation in a hotel performs an important threefold mission: (1) to produce an adequate profit; (2) to provide suitable food and beverage service within the hotel; and (3) to help support the role of the hotel in the community.

The importance of the hotel food and beverage operation may be illustrated by the history of two hotels in New York City. For years, The Waldorf Astoria New York has had one of the leading food and beverage divisions in the city. Today, it is considered one of the finest and most profitable hotels in the world. It enjoys a high room rate and a very high occupancy level, and does a very large food and beverage business. As a result, it continues to operate at a substantial profit.

175

Twenty years after the original Waldorf Hotel began operating, the Savoy Plaza Hotel was built. The Savoy Plaza was a more modern and, in some ways, far better hotel. Unfortunately, over the years, the Savoy Plaza's food and beverage division did not produce its proportionate share of profits. One problem was a very limited catering facility. As a result, the Savoy Plaza was torn down to make room for an office building.

A good food and beverage operation does more than help establish the quality of the hotel in the eyes of the traveling public. Such an operation may become a very valuable profit maker, may give the hotel a distinct competitive advantage over other operations, may help justify an increase in the average room rates, and may help to keep occupancy levels high.

Some Misconceptions About Food Service

Over the years, some misconceptions about the food and beverage business have arisen. One example is the old saying, "Hire good chefs and leave it to them." Blindly following this advice is one of the surest routes to failure. While a good food and beverage operation is almost impossible without a good chef, the entire food service operation must work as a team. The chef is an important member, but there are other equally important players. A complete team is necessary for a successful food and beverage operation. A chef who is capable of running an operation can be promoted to food and beverage manager and coordinate all the division's functions. However, as food and beverage manager, the former chef will still need a good chef to handle food production.

Another misconception is that successful food and beverage managers are "born." This is simply not true. A review of the hospitality industry's history reveals that all successful operators have one thing in common: the desire to get ahead. There is an old saying that states, "We do best the things we enjoy." It follows that people who are interested in food and beverage operations and who like to meet people are likely to succeed if they are committed to the job. Perhaps the observations of some successful hoteliers will make the point. Conrad Hilton said many times that he never saw a successful hotelier who did not have much curiosity. Ernest Henderson, founder of the Sheraton Hotels, said that all the successful people that he ever met, regardless of what business they were in, wanted to be the best. Other industry leaders have said that the success of a food and beverage operation corresponds directly to the time and effort the manager gives to it.

One sometimes hears of hotels that "the food and beverage division is a necessary evil," and that "it can't make any money anyhow—so just keep the losses down and forget about it." In fact, however, the leading accounting firms in the country indicate that practically every well-run food and beverage division in a hotel, regardless of size, does make a profit; the better the operation, the greater the profit and contribution to the overall operation.

Some people also believe that a hotel's food and beverage division has to be a loss-leader to attract rooms business. In truth, experience shows that a poorly run food and beverage division actually detracts from overall business. Any manager who would run a food and beverage division at a loss generally does not have the skill to run the rooms division at a profit either.

A Recipe for Success in Food Service

For every ten restaurants that open, only one will be open and making a profit after five years. This is a very low success rate. Of course, hotel restaurants do not go out of business with such frequency, since the property has the profit from the rooms to rely on; in many instances, the convenience of a restaurant to hotel guests keeps it going. However, in general, the operating profits of restaurants in hotels are actually less than the profits of independent restaurants.

There is an old saying that there are no secrets in any business. To find out how to prosper in the hotel and restaurant business, discover what successful operators do, and learn what causes other operators to fail. Comparing their activities can help unlock the "secrets" of hotel and restaurant business success.

Much of what is necessary for a successful food and beverage operation can be summarized in five distinct elements, the five E's. Although not all-encompassing, these factors are vital; no operation will thrive without all five of them. They are:

- Excellent environment
- Excellent service
- Excellent food and beverage products
- Excellent value
- Excellent management controls

Excellent Environment

Excellent environment starts with a good location. Some of the most successful operators say that an easily accessible location accounts for half of an operation's success. A restaurant has to be located in or near a community or near important intersections.

Studies consistently show that guests are very concerned about the restaurant building and grounds, especially its cleanliness, restrooms, and outside environs. Attention to these areas helps create repeat business for food and beverage operations in restaurants and hotels.

Environment also refers to the restaurant's theme. Many successful operators believe that the theme should create a mood that enhances guests' dining pleasure. The theme is created by coordinating the decorations, the menus and menu covers, food server uniforms, silver, china, glassware, linens, and the type of food and service offered.

Excellent Service

The surest sign of excellent service comes when customers feel so welcome that they are eager to return. Excellent service is primarily a matter of attitude and begins with that of management. If the manager is dedicated to giving friendly service and is courteous to employees and guests, this encourages the employees to be friendly and to make guests feel welcome.

Very few people can continually smile and be friendly to everybody they meet unless they are trained and encouraged to do so. One of management's most important jobs is to have a continuing training program for servers. Today, there are many training aids available from various sources so that even the smallest and most remote food operation can have an excellent training program.

Food service operations range from the classical French restaurant to the snack bar, each with different requirements for excellent service. A primary factor in all excellent service is that employees must be trained to recognize the importance of guests. They must realize that their livelihood depends on being courteous and friendly. The manager of any restaurant should understand that guests like to be recognized. When practical, the manager should learn guests' names and stop by their tables for polite conversation. If a problem arises, a little personal attention from the manager can often resolve it, and the guest will leave happy.

Excellent Food and Beverage Products

Many successful restaurant operators have said that excellent food is food that tastes better to the guest than the same food that the guest had somewhere else. Excellent food is basically a comparative matter; as long as the food that is being served tastes better, looks better, and receives favorable comments from guests, it is excellent food. The same principle applies to beverages. The formula is simply to purchase excellent products, store them properly, prepare the food and beverages according to proper standard recipes, control costs, package the food and beverages attractively, and satisfy guests with quality service provided by friendly employees.

Excellent Value

The way to measure whether a restaurant offers excellent value is to talk to guests and find out if they think that they got their money's worth. Repeat business is vital to a successful food service operation. Having many repeat guests proves that the restaurant is giving excellent value. Some restaurants are very expensive but generate repeat business. On the other hand, a low-check-average restaurant can lose guests if they feel that the food and service they get are not worth the price, no matter how low. Excellent value is in the mind of the guest.

Value may also relate to the size and cleanliness of the parking lot, the restrooms, the general appearance of the restaurant, the dishes on which food is served, the friendliness of the servers, the price of the food and beverages, and other factors. Sometimes, value is just a matter of the manager wishing guests a pleasant good evening and stopping to chat with them for a moment.

Excellent Management Controls

An operation can have the first four E's of this group, but if the manager does not practice excellent supervision and accounting control, the operation is likely to be another casualty in the food service business. No operation can succeed unless the manager gives the necessary personal supervision and ensures that the operation meets desired standards.

Management controls can be briefly summarized as the controls necessary: (1) to yield competitive prices; (2) to ensure that what is purchased is received, and that what is received is properly stored and issued; and (3) to ensure that the products are prepared and served properly, that all income is collected, that all money is deposited in the bank, and that all bills are paid. The internal control system also should ensure that there is a budget for the operation and that incurred costs do not become excessive. If the costs exceed the budget, the manager should find out why and take corrective action quickly.

Food Service Subsystems

There are many distinct but closely related subsystems or control points that must be managed if a food service operation is to meet its goals. These control points include menu planning, purchasing, receiving, storing, issuing, producing, and serving. The following discussion illustrates the interrelationships among these elements in a food service management system.[1]

Menu Planning

Food service management begins with the menu. Exhibit 1 shows some of the factors that menu planners must consider. The menu dictates what resources are needed and how they must be expended. It is also the property's most powerful marketing device. Menu planning is probably one of the most important but least understood aspects of today's food and beverage business. Many people can write a menu for a specific meal consisting of an appetizer, soup, entrée with potato, vegetable, salad, dessert, and coffee. However, it is much more difficult to develop an entire marketable and profitable menu for a particular restaurant. The menu planners (usually food and beverage directors and chefs) must determine who the guests are, how large the market is, and where potential guests are located. The next step is to define the types of food, beverage, and service these guests want. Planners must also consider the location of the property, transportation and parking facilities, the special concerns of the operator, and the competition.

Large chain organizations typically have marketing personnel who know what to consider when planning menus. The individual restaurant or hotel operator seldom has this specialized capability. There are, however, consultants who, for a fee, can create menus for restaurants and hotels. These specialists can work with the staff in developing a customer survey, creating the menu, and getting it designed and printed. They can also work with the chef and others in standardizing recipes and in training the staff in the proper preparation and service of the food and beverage products.

Menu planners emphasize marketing concerns and the guests' expectations while also recognizing the operation's budget constraints. In addition, the menu planning task must pay heed to the limitations imposed by the operation itself. When deciding whether to offer a wide or narrow range of choices, menu planners must keep in mind that, as the number of offerings increases, a wider variety of foods must be purchased, received, stored, issued, and otherwise managed. Compare, for example, the demands that a daily changing gourmet menu in a high-check-average property would place on operations with the demands of a fixed (seldom changed) menu in a quick-service establishment.

Exhibit 1   Priority Concerns of the Menu Planner

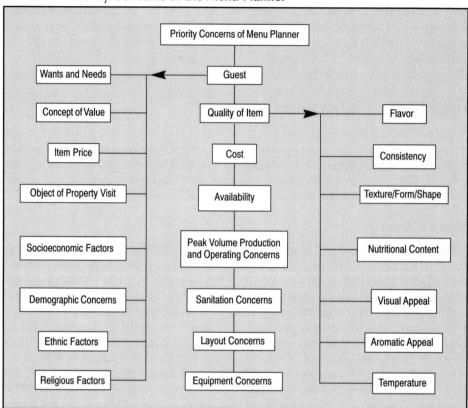

The menu affects a large number of resources, and these impose constraints that must be recognized as the menu is planned. Among these are:

- Labor—An adequate number of qualified employees with the appropriate skills are required to produce all menu items.

- Equipment—Equipment must be available to produce all items required by the menu.

- Space—Adequate square footage is required for all equipment and for receiving, storing, serving, clean-up, and other needs.

- Layout and design—The menu affects space and equipment necessary for efficient production.

- Ingredients—Recipes, which specify necessary ingredients, are important. All ingredients should be readily available at costs that support anticipated product selling prices.

- Time—The menu will affect the timing of food production and service.

- Cost implications—Equipment, space, personnel, and time concerns, mentioned previously, can all be translated into costs. Other expenses, such as utilities and supplies, will also be affected by the menu. Since a menu item's selling price will be influenced by its costs, at least in part, the menu planner must constantly guard against incorporating additional, unsupported costs into the operation by making unwise menu planning decisions.

Purchasing

Food and beverage items may be purchased by a food and beverage manager or by a purchasing agent in a special purchasing division or department. Whoever does the food and beverage purchasing must bear in mind that no amount of skill in food preparation can make up for food that is of poor quality to begin with; excellent food, to a large extent, depends on excellent purchasing judgment. Moreover, the control of food costs begins at the time of purchase. Profits lost through poor purchasing judgment or dishonesty cannot be recalled.

A good food and beverage purchaser cannot judge food items by price alone, or quality will suffer. By the same token, price must be an important purchasing consideration if the property is to remain financially viable. To make wise purchasing decisions, purchasers must understand:

- What the property's financial goals are and how purchasing decisions will affect them.

- How much food is needed to prevent both **stock-outs** and overstocking.

- How food and beverage items will be prepared and presented.

- What guests expect from the food and beverage service operation.

Receiving

After products are purchased, the same level of attention must be given to receiving them properly. In large properties, the receiving clerk is a member of the accounting division, independent of the food and beverage division; he or she is responsible only to the controller. This arrangement allows the clerk to receive and control any merchandise that comes into the hotel without being influenced by anyone else and provides one of the best means of reducing dishonesty in the purchasing system.

Even in small operations, food, beverages, and other supplies should not be received by the same person who does the purchasing. In some operations, however, receiving clerks still report directly to the food and beverage manager. Such a system may work in practice, but it certainly provides opportunities for dishonesty. Most food and beverage experts agree that hiring an independent receiving clerk who reports to the controller will pay dividends in any operation, regardless of its size.

Unfortunately, receiving functions in the past have often been neglected. Food service operations have suffered substantial losses because of the lack of trained receiving personnel and the use of ineffective receiving practices. Because a receiving clerk can be responsible for several million dollars' worth of merchandise in a year, the property obviously needs a well-paid and well-trained person in this sensitive position.

The receiving area should be located conveniently between the property's receiving dock and the storeroom so that the receiving clerk can see everything that goes in or out of the building. It should be equipped with an adequate floor scale and a small table scale. A complete set of purchase specifications should be developed to help in checking incoming merchandise. The proper tools should be available to open boxes and to check crates.

Everything that is received should be written up on a receiving clerk's daily report (see Exhibit 2). This report itemizes invoices that accompany the merchandise and indicates whether it is charged to that day's account for immediate use (listed under "**food direct**") or to the food storeroom (listed under "**food stores**"). This report should be completed each day, totaled, attached to the invoices that should accompany all incoming merchandise, and sent to the food and beverage controller for auditing. In turn, the report should go to the general manager, where each invoice should be initialed and sent on to the accounting division for payment.

The receiving clerk's office should also be equipped with a **credit memorandum** form and a form that can be used for recording merchandise received without

Exhibit 2 Receiving Clerk's Daily Report

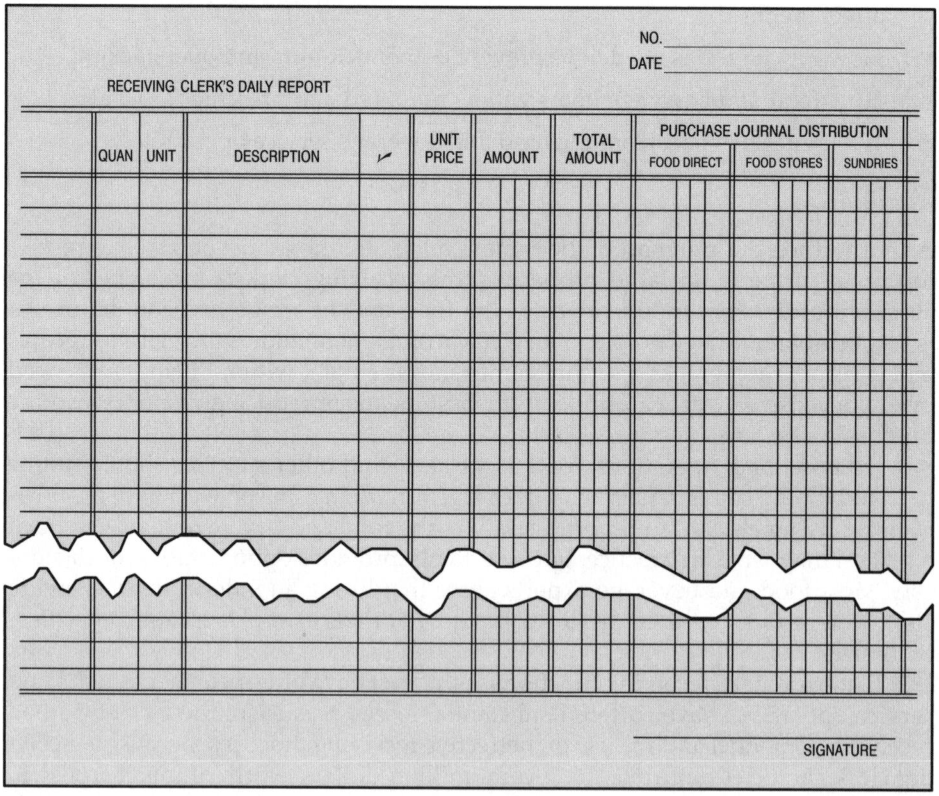

NO. ____________

DATE ____________

RECEIVING CLERK'S DAILY REPORT

QUAN	UNIT	DESCRIPTION	✓	UNIT PRICE	AMOUNT	TOTAL AMOUNT	PURCHASE JOURNAL DISTRIBUTION		
							FOOD DIRECT	FOOD STORES	SUNDRIES

____
SIGNATURE

invoice. By using these forms, the receiving clerk will help ensure that the property pays only for items actually received. It is important that all incoming items be weighed, counted, or measured to ensure that the orders are complete. The receiving clerk also must verify that the items being delivered were in fact ordered and that they match the property's purchase specifications. For example, if a property orders pre-cut steaks in 40-ounce packages containing five 8-ounce steaks, the receiving clerk must recognize the error if the delivery contains 40-ounce packages containing four 10-ounce steaks. This careful analysis of incoming items should be undertaken *before* the delivery invoice is signed.

The receiving clerk should quickly move all items to their proper storage areas. This practice helps to reduce theft as well as losses in product quality. The clerk should never permit delivery people to move products into inventory. It is important to limit access to storage areas to only those relatively few people who need to enter them.

Storing and Issuing

The next control points in the food service system are storing and issuing food and beverage products. In some properties, the storeroom is under the direction of the purchasing agent. In other, smaller operations, the storeroom is under the direction of the steward (who may also act as purchasing agent). In all properties, the controller should be responsible for the internal control system and for accounting for products that go into and out of the storeroom.

Food and beverage storage facilities, including refrigerated areas, can occupy a large portion of the food and beverage storage area. The entire storage area should be protected with locks. There should be only one entrance. Unauthorized personnel should be kept out of the storeroom at all times. Only one person should have the key to the liquor storage area (which should be separate from the food storage area) so as to be accountable for all the merchandise in that area. The area should be clean and properly lighted. Merchandise should be stored off the floor. Unpacked merchandise on shelves should be kept to a minimum, and regular storeroom hours should be adhered to. The food and beverage storeroom should be inspected every day by the food and beverage manager, the chef, or the general manager.

A properly authorized requisition should be required before merchandise is issued from the storeroom. To increase the accuracy of issuing control, every item in the storeroom should be priced with a marking pencil. This process is necessary for inventory purposes. Month-end inventories are the responsibility of the accounting division. Even though perpetual inventories are not kept on all storeroom items, they should be used for expensive and theft-prone items. **Perpetual inventories** provide a running balance of the quantity of items in stock. As items are received, the balance is increased; as products are issued, the balance is decreased. At the end of the month, the accounting division checks the perpetual inventory balance against the actual stock on hand; a list of overages and shortages should be prepared for management. A list of **dead stock** (items stored for more than a specified time) should be circulated monthly to the chef and food and beverage manager so that they can make plans to use these items.

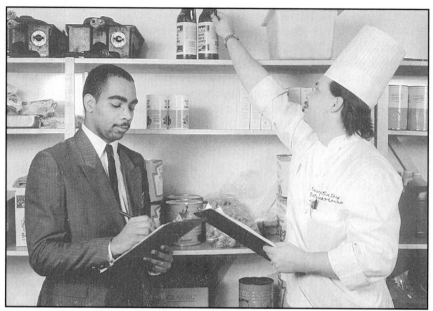

Regularly scheduled inventories of food and beverage items discourage theft and ensure that necessary products are always on hand.

Storeroom keys must be tightly controlled. Many properties use a log book that indicates to whom keys have been issued and for how long. When people with access to storeroom keys leave the organization, keys and locks should be changed.

Food Production (Cooking and Holding)

Excellent food is one of the five basic requirements for a successful food operation. Experience has proven that no restaurant or hotel food operation can continue to operate unless the food served is as good as or better than all nearby competing food service operations. Although we cannot provide details of food production in this chapter, we will point out certain basics about food production and kitchen operation that are always found in well-run food departments producing and serving excellent food at a reasonable profit.[2]

The first basic requirement is the proper management attitude—managers must want to serve excellent food. This means that the general manager of the restaurant or hotel has to be interested in food (although he or she does not necessarily have to know how to cook). A manager with the desire to offer quality food will motivate production personnel to prepare excellent food.

The hotel general manager typically has some involvement in the day-to-day operations of the food and beverage division, but most of the responsibility for this area falls to the food and beverage manager and/or the chef. In the past, the chef was often an excellent cook but less effective as a manager. Times have changed; today's top chefs are better kitchen managers, know how to control costs and

The Executive Chef

A property's executive chef is far more than a glorified cook. The executive chef may be responsible for all food production in the hotel or restaurant. He or she may also oversee the entire kitchen operation and manage the food production and clean-up staff as well. These responsibilities include preparing menus, working with the catering manager on banquet menus, and determining how much food is necessary to meet the forecast of business. The chef must make sure staff purchase and issue the proper quality of food. The chef must keep payroll costs in line and maintain contact with other department heads. The chef must be ready to correct any breakdown in food preparation.

A good executive chef who can produce good food at the right cost is getting to be a rarity. There are some excellent chefs' training courses in schools in the United States, but a former source of chefs, the European apprentice system, has all but disappeared.

Today, a good chef is well paid. In many instances, the salary may be similar to or higher than the general manager's. Many chefs receive more money than the food and beverage manager. Good chefs command a high salary and a bonus for performance. Their responsibilities are tremendous, the pressures are great, and the hours are long. The chef is a business executive and a valuable business associate. The chef's profession today is one that is highly respected.

merchandise foods, and have learned to work as a team with department heads and others with whom they come in contact.

Excellent food requires quality ingredients. To get the best results from quality ingredients, the food should be produced as close as possible to the time of service. One of the problems the chef in a large hotel confronts is that he or she may have four or five restaurant outlets plus as many as twenty different banquets going on in one day. It can be very difficult to produce all this food just prior to the time of service; consequently, some food must be prepared in advance. Unfortunately, some chefs regularly "cook for the refrigerator." They cook food ahead of time, place it in refrigerated storage, and then withdraw foods on an as-needed basis. This approach may keep payroll costs down, but it certainly does not yield excellent food.

The use of convenience foods also has quality implications. It is difficult to keep the flavor and taste of convenience foods comparable to the same foods cooked from scratch. Many synthetic ingredients are used in convenience foods to keep costs down and to maintain long shelf-life. Moreover, some synthetic foods may actually pose a health threat to people who are allergic to them. A good chef will be very wary of using any synthetic flavoring or convenience foods and will ensure that the property's quality and cost requirements can be met if they are used.

Proper cooking methods must be followed as food is produced. If a stew is to be simmered for two to three hours, it should be simmered and not boiled violently. If the standard recipe for lamb stew calls for cooking the lamb with fresh potatoes, onions, carrots, and celery, the various ingredients should not be cooked separately, and canned potatoes and carrots and dehydrated onion and celery flakes should not be substituted.

Another basic requirement is that food should be properly cared for after it is prepared and before it is served. Keeping food on the steam table too long reduces its quality; sanitation problems can result as well. Food must be kept hot or cold for the shortest possible time before service. Quality foods are typically those that are prepared in small batches on an as-needed basis.

Excellent food cannot be produced unless production staff have the proper tools and equipment with which to work. Employees cannot operate successfully using ranges that will not heat, refrigerators that will not cool, stock pots that will not boil, freezers that will not keep foods frozen, or warming cabinets that will not keep banquet foods hot. Likewise, measuring containers and other small equipment required by standard recipes must be available and in good working order.

A complete kitchen in a large hotel may consist of the range section (which includes the stock kettles, ranges, broilers, grills, steamers, fry kettles, and roasting ovens); the *garde-manger* (cold food) sections; the pantry (salad) area; the butcher shop; the pastry shop and sometimes a bake shop; the scullery (dish and pot washing) areas; an employees' cafeteria kitchen; the banquet kitchen(s); and the room service kitchen. In smaller operations, the *garde-manger* and pantry areas may be located in one section. The butcher shop is often eliminated if the operation uses pre-portioned meat and the pastry and bake shops are often combined or eliminated.

In a large hotel, each one of the kitchen production departments may be under the supervision of a department head, who works a shift and reports to the chef, either directly or through a sous (assistant) chef. Today, kitchen personnel are often paid well, and each year a more highly educated group is entering the kitchen. Chefs and cooks are producing better food in less time, and, in spite of problems with low productivity and high turnover, the cooking profession is more respected than ever before.

Serving

In all types of food service operations, management must establish and enforce minimum quality standards for employees in front-of-the-house areas.[3] Managers cannot rely on the employees' common sense to tell them to do the right thing at the right time. Planning is necessary to identify required tasks and to develop procedures for effectively performing them. Carefully consider the guest. The type of service provided should be that which is best from the guest's perspective. What does the guest desire, and how can the operation best provide for these wants and needs?

This question must be answered by each operation. While it is not possible to develop specific practices that apply to all properties, there are many general principles that can be used to develop consistent procedures for all front-of-the-house employees. Supervision is necessary to ensure that shortcuts that violate standard operating procedures are not used. Asking questions such as, "If I were a guest, what things would I like or dislike about the serving procedures?" offers ideas about which procedures should or should not be used. The answers to these questions also govern the development of standard operating procedures. They indicate where and even how training programs to teach required activities should be conducted.

Each property must strive to develop service that pleases guests. Dining room managers must inspect the facilities to ensure that they are clean and safe, assign food server stations so that guests are served efficiently, properly communicate with and train service staff, and make sure that server stations contain the necessary products and supplies. They must develop sales income control procedures to protect the property and guests from dishonest employees, and schedule and ensure that sidework (clean-up) duties are performed correctly.

Catering

In the early days of innkeeping, owners and managers learned the value of having function rooms on the premises. The importance then, as now, was twofold. First, it was necessary to provide ballrooms and meeting rooms of various capacities in order to book group business. Secondly, on-premises catering to groups can be quite profitable on its own. Hotels have long built small and large rooms that are offered to in-house, local, civic, and business groups, as well as weddings and other similar functions.

Catering, while a part of the food and beverage department, has to maintain a close relationship with the sales department as the success of each depends on the other. The catering staff services what the sales team sells and books.

Catering offers considerable profit even though there are many days and nights when the function rooms are not used. The profit in catering is favorable simply because the attendance at each meal function is guaranteed, which allows food service and food preparation to plan, schedule, staff, and prepare for a set number of people. The function group also buys things other than food and wine, such as flowers, music, and entertainment.

Off-premises catering has become big business and is very popular with businesses as well as individuals when entertaining for pleasure, business, weddings, sporting events, and other social events. In addition, the catering done by hotels and restaurant companies, both large and small, has flourished.

Until the late twentieth century, airline catering was significant. Early in this century, however, the airlines experienced down times and found that they could eliminate meals in coach and reduce the variety of meals in first class without any loss of payloads. When this took place, those caterers who served airlines consolidated, reduced their size, or went out of business.

Independent caterers usually operate by keeping their overhead low. They might have only an office for sales purposes. When an event is booked and about to take place, they arrange for independent banquet servers. Often the caterer will rent a kitchen from another caterer. There are independent caterers who maintain a kitchen and a staff of salespeople. They draw their servers and captains from an on-call pool of trained, part-time servers. Catering—whether in hotels or off-premises—is an important part of food service in America.

The Beverage Department

An exceptionally well-run food department can produce a departmental profit of 15 to 18 percent of sales. By contrast, a well-run beverage department can and often does produce a profit of as high as 50 percent of sales. The beverage operation is, then, an integral part of the property's financial and organizational structure. In fact, because of the many complex problems of food service, beverages alone often account for the entire profit of the operation.

Historically, the general supervision of the beverage department was the responsibility of a wine steward (sommelier), perhaps assisted by a head bartender. Today, the position has been renamed beverage manager or, in some cases, director of beverage operations. This official is responsible for the day-to-day operation of the bars, and reports to the food and beverage manager. In small hotels where there is no need for a food and beverage manager, the beverage manager normally reports to the general manager. In other small operations, a food and beverage manager may operate the beverage department.

In properties with union contracts, the head bartender (who assists the beverage manager) actually works at the bars, sets up the banquet bars, and, in many instances, relieves bartenders when necessary. The beverage manager typically cannot, by union rules, act as a bartender except in case of an emergency; but in non-union houses, especially in small operations, it is common practice for the beverage manager to relieve bartenders for meals and other occasions.

Beverage purchasing responsibilities are typically assigned to the purchasing agent. There was a time when beverage purchasing required a high degree of skill, but that is largely no longer true. With the beverage industry so closely regulated by the government and with all bottles of liquor and wine required to have a full disclosure of contents, the purchasing of this merchandise has been simplified. In fact, beverages are typically purchased by brand name from a supplier with exclusive distribution rights or from a state-operated store; there are relatively few decisions to make after brands are chosen.

Certain basic ground rules must be followed to achieve good beverage department operation. First, the decision concerning which brands to offer must be based on what the guest actually desires. Any attempt to force a lower-than-desired quality of liquors or wines on guests will merely drive away business. The profit in beverage sales is so great that it is often unwise to use anything other than high-quality merchandise. Using well-known brand names will give the guest confidence in the bar and its operations.

On the other hand, certain highly advertised brand names are often much more expensive than less advertised brand names. Management might want to consider making taste tests and experimenting with some of these lesser-known names to measure acceptance by the guest. In some states, it is possible to purchase private label merchandise, often of superior quality.

Some properties buy too many different brands of liquors and end up with funds tied up in a large inventory, which is an expensive practice. Ideally, inventory should turn over completely about once a month, depending on discounts offered for volume purchases. This is best accomplished when the property management approves a list of acceptable brands with a maximum and minimum quantity established for each.

The receiving of beverages, like the receiving of food supplies, should be done by the receiving clerk of the property under the control of the accounting division. The receiving clerk should be given a list of the merchandise expected to arrive each day and should check it off as it arrives. Beverage receipts may be written on a special receiving sheet or on the same form used for food supplies. These receiving sheets should be written in duplicate and totaled each day. The original should be attached to the approved invoices and routed through management, purchasing, and accounting channels in the same way that food purchases are. The food and beverage controller should use the duplicate of the receiving sheet for establishing perpetual inventory controls. In large operations, it is also wise to use bin cards, which show receipts and issues to keep a running balance of the merchandise. This information serves as a basis for submitting a purchase request for additional supplies.

Supplies of liquor and wine should be stored in areas separate from food supplies and should be issued only upon the receipt of a signed requisition in accordance with the instructions set up by the food and beverage control department. Par stocks should be maintained on all the bars; the empty bottles should be returned to the storeroom as a basis for bottle-for-bottle exchange when the bars are restocked. (**Par** is the number of bottles management has determined must be behind the bar at the beginning of a shift in order to avoid run-outs.) The keys to the liquor and wine storage area should be in the hands of one person who is held responsible for the security of all the merchandise in the storeroom. The accounting division should keep a perpetual inventory of these products and should take a physical inventory at the end of each month with the person responsible for the keys to the area.

In any property doing a substantial amount of banquet business, a banquet beverage storeroom should be set up and all issues to banquets should be made to this area. Merchandise can be issued to the various banquet bars and any liquor remaining from a banquet bar can be returned and recorded. With such a setup, a banquet bar can operate with a par stock, and a daily banquet cost can be determined if required by management.

It is just as important for a restaurant or hotel to be known for having a good bar as it is for serving good food. Smart managers insist that standard drink recipes be followed and that proper measuring tools, such as jiggers and shot glasses, be used by the bartender. The head bartender must train and supervise the bartenders to ensure that no shortcuts are taken, that drinks are the correct size, and that, whenever possible, fresh juices and ingredients are used to prepare drinks.

One of the best ways to obtain consistent quality of drinks is to prepare a bar operation manual. The manual should be prepared specifically for the operation by the beverage manager and/or the head bartender and should include all the standard recipes of the operation plus instructions about service, the glasses to be used, and how to merchandise certain drinks, as well as a complete wine list, instructions on banquet bar setups, and an outline of the internal control system of the property as it applies to bar operations. The control system outline covers such things as accountability of bar checks and the collection of money, accountability for cash and charges, register readings, and security measures.

Beverage Sales and Promotions

There are some proven ways to increase beverage sales and to merchandise beverages and wines. The first step is to provide a training program for all bartenders and servers. The more these employees know about products and merchandising, the greater the sales and profits will be. Frequently, key beverage suppliers can assist in promotions, providing necessary ingredients from displays to staff training.

Today, the great and legitimate concern about drunken driving is changing the promotion of alcoholic beverages. Many properties and some states have halted certain types of promotions, such as happy hours featuring two drinks for the price of one. Promotions must recognize the responsible and safe use of alcoholic beverages. Alcohol awareness programs (for guests and employees), designated driver programs (in which one member of a group does not consume alcohol), and merchandising no- or low-alcohol drinks all stem from today's concern about alcohol abuse.

Many books have been written on how to sell wine, but the writers usually fail to discuss pricing. New pricing strategies have unquestionably contributed to the rapid increase of wine sales. In-house marketing of house wines has yielded increased revenues for many properties. So too has the sale of more expensive premium wines by the glass, a development made possible by dispensing equipment that injects nitrogen into opened bottles, enabling high-quality wines to be kept for very long time periods. One of the best ways to sell wine is to package a bottle or a carafe of wine with banquet meals or with dining room meals where state laws permit. Another good strategy is not simply asking the guests if they would like wine with their dinners, but actually suggesting the type of wine that would go well with an entrée.

Every bar operation should have at least one or two specialty drinks. Such drinks are often just a variation of some of the old standbys served in a specialty glass or container and in a manner designed to attract attention. These drinks (which do not need to be alcoholic) can be attractively packaged with unique glassware and garnish, and can be merchandised by the menu, tent cards, suggestive selling, or in any other appropriate manner.

To help promote beverages, a short but interesting list of cocktails, beers, and wines can be made available to guests. Some properties use long wine lists, but it is hard to maintain complete stocks. Moreover, long lists may overwhelm guests and discourage them from ordering wine at all. Useful for elegant, classical restaurants, these wine lists should be replaced in more casual properties by an abbreviated list or wine card that offers a limited variety at prices designed to encourage the guest to buy.

Food and Beverage Control

Food and beverage control systems have been used widely since Prohibition began (1920). Before that time, most of the better hotels and restaurants had no trouble making money in the food and beverage operation, primarily because of the large profits made on beverages. During Prohibition, the profits in the beverage department disappeared overnight. Restaurant and hotel operators realized that to stay in business they had to get control of operating costs in the food department.

Hotel and restaurant accountants in the early 1920s did not have food control systems as such, but some of the more progressive hotel and restaurant accounting firms quickly devised food control systems to meet the needs of the hotel and restaurant industry. After Prohibition was repealed in 1933, the hotel and restaurant industry found that it still needed a good food control system. It also had to create a good beverage control system so food and beverage operations could make a profit.

Most operators agree that large operations need one control system, while smaller operations need a smaller, less expensive system. Many operators are working to computerize systems that will be more efficient and less costly in labor hours. A computerized standard beverage control system is now available from a number of companies. In addition, various phases of the food control system, such as inventory, sales income, and menu engineering, have been computerized.

Sometimes food and beverage control personnel become involved in the management of operations and the development of policy. This naturally causes trouble. When there are disagreements between the operating staff and the controller, it is often due to a lack of understanding of what a controller does. In fact, the controller is in a staff (advisory) position. He or she reports facts and makes suggestions to managers, but it is the managers who must make policy and operating decisions. See Exhibit 3 for a discussion of the proper duties of a food and beverage controller.

Production Forecasting

One of the most important questions about food and beverage control is: how many meals/guests will we serve in the future? Knowing the right answer helps ensure acceptable food and payroll costs. The food controller tries to anticipate that answer by forecasting. In hotels, for example, the forecaster considers facts and figures for a given period of time, which then determine the number of guests served based upon the number of guests in the hotel.

Assume, for example, that a hotel food controller uses a factor of 70 percent for breakfast guests in the coffee shop (that is, 70 percent of hotel guests without group banquet meal commitments eat breakfast in the coffee shop). The house count is 1,400, and the banquet office indicates that 200 people staying in the hotel will have breakfast in a banquet room. From this information, a preliminary forecast can be made as follows:

House count	1,400	
Less banquet	200	
	1,200	Guests without banquet commitments
	× 70%	Breakfast factor
	840	Guests estimated for coffee shop breakfasts

(While any hotel can use this method for forecasting, each must determine its own factors.)

One forecast is typically made a week in advance. Such a forecast could, of course, become obsolete, but this is just a preliminary forecast. Every day, the food controller adjusts a three-day forecast as well. Factors are developed from the previous year's record of guests served and house count, and are re-checked to maintain accuracy.

Exhibit 3   Duties of the Food and Beverage Controller

The food and beverage controller is a member of the accounting division. He or she must:

- Help the property's accountant prepare the annual budget, monthly forecasts, and related financial information applicable to the food and beverage division.

- Keep a daily review of the manner in which the receiving clerk carries out his or her duties and observe daily the quality of merchandise coming into the property through the receiving department.

- Check daily food and beverage requisitions and production tests and confirm that a daily sales analysis is being made on entrée sales.

- Review purchase records for price comparisons, for trends in seasonal foods, and for cost figures in order to correctly cost out menus.

- Prepare daily food cost reports and weekly beverage potential cost reports.

- Keep perpetual inventories on beverage storerooms and on the frozen and expensive dry ingredients.

- Assist in or take month-end inventories of both food and beverage.

- Prepare food and beverage reconciliations of costs for the accounting division.

- Attend weekly food and beverage meetings and provide cost information to management or the food and beverage manager for operational decisions.

- Work closely with top management, the food and beverage manager, chef, and purchasing agent in the testing program designed to set up standard purchase specifications and to provide a continuous check on portion costs.

- Help the food and beverage manager and the chef prepare and maintain standard portion size lists posted in the appropriate operating departments.

- Assist management in the preparation, maintenance, and continuous use of the standard recipe files.

Other considerations in determining the number of people to be served are the weather and the day of the week. For example, Friday evening meal counts may be small in food service operations catering to travelers. On Sundays, a hotel's lunch business may be low if most lodgers eat a late breakfast, skip lunch, and then have an early dinner. There are other considerations, and each restaurant and hotel will have its own explanation for rises and falls in the number of guests served.

A forecast has various uses. First, it determines staffing. For example, the dining room manager uses the forecast of meals to be served to decide how many food servers and buspersons will be required. The chef then determines the number of cooks and pantry workers required. It is essential that the correct number of people be scheduled—enough to get the job done well, but no more than actually necessary.

The chef also uses the forecast to ascertain how much food should be prepared. Therefore, the forecast helps maintain low food costs, since overproduction often increases costs more than any other factor. The purchaser uses the forecast to purchase, as accurately as possible, the amount of food necessary for a given period. The food and beverage manager can use the information provided by the forecast for planning other purchases. By knowing the approximate income to expect, he or she can determine expenses and arrive at a profit figure that will help clarify how much money can be spent.

Calculating Food and Beverage Costs

Actual food and beverage costs are calculated and indicated as *cost of goods sold* on monthly income statements. However, food and beverage management personnel need food cost information more frequently in order to make timely control decisions. One of the chief duties of the food and beverage controller is to prepare and distribute the daily food cost report. All food and beverage department heads receive this report, which indicates whether food costs are running higher than the budgeted standard cost set up by management.

Daily food cost information is also frequently tabulated for the general manager's daily food report. This rather simple report (see Exhibit 4) keeps managers informed about the food costs for the day and to date and how these food costs relate to the same period of the previous year. Properties with several food outlets may best record food costs separately for each restaurant. If the costs run higher than they should, managers and the food and beverage controller analyze the operation to find out why food costs are high.

Exhibit 4   Daily Food Report

	DAILY FOOD REPORT				
Hotel_____			Day and Date _____		
	TODAY		TO DATE		Last Year to Date %
EXPLANATION	Amount	%	Amount	%	
Sales—Restaurants					
—Banquets					
—Total					
GROSS PROFIT OF FOOD CONSUMED					
Less: Employee Meal Credits					
Net Cost of Food Sold					
PAR NET COST—Restaurants					
—Banquets					
—Total					
DIFFERENCE					
Remarks					
			Food Controller		

Fortunately, beverage costs do not fluctuate greatly from day to day, and it is not necessary for the controller to publish a daily beverage cost report. Experience has shown that excellent results can be attained through the use of the analysis of beverage sales and costs report (see Exhibit 5). This report—which can be prepared on a weekly, semi-monthly, or monthly basis—shows what the sales actually were, what the costs were, and what the sales should have been (potential sales) for each individual bar based on the sales price per drink, the current cost of liquors, and the standard size drink being served at the various bars. The report also shows sales and costs for full bottles (wines, beers, mineral waters, and full-bottle liquor sales) separate from the sales and costs of mixed drinks. From this information, management can readily locate possible losses in the bar operation and take steps to correct them.

Payroll Costs and Controls

Wages and salaries paid to managers and employees make up a large percentage of the operating expenses incurred by a food and beverage operation. *Prime cost* is a concept managers use in all types of food and beverage operations. To explain, Prime Cost = Food Cost + Labor Cost, each expressed as a percentage of sales. The general rule of thumb says that prime cost should not exceed 65 percent if the operation is to be profitable. The reader should note that two very dissimilar operations—one with a high food cost but a low labor cost and the other with a low food cost but high labor cost—can have identical prime costs and be profitable.

Exhibit 5   Analysis of Beverage Sales and Costs Report

November 20—   ANALYSIS OF BEVERAGE SALES AND COSTS

	Combined Operations	GREEN ROOM BAR	BANQUET BAR	LOUNGE
SALES				
Drink	62,039.80	51,339.40	7,364.95	3,335.45
Bottle	18,687.25	5,725.50	12,961.75	
Total Sales	80,727.05	57,064.90	20,326.70	3,335.45
Potential	81,198.75	57,578.10	20,223.55	3,397.10
Bar Difference (over or short)	471.70	513.20	103.15	61.65
Percent of Difference	.6	.9	.5	1.8
COST OF SALES				
Drink	19,229.88	16,052.02	2,147.54	1,030.32
Bottle	8,642.04	2,711.87	5,930.17	
Total	27,871.92	18,763.89	8,077.71	1,030.32
PERCENTAGE COST				
Drink	30.9	31.3	29.2	30.9
Bottle	46.2	47.4	45.7	
Actual	34.5	32.9	39.7	30.9
Potential	34.3	32.6	39.9	30.3
Difference	.2	.3	.2	.6

The increase in payroll costs is not due only to increased payroll rates (although rates have gone up substantially in the past twenty years). One of the biggest factors in increased payroll costs has been the cost of benefits such as vacation pay, pensions, medical and dental benefits, life insurance, unemployment benefits, workers' compensation, personal holidays, and sick leave. In 1950, the cost of benefits in a food and beverage operation, including employee meals, was about 5 percent of the payroll. Today it is approaching 40 percent.

Rising labor and benefits costs will unquestionably force a change in the facilities and service offered to the commercial food service customer. Some restaurants have begun eliminating a great deal of service and moving toward self-service bars featuring pre-prepared food. In hotels, banquet service is sometimes offered as buffet service. Even many high-check-average restaurants are now offering buffet service at noon, and salad bars, soup bars, and dessert bars for dinner. There are even restaurants offering guests the opportunity to do their own cooking. Innovation seems to be the key in hotel and restaurant operators' attempts to offset high payroll costs.

Excessive Payroll Costs. While average payroll costs are about 40 percent of sales, a great many operations incur much greater payroll costs. Such a situation requires concentrated efforts to find out why payroll costs are so high and what can be done about it. Excessive payroll costs generally stem from poor management.

Some situations exist in which the location, the physical setup, or the need to offer a service makes it impossible to reduce payroll costs. Fortunately, these situations are relatively rare. Excessive payroll costs are generally caused by one or more of the following reasons:

- No basic staffing guides

- Poor or no budgeting and forecasting

- No work schedules

- No control of overtime

- No control over variable staffing for banquet service

- Poor payroll cost reporting

- Union job restrictions

- Poor communication between managers and employees (further complicated by poor communication between management and unions)

To control payroll costs, managers must first recognize the problem and then make a commitment to resolve it. Top-level managers must coordinate the efforts of the various people involved. It is their job to follow up and ensure that plans are carried out. The actual program for controlling payroll costs should be developed by someone with the time and ability to do the job. It does not matter whether this is the human resources manager, an operations analyst, the controller, or an assistant manager. The person must be familiar with the operation as a whole, have the ability to read and analyze operating statements, be methodical, and have empathy for the employees.

Many hotels and restaurants have a bargaining agreement with one or more employee unions, and consequently some payroll control procedures may require changes to abide by the union contract. The person who is in charge of payroll control must know the conditions of the union contract and must know how to work with union representatives in order to protect the best interests of the hospitality operation.

The following is a step-by-step program for controlling costs:

1. An annual operating budget (compiled from monthly operating budgets) for the food and beverage operation should be prepared under the supervision of management.

2. A staffing guide that incorporates required performance standards should be developed. Allowable labor hours permitted by the staffing guide should be in harmony with the operating budget standards.

3. A revised budget or forecast should be prepared by the 25th of each month for the coming month by the food and beverage manager with the help of department heads; it should then be approved by upper management. This labor budget should reflect the forecast of expected business volume.

4. Personnel in all positions should be scheduled on a weekly (or another regular) basis, according to the business forecast and staffing guide requirements.

5. There should be a regular monthly comparison of the actual results of the operation with the annual and revised budget as soon as management receives the monthly operating statement. Actual hours worked should also be compared with hours scheduled.

6. Each department within the food and beverage operation should have a current organization chart and a basic staffing guide that shows the number of employees and hours allowed in the basic staff, day by day, for the week.

In addition to the basic staffing guide that shows the regular salaried employees, there should be standards set up for variable staff such as dishwashers, extra banquet help, extra food servers, housepersons, buspersons, and other help that are hired on an hourly basis as the workload requires. These standards are, in many cases, specified in the union contract. However, in other instances they are subject to negotiation; this is where goodwill on the part of everyone can pay off for both sides.

Overtime becomes extremely costly unless it is strictly controlled. There should be a procedure for pre-approval of overtime by the food and beverage manager or another appropriate official. There should be a policy of no built-in overtime for anyone. This policy should be diligently followed by the general manager.

Most operations make use of a weekly report of the payroll showing regular time, extra time, and overtime, and a comparison between the actual and the allowable time and cost in these categories. This report should be discussed in the weekly food and beverage meeting.

Endnotes

1. Readers desiring more detailed information about the management of a food service operation are referred to Jack D. Ninemeier, *Management of Food and Beverage Operations,* 5th ed. (Lansing, Mich.: American Hotel & Lodging Educational Institute, 2010).
2. The Educational Institute has developed an entire course dealing with food production. Contact the Institute (www.ahlei.org) for details.
3. The remainder of this section is adapted from Ninemeier.

Key Terms

credit memorandum—A form that is to be completed by the purchaser when merchandise received from a supplier does not match the specifications of the purchase order.

dead stock—Items that have been kept in storerooms for more than a specified time; a list of such items should be circulated to the chef and food and beverage manager on a regular basis so that they can make plans to use them.

food direct—Food purchased that will be used immediately.

food stores—Food purchased that will be stored before being used.

par—The standard number of a particular inventory item that must be on hand to support daily operations.

perpetual inventory—An ongoing tally of the quantity of items in stock.

stock-outs—Depletion of an inventory item.

Review Questions

1. What factors can cause food and beverage profits to fluctuate tremendously?
2. What factors enter into creating a restaurant's environment?
3. What five elements must be present if a food and beverage operation is to succeed? Briefly discuss them.
4. What are the factors involved in planning a menu?
5. Why does the receiving clerk in larger properties work in the accounting department rather than the food and beverage department?
6. What precautions should food and beverage operations take when storing and issuing supplies?
7. What is a perpetual inventory?
8. What are the advantages and disadvantages of convenience foods in hotel kitchens?
9. Why is forecasting of sales so important to food and beverage operations?
10. What are some of the basic ground rules that must be followed to ensure that the beverage department operates smoothly?

Internet Sites

For more information, visit the following Internet sites. Remember that Internet addresses can change without notice. If the site is no longer there, you can use a search engine to look for additional sites.

Food Service and Related Associations

Academy of Nutrition and Dietetics (formerly American Dietetic Association)
www.eatright.org

American Culinary Federation
www.acfchefs.org

American Hotel & Lodging Educational Institute
www.ahlei.org

Association of Nutrition & Foodservice Professionals (formerly Dietary Managers Association)
www.anfponline.org

Educational Foundation of NRA
www.nraef.org

School Nutrition Association (formerly American School Food Service Association)
www.schoolnutrition.org

Part IV

Functional Areas in Hospitality Operations

Chapter 10 Outline

The Changing Nature of Engineering
    The Engineering Division as a Savings
      Center
    The Need for Effective Management
The Work of the Engineering Division
    Electrical Systems
    Plumbing Systems
    HVAC Systems
    Refrigeration Systems
    Life Safety Systems
    General Maintenance and Repair
    Preventive Maintenance
    Renovation
    Water Management
Energy Management
    Energy Problems
    Energy Management Programs
    Recent Developments

Competencies

1. Describe the general role of the engineering and maintenance division in hospitality operations. (pp. 201–203)

2. Identify engineering's responsibilities in relation to electrical, plumbing, HVAC, refrigeration, and life safety systems. (pp. 203–207)

3. Explain the role of the engineering and maintenance division in relation to general and preventive maintenance programs and renovation projects. (pp. 207–210)

4. Explain the role of the engineering and maintenance division in relation to water management. (pp. 210–212)

5. Explain the role of the engineering and maintenance division in relation to energy management and other conservation practices. (pp. 212–217)

10

The Engineering and Maintenance Division

I<small>F ONE WERE TO DESIGNATE</small> an unsung hero in hotels and restaurants, the engineering division would win the competition hands down. Until recently, engineering has been undervalued, underappreciated, and underrecognized by both owners and managers. A hotel or restaurant requires a huge investment in land, building, and equipment. The building and the equipment both have a projected life span that must be achieved if profit and return on investment projections are to be realized. Every division uses the building and the equipment, but only one—engineering—has the responsibility for keeping them in efficient working order. When it comes to overall importance, the engineering division takes a backseat to none.

A property of any size must have a chief engineer who can meet the management and technical needs of this division. The chief engineer directs the activities of the division and supervises a staff of skilled technicians. The exact titles of engineering positions and the degree of specialization each position requires depends on the size of the operation and on whether or not the division is unionized.

The engineering divisions of hotels are typically larger and more elaborate than those of restaurants. Therefore, this chapter will focus on those of hotels. Large hotels have electricians, carpenters, formative repair specialists, and many others on staff. Smaller properties must rely more on general maintenance and repair crews. As staff specialization decreases, outside help may be required to help maintain the building and equipment, especially as properties use more sophisticated computerized equipment.

Although some people use the terms *engineering* and *maintenance* almost interchangeably, in the hospitality industry (and in this chapter), engineering technically involves the operation of the systems and equipment necessary to provide the building support services. Maintenance is the servicing of equipment and systems.

The Changing Nature of Engineering

Traditionally, engineering's main goal was to minimize equipment maintenance and repair expenses. While this task was never easy, equipment was less complex than it is today, so the overall cost of operating this division was not high. Guests also expected less. Now-common Jacuzzis, saunas, and other amenities did not appear before the early 1970s. As guest demands for higher levels of comfort and service have increased, the knowledge, skills, and abilities of the engineering staff have had to increase accordingly.

The job of the engineering division can no longer be taken for granted. The systems and equipment that it operates are expensive to purchase and to maintain. Energy costs are also affected by the way the division is operated. Most importantly, the division has a direct impact on how guests react to the lodging and dining facilities.

The engineering division is an integral part of the entire property and participates in all property management functions with full knowledge of the operation and its goals. Engineering should be thought of as a staff division: a specialized and technical advisory team providing managers with useful advice and assistance in areas such as energy management, equipment operation and repair, and guest comfort.

The Engineering Division as a Savings Center

The engineering division has traditionally been seen as a cost center. That is, instead of generating revenues as the rooms or the food and beverage divisions do, engineering merely costs money. It is really more appropriate to see the division as a cost savings center. Efficient management principles and energy management procedures in this division can save money and increase the property's profit.

Consequently, the chief engineer should understand basic management principles. The average hotel incurs operating, maintenance, and energy costs equal to about 40 percent of its **undistributed operating expenses**. Managers can reduce approximately 15 to 30 percent of this cost with good management procedures. Top-level managers in the property need to recognize the important role that the engineering division plays in attaining the property's economic goals and other objectives. Suggesting that the division merely keeps the equipment going and delays the need for capital expenditures ignores this division's ability to increase profit significantly.

While top management needs to recognize that the engineering division can help save money, the engineering division should try to demonstrate this ability whenever possible. For example, when the engineering division proposes improvements that cost money, the most effective way to approach management is not to focus on how much the equipment costs, but on how much the equipment will save. This approach concentrates on profit and puts the proposal in the same terms as those from revenue centers, such as the rooms or food and beverage divisions.

The Need for Effective Management

It is easy to argue that the chief engineer must be a technical specialist, considering the extensive knowledge needed to understand refrigeration, heating, ventilation, electrical, and mechanical control systems. In many areas, engineers who work with the equipment and systems must be licensed. Licensing requires training, experience, and completion of a battery of tests covering the highly technical information that the engineer must possess.

As noted previously, however, the chief engineer must be a good manager. In addition to possessing highly specialized technical skills, he or she must also know how to manage available resources—people, money, time, and so forth. Many top managers in the hospitality industry agree that chief engineers generally have better technical than managerial skills. Engineers who have problems on the job more often need help mastering general management techniques than specialized technical knowledge. Some of these techniques include managing time, setting priorities, developing budgets, keeping records, or effectively selecting, orienting, training, supervising, and managing staff.

General managers often assume that the engineer who can effectively repair and maintain equipment and make decisions about new high-technology systems can also manage people, time, money, and procedures. However, effective supervisory skills and knowledge of basic management principles should never be taken for granted. Top management must ensure that all members of the engineering staff are being provided with the information necessary to succeed in their jobs.

A good chief engineer can effectively perform all required job tasks. Exhibit 1, a sample job description for a chief engineer, provides examples of commonly required tasks.

The Work of the Engineering Division

The engineering division performs work in several areas: electrical; plumbing; heating, ventilation, and air conditioning (HVAC); refrigeration; life safety; general maintenance and repair; preventive maintenance; renovation; and water management. The property's own engineering staff concerns itself primarily with maintenance in each of these areas. Local building codes and/or lack of time or personnel in the engineering division may dictate that outside contractors must handle large installations, changeovers, or new construction. The use of contractors is often dictated by applicable codes and by the fact that the engineering staff frequently has insufficient time and personnel to handle such work while attending to regular repair and maintenance.

Electrical Systems

Hospitality operations use a tremendous amount of electrical equipment, and electrical repair takes the engineering division to every corner of the building. An elaborate electrical system with its many circuits requires hundreds of fuses and/or circuit breakers. Should a fuse continue to burn out or a circuit breaker continue to trip, the short circuit must be located and repaired. All electrical fixtures, outlets, and switches must be kept in good working order. Maintaining and servicing a *modern* electrical system is very complicated, but consider the woes of an engineer whose property may be fifty to one hundred years old who must contend with obsolete equipment and wiring. Engineering personnel also handle display lighting, spotlights, movie projectors, and appliances for sales meetings or conventions.

Today, most properties buy electrical power from public utilities. However, many properties have an emergency generator ready in case the regular source

Exhibit 1   Job Description for a Chief Engineer

Job Title ___Chief Engineer_____   Date _____

Basic Function:

Performs, manages, or supervises maintenance operations for exterior and interior facilities including electrical, refrigeration, plumbing, heating, cooling, structural, groundcare, parking areas, and other maintenance work necessary to maintain the property in an optimum and efficient condition. Also, ensures the safety and comfort of the guests and employees.

Responsibilities:

1. Maintain all distribution systems for electricity, water, steam, gas, etc.
2. Maintain and operate air conditioning, heating, ventilation, and refrigeration systems.
3. Maintain buildings and grounds.
4. Monitor and coordinate the services performed by outside contractors in accordance with all contracts, leases, service agreements, and warranties.
5. Keep all records pertaining to heat, light and power, and costs of the facility.
6. Ensure timely response to requests for services by guests, employees, and management to include repair or replacement of all interior fixtures and furnishings.
7. Schedule all work to be done on a daily basis at a minimum of inconvenience to guests and employees.
8. Plan, implement, and administer an effective preventive maintenance program in accordance with good engineering practices.
9. Plan, implement, and administer an energy management program.
   - Maintain appropriate equipment operating logs.
   - Maintain utility consumption records.
   - Educate other operating departments in energy management.
   - Establish annual energy reduction objectives.
   - Analyze and modify operation of the physical plant to conserve energy.
10. Assist in the preparation of capital expenditures and maintenance budgets.
    - Select vendors and contractors that meet quality standards and pricing specifications.
    - Initiate purchase orders.
    - Approve invoices.
    - Maintain adequate inventory of parts, tools, and supplies.
    - Maintain purchasing records.
11. Train and supervise subordinates and assist in safety and emergency training for other employees.
12. Conduct continuing inspection of buildings and grounds to ensure compliance with OSHA, fire and safety laws.
13. Recommend and/or take action to ensure compliance.
14. Maintain a clean and orderly work area free of hazards.
15. Perform other duties as assigned.

Supervision Exercised:

Assistant chief engineer, carpenters, electricians, grounds maintenance, lock and key maintenance, painters, plumbers, refrigeration mechanics, and sound technicians.

Supervision Received:

General Manager

Exhibit 1   *(continued)*

Minimum Requirements:

- Education: high school or equivalent.

- Mechanical or equivalent training in the following: refrigeration, boilers, plumbing, air conditioning, power or building construction. Higher education or experience of such kind and amount as to provide a comparable background required.

Experience:

Five years in any combination of mechanical trades with hotels/motels, hospitals, high-rise apartments, or similar duties with the armed services. Must have license where required or qualifications to become licensed. Knowledge of carpentry and painting required.

Other:

1. Applicant should possess the following traits:
   - Effective communication skills
   - Administrative abilities
   - Good personal relations skills
   - Self-motivation
   - Mechanical aptitude
2. Applicant must be willing to relocate when and where directed.

---

fails. A few hotels generate their own power, but this requires added staff and equipment.

Plumbing Systems

Maintaining a plumbing system, especially that of a hotel or institution, is no small job. With a bathroom in every guestroom and elaborate restaurant kitchen equipment, a good-sized hotel often has a larger plumbing system than many American communities. In addition to the circulating hot water system, hotels have a separate and complete cold water system. A guest without either hot or cold water wastes no time making this fact known, and engineers must remedy the situation immediately. Faucet washers are bound to wear out, and many hours are spent replacing them. Drains can become stopped in the course of everyday use, or guests may discard objects that plug up sinks or bathtubs. On upper floors, plugged drains may cause flooding. Even minor flooding can cause extensive damage.

The engineering division also frequently receives calls about toilets. Basic tools can generally be used to resolve problems, but, in serious cases, the toilet may have to be removed to let the plumber locate the source of difficulty. Water-closet valves must be frequently checked and kept in good working order to avoid noises.

Some plumbing work can be rather messy. One example is cleaning the kitchen grease traps and the basement grease line. Chemicals can help keep these lines open, but, occasionally, cleaning must still be done manually. An additional problem for hotel engineers is the fact that the original plumbing in most hotels probably was not intended for all the use it now gets. Properties can modernize systems gradually, but few properties can undertake such a job in a short period of time.

HVAC Systems

In many parts of the world, the engineering staff must keep the property heated for a good part of the year. In the winter, this means simply maintaining a comfortable, even temperature. During spring and fall, however, it is desirable to take off the chill without overheating the building—no small task if the heat is manually controlled.

Hot water heating systems are still used in some properties, but steam systems are more common. While many properties purchase their steam from public utilities, others operate their own boilers. Coal-stoked boilers are dirty. Gas or oil burners are clean, but they require additional employees. Buying steam reduces the number of employees required to maintain the boilers, but even hotels that buy steam usually maintain standby boilers. As a result, the engineering crew must have the technical knowledge and skill to handle them. Both the kitchen and the valet service require high-pressure steam, which is usually provided by a separate boiler.

Maintaining a heating plant requires highly technical knowledge. Burners must be maintained and repaired, thermostats must be kept in good working order, radiators and valves need attention. New types of controls are being developed that will bring heating closer to an automatic operation, but the automated repair and maintenance engineer just does not exist and probably never will.

Another responsibility of the engineering division is the ventilation and air conditioning system. Regular changes of air are required, and it takes machinery to provide this. The public today demands air conditioning in all first-class hospitality operations. A central system provides a central point for maintenance and repair. Air conditioners in each guestroom greatly increase work.

Refrigeration Systems

Every food service operation requires refrigeration equipment. Large **walk-ins**, reach-ins, and other types of refrigerators and freezers must operate twenty-four hours a day. The failure of a reach-in refrigerator may not be too serious if detected reasonably soon, since the unit's contents can be transferred. Even if the contents of a reach-in were to spoil, it would not involve a major sum of money. The failure of a well-stocked walk-in, however, would be a different story, since spoilage here would mean a major loss. Preventing such failures requires continual maintenance by the engineering division.

Life Safety Systems

Guest and employee safety is a major concern of all hospitality businesses. Fire and building codes are very stringent and have led to complex and complete life safety systems. These systems include sprinkler systems, smoke detectors, general fire alarms, an annunciator communication system, special systems for the kitchen area, pull alarms, and individual fire extinguishers. (This listing is representative only.) Modern systems have a centrally located map board of the property that immediately reveals the location of the fire when an alarm is triggered. The hotel alarm system is usually linked to the local fire station, which can save precious minutes when answering an alarm.

These systems must be maintained, kept in perfect working order, and tested on a regular basis. Most of this responsibility rests on the shoulders of the engineering division.

General Maintenance and Repair

When it becomes necessary to break through walls to make plumbing or electrical repairs, engineers make the subsequent repairs. The engineers also handle small welding jobs and maintain door hinges and locks. Engineering staff may also be involved in a wide range of miscellaneous tasks such as replacing windows, painting, installing carpet, and so forth. An outside firm is usually contracted for the maintenance, repair, and inspection of major equipment such as elevators.

Preventive Maintenance

A quick look at the history of the hospitality industry reveals that thousands of restaurants and hotels have gone out of business unnecessarily because of deferred maintenance. Whenever the budget got a little tight, management deferred equipment maintenance for a year or so. Unfortunately, maintenance was deferred so often that sales, occupancy, and profits diminished, and then there was not sufficient money to bring the building and equipment back to a satisfactory state. Deferred maintenance had taken its toll. The old saying, "Never put off until tomorrow what should be done today," certainly applies to the engineering division. Progressive ownership and management stress **preventive maintenance**, which is the perfect antidote to the poisonous deferred maintenance.

A preventive maintenance program offers a systematic approach to equipment operation. Every item of equipment receives scheduled attention to make sure that it is operating efficiently and to reduce downtime for emergency repairs or service.

Most hotels buy equipment with warranties that cover most or all of the equipment's expected lifetime. Unfortunately, some properties treat the warranty as sufficient insurance against equipment breakdowns. The property simply installs the equipment, puts it into operation, and forgets about it. This is a poor management practice. Even when equipment continues to operate, there is constant deterioration and decline in its efficiency resulting from normal wear and tear, age, and accumulation of dirt and debris. This eventually causes costly service calls—usually emergencies—and a loss of revenue.

A good preventive maintenance program provides many benefits to a property. Not only will the equipment last longer (bringing a better return on investment), but it will use less energy. Service calls and their costs will diminish, and inventory levels for spare parts will be reduced. Furthermore, overall property operation will be enhanced, since service breakdowns can be largely eliminated. Equipment that is beginning to fail (as all equipment will do eventually) can be repaired or replaced before breakdowns interrupt the normal operation of the property.

Procedures. A preventive maintenance program is really a catalog of manufacturers' recommendations regarding the maintenance of all the property's equipment and systems. The engineering division develops a program by first identifying all property equipment requiring periodic checking and/or maintenance. Once this equipment has been identified, a schedule of routine inspections and maintenance activities can be established based on the equipment manufacturers' recommendations for proper maintenance. The inspection schedule will also list activities to be performed during the inspection. Exhibit 2 illustrates a **preventive maintenance schedule** that can help schedule inspections. These schedules can be simple or detailed, depending upon the property and equipment.

Supervision. The maintenance program must be supervised by responsible individuals. All staff must be familiar with the inspection and maintenance activities schedule and know who is responsible for the duties it requires. Maintenance shifts, for example, can be responsible for checking certain areas of the property. It is also possible to divide the property into areas or sectors for which individual engineering personnel are responsible. Under this system, personnel in any given

Exhibit 2 Preventive Maintenance Schedule

PREVENTIVE MAINTENANCE SCHEDULE

Description of Work	No. Items	Month																				
		Week	1	2	3	4	1	2	3	4	1	2	3	4	1	2	3	4	1	2	3	4

Section/Person Responsible: ____________ Signature (When Completed): ____________

Source: *Energy Maintenance Manual: Volume II* (San Antonio, Texas: Technical Services Center and The Hospitality, Lodging & Travel Research Foundation, Inc., undated), p. A5.

department are responsible for checking their own equipment and reporting any problems to the engineering staff. The benefit of this procedure is that it keeps the established in-house engineering staff at a minimum number. The main disadvantage is that it adds to the responsibility of various department and division heads.

How does management control the activities of assigned engineering staff? The answer to this question provides the key to a successful maintenance program. Managers need to ensure that activities are taking place when required. In addition, checks must ensure that repairs have been performed. **Work orders** (see Exhibit 3) sent to the engineering staff from other departments can be an excellent control mechanism if they are filed after the required work has been completed. A review of completed work orders will reveal what was required for various units of equipment, what was performed, and when it was completed.

Another valuable checking aid is a file containing an information card for each piece of equipment. Completed inspections, maintenance activities, and repairs can be noted on the cards and signed and dated by the person performing them. Other variations of this system could be developed. The system should remain as simple as possible while retaining data required for future reference.

Exhibit 3   Work Order

WORK ORDER   No. _____

Requested Service: _____

_____

Person Requesting: _____

Nature of Problem: _____

_____

_____

_____

_____

Work Performed: _____

_____

_____

_____

Person Completing Work: _____

Date Performed: _____

Maint. Supervisor Signature: _____

Source: *Energy Maintenance Manual: Volume II* (San Antonio, Texas: Technical Services Center and The Hospitality, Lodging & Travel Research Foundation, Inc., undated), p. A7.

Renovation

A restaurant changes its theme or modernizes its food production equipment and space more frequently than a hotel. This is because it costs far less to overhaul a restaurant than to renovate an entire hotel, especially a luxury property.

As long as **renovation** is cheaper than the cost of demolition and new construction, hotels will continue to renovate. All hotel brands require owner-managed and franchised properties to periodically update their facilities along mandated guidelines (commonly referred to as property improvement plans). Some of this renovation work can be performed by the hotel's engineering staff, but most often it requires the work of outside contractors, architects, and planners. Most hotels earmark 3 to 7 percent of budgeted sales for capital improvements, including renovations. This figure will vary by the life of the hotel and brand requirements. Sometimes, age and competitive circumstances dictate significant overhauls. On occasion, major hotels and resorts have even closed operations to perform this work. Barron Hilton referred to such major renovations on Hilton's classic hotels as "polishing our Picassos." A world-class resort property, The Breakers, underwent a major capital improvement program, far exceeding normal costs per budgeted sales, to address the loss of a coveted *Mobil Travel Guide* star. Within a matter of years, The Breakers regained its prestigious fifth star.

When hotels change ownership, as they commonly do, renovation almost always is a significant factor. Hotel brands see ownership change as golden opportunities to mandate refurbishing. It is common to see multimillion-dollar expenses factored into hotel ownership changes. New owners invariably see purchase price plus renovation cost as well below replacement costs for these hotels.

Water Management

Hotels and restaurants cannot operate without a clean, plentiful supply of water for drinking, cleaning, sanitizing, cooking, cooling, and fire sprinkling systems. In hotels, water is also needed for bathing and often for swimming.

Hotels and restaurants need two kinds of water systems: a **potable water** system, which brings water suitable for drinking into the property, and a sewer system, which channels wastewater away from the property. Purchasing and installing water and wastewater systems constitute 5 to 12 percent of the total building costs of a new hotel. Water and wastewater systems account for 5 to 15 percent of total energy expenses once the hotel is built.

Most properties purchase potable water from a local utility, but occasionally a hotel has its own water supply. Properties that provide their own water must carefully treat it to maintain state and federally mandated drinking water standards. However, even properties that buy water from local utilities may need to treat water further.

The cleanliness, quantity, and appearance of a property's water supply not only affect guest satisfaction, but the staff's ability to perform their duties. The engineering department must evaluate water for:

- Hardness—Guests may complain about hard water that prevents soap from lathering. Hard water will also make cleaning duties for housekeeping and kitchen staff more difficult. Hard water can be softened with chemicals that are safe to drink.

- Taste/odor—Water that smells or tastes bad may be completely safe to drink, but it may be difficult to convince guests of that fact. Such water can also affect the taste of coffee and tea. Properties can treat their water supply to eliminate undesirable odors and tastes.

- Color—Minerals in the water can stain linens and porcelain. Again, water can be treated to eliminate these problems.

- Turbidity—Turbid water appears cloudy because it contains a large number of solid particles. In addition to looking unappetizing to guests, turbid water may also clog pipes and machinery. Water filters can correct this problem.

- Corrosion—Water with high acidity can corrode pipes and other equipment. Corrosion leads to extra maintenance and repair. Water treatment can help reduce acidity and thereby prevent corrosion.

Water pressure also concerns the engineering department. Generally, a water main will provide enough pressure for a four- to six-story building. However, high-rise properties often need pumps to provide additional water pressure.

Until recently, in most areas of the United States water shortages appeared only when a severe drought occurred. The availability and cost of water were not major concerns in hospitality operations except in very remote areas. However, this is changing as the production of clean water becomes more difficult and expensive both at home and abroad. On the island of Aruba, for example, where fresh water is produced through desalination plants, the cost of water for hotels equals that of energy.

In the years ahead, certain concerns about water will become more and more important to hospitality industry engineers and managers. These concerns include water potability, rising costs and shortages of water, and hot water use.

Potability. Pollutants such as herbicides, insecticides, fertilizers, household wastes, industrial wastes, and urban runoff (rubber, salt, gas, and oil deposits washed from city roads) pose threats to the **potability** of the water supply. Hotels and restaurants must be vigilant about protecting their water supplies. Moreover, state and federal regulations designed to curb pollution may dictate how and in what amounts hotels and restaurants can dispose of certain kinds of wastes.

Rising Water Costs and Shortages. Potable water costs can vary widely. A recent study of fourteen countries found that the average cost per 1,000 gallons in the United States was $2.50 (or $0.66 per cubic meter), while the cost in both Germany and Denmark averaged $8.51 per 1,000 gallons ($2.25 per cubic meter).[1] Costs can climb significantly higher in regions where water is scarce and where desalination is required. Sewer rates often equal or exceed the water rates. While the average property uses about 218 gallons of water per occupied guestroom per day, actual use varies considerably from property to property. An American Hotel & Lodging Association study showed that water use is lower at smaller properties without food service and higher at large convention and resort properties with pools and restaurant operations.

Whatever its use level, however, virtually every property wastes a certain portion of its water supply. Preventive maintenance and other conservation measures can eliminate much water waste, saving the property more and more money as water and sewer rates increase. For example, a one-sixteenth-inch leak in a toilet wastes enough water in one month to supply a single-occupancy guestroom for 220 nights. Water can be conserved in kitchen areas by cutting the amount of water used for washing, thawing, and cooling. Tunnel washers in laundries can recycle water from some rinse cycles. Showerheads that restrict water flow prevent guests from wasting hot water. Irrigation—watering lawns and shrubs—consumes 25 to 30 percent of a hotel's water supply. This amount can be reduced by watering plants every two or three days instead of every day, a schedule that not only saves water but promotes better plant growth. Other properties are using **gray water** (treated sewer and laundry rinse water, for example) for irrigation or other non-drinking purposes.

Hot Water Use. Wasted hot water not only depletes water resources, but the energy used to heat the water as well. In many U.S. properties, heating water consumes more energy than any other function. The cost of heating the water may be four to twenty times the cost of the water itself.

Some properties are using the latest conservation technology to save on water heating costs. Heat rejected by refrigerators and freezers, for example, can be captured and used to help heat water. Some washers can use hot waste water from one laundry cycle to heat the water for the next cycle. And some hotels have turned to solar technology to help heat water.

Increasingly, hotels are encouraging guests who stay for more than one night to become more "green sensitive" by limiting the frequency of cleaning bed linens and bathroom towels. It was once standard to receive all new linens and towels on a daily basis, but now it is up to guests to indicate when they want these changes. The result has been a big reduction in hot water and detergent usage as well as longer life for linen and terrycloth goods.

Energy Management

Energy management is a fairly new responsibility of the engineering division and deserves some detailed attention here. In the past, energy in the United States was readily available and relatively inexpensive. The United States has 6 percent of the world's population. However, before 1973, it consumed approximately 36 percent of the world's energy resources. The hospitality industry, of course, was not immune to the false sense of security created by a seemingly endless supply of energy resources. In 1977, the average energy consumption of hotels in the United States was 29 percent greater than it was by 1982.[2] The dramatic reduction in consumption illustrates how energy-wasteful the operating and management philosophies had been for many properties. Although many operations have made great strides in energy management, many of the easy steps have been accomplished, and further gains must be achieved through more difficult processes.

Energy Problems

Energy problems in the hospitality industry are multi-faceted, but the causes essentially break down into the following categories:

- Lack of awareness
- Inadequate maintenance or personnel
- Poor design
- Little or no tracking of energy consumption
- Attitude problems

Lack of Awareness. There are numerous properties where energy-saving measures have been implemented to no avail. The problem is that managers do not understand how a property consumes energy. Wise professionals perform energy audits to determine how a property really uses energy and, thus, how to conserve it.

Inadequate Maintenance or Personnel. Preventive maintenance programs in the hospitality industry were almost unheard of in the early 1970s. Since the energy crisis, they have proliferated, but many managers still do not recognize them as tools for savings. Consequently, not enough staff is hired to carry out preventive maintenance programs.

In many cases, unqualified personnel in the engineering divisions of the hospitality industry have been both the cause and the result of many of the problems. In many properties, janitors perform maintenance functions—even though it is hard to believe that several million dollars would be invested in the construction of a property and people would be hired at minimum wage to maintain it. The obvious result is inadequate maintenance, inoperative equipment, disconnected controls, and numerous leaks.

Poor Design. In the past, property designers were basically unconcerned with energy consumption because it was not a big factor in operations. Today, many people feel that energy consumption is still not a high priority in the development of a property, so poor design frequently continues. There is a common belief that an energy-efficient building must cost more to build. This is a myth. Companies today such as Hilton Hotels make energy evaluations on new construction and major renovations. This has resulted in energy consumption reductions of at least 25 percent for new properties.

Little or No Tracking of Energy Consumption. In the past, properties often did a poor job of tracking energy costs—and still do today in some cases. These costs merely appear on the monthly financial statement as a group of bills that were paid that month with little correlation to the property's operation. If energy is managed properly, consumption is accurately tracked and identified. Property managers must realize that utility bills do not necessarily cover the same operating periods and that some effort must be made to match energy use and cost.

Attitude Problems. Several—or perhaps most—of the factors that have contributed to energy problems in the hospitality industry can be traced to attitude problems. Consider, for example, staff who are not concerned about energy management problems and do not want to develop operating, maintenance, and design systems to reduce energy usage. Or how about the manager who believes that energy consumption cannot be reduced and is relatively unimportant anyway, since the costs are passed on to guests? Some management staff express concern, but place a relatively low priority on energy management in the belief that "we'll get around to it someday." As a final example, consider the often-expressed thought that only pennies can be saved unless major capital investments are made. In fact, this is usually not true, but a bad attitude can make it seem true.

Energy Management Programs

The hospitality industry has made great progress in developing comprehensive programs to help reduce energy consumption. It understands the following benefits of good energy management practices:

- Education—Local utility companies can offer information to pass along to employees and guests about ways to conserve energy and water. Furthermore, as today's guests continue to show more and more interest in "green" (ecologically designed and driven) practices, many are beginning to base their travel purchase decisions in part on what a potential lodging provider is doing to promote conservation and environmental sustainability. Sharing such information with guests can increase loyalty and repeat business.

- Reduced consumption—Effective maintenance, a prerequisite of a good energy management program, can reduce energy consumption by as much as 20 percent.

- Improved equipment performance—The equipment and the systems last longer and perform better.

- Increased guest satisfaction—Reducing energy costs through adequate maintenance can lead to increased guest satisfaction. The guest's comfort need not be sacrificed to save energy. On the contrary, an efficient, adequately maintained system is a better guarantee of guest comfort and satisfaction. How much revenue is lost, for example, when guests never return because a poorly maintained air conditioning system cannot meet their demands? Guest satisfaction may also rise when guests recognize and appreciate a hotel's green practices.

- More accurate forecasting—Energy management allows more accurate forecasting of energy and maintenance costs and minimizes emergency expenditures for unforeseen repairs.

Organizing an Energy Management Program. To coordinate and monitor the development of an ongoing energy management program, several basic steps must be followed. They are:

- Obtain top management commitment.
- Establish an energy coordinating committee.
- Establish an ongoing energy consumption tracking program.
- Summarize the current consumption data.
- Survey/audit the property.
- Determine energy management opportunities.

- Establish measurable goals.

- Establish operating procedures and policies for no- or low-cost energy management improvements.

- Consider building modifications and equipment-needs programs.

- Implement high-cost energy management improvements (but only after no- or low-cost improvements have been made).

- Modify and revise goals as necessary.

- Evaluate and continually monitor/improve the energy management program.

- Evaluate and install an appropriate energy management system (EMS).

Energy Management Systems. Computer and other electronic devices called **energy management systems** (EMS) have been developed to control peak power demand; regulate the heating, ventilating, and air conditioning throughout the building as needed; use photoelectric sensing to control lighting intensity; and, generally, control every aspect of energy usage in the operation. The EMS is a subsystem of the property management system.

A good example is guestroom HVAC control. Sensors located in guestrooms detect whether a room is occupied and adjust temperatures accordingly. Management can program default temperature settings—both minimum and maximum—to kick in while the guest is away from the room. When the guest returns, the temperature he or she had chosen is restored. Statistics indicate that a rented room is unoccupied 60 percent of the time, and an unsold room nearly all the time, so most energy is wasted heating and cooling an empty room. It is also a fact that a property's HVAC cost is second only to its payroll expense. Payback time to install this system runs from two to three years.

These systems are all technically very complex and require a knowledgeable and experienced staff to operate and maintain them. One seasoned hotel manager with no previous experience with an EMS said of the system after a few weeks: "It's great, I guess. The only problem I see is that I am convinced one needs a Ph.D. in physics to understand and operate it!" The point, of course, is that the EMS is only as good as the staff's ability to operate it, and managers should do some research and comparison shopping to make sure the system they choose is right for their staff. The complexity of energy management systems also underscores the need for better training and education of the engineering staff.

Energy Management Advancements. Successful hotels will always seek ways to reduce costs without reducing guest satisfaction. In periods of low or no growth in either room rate or occupancy, new savings on expenses often make the difference in attaining profitability goals. Energy costs equal about 6 percent of a typical hotel's revenue. This is a significant cost to tackle.

In the late 1990s, deregulation of gas and electric utilities in many states caused forward-thinking hotel companies to negotiate together, a practice that yielded a bulk discount. In 1999, Wyndham Hotels enjoyed an impressive 15 percent reduction in its gas expenses among hotels that were included in bulk purchase arrangements, according to its chief procurement officer, Jay Litt. He had seen savings in the purchase of electricity in bulk buy, though at a lower percentage than with gas, due to higher infrastructure costs. Still, he showed a six-percent drop in electricity expenses over the previous year.

Traditional energy cost savings programs that focus on employee awareness of energy waste will always prove beneficial. Such programs include reminding staff members to turn off lights when leaving rooms and to leave air conditioning at prescribed settings.

Recent Developments

All energy users have become acutely aware of rapidly escalating energy costs in recent years. Dwindling supplies of fossil fuels and rising demand from emerging economic giants like China and India promise to keep oil and natural gas prices high for the foreseeable future.

In light of these rising costs, some hotels have begun ambitious energy saving programs. Starwood Hotels and Resorts Worldwide outsourced energy management for all its North American properties to a subsidiary of a major energy corporation. The energy corporation supplies or buys electricity and natural gas, manages the energy infrastructure, and provides energy price stability. In addition, Starwood invested $50 million in programs and procedures designed to reduce energy costs. Savings are projected to be $20 million per year over the life of the contract. While the investment is not visible to the public, it provides compelling financial and environmental benefits.

Choice Hotels International has contracted with Chevron and Tharaldson Energy Group to perform services for its franchisees including installation of high-efficiency equipment; water conservation measures; power supply upgrades; and energy rate analysis. Tharaldson Energy Group, an energy-purchasing consortium developed by hospitality company Tharaldson Enterprises, negotiates cost-efficient energy supply contracts for franchisees in deregulated areas.

A particularly ambitious program is the thirty-six-kilowatt solar project constructed by Gaia Napa Valley Hotel and Spa. This clean, renewable energy source is projected to produce 12 percent of the hotel's total energy supply.

The Proximity Hotel in Greensboro, North Carolina, which opened in late 2007, dramatically shows how environmentally oriented new hotels can become. The hotel uses one hundred rooftop panels for energy; recycled 75 percent of its construction waste; and captures rainwater to irrigate gardens and grow vegetables on its roof. By using an air exchange unit, it uses about half the energy of a traditional hotel. These advancements helped the Proximity Hotel earn the second-ever gold rating from LEED.

New hotel construction since 2000 has steadily become more compliant with LEED guidelines. LEED (Leadership in Energy and Environmental Design) is the recognized benchmark for design, construction, and operation of high-performance green buildings. LEED promotes a five-step approach to sustainability including site development, water savings, energy efficiency, materials selection, and indoor environmental quality.

By 2007, more than one hundred LEED-certified hotels were open, in development, or under construction. These include properties under the brands of Marriott Renaissance, Hilton, Starwood, and Holiday Inn Express.

Many hotels and restaurants now seek out Energy Star–labeled commercial food service equipment guaranteed to save 10 to 30 percent in energy costs over other equipment. For example, typical gas burners run at approximately 35 percent efficiency. This means 65 percent of the energy is wasted, going directly into the exhaust hood. Lower BTU appliances coming onto the market with the Energy Star label are able to produce the same amount of food as their less-efficient, higher-BTU alternatives. As technology advances, it can be expected to create lower-cost Energy Star equipment, making it easier to justify the purchase of such equipment.

Energy-saver fluorescent bulbs for lamps are now commonly available, affording up to a 500-percent longer life span than incandescent bulbs. In a typical hotel guestroom, this can represent a reduction in watts from over four hundred to less than one hundred. Use of compact fluorescent lighting in hotel corridors and lobbies will enable hotels to further reduce wattage and energy costs.

Ozone systems installed in hotel laundries are becoming more common. The injection of ozone into the wash cycle reduces the temperature of the water needed to a lukewarm level, while also helping to sterilize the laundry. With this system, detergent use is greatly reduced. Jurys Doyle in Boston found the payback time on the system—installed for $45,000—to be sixteen months.

Another interesting energy-saving concept is a waste heat recovery system for dishwashers. The waste heat generated by the machine is reclaimed as free energy and then used to preheat incoming rinse water. The machine, thus, is able to use the cold water supply because heating is completely generated inside the machine. We can expect to see this process become common in new dishwashing systems in hotels and restaurants.

 ## Endnotes

1. Edwin H. Clark, II, "Water Prices Rising Worldwide," March 7, 2007. Earth Policy Institute. www.globalpolicy.org/socecon/gpg/2007/0307waterprices.htm.

2. Technical Services Center, "Annual Energy Use Surveys: 1977–1982" (San Antonio, Texas: American Hotel & Lodging Association Technical Services Center and The Hospitality, Lodging & Travel Research Foundation, Inc., 1982), p. ii.

 ## Key Terms

energy management system—A device, usually computer or microprocessor based, that is designed to be programmed on-site to control energy-consuming equipment and to reduce overall energy consumption.

gray water—Relatively clean wastewater, such as that produced from certain laundry cycles and effluent from wastewater treatment systems, that can be used to supply needs for landscape water and other non-potable uses.

potability—Suitability for drinking.

potable water—Water that is suitable for drinking.

preventive maintenance—Maintenance stressing inspections, lubrication, minor repairs or adjustments, and work order initiation. Generally performed using manufacturers' information as a guideline.

preventive maintenance schedule—A schedule for maintaining elements of the hotel building that are critical to guest satisfaction, overall property image and marketing, safety and security, and the performance of other departments' duties.

renovation—The process of renewing and updating a hospitality property to offset the ravages of use and modify spaces to meet the needs of changing markets.

undistributed operating expenses—Costs a property incurs as a whole; they are not assigned to any particular division or department.

walk-in—A large refrigerator or freezer used in high-volume kitchens for storage of perishable items.

work order—A document used to initiate requests for maintenance services.

 ## Review Questions

1. In what ways does the engineering and maintenance division deserve the title of unsung hero in hotels and restaurants?

2. How does the engineering department operate as a cost savings center?

3. What are the effects of deferred maintenance? What are the effects of preventive maintenance?

4. What are the possible reasons for the tremendous amount of renovation of hotels occurring in the 1980s and early 1990s?

5. What usual evaluations of water must the engineering division conduct?

6. What approaches could a hotel take to reduce water waste and realize savings in the process?

7. What are some of the advantages of an energy management program?

8. What is a hotel "green room" program?

9. What are the basic steps in a preventive maintenance program?

10. What four major areas of work is the engineering department involved in? Describe them.

 ## Internet Sites

For more information, visit the following Internet sites. Remember that Internet addresses can change without notice. If the site is no longer there, use a browser to look for additional sites.

Associations

American Culinary Federation
www.acfchefs.org

American Hotel & Lodging Association
www.ahla.com

American Hotel & Lodging Educational
  Institute
www.ahlei.org

Club Managers Association of America
www.cmaa.org

Commercial Food Equipment Service
  Association
www.cfesa.com

Educational Foundation of NRA
www.nraef.org

Hospitality Financial & Technology
  Professionals
www.hftp.org

Publications—Online and Printed

Food Channel
www.foodchannel.com

Foodservice and Hospitality
www.foodserviceworld.com/
foodservice-and-hospitality-mag.html

Lodging
www.lodgingmagazine.com

Nation's Restaurant News
www.nrn.com

Chapter 11 Outline

The Modern Marketing Emphasis
Product and Service Marketing: The Sale of
    Hospitality
Planning for Guest Needs
    The Feasibility Study
    Situation Analysis
The Marketing Planning Process
    Six Elements
The Organization of the Marketing and
    Sales Division
    Interdepartmental Relationships
    Bringing Business to the Property
Hotels and Airlines: Birds of a Feather
The Business of Selling
    Rooms Business
    Public Space
    Food and Beverage Business
    Internal Selling
    Personal Selling
Star and Other Rating Systems
Advertising, Special Promotions, and
    Public Relations
    Advertising
    Special Promotions
    Public Relations

Competencies

1. Define the terms marketing, market, market segment, market mix, and marketing strategy, and discuss the importance of marketing to hospitality businesses. (pp. 221–222)

2. Explain the function and identify the components of a feasibility study. (pp. 222–224)

3. Explain the function and identify the components of a situation analysis. (pp. 224–225)

4. Explain the function of a market plan and identify components of the marketing planning process. (pp. 225–226)

5. Identify the responsibilities of positions within a marketing and sales division. (pp. 226–232)

6. Describe the business of selling hospitality products and services, discuss the similarities between marketing hotels and airlines, differentiate between internal selling and personal selling, and describe the importance of stars and diamonds rating systems. (pp. 232–239)

7. Identify the advantages and disadvantages of major advertising media used by hospitality companies. (pp. 239–243)

8. Explain the purpose of special promotions, and differentiate between publicity and public relations. (pp. 243–245)

11

The Marketing and Sales Division

PEOPLE OFTEN THINK OF MARKETING as selling or advertising and public relations. But marketing involves many more activities than these. Marketing strives to produce the maximum profit through sales, advertising, public relations, promotions, merchandising, and pricing activities. Marketing brings buyers and sellers together. Put another way, marketing matches product with customers. A hotel or restaurant must accurately determine what types of customers are attracted to its location and features. The job of marketing should begin well before a new property opens; in fact, it should begin even before the hotel or restaurant is designed. This phase will be discussed in more detail later in this chapter.

Marketing also helps identify groups of current or potential guests by (1) geographic location, (2) industry, (3) economic status, or (4) behavioral characteristics. Marketers call these groups **markets**. Marketing also helps identify groups with common buying traits called **market segments**. Marketing activities can help reveal a property's **market mix**—that is, the various market segments it hopes to attract. In addition, marketing indicates the approaches and tools—the **marketing strategy**—that can be used to attract the market mix.

Another benefit of marketing is to help managers see their operations from the guest's perspective. For example, marketers may conduct feasibility studies and situation analyses to help them determine what guests want and need and how to provide it. Marketers also may help managers to make pricing decisions and develop competition strategies, activities critical to the success of today's hospitality operation.

The Modern Marketing Emphasis

During the early years of the twentieth century, companies in the United States marketed goods and services in mass quantities hoping to persuade consumers to buy them. Mass production allowed the companies to make products cheaply so that the average consumer could buy them. Consumers purchased these products as fast as companies could produce them. The job of marketing was simply to sell products.

During the hard times of the Great Depression, consumers could no longer afford to buy all the goods and services that companies produced. Companies were forced to produce only goods that consumers really wanted. As a result, marketing strategies became more consumer-oriented.

Today, most producers of goods and services use consumer-oriented marketing. Marketing activities determine what consumers want, and marketers then inform production so that goods and services meet those wants. Marketing also informs consumers—through selling, advertising, and promotion—that the goods and services are available.

Product and Service Marketing: The Sale of Hospitality

A hotel or restaurant sells products (rooms, food, and beverages) and services (hospitality). There are significant differences between marketing services and marketing products. A product can be demonstrated or shown, and thus guests can assess its value rather easily. Marketing service is more difficult because it is intangible. Every service provided must meet the expectations of the guests the property hopes to attract and satisfy. Otherwise, the guests will be either disappointed or overwhelmed. For example, a room escort might surprise and even embarrass guests in an economy hotel, and an extensive wine list might make visitors to a casual diner feel out of place. On the other hand, guests might feel cheated if a nightly turn-down service were omitted at a deluxe hotel or if they were greeted with a "Hey" at a formal restaurant.

When a property is marketed well, its image and position relative to the competition are so clear that the specifics of its service become an instantly recognizable, permanent signature. For example, what frequenter of resort hotels has not heard of the impeccable service of The Greenbrier? Similarly, who can think of The Waldorf Astoria and not think of the highest standards of service and the highest quality of food and drink? And, among conventioneers, what hotels conjure up more positive images as convention headquarters than the Sheraton Waikiki in Honolulu or the Gaylord Opryland Resort & Convention Center in Nashville?

Hospitality is not something a property presents to a guest on a plate or in a glass. It includes every aspect of the guest's stay and must meet or exceed the guest's expectations. Hospitality can be thought of as the property's personality. Developing that personality begins with the attitude of owners and managers and includes the hospitable service that all employees provide to guests.

Planning for Guest Needs

How does the marketing and sales division tackle the difficult job of selling hospitality to potential guests? The task begins with proper planning and continues through the delivery of products and services to guests. It also must consider how to draw potential markets to the property.

The Feasibility Study

The goods and services that potential guests want must be determined even before a property is built or purchased. A **feasibility study** analyzes a proposed site to determine what type of property has the best chance for success. The feasibility study ultimately determines whether investors should construct or purchase an operation. It concentrates on four areas: location, guest demographics, the competition, and financial analysis.

Location. Location is the most important element in the success of any property. A hotel may have great food and service, beautiful decor, a wonderful atmosphere, the newest guestrooms, and low prices. However, it can fail if it is poorly located. On the other hand, a poor-quality property may succeed *in the short run* if it is in a good location. Some of the criteria that determine whether or not a proposed site is in a good location include:

- Population of the surrounding area.
- Number of people living or working in the immediate area.
- Number of people within easy driving distance.
- Types of business in the immediate area.
- Availability and convenience of parking.
- Traffic flow patterns.
- Distance from exits off main highways.
- Location of air transportation.

The type of property envisioned must also be considered. Most hotel properties fit into one of three basic categories, though there is some overlap. These basic types are commercial hotels, convention hotels, and resort hotels. Each of these types must consider location in order to determine its appropriateness for the kinds of customers it hopes to attract. For example, a commercial hotel must know how many companies are located in reasonable proximity and determine how much business can be generated. A convention-oriented hotel must have easy access to a convention or trade center. Distance from a major airport is critical for a resort hotel.

Not all restaurants fit quite as easily into a few basic categories, but the same principles apply. In order to have the best chance of success, a restaurant owner must give careful consideration to the clientele he or she seeks to attract and then determine whether a particular location will make that possible.

Guest Demographics. Demographic studies identify such statistical characteristics as average age, sex, marital status, average number of children, average family income, and occupation of potential guests. Surveys can identify preferences of potential guests: What kind of dining do they like? What do they want in a guestroom? How much are they willing to pay for certain goods and services? Will they be using banquet/catering facilities? Marketers can conduct surveys via personal interviews, telephone interviews, or direct mail questionnaires.

After marketers obtain guest demographic and preference information, they decide what level of service and prices, type of food and beverage service, decor, and so forth best match potential guests.

Competition Analysis. To determine whether their own property will succeed, marketers must know how financially successful their competitors are and how well they are meeting the needs of their guests. This analysis should identify the strengths and weaknesses of each competitor, how long each competitor has operated at its current location, how busy each competitor is on various days of the week, and how current guests feel about each competitor.

After analyzing the competition, the investors can reasonably estimate the number of guests the new property can expect to attract. This figure is determined by adding the number of potential guests not currently satisfied by the competition and the number of potential guests who would patronize the new operation instead of competing facilities. The estimated number of expected guests becomes the basis for the financial analysis of the feasibility study.

Financial Analysis. Unless the property can make a profit, it should not be constructed or purchased. If the other parts of the feasibility study have been conducted properly, they will offer reliable data to help investors estimate expected revenues and expenses.

Situation Analysis

After a property opens, a **situation analysis** determines what guests like and dislike about the operation.[1]

Situation analysis gathers information about a property's current market position and promotion opportunities. Situation analysis does not rely on hunches, intuition, or lucky guesses. It requires thorough, careful research and analysis of five basic components: the product, the market, the competition, guest segmentation, and evaluation.

The Product. The product is the goods and services the property sells. Analysis of the product considers both physical and psychological factors. These may include the strengths and weaknesses of the property, the number of guestrooms, the property's image, and the atmosphere created by its furnishings. Current marketing efforts should be evaluated. These include the marketing objectives and how well the property accomplishes its goals.

The Market. The marketing and sales division should identify and analyze past and current guests to determine group and individual markets. Market analysis yields a picture of "what guests look like" and "what they think and do." Market analysis should be completed for the whole property and for each of its separate facilities.

The Competition. A property should also conduct product and market analyses of all competitors in the local area and in other cities and locations. What are the competitors' strengths and weaknesses? How does the competition differ from the property under study? How is it similar? Which of the differences will be significant to which markets?

Guest Segmentation. This portion of the situation analysis matches property needs with guest needs. First, marketers identify revenue centers that need to generate additional sales. The analysis should note guest preferences for physical facilities (for example, meeting rooms) and their desired level of luxury, convenience, security, and so forth. Once property and guest needs are determined, marketers can classify market segments and choose target markets to fulfill property needs. For example, if the hotel has a cocktail lounge, which guest segments will increase its early evening sales? Developing a position and a mission statement will define the property's place in the market and its marketing objectives.

Evaluation. Situation analysis is not a onetime activity but an ongoing process that monitors the property's success in the marketplace. Updating the market plan allows staff to compare objectives with actual results so that new strategies can be developed. Research should constantly monitor changes in the market and the environment and develop plans to help the property maintain a competitive edge.

Guest surveys and comment cards help managers understand what guests want and need. In turn, this helps the operation maintain long-term profitability. Individuals and groups can be surveyed at the time of room check-out, after they have eaten meals, or after they have attended banquets or other functions. These surveys attempt to find out how guests liked the food, service, cleanliness, price, and atmosphere. Guest comment cards are very similar to guest surveys. The property places these tent-shaped cards on dining room tables or in guestrooms. Guests can then rate various aspects of the property. The back of guest checks in a restaurant or lounge can also be used for guest comments.

The Marketing Planning Process

The completed situation analysis tells the marketing and sales division what it sells, what business it currently attracts, and who its competitors are. Its target markets have been defined. The situation analysis thus paves the way for the market plan. The market plan identifies both short- and long-term approaches to attracting and retaining guests.

Marketing planning is not just for large properties with marketing and sales divisions. In fact, it is even more vital for a small property to have a written market plan. Jobs are often more generalized in smaller properties. It is therefore easy for employees to overlook marketing activities in favor of other duties. In small properties, managers can get distracted from sales goals and spend far less time on marketing and sales than they intend. A written market plan helps prevent staff from neglecting marketing functions.

Regardless of the size of a property, its market plan should be easy for owners and senior managers to understand. Key employees in every department or outlet of the property should contribute to the plan. This builds team spirit, which is especially important if unpredicted major setbacks occur.

Six Elements

A good market plan helps marketing and sales division staff sell the right products and services to the right markets at the right time. The marketing planning process includes six basic elements:

1. A mission statement—The mission statement should clearly state what the property is and what markets it intends to serve.

2. A situation analysis—The situation analysis should compare the property to competitor properties based on rates, occupancy, etc., both historically and in projections for the coming year.

3. Comparative statistics—Actual business volume during the current year should be compared with projections for each month of the next year. Such

comparisons help properties plan business activities for the future. Hotels, for example, need statistics on occupancy rate, rooms volume, food and beverage volume, marketing overhead expenses, and, if possible, **gross operating profit**. The hotel should project its individual and group business for upcoming years. Managers can determine the status of bookings by comparing the amount of future business already on hand for a given date with the amount of business booked on the same date a year earlier. These statistics should lead to specific revenue and booking goals for each salesperson on staff.

4. Action plans—The property needs to produce a monthly plan for each market segment—group, social/recreational, business traveler, and the like. Each plan should include: assignment of accountability (assigning individual managers specific parts of the plan for which to be responsible), sales activities, target dates, and standards of measurements (criteria by which the success of the plan will be measured). Media for advertising can then be considered, and a marketing budget to guide expenses can be planned. A **key account** list can be compiled along with an action plan for attracting these key accounts during the upcoming year. Using this information, management can develop sales quotas for the year.

5. A calendar of promotional events—Managers should compile a calendar of the property's promotional events. The objectives of the promotion, the advertising media to be used, and any creative managerial recommendations should be noted for each event.

6. A catering plan—The catering plan should present the property's competitive positioning, pricing, menu selections, and a specific catering action plan with goals for bookings.

The Organization of the Marketing and Sales Division

The organization of the marketing and sales division depends on the property's needs and size. For example, independent restaurants need someone to handle marketing and sales activities. However, unlike restaurant chains and many hotels, they seldom have a separate marketing and sales division. Most of the examples in this chapter deal with hotel marketing and sales functions, which are often more detailed than those in restaurants. Nevertheless, many of the concepts presented here apply to all types of hospitality operations.

Exhibit 1 shows one possible organization of a marketing and sales division in a large hotel. As the exhibit shows, the director of the marketing and sales division reports to the general manager. The division director supervises four separate departments headed by the following managers:

- Director of Sales—The director of sales heads the sales department. He or she supervises sales managers (increasingly called account executives) and clerical staff. This department generates group business from conventions and meetings of associations and corporations and from tour/travel companies. After the sales department books group business, the convention services department generally handles further contact with the group. This includes

Exhibit 1 Sample Organization Chart of a Marketing and Sales Division in a Large Hotel

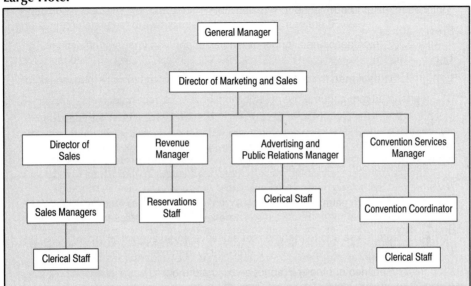

making arrangements for food and beverage services or guestrooms. When groups do not require food and beverage services or meeting rooms, the director of sales must work with other divisions, such as the front office, to coordinate service to the groups.

- Revenue Manager—This manager is responsible for implementing the property's ever-changing revenue strategy. The revenue manager compares booking patterns to historic trends in order to determine the prices the property will offer to various markets as given dates approach. For example, if booking is running lighter than usual, prices might be lowered. This manager typically oversees the onsite staff handling reservations and is the property's chief liaison with chain reservations and outside booking sources such as Internet wholesalers and third-party reservation organizations. The revenue manager works closely with the director of sales to ensure that group bookings comply with established selling strategies.

- Advertising and Public Relations Manager—This manager oversees the advertising and public relations department(s). He or she develops the advertising budget, determines which media offer the most effective outlets for the property's advertising efforts, and develops advertising messages or works with the hotel's advertising agency. This manager also develops and carries out short- and long-range plans so that guests and the general public receive a positive and consistent image of the property through brochures and fliers. Increasingly, these functions are handled by the director of marketing, frequently in conjunction with outside agencies specializing in advertising or public relations.

Insider Insights

Steven Jones
Senior Revenue Manager
Marriott Hotels and Resorts
Orange County, California

Hotel revenue management can be summed up as trying to maximize the revenues of a hotel. When the concept first came along, it was exclusively used for guestrooms. As we have continued to learn new tools and techniques, it has been applied to more areas of the industry. The result is that we now have total hotel revenue management, which seeks to maximize the combination of guestrooms and meeting spaces.

The major hotel companies use advanced mathematical algorithms to help revenue managers make their decisions. These new tools can save an immense amount of time. For example, revenue managers now have data analysis tools that allow them to look at demand over many years and to track rate shops across multiple platforms, as well as pricing optimizers that provide a rate recommendation and forecasts that look further into the future than ever before. Nevertheless, even though the computer programs continue to get smarter, revenue managers must keep the human element involved. Just because a program forecasts something doesn't mean that it can be trusted 100 percent of the time.

As the hotel shopper has become more Internet-savvy and cost-conscious, hotel booking trends have changed. One part of this is the emergence of third-party online sites such as Expedia.com and Travelocity.com, which allow guests to examine multiple hotels at the same time. Another key development has been the introduction of opaque bidding sites such as Priceline.com and Hotwire.com, which give guests access to low rates that can severely reduce a hotel's average daily rate. These online options have changed the loyalties of many guests, forcing hotels to adapt. One consequence has been the further expansion of hotel brands, with each brand designed to target certain guests.

Revenue managers need to remember that no single rule applies to every situation. Instead, it is essential to look at all of the characteristics of a market. For example, one important consideration is whether the travelers who visit that market are corporate travelers, leisure travelers, or wholesalers. A market such as Denver is primarily a corporate destination, which gives a good basis for setting price points. However, a market like Anaheim, California, which has a tourist destination in Disneyland, but is also in the heart of Orange County, has all three types of travelers. This makes it necessary to look at different price points during different seasons and even on weekdays versus weekends. If there is a large convention center in either of these cities, that adds another factor that must be taken into account. Finally, some markets mostly have brand hotels, but others (such as Anaheim) have quite a few independent hotels as well. Since independent hotels tend to generate more business from the third-party sites, Anaheim's brand hotels need to place more emphasis on competing with them.

Overall, revenue management continues to advance each year. Revenue managers who don't learn and use these new tools will be left behind. And in the business world, the person who is left behind is out of a job.

- Convention Services Manager—This manager, head of the convention services department, coordinates meeting rooms needed for group business sold by the sales department. Frequently, this department handles all contacts with the new account after the sale. Sometimes the convention services director handles only the setup for the meeting. When the meeting requires food and beverage service, this department must work closely with the food and beverage division.

Interdepartmental Relationships

The marketing and sales division's primary mission is to sell the property's products and services. As a result, its staff must work closely with many other departments and divisions within the operation. The following examples help illustrate the close working relationship between the marketing and sales division and other divisions:

- Suppose the sales staff sells a group meeting that requires food and beverage services. In a large property, the sales department may turn over final arrangements for the group to the convention services department. Convention services would then coordinate the group's arrangements with catering and other departments.
- The sales department may sell a group meeting that requires guestrooms. In this instance, sales staff would work closely with the front office or reservations manager to make sure enough rooms would be available.
- Suppose the catering sales manager sells food and beverage events to a group that does not require any other property services. (This may be for a wedding reception, social party, anniversary party, or the like.) While some out-of-town guests may stay at the property overnight, the food and beverage division generates the primary sales revenue. Before the catered event can be booked, marketing and sales must check with the colleague in charge of scheduling meeting rooms. If a specific room has already been scheduled, it obviously will not be free for catered functions.

Making a guest's special event truly special depends on good planning, which happens only if the marketing and sales division effectively communicates the guest's needs to other departments.

Bringing Business to the Property

Besides working closely with divisions within the property, marketing and sales staff must maintain close ties with outside businesses that can bring guests to the property.

In addition, there are a number of methods by which guests can be brought to the hotel. The marketing and sales division plays an important role, directly or indirectly, in these methods. Some ways guests can be brought to the hotel are outlined in Exhibit 2 and discussed in the following sections.

Personal Contact. Guests may come to the hotel through direct personal contact. Perhaps the guest wants to stay at a certain chain-affiliated property. He or she can make

Exhibit 2   Bringing the Traveler to the Hotel

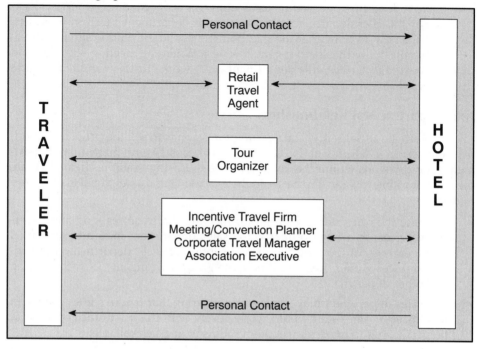

reservations by calling a toll-free reservation service. Guests can also make reservations by calling a local affiliated property. Reservations staff there will then reserve a room at any other property in the same chain. In either case, the marketing and sales division will play an important part in promoting these reservation services.

The explosive emergence of the Internet onto the commercial scene has offered brand-new ways for hotels to promote themselves. It is now virtually mandatory for hotels to have websites of their own or as subsets of chain websites. Many such sites can give virtual tours of a hotel's facilities and features as well as provide all of the copy and photos included in a traditional printed brochure. Requests for hard copy material can be made electronically, and many hotel websites can receive booking requests and can confirm reservations online. Online bookings from property, chain, and third-party websites represent an increasingly important and ever-growing segment.

The guest may also stop by chance at the property or make a reservation there on the recommendation of a friend or business associate. Word-of-mouth recommendations show that the hotel's marketing and sales division has done a good job promoting the property's image and that employees are aware of their own role in good public relations.

Advertisements on billboards, in airline magazines, and on radio and television may all influence a guest to check into a particular property. These advertisements are developed by the marketing and sales division, who choose the media most likely to reach the target markets.

The hotel may initiate contact with guests through sales blitzes, outside sales agents, and other types of personal selling coordinated by the marketing and sales division. In today's competitive economy, the use of outside sales calls is increasing, especially in areas where the number of hotels exceeds guest demands. If a hotel can persuade local businesses to encourage clients to stay there, its occupancy rates will improve significantly.

Companies and Associations. In developing accounts for their hotels, sales and marketing managers concentrate most of their attention on companies and professional or trade associations that have or may have occasion to book groups into their properties.

Sales managers carefully research the ranks of companies to determine which employee or department books hotels for individual reservations or group programs. In some large companies, a special department is responsible for travel planning.

Associations on a local, state, regional, and international level plan thousands of seminars, trade shows, and conventions annually. This is a very important business segment for most hotels, so their sales departments expend considerable time and effort cultivating good relations with these associations' travel staff and executives.

Travel Agents. Retail travel agencies can play a significant role in the booking of hotel business. Travel agents have seen that they can augment their traditional source of revenue (from airline commissions) by also selling hotel rooms to leisure and business customers. Many businesses have found that they can save travel expenses by booking through travel agencies. Both companies and individual travelers are discovering the convenience of booking air, hotel, and car rental reservations through one agency. Hotels now recognize the importance of having their sales departments solicit business and negotiate contracts directly with agencies and agency groups.

Travel agents learn about hotels through special directories that list facilities and rate information for hotels worldwide. Increasingly, this same information and the ability to book reservations is available to agencies through the computer reservation systems developed by the major airlines. Many large hotel companies have modified or newly created their own computer reservation systems to accommodate agencies.

Hotels cater to travel agencies by encouraging agency staff and principals to visit their properties on individual or group familiarization tours.

Other Third-Party Business Sources. Travel wholesale companies package destinations and many aspects of travel, including hotel stays, into tours that they display in brochures and sell to the general public through retail travel agencies. The role of the wholesaler is extremely influential in travel outside of the United States and to vacation destinations.

Many companies offer travel as an incentive to encourage their sales staff to make more sales. Travel wholesalers who specialize in incentive travel have emerged. They sell tailor-made travel programs to companies with large sales forces.

While most hotels have their own websites, more and more travelers today book their reservations through third-party Internet sources like Expedia.com, Travelocity.com, Orbitz.com, Hotels.com, and similar sites. Many travelers find such websites attractive because they allow travelers to book their flights, hotel rooms, and rental vehicles all in one place.

Hotels and Airlines: Birds of a Feather

Although it might not be immediately obvious, there are many similarities between the hotel and airline industries. Both offer products that are among the most fragile to be found anywhere. An unfilled seat on any flight, or an unoccupied hotel room on any night, cannot be stored in inventory and used later—they are gone forever.

The business traveler is a key market for the hotel and airline industries and the target of many marketing campaigns. Both industries have experienced the full brunt of the consolidation steamroller through acquisitions and mergers.

In the mid-1980s, several major U.S. airline carriers initiated frequent traveler programs designed to increase customer loyalty and attract new customers by offering rewards for a certain number of miles flown. The more miles flown, the richer the reward. Within two years, several major hotel companies introduced frequent traveler programs. Holiday Inn and Marriott created their own programs, while other companies joined existing airline programs. By 1988, most lodging firms had adopted some kind of frequent traveler program. The airline and hotel industries continue to feature many of these programs.

Next, the airline marketers devised the advance purchase discount practice in which the customer gets a significant discount on the regular fare by reserving and paying for the ticket at least fourteen days in advance. The ticket usually is nonrefundable and flights cannot be changed. Advance purchase discounts worked for the airlines, and hotels quickly took notice of this success. As a result, hotel companies have experimented with pricing strategies adopted from the airline procedures. At one point, there were high expectations that discounted, non-refundable advance purchase room rates would become commonplace in hotels. This has not occurred to any major degree except in some limited situations with leisure travelers.

A strategy borrowed from the airlines that has become much more prevalent in hotels is the concept of yield management, also called revenue management. In simplified terms, this concept means that rates and room availability are controlled to allow the best rate and occupancy for each night. When demand justifies, discounts will be eliminated, certain dates may be closed to arrival, and multiple night stays may be required. Likewise, when demand is low, yield management will ensure that discounts will be readily available to generate maximum occupancy. Computerized reservation systems are now in use in many hotels to facilitate effective yield management activity.

The Business of Selling

To many young people interested in hospitality employment, a career in sales appears glamorous and fun. That is indeed the case, but success in sales also

Insider Insights

Julie Dow
Director of Development Services
Dow Hotel Company
Seattle, Washington

The travel industry was one of the very first to embrace computers in the form of airline reservation systems. Today, those systems form the basis for the Global Distribution System (GDS). For the first forty years or so, only travel agents used the GDS to access hotel (as well as airline) inventory. Consumers and meeting planners booked using traditional telephone methods.

With the advent of the Internet, certain intermediaries were able to use the GDS to put hotel inventory "out there" directly for consumers to view. Then wholesalers, such as Hotels.com, entered the picture, offering steep discounts for volume. Then "opaque" vendors came into play, where the rate was published, but the hotel was not until after purchase. These three types of Internet distribution created a downward spiral in rates, and many unsuspecting hotels and brands lost significant market share by not keeping up with the trends. Ultimately, most of these providers either merged or adopted multiple distribution models.

The hotel brands were understandably frustrated by the rate drop—without demand increase—and the lack of control of hotel inventory. Recently, the best value guarantees that brands offer at their own websites have begun to level the playing field for the brand-loyal customer. Brands have also begun restricting the availability that both franchised and corporately managed hotels can distribute with third-party providers in consumer-direct channels, unless opaque. Fortunately, the public steep discounting appears to be ending.

Hotels that use the Internet to actively market packages, and pursue links to area demand generators/attractions and opaque channels, can really increase revenues, even in periods of low demand. The most successful hotels work at electronic marketing daily; it is a conscious job responsibility, not something that is a side duty of an already busy professional. There are several vehicles hotels can use to assess their competitive price position daily. They are critical tools for success.

Still emerging is the customer relation management function, where hotels and brands can communicate, to repeat customers and group decision-makers, offers relevant to their buying-specific patterns. One of the biggest challenges has been the accurate collection of data, particularly e-mail addresses, at hotel check-in and reservation creation. Some of the frequent traveler programs have done a better job of this than others, but, as with traditional marketing, electronic marketing is only as good as the database it uses.

The Internet has completely changed interactions with meeting planners as well. Some brands have search engines that allow regional salespeople and group desks to search availability via the sales POS system without having to interact at all with an individual at the hotel. A meeting planner can create standardized group RFPs and distribute them to many brands and CVBs, and the planner expects immediate response.

(continued)

Insider Insights *(continued)*

Let's not forget the business travel manager, who can use one of several standardized RFPs (as created by the National Business Travel Association, among others) and collect responses by automated functions, completely sidestepping the sometimes-emotional buy of hotels. Some travel managers also set up online reverse auctions, having several hotels in a given city bid for all their volume online at the same time. Many companies have standardized their travel policies with online providers, which lowers the cost of direct reservations for both the companies and the hotels.

In our experience, one of the largest ways in which hotels can affect their revenue is by paying active attention to today's electronic world. Daily care in the following areas makes a measurable difference: immediate response to electronic inquiries, timely and attractive rate positioning and packaging, active outreach to opaque distributors to fill otherwise-empty rooms, mining of the Internet for leads and customer knowledge, and meaningful (to the customer) outbound electronic marketing.

And travel agents? They remain our best source for the repeat guest who is willing to pay the highest price, even though Internet marketing has exploded.

---

requires hard work. A successful operation focuses group sales efforts on guest segments most likely to use the property. Staff responsible for obtaining business from these segments make up the core of the sales department. Each day they meet potential guests face-to-face.

It is important to sell all products and services, but the most profitable must take precedence. By far the most profitable offering is rooms.

Rooms Business

Room sales are focused in two distinct directions: group business and individual business, each of which can be divided into pleasure and business segments.

A good sales department staff must maintain balance in the amount of group business booked for guestrooms and space. This requires staying abreast of past and current booking trends. A hotel cannot overcommit space to groups and conventions at the expense of turning away individual business. At the same time, a hotel must attract groups that will book a good mix of guestrooms and function space.

Maintaining these balances in the **business mix** requires good interdepartmental coordination. Thorough knowledge of the property's booking trends helps marketers place limits on group rooms committed by season and night of the week. A salesperson must get approval from an appointed executive committee member to exceed a limit. Likewise, catering staff need guidelines for booking advance times and the amount of space assigned. If caterers must exceed time and space guidelines, they should obtain permission from the director of sales first. Following these guidelines helps the property draw the best mix of business for the hotel overall.

Booking conventions requires considerable planning and skillful execution. Senior sales staff in smaller properties and specialized departments in large hotels usually perform these jobs.

Conventions. About 25,000 professional, trade, and fraternal organizations provide big business each year for hospitality operations and cities. Major conventions bring enormous amounts of money into properties and the community, so the competition for this market segment is intense. Hotels and convention centers try hard to book major groups during slack times.

Associations holding conventions and meetings vary widely in size and scope. They may be international or local and include fewer than 100 or more than 100,000 people. Such a wide range allows many properties and cities to find their niche in the market.

Booking conventions into hotels that do not depend primarily on this business can be risky. Conventions may lower the availability of rooms for repeat individual guests and, worse yet, may create noise and partying, which could drive away regular guests permanently. These risks are even greater for resorts where the individual guest stays to "get away from it all."

In recent years, resort properties have begun searching for convention business to fill **shoulder periods** (pre- and post-season periods) and off-season periods. Even major destination resorts have now begun to compete for conventions. They offer good meeting facilities with many recreational amenities that appeal to convention delegates.

Contract Rooms. Companies such as airlines that need hotel space regularly may negotiate annual contracts for the rooms needed. Such a company usually receives a discount for those rooms.

Company Business Meetings. Corporate travel (individuals and groups) is the biggest segment of rooms sales in most hotels and many resort properties. Hotel sales departments expend a lot of effort attracting company meetings and special events. Except for hotels in popular destinations, hotels often count on local companies to use their facilities. Company needs include sales meetings, human resources and training programs, executive sessions, and reward programs. Resort sales departments look primarily for gatherings requiring attractive locations with extensive recreational facilities or tourist attractions.

Tour Groups. The travel industry books more and more hotels and resorts each year for individuals, groups, and business travelers. As noted earlier in this chapter, travel wholesalers create individual or group packages and market them through retail travel agencies. Retail travel agents directly handle individual bookings for business and pleasure purposes. Travel agents and special incentive travel companies book company meetings and special event groups. Hoteliers know that, to remain competitive, their sales departments must have one or more managers skilled in dealing with the travel industry.

Individual Business. Competition for individual business has increased as much as it has for group business. Marketers use a wide range of advertising methods to attract individual business. Business travelers are extremely important to most hotels, since they represent a continuing source of business.

Insider Insights

Clare Sullivan Jackson
CSEP & CEO
Sullivan Group
Houston, Texas

At the risk of seeming obvious, a special event calls for special people to make the "magic" happen.

The particular occasion is at the heart of *why* any event is special. It may be special to the company, as in a product introduction, a grand opening, the launch of an advertising campaign, or a holiday party. Or the occasion may be special to an industry, as in a professional association's annual convention or trade show featuring related special activities. Examples range from fairs to festivals to society galas, from fundraisers to company picnics, from golf tournaments to political conventions. Then there are the Super Bowl halftime production and the Olympics opening/closing ceremonies.

The special events professional ensures that each occasion is indeed special and memorable for all the right reasons. Memories that attendees take away from special events must be "warm and fuzzy" because the attendees had a good time and a positive attitude toward the host—not that something went wrong. The special events professional must constantly keep Murphy's Law out of the picture.

How does one become a special events professional? Entry points are virtually as open-ended as the events themselves. Since few schools offer even one course in special event planning, professionals tend to emerge from related backgrounds. Most often they come from the hospitality, theatrical production, and public relations fields.

The personality traits, skills, and knowledge of a special events professional are counterintuitive. Some of the disparate qualities or skills required are attention to detail, flair, project management, writing, budgeting, marketing, effective oral presentation skills, and management. Then add food and beverage selection, sanitation and trash disposal, audiovisual production, staging, loss prevention, etiquette and protocol, ethics, entertainment selection, basic electricity, and contracts.

And don't forget client relations, theme design, logistics, and "thinking on your feet." Techniques in some of these change daily, especially the high-tech applications involving the production side of an event. Staying abreast of trends and changes is critical.

Many special events professionals produce the entire event. Others are vendors to the overall production. Some of the vendors with which a special events professional would work, or function as, are caterers, hoteliers and restaurateurs, athletic facilities, theaters or performing arts centers, convention centers, electricians, plumbers, security experts, entertainers and their agents, florists, designers, printers, typographers, writers and publicists, incentive/corporate gift providers, limousine and other transportation services, photographers, tour operators, resorts; audio/video, sound, and related high-tech experts; pyrotechnic, lighting, and other special effects professionals; rental services for tents, props, tablecloths; and a multitude of other necessities.

Insider Insights *(continued)*

Most special events require "thinking outside the box." Additionally, the bar is constantly being raised. Last year's most memorable occasion was just that—last year's.

If this sounds like a lot of work, it is. But it can be rewarding. And you will not be alone, thanks to an invaluable support network of other special events professionals. The International Special Events Society (www.ises.com) was formed in 1987 "to foster enlightened performance through education while promoting ethical conduct. ISES works to join professionals to focus on the 'event as a whole' rather than its individual parts."

What kinds of job opportunities are available? A spot-check of recent listings in *Special Events* magazine included these examples:

- "Well-rounded, self-motivated and creative event coordinator" for a caterer
- Event marketing manager for a confectioner
- "Highly motivated individuals who are multi-faceted and need growth potential" for a "leading event production design firm with over 10 years in the business"

Interested? While still in school, use every opportunity possible to gain experience with a special events professional at both the total production level and with vendors. Initiative, skill, acquired knowledge, and hard work are definitely rewarded. Cultivate these, and in a few years you, too, can be a special events professional making magic happen.

Public Space

Besides promoting guestroom sales, the sales department must sell ballrooms and other meeting rooms. Local and out-of-town groups use this **public space** for meetings. Many larger operations have a separate sales team devoted to booking local functions. In smaller properties, this is an additional function of the sales department. While hotels need local business and promote their facilities to local groups, guestroom sales remain the biggest source of income. As a result, the sales department's first priority will be to accommodate out-of-town groups who will book both meeting facilities and guestrooms.

Often conventions select hotels based on the availability of public space. Sales staff must know about booking trends, lead time for bookings, and public room layouts and capacities. Cooperation between sales and the department that handles banquet and local meeting sales helps ensure the most profitable use of public space and guestrooms. Likewise, the sales department must work with the front office to develop group room plans for specific seasons or nights of the week.

Food and Beverage Business

In many hotels, food and beverage sales generate 30 percent or more of total revenues. Complaints from group meeting attendees often involve food and beverage services. Properties serving quality food and beverages make the job of the marketing and sales division easier. Group business planners are most interested in properties with a good reputation for food and beverages. Staff in "problem" food and beverage operations must work harder to assure prospective clients that food and beverage needs can be met.

Besides catering services for large groups, many operations offer one or more restaurants or lounges that cater to small groups and individuals. In today's competitive marketplace, freestanding restaurants of all types compete with hotel food and beverage operations. Marketing hotel food and beverage services can be challenging and difficult.

Properties need a great deal of space and equipment to make food and beverages available. Many properties use prime space, such as hotel lobbies, for food and beverage service areas. Some have outside entrances to food and beverage facilities. Few hotels can afford to rely on overnight guests alone to make their food and beverage operations successful. Community business fills seats in restaurants and lounges, and marketers therefore conduct aggressive advertising campaigns to attract local residents.

The property's marketing and sales staff help food and beverage operations by conducting a situation analysis and by developing market plans. Typically, food and beverage operations receive attention when these marketing tools are developed for other aspects of the property. Likewise, selecting advertising media, developing advertisements, and maintaining a food and beverage public relations program involve the marketing and sales staff.

Internal Selling

Internal selling is a marketing technique for increasing sales and profits. Internal selling occurs when front desk agents sell more expensive rooms first and when servers use suggestive selling techniques to move high-profit items, such as orange juice, appetizers, cocktails, glasses of wine, and desserts. Internal selling also refers to in-house signs and displays that promote the sale of the operation's products and services. Examples include signs in the entrance listing daily food and beverage specials, menu clip-on cards promoting specialties of the house, and tent cards with promotional messages in guestrooms.

Personal Selling

Personal selling (outside selling) is a marketing technique that is used in the lodging industry but rarely in food service. Personal selling involves salespeople who are employed specifically to generate sales for the operation. Manufacturers, wholesalers, and retailers of products use salespeople extensively. Lodging operations with large banquet or restaurant facilities may need salespeople to generate profitable bookings for these facilities.

Marketing and sales division staff may send out brochures, banquet menus, or packages to prospective groups and follow up these mailings with personal sales calls. They also handle all group inquiries and personally discuss the details involved with putting on special meetings. Salespeople work with other management people in designing packages or package plans. Then they sell these packages to help increase the total revenue of the entire operation. The difference between personal selling and internal selling is that personal selling uses salespeople to sell groups, whereas internal selling uses service employees to suggestively sell to individual guests.

Star and Other Rating Systems

All hotel owners and executives are very conscious of the various rating systems that judge their hotels and publish the results in terms of star, diamond, or other ratings. Perhaps most directly concerned are the marketing executives who are responsible for building room, food, and beverage sales at the property.

Hotels throughout the world are classified by one or more of these rating systems. In a number of countries, including Greece, Spain, and Jamaica, the government controls the classification of hotels. In these countries, the classification is based on published standards of design and service for each category. In Switzerland, the system is set up by the National Hotel Association, although it is essentially voluntary and based on the hotel's self-assessment. In the United States, the Mobil Star Guide and the American Automobile Association Diamond Rating are by far the best known. The highest ratings are five stars and five diamonds, respectively.

There is no truly international star rating system applicable throughout the world. One country's four-star rating may be another's five-star designation. France and Spain both have a maximum of four stars but also feature a Four Star Deluxe category for which very few hotels qualify. In all of Spain, only nine hotels are ranked in this category. Because of the different rating systems with their varied standards, to equate hotels by their star or diamond ratings provides, at best, only a partial measure of their comparative quality levels.

However, these rating systems strongly affect guest selection of lodging accommodations. The loss of a single star or diamond can have a devastating effect on a hotel's sales and profit picture and has, on occasion, resulted in the release of a top-level executive.

Advertising, Special Promotions, and Public Relations

Advertising

Advertising is a major part of marketing and several communications media are used to reach target markets. Each medium's advantages and disadvantages are discussed here.

Newspapers. The only print medium that regularly goes to many family homes is the local newspaper. It is not surprising, then, that many hospitality operations advertise in newspapers often. Newspaper ads have a well-defined circulation, reach many people, offer intensive coverage of the local market, and have targeted readership, immediacy, and flexibility.

Newspapers, however, have a short life. Readers typically skim papers and discard them. Reproduction quality is often poor. In addition, newspapers are not well suited to reaching a specific market segment. For example, a luxurious property advertising expensive food service in a local newspaper will reach many readers who cannot afford such service.

Magazines. Magazine advertisements offer many advantages over newspapers. These include high-quality reproduction, color availability, prestige, audience selectivity, and a long life. Advertisers can take advantage of high-quality paper, excellent reproduction, and lifelike color in magazine advertisements to show off their operation's appetizing food items, attractive guestrooms, recreational facilities, and so forth.

Magazine advertisements, however, usually take longer to prepare than newspaper ads, sometimes weeks or months. They also cost more and reduce an advertiser's ability to repeat ads.

Radio. Almost 99 percent of U.S. households have at least one radio. Local radio stations reach people within a convenient driving distance of a property. Radio advertisements can saturate an entire local area.

In addition, advertisers can reach specific target markets by matching the radio station's format or the time the ad is aired with the property's target market. For example, if an operation features jazz in its lounge, advertising on a jazz station or during a jazz program will reach the target market directly. If business-people are a target market, advertising on an "easy listening" station during rush-hour would make sense. Unless repeated, however, radio messages have a short life span and offer only audio messages.

Television. Television's main advantage over radio is that it combines sight with sound. Television commercials can show friendly front desk agents greeting guests or chefs preparing magnificent food. Television also commands a high attention level in its audience, so viewers retain many advertising messages.

Another advantage is saturation. That is, commercials can run many times daily and reach many households. Also, advertisers can reach specific audiences by selecting shows they prefer.

Disadvantages include high costs and extensive lead times necessary to produce commercials.

Internet Websites, E-Mail, and Social Media. It is common for hotels to promote themselves in various ways through the Internet. A hotel's own website or link on other websites gives the hotel wide exposure for its products and services. Like television, a website can present videos that combine sight and sound. The interactive link of e-mail allows a potential guest to send direct inquiries to the hotel. Hotel websites often can give the user a virtual tour of facilities in a more personal way than a hard-copy brochure can. A major advantage of having a website is the ease with which changes can be made in both copy and images (photos and videos). The role of a webmaster is becoming important to a hotel's marketing efforts. Hotels are also beginning to make use of social media platforms to connect with guests and potential guests.

Outdoor Advertising. Outdoor advertising is widely used in the hospitality industry. Billboards along highways are vital to hospitality establishments. Billboards are also used in and around large cities to promote local facilities. Almost

Insider Insights

Randall M. King
Vice President of Corporate Marketing and Development
Dow Hotel Company
Seattle, Washington

There was a time when news stories were generated from current events of the day or week. You could always count on the news anchor informing you of the latest tragedy or updating you on the current overseas conflict. The lead story was chosen from the news desk on the basis of what would scoop the other networks. Today, however, most news stories are determined by social media. News analysts research what is popular on the Internet and the subjects become the story of the day.

The same principle now applies to the hospitality industry as a result of the onslaught of social media. TripAdvisor recently did a study of 1,700 travelers and discovered that 42 percent use social media for travel planning and 40 percent use it for travel inspiration. A stunning 39 percent share travel experiences on social channels after they return home and 52 percent share their details while traveling. In all, 76 percent of U.S. travelers share travel experiences on social networks.

Facebook, Twitter, TripAdvisor, and YouTube are recognized as new forums for marketing. Nevertheless, many hotels are still unconvinced that these channels can increase bookings and are therefore deterred from implementing the necessary strategies. One in three hotels has no social media strategy, and only one in eight use any form of social media as a marketing tool. Hotels are still too focused in offline strategies. Even the ones that do invest in social media often fail to realize that it is not primarily a numbers game. It is not about having the *most* reviews on TripAdvisor; rather, a hotel needs to have high-quality reviews depicting a positive guest experience.

So how does a property go about finding likes, followers, fans, or good reviews that will bring in new guests? The answer is customer service, the one trait that all great hotels share. Treat your guests right and go the extra mile by embedding this approach in your corporate culture and training programs. All too often, hoteliers believe it is the guest with bad experiences who dominates online discourse. Not true! A 2012 survey of 1,300 online reviewers conducted by the Keller Fay Group found that "The vast majority of consumers who post online reviews are overwhelmingly motivated by goodwill and positive sentiment."

Hotels can take advantage by utilizing the front desk to garner positive reviews. When a guest has had a good experience, the front desk agent should ask the guest to go online and write a review on TripAdvisor. Hotels can also encourage positive feedback by printing the URLs for their Facebook and Twitter pages on the bottom of guests' settlement receipts and by rewarding them for posting their experience on these sites. For example, hotels can create special packages and discounts that are only available to their fans. They can also encourage guests to use location-based features on social media sites such as Facebook places or Foursquare by offering a free meal to the guest who checks in most frequently.

Many of us fall under the misconception that social media is only for the young. This could not be further from the truth. According to a 2012 Mashable

(continued)

Insider Insights *(continued)*

study, 62 percent of adults worldwide use some type of social medium daily. With today's smartphones, grandparents and grandchildren alike use social media while at home and on the go.

The biggest challenge for hotels is to find the right person to oversee their social media campaigns. Some hotels opt to use social media companies because of their tracking software, multi-platform update capabilities, reputation alerts, and consultancy expertise. These tools can be of great value in obtaining an accurate picture of your efficacy in multiple networks. However, it can be a mistake to entrust social media content to a firm that knows little about the property and may be unable to answer incoming questions. For this important responsibility, it is best to find a staff member who is familiar with the property and culture.

A wide range of skills are needed to do social media effectively. Not only is it critical to be able to navigate the site, spell correctly, and avoid grammatical errors, it is also necessary to be good at marketing, strategy, analytics, reporting, customer service, and communication. Just as important is the capacity to remain calm in the face of stress. There are not many people who possess all of these attributes, so a considerable amount of mentoring and patience may be needed. This is time well spent, however, because a lot of damage can be done by poor use of social media and months can be spent repairing the blunders.

The beauty of social networks is their ease of use and quick response time. A key limitation is that fatigue can set in quickly, which is why new social networks are popping up every six months. Everyone will have their favorite forums that they enjoy over others, but it is important to gauge what kind of results each site brings in and whether followers are re-blogging or posting your content. Social media campaigns fail because they forget to make it about the user, so the key is figuring out what users want you to talk about. Research your target audience and find out what topics interest them. Simply ask them what they would like to hear on a regular basis. Remember to keep your content interesting to your users, which means frequent contests and lots of user-generated content.

all managers use exterior signs to attract guests and to advertise the establishment's name and features. Outdoor advertising is basically a reminder that tries to attract the attention of potential guests who pass by the billboards or signs. Outdoor advertising must be bold, dynamic, and graphic so that passersby can get the message at a glance. Advantages of outdoor advertising include large circulation, broad reach, and low cost. A primary disadvantage is the limited message length.

Direct Mail. Direct mail simply involves the mailing of the advertising message in brochures, coupons, or other formats. Many managers use direct mail advertising, especially in clubs and other establishments with private memberships. Direct mail advertising allows audience selectivity and specific target marketing. Only those people who fit the operation's target market receive advertising material. Another advantage of direct mail advertising is that it can be personalized. It is also flexible, and the markets it reaches can be easily measured.

A primary disadvantage of direct mail is the high cost of developing and mailing a high-quality professional brochure or information packet. The cost per unit of circulation for direct mail advertising is generally greater than that for any other advertising method.

Special Promotions

Special promotions are widely used in almost all hospitality operations. They are limited only by one's imagination. Examples include couponing, product sampling, contests, packages, premiums, gift certificates, discounting, and bonus offers.

Couponing. Coupons attract potential guests with a special offer, such as a free night's lodging after a specific number of credits. Coupons can be given out personally, included in direct mail advertising, printed in newspapers and magazines, or made available through a website. The property may also increase slack-time business by using coupons with other special promotions, such as bonus offers or discounting.

Product Sampling. Product sampling acquaints guests with new food items. Samples help determine whether guests like a new product and also encourage them to order the item if they do.

Contests. Contests organized by the marketing and sales division can increase sales. A contest should be cost-effective; that is, increased sales should offset the cost of contest promotion and prizes.

Packages. Properties can offer products or services in packages at a discount price to attract new guests and to increase sales. One example is a weekend package complete with lodging, champagne, meals, and tickets for a local attraction. The package would cost considerably less than each item paid for separately.

Premiums. Premiums are given to guests who pay the regular prices for certain products or services. For example, an upgraded room might be provided or free movie tickets might be given to each adult eating dinner on Wednesday night, the slowest night of the week for most restaurants.

Gift Certificates. Gift certificates are used most often by chains or exclusive properties to increase sales. They are handled the same way as gift certificates sold in retail stores.

Discounting. Many properties discount prices to attract more guests and increase total sales. For example, one entrée on the menu might be reduced by 50 percent. Offering discounts through coupons allows the property to track how many guests use the offer.

Bonus Offers. This promotional technique, very similar to discounting, is also widely used in the food industry. In a bonus offer, the guest buys a product or service at the regular price and then receives a bonus. For example, guests receive three dinners at the regular price and a fourth dinner free. Bonus offers can be used with coupons. These can be very effective in attracting new guests and increasing food and beverage revenue.

Public Relations

Marketing and sales staff will probably spend a significant amount of time on various public relations activities. Public relations, as the term indicates, fosters a good relationship between the operation and the public. It also maintains good relations with the media, competitors, chambers of commerce, convention bureaus, trade and visitors' bureaus, business groups, trade associations, government groups, employees, and, especially, current and future guests.

Publicity and the Media. Public relations departments work most often with television, radio, newspapers, and magazines. One of the challenges the marketing and sales staff faces is getting **publicity** in the media. Publicity refers to editorial coverage as opposed to advertising.

Publicity is important because it helps create a public image for the property. While the property has less control over publicity than advertising, publicity is often more credible—that is, the public generally gives more credence to something reported in the media than to paid advertising.

Some people think publicity is free. Though the property does not pay the media directly for publicity, it spends a good deal of money to generate it. Merely hiring someone at the property to generate publicity requires money. The property may also spend money on a variety of events or activities that will generate publicity.

To get publicity, the property must make news in some way. The public relations department anticipates newsworthy events involving the property and informs the media about them. Staff members hope that the media will then cover these events and create a favorable impression of the property. Newsworthy events might include the grand opening of an operation, the opening of a new wing or remodeled section, the opening of the facility under new ownership or new management, or the celebration of a significant anniversary of the property. Often, managers host a party along with these events and invite members of the media.

Public relations staff frequently ask media travel writers, restaurant reviewers, or freelance writers eager for a good story to visit the operation. The hope is that these reviews will be positive and will generate additional sales.

Even handling emergencies and accidents effectively can create a favorable public impression of the operation and improve its chances for long-term survival.

Public Relations and the Community. Hospitality operations of all sizes may participate in charity work. For example, they can collect donations from employee paychecks, sponsor fund-raising activities, support telethons, and contribute company funds. Other examples of community public relations activities include sponsoring Little League teams, bowling teams, Boy Scout and Girl Scout troops, and other local organizations.

The Employee's Role in Public Relations. Meeting and exceeding guest expectations contributes to good public relations and to the success of the operation. Hospitality managers keep employees well-informed of special programs and important groups meeting in the facility. A well-informed employee can greatly aid the property's selling efforts. Since marketing and sales is the only division with an overall view of the operation, its staff members are in the best position to help managers deliver the best products for guests.

Endnote

1. This discussion of situation analysis is drawn from Julia Crystler, *Situation Analysis Workbook* (Lansing, Mich.: American Hotel & Lodging Educational Institute, and Hotel Sales and Marketing Association International, Washington, D.C., 1983), pp. 1–3.

Key Terms

business mix—A hotel's desired blend of business from various segments such as business transient, corporate group, leisure, and convention.

feasibility study—A study that analyzes a proposed site to determine what type of property has the best chance for success. It ultimately determines whether investors should construct or purchase an operation. It concentrates on four areas: location, guest demographics, the competition, and financial analysis.

gross operating profit—Departmental profits minus other overhead costs.

key account—A prospective guest that the property especially wants to attract.

market—A group of current or potential guests identified by geographic location, industry, economic status, or behavioral characteristics.

market mix—The various market segments a property hopes to attract.

market segment—A group of consumers with similar needs, wants, backgrounds, incomes, buying habits, and so on.

marketing strategy—The marketing approaches and tools used to attract a property's market mix.

publicity—Editorial coverage as opposed to advertising.

public space—Areas of a hotel that groups can privately reserve.

shoulder periods—The periods between the busy season and the off-season for resort properties.

situation analysis—A survey commonly performed by a marketing department using customer input and feedback to analyze a marketing strategy.

Review Questions

1. In what three ways can markets be divided and tracked? Describe them.
2. What major effect did the Great Depression have on marketing?
3. What are the basic responsibilities of a convention services department?
4. In what ways have hotels imitated marketing practices used by airlines?
5. What role does marketing play in a hotel's feasibility study?
6. What location-related criteria are used in feasibility studies?

7. What useful purpose do guest comment cards serve to a hotel?

8. What are the pros and cons of convention business for hotels of different types?

9. What is internal selling? Cite examples of it.

10. What are the differences between publicity and advertising?

11. What services can a hotel website provide?

 Internal Sites

For more information, visit the following Internet sites. Remember that Internet addresses can change without notice. If the site is no longer there, you can use a search engine to look for additional sites.

Associations

American Hotel & Lodging Association
www.ahla.com

American Hotel & Lodging Educational
Institute
www.ahlei.org

Association of Corporate Travel
Executives
www.acte.org

Destination Marketing
Association International
www.destinationmarketing.org

Educational Foundation of NRA
www.nraef.org

Hospitality Sales and Marketing
Association International
www.hsmai.org

International Association of
Exhibitions and Events
www.iaee.com

International Hotel & Restaurant
Association
www.ih-ra.com

Meeting Professionals International
www.mpiweb.org

National Restaurant Association
www.restaurant.org

Publications—Online and Printed

Convene
www.pcma.org/convene-content/
archives

Event Solutions
www.event-solutions.com

M&C
www.mcmag.com

The Meeting Professional
www.mpiweb.org/Magazine/Archive

Meetings
www.themeetingmagazines.com/index/

Successful Meetings
www.successfulmeetings.com

The Trade Show News Network
(TSNN)
www.tsnn.com

Chapter 12 Outline

What Is Accounting?
  Who Manages the Accounting
    System?
  Who Uses Financial Information?
  Technology
Accounting Principles and Practices
  Generally Accepted Accounting
    Principles (GAAP)
  Uniform Systems of Accounts
Accounting Tools
  Operating Budgets
  Income Statements
  Balance Sheets
  Ratio Analysis Techniques
Managerial Accounting
  Internal Controls
  Other Managerial Accounting
    Techniques
Routine Activities of the Accounting
  Division
  Revenue Accounting
  Expense Accounting
  Salary and Wage Accounting
Purchasing
  Objectives of Effective Purchasing
  Purchasing Food, Equipment,
    Supplies, and Services
  E-Commerce and Central Purchasing
  Ethics and Supplier Relationships

Competencies

1. Define accounting, identify who manages the accounting system, distinguish internal users from external users of information provided by the accounting division, and describe automated accounting systems. (pp. 249–251)

2. Apply generally accepted accounting principles to hospitality situations and distinguish between cash basis accounting and accrual basis accounting. (pp. 251–253)

3. Explain the advantages of adhering to a uniform system of accounts. (p. 254)

4. Explain the purpose of the following accounting tools: operating budgets, income statements, balance sheets, and ratio analysis techniques. (pp. 255–266)

5. Identify managerial accounting techniques useful in making planning and control decisions. (pp. 266–271)

6. Describe the routine activities of the accounting division. (pp. 271–273)

7. Identify the nature and typical responsibilities of a purchasing department. (pp. 273–279)

12

The Accounting Division

IN THE HIGHLY COMPETITIVE FIELD of hospitality, successful careers often depend on the ability of managers to make daily operating decisions based on their analyses of financial information. The primary responsibility of the accounting division is to provide management with the financial information necessary to make these decisions. In order to achieve satisfactory profit objectives for their areas of responsibility, managers must thoroughly understand how the accounting division accumulates and processes financial information. Moreover, the results of operating decisions are reflected in the information gathered by the accounting division, and managers themselves are evaluated, in part, by whether their decisions improve the profitability of the business.

What Is Accounting?

Accounting can be thought of as the "language of business," a language with its own vocabulary, rules, and procedures that turn financial data into useful reports. Basic accounting activities include recording, classifying, and summarizing financial information. *Recording business transactions* refers to the procedure of entering the results of transactions in an accounting document called a **journal**. *Classifying* refers to the process of assembling the numerous business transactions into related categories. *Summarizing* refers to the preparation of financial information according to the formats of specific reports or *financial statements*.

Simply put, accounting is a language that "translates" ideas, decisions, and actions into dollars and cents. For example, a manager may have very creative ideas for new menus or for innovative guest services, but, before these become reality, the ideas must be reduced to numbers—the symbols of accounting. Accounting systems provide a framework for evaluating the potential worth of ideas, and, once concepts are implemented, these systems help to assess how successful those ideas have been in reality.

Those new to the field of hospitality sometimes think that only specialists who thrive on "number crunching" can understand accounting. However, accounting theory and practice is not based on complicated mathematics; it is based on *logic* and uses basic terminology, fundamental concepts, and relatively straightforward procedures. Applying the logic of accounting requires only the most basic math skills: addition, subtraction, multiplication, and division. Once the terminology, concepts, and procedures of accounting are mastered, accounting practices are not as difficult to understand as some people tend to believe. The important point is that accounting is a means to an end (a profitable or efficient operation) and not an end in itself.[1]

Who Manages the Accounting System?

Top-level managers are ultimately responsible for the financial status of the property, but, since the general manager is extremely busy with a wide range of responsibilities, staff (advisory) personnel are employed to manage the accounting system. Small properties may employ a staff **bookkeeper** (someone who records and classifies business transactions) and/or hire an outside accountant to design and manage the accounting system. Large properties require a division of several people headed by a **controller** to account for and summarize the results of the numerous transactions that take place in a hotel or restaurant. Regardless of property size, accounting personnel must possess specialized technical knowledge and skills and must have experience and objective judgment.

Those unfamiliar with accounting activities often believe that a controller is simply a glorified bookkeeper. However, there are many important differences between the two. Bookkeepers conduct only one part of the overall accounting function. The controller supervises the work of bookkeepers and also interprets accounting data. Because the controller's job is more demanding than the bookkeeper's, it requires more training.

The controller oversees the development of systems for recording, classifying, and summarizing financial information. In addition, the controller may also design and monitor internal controls, prepare forecasts, coordinate the budgeting process of the property, conduct cost and feasibility studies, prepare tax returns, analyze the results of operations, and advise management.

Who Uses Financial Information?

The users of financial information are classified as internal and external users. In hotels and restaurants, all managers are internal users of financial statements. These managers use financial statements and reports to analyze and control revenues and expenses and to manage the financial position of the business. External users include:

- Owners and investors—Owners include stockholders, partners, and proprietors. Investors are potential owners. The primary concern of owners is the past, present, and future profitability of the business. Dividends to the stockholders and increases in ownership to partners and proprietors depend on the profitability of the business.

- Creditors and lenders—Short-term creditors want to know that there are sufficient assets (resources of value) that could be converted to cash to repay loans made to the business. Long-term lenders are more interested in current and future profits available to the hospitality operation that can be used to make future loan payments.

- Government agencies—A business pays many different taxes to various government agencies—federal, state, and local—that want to ensure that they collect the proper amount of tax. Some of the taxes are: income taxes, payroll taxes, sales taxes, property taxes, hotel occupancy taxes, and alcoholic beverage taxes.

- General public—Community pride and growth is often fostered by successful hospitality properties in the area. The general public has an economic interest in the success of any business that provides jobs.

Technology

Although some small hotels and restaurants still maintain their accounting records by hand, most accounting systems today are automated. In a hotel, these systems are generally categorized as front-of-the-house and back-of-the-house systems.

Front-of-the-house systems include front office terminals used for checking guests in and out; reservation terminals used for booking reservations; and point-of-sale terminals located throughout the hotel in its restaurants, bars, and other retail locations.

Back-of-the-house systems focus on maintaining accounts receivable, accounts payable, payroll, and general ledger records. They automatically prepare payroll checks, accounts payable checks, and monthly financial statements.

Other back-of-the-house systems include those designed to track sales prospects, sales calls made by marketing staff, and group bookings; and those that manage food and beverage inventories and costs, conserve energy, and prepare operating budgets.

Accounting Principles and Practices

As noted previously, accounting is the language of business, and it must be widely understood to be useful. Uniformity in accounting terminology and in methods of recording financial transactions helps make accounting more widely understood. The American Institute of Certified Public Accountants (AICPA) has been instrumental in making such uniformity possible by developing the generally accepted accounting principles used in the United States.

Generally Accepted Accounting Principles (GAAP)

For almost every profession there are guidelines and rules to ensure that members carry out their responsibilities according to accepted standards. In the field of accounting, these standards are known as **generally accepted accounting principles (GAAP)**.

The application of generally accepted accounting principles ensures that business transactions are recorded and financial statements are prepared according to consistent accounting procedures. This consistency allows internal and external users of financial statements to make reasonable judgments about the overall financial condition of a business and the success of business operations from period to period. Some of the generally accepted accounting principles that hospitality managers should know are discussed in the following sections.

Unit of Measurement. Money is the standard medium of exchange in virtually every nation. Financial statements are based on transactions expressed in monetary terms. A common unit of measurement permits the users of accounting data to compare current and past business transactions.

Historical Cost. The principle of historical cost states that the value of merchandise or services obtained through business transactions should be recorded in terms of actual costs, not current market values. For example, assume that a truck having a market value of $15,000 is purchased from a seller for $12,800. The amount recorded as the cost of the truck is $12,800. As long as the truck is owned by the business, the value (cost) shown in the accounting records and on the financial statements will be $12,800. However, a depreciation expense may also be carried on the books to reflect the asset's declining worth.

Going Concern. The principle of going concern (also known as *continuity of the business unit*) requires financial statements to be prepared under the assumption that the business will continue indefinitely and thus carry out its commitments. Normally, a business is assumed to be a going concern unless there is objective evidence to the contrary. The principle of going concern can be used to defend the use of historical costs in the presentation of financial statements. Since the assumption is that the business will not fail in the immediate future, the use of market values would not be appropriate unless the principle of conservatism applies.

Conservatism. The principle of conservatism guides the decisions of accountants in areas that involve estimates and other areas that may call for professional judgment. However, it is important to stress that this principle applies only when there is uncertainty in reporting factual results of business transactions. The principle of conservatism provides accountants with a practical alternative for situations that involve doubt. When doubt is involved, the solution or method that will not overstate assets or income should be selected.

Objectivity. The principle of objectivity states that all business transactions must be supported by objective evidence proving that the transactions did in fact occur. Obtaining objective evidence is not always a simple matter. For example, a canceled check serves as objective evidence that cash was paid. However, it is not evidence of the reason for which the check was issued. An invoice or other form of independent evidence is necessary to prove the reason for the expenditure. When independent evidence is not available to document a business transaction, estimates must be made. In these cases, the choice of the best estimate should be guided by the principle of objectivity.

Realization. Under the realization principle, revenues resulting from business transactions are recorded only when a sale has been made *and* earned—when a hotel receives cash from a guest served in the dining room, for example. The results of the transaction are recorded to the proper accounts.

However, according to the principle of realization, if a hotel receives cash for services that have not yet been earned, the transaction cannot be classified as a sale. For example, if a hotel receives an advance deposit of $500 for a wedding banquet to be held two months later, the cash received must be recorded—but the event cannot be classified as a sale. This is because the business has not yet earned the revenue; services have not been performed or delivered.

Matching. The matching principle states that all expenses must be recorded in the same accounting period as the revenue that they helped to generate. When expenses are matched with the revenue they helped to produce, external and internal users of financial statements can make better judgments about the financial position and operating performance of the hospitality business. There are two accounting methods for determining when to record the results of a business transaction: cash accounting and accrual accounting.

Cash accounting. The **cash accounting** method records the results of business transactions only when cash is received or paid out. Small businesses usually follow cash accounting procedures in their day-to-day bookkeeping activities. However, financial statements prepared solely from cash accounting sources may not necessarily comply with generally accepted accounting principles. If expenses are recorded on the basis of cash disbursements, expenses will not necessarily match the revenue that they helped to generate. This may occur for any number of reasons.

For example, assume that each month a new accounting period for a particular restaurant begins. During each month, the restaurant follows the principle of realization and records revenue only as sales are made and earned. The restaurant also records expenses only as cash payments (which include payments by check) are made to various suppliers and vendors. Cash accounting will not ensure that expenses will match the revenue generated during the month because many expenses will be incurred during each month but not paid until the following month. These expenses include utility bills, laundry bills, and telephone bills that the restaurant may not even receive until the first week of the following month.

The Internal Revenue Service generally will accept financial statements prepared on a cash accounting basis only if the business does not sell inventory products and meets other criteria. Since food and beverage operations sell inventory products, these establishments must use the accrual method.

Accrual accounting. To conform to the matching principle, most hospitality operations use the accrual method of accounting. **Accrual accounting** adjusts the accounting records by recording expenses that are incurred during an accounting period but that (for any number of reasons) are not actually paid until the following period. Once the adjusting entries have been recorded, financial statements and reports for the accounting period will provide a reasonable basis for evaluating the financial position and operating performance of the hospitality business.

Consistency. There are several accounting methods that determine certain values used as accounting data. For example, there are several methods for determining inventory values. Deciding which accounting method to use is the responsibility of the property's high-level managers. The generally accepted accounting principle of consistency states that, once an accounting method has been adopted, it should be followed consistently from period to period. In order for accounting information to be comparable, there must be a consistent application of accounting methods and principles. When circumstances warrant a change in the method of accounting for a specific kind of transaction, the change must be reported along with an explanation of how this change affects other items shown on the operation's financial statements.

Uniform Systems of Accounts

While generally accepted accounting principles ensure that accountants carry out their responsibilities in accordance with accepted standards, uniform systems of accounts standardize formats and account classifications and guide accountants in the preparation and presentation of financial statements. Standardization permits users of financial statements to compare the financial position and operational performance of a particular property to similar types of properties in the hospitality industry. For new businesses entering the hospitality industry, a uniform system of accounts serves as a ready-made accounting system that can be quickly adapted to the needs and requirements of the business.

A uniform system of accounts also serves as an instructional handbook because it identifies and explains many of the **line items** that may appear on the financial statements of a particular kind of business. Some line items may not apply to every kind of property in the industry, but accountants can easily adapt a uniform system to meet the individual needs of their properties by deleting or adding line items as necessary.

The idea of a uniform system of accounts is not new or unique to the hospitality industry. The *Uniform System of Accounts for Hotels* was first published in 1926 by a group of hoteliers who had the foresight to recognize the value of such a system to the hotel industry. Although there have been many revised editions since 1926, the fundamental format of the original uniform system survives as testament to the success of the system in meeting the basic needs of the industry. The current version is titled the *Uniform System of Accounts for the Lodging Industry*.[2]

Following the lead of the lodging industry, the National Restaurant Association published the *Uniform System of Accounts for Restaurants* in 1930. Its objective was to give restaurant operators a common accounting language and to provide a basis upon which to compare the results of their operations. This uniform accounting system has been revised several times, and today many restaurant operators find it a valuable accounting handbook.[3]

There are also uniform systems of accounts for clubs, hospitals, condominium operations, and conference centers. The uniform accounting systems for the hospitality industry are continually revised to reflect changes in acceptable accounting procedures and changes in the business environment that may affect hospitality accounting. They now enjoy widespread use within the industry and recognition by banks and other financial institutions, as well as the courts.

Hotels, motels, restaurants, and other segments of the hospitality industry benefit from adopting the uniform system of accounts appropriate for their operations. Perhaps the greatest benefit provided is the uniformity of recording business transactions. This uniformity allows local, regional, or national statistics to be gathered, alerting the industry to threats and/or opportunities of developing trends. In the past, accounting firms serving the hospitality industry have been instrumental in standardizing reporting procedures. Today, STR collects and publishes statistical data on hotels. The National Restaurant Association and the Club Managers Association of America compile statistical data on restaurants and private clubs, respectively. Exhibit 1 lists a number of important sources of financial information for the major segments of the hospitality industry.

Exhibit 1   Major Hospitality Statistical Publications

Publication	Industry Segment	Firm
Trends in the Hotel Industry, USA Edition	Lodging	PKF Consulting
Clubs in Town & Country	Clubs	PKF Consulting
The HOST Study	Lodging	STR
Restaurant Industry Operations Report	Restaurant	National Restaurant Association

Accounting Tools

Some managers prefer to leave accounting to the controller. They may reason, for example, that the subject is too difficult and specialized and that they have enough work to do in taking care of the physical levels of production and service. However, a fact of business life is that a manager must be able to apply the basics of managerial accounting.

Managerial accounting systems provide financial information to managers at all organizational levels. Financial information is used to develop operating plans (for example, an operating budget), to assess how well the operation is doing (an income statement can be used for this purpose), and to make operating decisions.

Operating Budgets

Wise managers understand the need to plan for the future. To help do this, they use operating budgets, which are formal plans indicating the property's estimated revenue and expenses. The purpose of the budget is to state how to achieve the maximum financial benefits from available resources.

The annual operating budget acts as a profit plan for the property, addressing all revenue sources and expense items. Annual budgets are commonly divided into monthly plans. These monthly plans become standards against which management can evaluate the actual results of operations. Thus, the operating budget enables management to accomplish two of its most important functions: planning and control.

The budget process requires a closely coordinated effort involving all supervisory and management personnel. Each manager responsible for a functional area within the property should participate in the budget process. When managers are allowed real input into the budget process, they often become more motivated to implement the property's profit plan and are less likely to adhere blindly to budget numbers they feel are imposed upon them.

The accounting division normally supplies department managers with statistical information from which they can project sales volume and revenue and estimate expenses for their areas of responsibility. The accounting division is also responsible for coordinating the budget plans of individual department managers. The controller then combines these plans into a comprehensive operating budget for the general manager's review.

The general manager and the controller review the departmental budget plans. If additional adjustments are required, they meet with the appropriate managers to identify how the adjustments will be made. If major adjustments are made, the effects of such changes on the budgets of other departments and/or the total budget package are carefully analyzed. After reviewing the final budget report with department managers, the general manager and the controller present the operating budget to the owners of the property. If the budget is not satisfactory, elements requiring change are returned to the appropriate department managers for review and revision.

To ensure that adequate time is available for preparing the operating budget, a schedule should be set and closely followed. Exhibit 2 presents a sample timetable that could be used by properties whose fiscal year coincides with the calendar year.

Budgets take time and money to prepare, but, done properly, they are management's primary hedge against the uncertainty of the future and an important tool in planning and control. Once developed, the budget becomes a road map to achieving profit goals and a benchmark against which actual operating results can be compared. For example, if the budget plan suggests a specified income level and certain dollar (or percentage) limitations on expenses, it will be possible to compare actual income/expense levels (from the income statement) with the operating budget. Realistically, almost all budgeted revenue and expense items will differ from actual results of operations because no budgeting process is perfect. However, significant variances should be analyzed, and managers should follow through with appropriate corrective actions.

Income Statements

The operating budget indicates the ideal financial picture of an operation, that is, its situation if nothing goes wrong. At regular intervals (typically, at the end of

Exhibit 2   Timetable for Operations Budgeting

Who	What	When
General Manager, Controller, Department Heads	Budget planning meetings.	October 1–31
Department Heads	Preparation of departmental budget plans.	November 1–9
Accounting	Consolidation of departmental budget plans.	November 10–19
General Manager, Controller	Preparation of the General Manager's Budget Report.	December
Owners	Review and approval of the General Manager's Budget Report.	December

each month), the accounting division develops an income statement that indicates *actual* revenue, expense, and income levels. Because this statement reveals the business's profitability for a given period, it is one of the most important financial statements managers use to evaluate the success of operations. It is also an important measure of the effectiveness and efficiency of management.

In the case of a restaurant, the income statement pertains to the entire property. Exhibit 3 presents a sample income statement for a small restaurant corporation.

Most hotel income statements are a consolidation of the revenues, expenses, and income reported on departmental schedules. Exhibit 4 presents a sample income statement for a full-service hotel. Exhibits 5 and 6 show a rooms schedule and an administrative and general schedule, respectively. Once calculated, the results of these schedules are then transferred to the hotel's income statement.

While there are some obvious differences between the forms used by lodging and restaurant properties (many relating to differences in terminology), the basic purposes for, and uses of, the statements are exactly the same.

Balance Sheets

The balance sheet provides important information regarding the financial position of a hospitality business *on a given date*. The phrase *on a given date* carries an entirely different meaning from "for a period of time." A balance sheet dated December 31, 20X2, shows the financial position of the business *on December 31, 20X2*, not for the month of December or any other period of time. The balance sheet is like a snapshot of the financial condition of the business. The exposure captures just one moment of the business's financial condition.

Hospitality managers have a more direct and immediate need for information on income statements, but, at the same time, find balance sheets useful for conveying financial information to creditors and investors. Understanding how the statement is used to reveal the financial position of a business is the key to understanding the logic behind the sequence of categories that appear on the statement. The major categories that appear on the balance sheet are assets, liabilities, and equity.

Simply stated, assets represent anything a business owns that has commercial or exchange value. Liabilities represent the claims of outsiders (such as creditors) to assets, and equity represents the claims of owners to assets. On every balance sheet, the total assets must always agree (that is, balance) with the combined totals of the liabilities and equity sections. Therefore, the very format of the balance sheet reflects the fundamental accounting equation:

$$\text{Assets} = \text{Liabilities} + \text{Equity}$$

Exhibit 7 illustrates a balance sheet of a hotel corporation. Exhibit 8 shows a balance sheet of a small restaurant corporation.

Ratio Analysis Techniques

Financial statements issued by hotels and restaurants contain a considerable amount of information. A thorough analysis of this information requires more than a simple read of the reported figures and facts. Users of financial statements need to be able to make the figures and facts reveal aspects of the property's financial

Exhibit 3   Sample Income Statement for a Small Restaurant

Statement of Income
For the Year Ended December 31, 20X2

REVENUE
    Food Sales $
    Liquor Sales
        Total Revenue $

COST OF SALES
    Food
    Liquor
        Total Cost of Sales

GROSS PROFIT

OPERATING EXPENSES
    Salaries and Wages
    Employee Benefits
    China, Glassware, and Silverware
    Kitchen Fuel
    Laundry and Dry Cleaning
    Credit Card Fees
    Operating Supplies
    Advertising
    Utilities
    Repairs and Maintenance
        Total Operating Expenses

INCOME BEFORE FIXED CHARGES AND INCOME TAXES

FIXED CHARGES
    Rent
    Property Taxes
    Insurance
    Interest Expense
    Depreciation
        Total Fixed Charges

INCOME BEFORE INCOME TAXES

INCOME TAXES

NET INCOME $

Exhibit 4 Sample Income Statement for a Full-Service Hotel

STATEMENT OF INCOME

	Current Year	Prior Year
	Period	
REVENUE		
Rooms	$	$
Food and Beverage		
Other Operated Departments		
Rentals and Other Income		
Total Revenue		
EXPENSES		
Rooms		
Food and Beverage		
Other Operated Departments		
Administrative and General		
Sales and Marketing		
Property Operation and Maintenance		
Utilities		
Management Fees		
Rent, Property Taxes, and Insurance		
Interest Expense		
Depreciation and Amortization		
Loss or (Gain) on the Disposition of Assets		
Total Expenses		
INCOME BEFORE INCOME TAXES		
INCOME TAXES		
Current		
Deferred		
Total Income Taxes		
NET INCOME	$	$

Source: *Uniform System of Accounts for the Lodging Industry*, 10th rev. ed. (Lansing, Mich.: American Hotel & Lodging Educational Institute, 2006), p. 18.

situation that might be overlooked. This is accomplished through ratio analysis. A ratio mathematically expresses a significant relationship between two figures and is calculated by dividing one figure by the other.

Ratios are useful only when compared against useful criteria. Useful criteria against which to compare the results of ratio analysis include: (1) the corresponding ratio calculated for a prior period, (2) other properties and industry averages, and (3) planned ratio goals. Users of ratio analysis must be careful when comparing two different properties because the accounting procedures used by the properties may differ and their ratios may not be comparable.

Ratio analysis can help owners, managers, and creditors evaluate the financial condition and operation of a hotel or restaurant. However, ratios are only indicators; they do not resolve problems or actually reveal what the problems may be. At best, when ratios vary significantly from past periods, budgeted standards, or

Exhibit 5   Sample Rooms Schedule

	CURRENT MONTH						YEAR-TO-DATE					
	ACTUAL		FORECAST		PRIOR YEAR		ACTUAL		FORECAST		PRIOR YEAR	
	$	%	$	%	$	%	$	%	$	%	$	%
REVENUE												
Transient Rooms Revenue												
Group Rooms Revenue												
Contract Rooms Revenue												
Other Rooms Revenue												
Less: Allowances												
Total Rooms Revenue												
EXPENSES												
Payroll and Related Expenses												
Salaries, Wages, and Bonuses												
Salaries and Wages												
Bonuses and Incentives												
Total Salaries, Wages, and Bonuses												
Payroll-Related Expenses												
Payroll Taxes												
Supplemental Pay												
Employee Benefits												
Total Payroll-Related Expenses												
Total Payroll and Related Expenses												
Other Expenses												
Cable/Satellite Television												
Cleaning Supplies												
Commissions												
Commissions and Rebates—Group												
Complimentary Services and Gifts												
Contract Services												
Corporate Office Reimbursables												
Decorations												
Dues and Subscriptions												
Equipment Rental												
Guest Relocation												
Guest Supplies												
Guest Transportation												
Laundry and Dry Cleaning												
Licenses and Permits												
Linen												
Miscellaneous												
Operating Supplies												
Printing and Stationery												
Reservations												
Royalty Fees												
Telecommunications												
Training												
Travel—Meals and Entertainment												
Travel—Other												
Uniform Laundry												
Uniforms												
Total Other Expenses												
TOTAL EXPENSES												
DEPARTMENTAL INCOME (LOSS)												

Source: *Uniform System of Accounts for the Lodging Industry,* 10th rev. ed. (Lansing, Mich.: American Hotel & Lodging Educational Institute, 2006), p. 38.

Exhibit 6   Sample Administrative and General Schedule

	CURRENT MONTH			YEAR-TO-DATE		
	ACTUAL	FORECAST	PRIOR YEAR	ACTUAL	FORECAST	PRIOR YEAR
EXPENSES	$ | %	$ | %	$ | %	$ | %	$ | %	$ | %
Payroll and Related Expenses						
Salaries, Wages, and Bonuses						
Salaries and Wages						
Bonuses and Incentives						
Total Salaries, Wages, and Bonuses						
Payroll-Related Expenses						
Payroll Taxes						
Supplemental Pay						
Employee Benefits						
Total Payroll-Related Expenses						
Total Payroll and Related Expenses						
Other Expenses						
Audit Charges						
Bank Charges						
Cash Overages and Shortages						
Centralized Accounting Charges						
Complimentary Services and Gifts						
Contract Services						
Corporate Office Reimbursables						
Credit and Collection						
Credit Card Commissions						
Decorations						
Donations						
Dues and Subscriptions						
Equipment Rental						
Human Resources						
Information Systems						
Laundry and Dry Cleaning						
Legal Services						
Licenses and Permits						
Loss and Damage						
Miscellaneous						
Operating Supplies						
Payroll Processing						
Postage and Overnight Delivery Charges						
Printing and Stationery						
Professional Fees						
Provision for Doubtful Accounts						
Security						
Settlement Costs						
Telecommunications						
Training						
Transportation						
Travel—Meals and Entertainment						
Travel—Other						
Uniform Laundry						
Uniforms						
Total Other Expenses						
TOTAL EXPENSES						

Source: *Uniform System of Accounts for the Lodging Industry*, 10th rev. ed. (Lansing, Mich.: American Hotel & Lodging Educational Institute, 2006), p. 130.

Exhibit 7   Sample Balance Sheet for a Hotel

BALANCE SHEET

Assets

	Current Year	Prior Year
CURRENT ASSETS		
Cash		
House Banks	$	$
Demand Deposits		
Temporary Cash Investments		
Total Cash		
Restricted Cash		
Short-Term Investments		
Receivables		
Accounts Receivable		
Notes Receivable		
Current Maturities of Non-current Receivables		
Other		
Total Receivables		
Less Allowance for Doubtful Accounts		
Net Receivables		
Due To/From Owner, Management Company, or Related Party		
Inventories		
Operating Equipment		
Prepaid Expenses		
Deferred Income Taxes—Current		
Other		
Total Current Assets		
NON-CURRENT RECEIVABLES, NET OF CURRENT MATURITIES		
INVESTMENTS		
PROPERTY AND EQUIPMENT		
Land		
Buildings		
Leaseholds and Leasehold Improvements		
Furnishings and Equipment		
Construction in Progress		
Total Property and Equipment		
Less Accumulated Depreciation and Amortization		
Net Property and Equipment		
OTHER ASSETS		
Intangible Assets		
Cash Surrender Value of Life Insurance		
Deferred Charges		
Deferred Income Taxes—Non-current		
Operating Equipment		
Restricted Cash		
Other		
Total Other Assets		
TOTAL ASSETS	$	$

Exhibit 7 *(continued)*

BALANCE SHEET

Liabilities and Stockholders' Equity

	Current Year	Prior Year
CURRENT LIABILITIES		
Notes Payable		
Banks	$	$
Others		
Total Notes Payable		
Due To/From Owner, Management Company or Related Party		
Accounts Payable		
Accrued Expenses		
Advance Deposits		
Income Taxes Payable		
Deferred Income Taxes—Current		
Current Maturities of Long-Term Debt		
Other		
Total Current Liabilities		
LONG-TERM DEBT, Net of Current Maturities		
Mortgage Notes, other notes, and similar liabilities		
Obligations Under Capital Leases		
Total Long-Term Debt		
OTHER LONG-TERM LIABILITIES		
DEFERRED INCOME TAXES—Non-current		
COMMITMENTS AND CONTINGENCIES		

Stockholders' Equity

	Current Year	Prior Year
____% Cumulative Preferred Stock, $ ____ par value, authorized ____ shares; issued and outstanding ____ shares	$	$
Common Stock, $____ par value, authorized ____ shares; issued and outstanding ____ shares		
Additional Paid-In Capital		
Retained Earnings		
Accumulated Other Comprehensive Income (Loss), Net of Income Tax		
Less: Treasury Stock, ____ shares of Common Stock, at cost		
Total Stockholders' Equity	$	$
TOTAL LIABILITIES AND STOCKHOLDERS' EQUITY	$	$

Source: *Uniform System of Accounts for the Lodging Industry*, 10th rev. ed. (Lansing, Mich.: American Hotel & Lodging Educational Institute, 2006), pp. 4–6.

Exhibit 8   Sample Balance Sheet for a Small Restaurant

Balance Sheet
December 31, 20X2

ASSETS

Current Assets
  Cash $
  Accounts Receivable
  Inventories
  Prepaid Expenses
    Total Current Assets   _____ $

Property and Equipment

	Cost	Accumulated Depreciation
Land	$	
Building		$
Furniture and Equipment		
China, Glassware, Silver	_____	_____
Total		

Other Assets
  Security Deposits
  Preopening Expenses
    Total Other Assets   _____

Total Assets $ _____

LIABILITIES

Current Liabilities
  Accounts Payable $
  Sales Tax Payable
  Accrued Expenses
  Current Portion of Long-Term Debt
    Total Current Liabilities   _____ $

Long-Term Liabilities
  Mortgage Payable
  Less Current Portion of Long-Term Debt   _____
    Net Long-Term Liabilities   _____

Total Liabilities

OWNER'S EQUITY

Capital, Owner—December 31, 20X2   _____

Total Liabilities and Owner's Equity $ _____

industry averages, they indicate that problems *might* exist. When problems appear to exist, considerably more analysis and investigation is necessary to determine the appropriate corrective actions. A full discussion of ratio analysis is beyond the scope of this chapter; however, the following paragraphs introduce common operating ratios analyzed by restaurant and hotel managers.

There are several ways to express ratios. A common way is to use a percentage. For example, a food cost percentage results when cost of food sold is divided by food sales. If a restaurant's cost of food sales is $42,000 and its food sales are $120,000, the food cost percentage for the restaurant can be calculated as follows:

$$\text{Food Cost Percentage } = \frac{\text{Cost of Food Sales}}{\text{Food Sales}}$$

$$= \frac{\$42,000}{\$120,000}$$

$$= .35, \text{ or } 35\%$$

In this example, food costing $42,000 is sold for $120,000. That is, for every dollar of food sold, 35 cents was required to cover the cost of food sales. Food cost percentages are often calculated on a daily basis. Most food and beverage managers separate food income and costs from beverage income and costs to more closely monitor these important revenue centers. If this is not done, food or beverage income may be too low or expenses too high without the manager being able to isolate the specific problem.

A second way to express a ratio is to use *per-unit* information. For example, an average breakfast check may be calculated for a meal period by dividing the total breakfast sales by the number of breakfasts served. Another way to express a ratio is to use a turnover rate. For example, seat turnover for a meal period can be determined by dividing the number of customers served by the number of dining room seats available.

Three key ratios for hotel management are occupancy, average daily rate (ADR), and revenue per available room (RevPAR). Occupancy is the ratio of occupied rooms to available rooms and is calculated by dividing the number of rooms occupied for a period by the number of rooms that were available to sell. Average daily rate is the price that the average room was sold for during a period. It is calculated by dividing total rooms revenue by the number of occupied rooms. RevPAR takes into consideration both the number of occupied rooms and the average daily rate they were sold for. An easy way to calculate RevPAR is to multiply the percentage of occupancy by the average daily rate.

> **Example.** Assume that a hotel has 100 rooms, and 2,100 are occupied during June. The occupancy percentage for the month would be 2,100 divided by 100 times 30, since there are 100 available rooms each day and there are 30 days in June. This calculates to an occupancy percentage of 70 percent.
>
> If this same hotel had $105,000 of rooms revenue for the month, its average daily rate would be $105,000 divided by 2,100 (the number of occupied rooms for the month), or $50.

Finally, to calculate the hotel's revenue per available room (RevPAR) for the month, you would multiply its occupancy percentage of 70 percent by its average daily rate (ADR) of $50, which would result in a RevPAR for the month of $35.

An important financial ratio for ownership is return on investment (ROI). ROI measures the profitability of a hotel or restaurant against the amount of equity that the owner has invested in the business. Return on investment is calculated by dividing annual net income by the owner's equity.

> **Example.** If a hotel generated a net income for the year of $150,000 and the owner had invested $1,000,000 of equity in the business, the owner's ROI would be $150,000 divided by $1,000,000, or 15 percent.

Operating ratios useful to hotel managers relate revenue or expenses to total revenue. For example, say that the XYZ Hotel had rooms department revenue of $900,000 for a given year and that the hotel's total revenue for the year was $1,600,000. Dividing rooms revenue ($900,000) by total revenue ($1,600,000) yields a percentage amount of approximately 56 percent. This means that room sales accounted for roughly 56 percent of the total revenue taken in by the XYZ Hotel for the year. If the XYZ's administrative and general expenses for the year were $100,000, these expenses can be expressed as a percentage of total revenue by dividing $100,000 by $1,600,000. The ratio result yields a percentage amount of approximately 6 percent. This means that for every $1 of revenue generated during the year, about six cents went to cover administrative and general expenses.

Revenue and expense ratios can also be calculated from figures on departmental income or expense statements. These ratios are useful for control purposes when the ratio results are compared to budgeted or planned ratio goals. There are hundreds of operating ratios that can be calculated. Exhibit 9 suggests more than two hundred of them.

Managerial Accounting

Managerial accounting is the branch of accounting that uses various techniques and concepts to process historical and forecasted information for planning and control decisions. Data generated by the accounting system must be analyzed and interpreted if it is to be useful. Hospitality managers can use a variety of analytical techniques and reports for controlling and planning operations.[4]

Internal Controls

A small owner-operated hospitality business often restricts its recordkeeping and control systems to those required by governmental agencies and creditors. Since the owner handles all incoming cash and makes all payments, his or her presence helps ensure smooth and efficient operations. However, as an operation increases in size or becomes multi-unit, managers increasingly need timely and accurate reports and analysis systems to control and manage the business.

Internal controls are those procedures and methods adopted by the manager to safeguard the assets of the business, to ensure proper accountability, and to promote efficient operations. Internal control begins with an organization plan

Exhibit 9   Operating Ratios Useful in Analysis

CERTAIN OPERATING RATIOS USEFUL IN ANALYSIS	% of Total Revenues	% of Depart. Revenues	% of Depart. Total Cost	% Change from Prior Period	% Change from Budget	Per Available Room	Per Occupied Room	Per Available Seats	Per Cover/Guest	Per Square Foot	Per Full-time Equiv. Employee	% of Total Salaries & Wages	Per Unit Produced or Used
Total Revenues				•	•	•	•			•	•		
Rooms													
Revenue	•			•	•	•	•				•		
Salary, Wages & Burden		•	•	•	•	•	•					•	
Other Expenses		•	•	•	•	•	•						
Departmental Profit		•		•	•	•	•						
Food													
Revenue	•			•	•	•	•	•	•	•	•		
Cost of Sales		•	•	•	•				•				
Salary, Wages & Burden		•	•	•	•			•	•			•	
Other Expenses		•	•	•	•				•				
Departmental Profit		•		•	•			•	•	•	•		
Beverage													
Revenue	•			•	•	•	•	•	•	•	•		
Cost of Sales		•	•	•	•								
Salary, Wages & Burden		•	•	•	•			•				•	
Other Expenses		•	•	•	•								
Departmental Profit		•		•	•			•		•	•		
Minor Departments													
Revenue	•			•	•								
Cost of Sales		•		•	•								
Salary, Wages & Burden		•		•	•							•	
Other Expenses		•		•	•								
Departmental Profit		•		•	•								
Administrative & General													
Salary, Wages & Burden	•			•	•	•	•					•	
Other Expenses	•			•	•	•	•						
Departmental Total Cost	•			•	•	•	•						
Marketing													
Salary, Wages & Burden	•			•	•	•	•					•	
Other Expenses	•			•	•	•	•						
Departmental Total Cost	•			•	•	•	•						

(continued)

Exhibit 9   *(continued)*

CERTAIN OPERATING RATIOS USEFUL IN ANALYSIS	% of Total Revenues	% of Depart. Revenues	% of Depart. Total Cost	% Change from Prior Period	% Change from Budget	Per Available Room	Per Occupied Room	Per Available Seats	Per Cover/Guest	Per Square Foot	Per Full-time Equiv. Employee	% of Total Salaries & Wages	Per Unit Produced or Used
Property Operation & Maintenance													
Salary, Wages & Burden	•			•	•	•	•				•		
Other Expenses	•			•	•	•	•						
Subtotal Maintenance	•			•	•	•	•						
Energy Cost	•			•	•	•	•						•
Departmental Total Cost	•			•	•	•	•						
House Laundry													
Salary, Wages & Burden	•			•	•	•	•					•	•
Other Expenses	•			•	•	•	•						•
Departmental Total Cost	•			•	•	•	•						•
Food & Beverage (or Outlets)													
Revenue	•	•		•	•		•						
Salary, Wages & Burden		•		•	•						•		
Other Expenses		•		•	•								
Departmental Total Cost		•		•	•								
Total Other Expenses	•			•	•	•	•						
Payroll Burden Items	•			•	•						•	•	
Total Salary & Wages	•			•	•	•	•				•		
Capital Expenses													
Property Taxes	•			•	•	•	•			•			•
Insurance	•			•	•	•	•						•
Rent/Lease	•			•	•	•	•						
Interest	•			•	•	•	•						•
Management Fee	•			•	•	•	•						
Debt Service	•			•	•	•	•						•
FF&E Reserve/Replacement	•			•	•	•	•						

that clearly establishes lines of communication and levels of authority and responsibility throughout the operation. A good organization plan separates recordkeeping of assets from the actual control of assets. Additionally, the responsibility for related transactions should be separated so the work of one person can verify that of another. For example, an accounts receivable clerk should not both receive payments (control of assets) and post those payments to the accounts receivable register (recordkeeping of assets). These related transactions should be separated so that one person receives the payments and another person posts the records.

Internal controls require forms and procedures that measure the efficiency and effectiveness of employees and provide accounting information that, when analyzed, will help identify problem areas. These controls must also be cost-effective. The potential cost savings of a particular control must outweigh the cost of implementing and continuing the control procedure.

Another element in a sound system of internal control is the effective selection, training, and supervision of personnel. The hospitality operation must have policies that define employee skill levels, education, and job responsibilities.

In addition to checks and balances inherent in a well-designed system of paperwork controls (such as pre-numbered guest checks and sales tickets) and correct use of cash registers, internal control also includes the following areas:

- Comparative statistical analysis
- Planning and forecasting sales and the cost of goods sold
- Departmental budgeting controls

The Role of Accounting in Control

What is control? Some people think that the management task of control merely involves physical activities such as locking up money in a safe, limiting access to keys, using a perpetual inventory system for expensive items, and so forth. While these tasks are part of control, an effective control system is much broader in scope. It actually involves five steps:

1. Establish ideal standards indicating what things would be like if nothing went wrong. For example, the food and beverage manager may determine that a 35 percent food cost in the coffee shop is a realistic goal. (That is, of all the income generated by sales in the coffee shop, 35 percent of this income will be used to pay for food used to generate the income.)

2. Assess actual costs. At this point, accounting procedures come into focus. Pre-established, acceptable accounting procedures must be used to determine actual food costs. The food and beverage manager must work with the accountant to determine how to collect information about applicable costs. The report of actual costs is typically presented in the income statement in a restaurant operation or in records generated in support of that document in a hotel operation with more than one food service outlet.

3. Compare standard costs with actual costs.

4. If the comparison reveals a variance between what costs are and what they should be, corrective action is required to bring costs closer to the planned standard cost level. At this point, physical actions such as securing income, limiting access to food storage areas, and keeping perpetual inventory are implemented.

5. Evaluate the extent to which the corrective actions have been effective. This evaluation must look at both the specific problem (such as high food costs) and related areas (such as marketing concerns if food costs are lowered by reducing portion sizes).

- Predetermined standards and evaluation reports

- Properly designed and secured storage areas

- A system for the ongoing review and evaluation of the entire internal control system

No internal control system is foolproof. However, a soundly designed and well-maintained system may reveal areas where fraudulent conversions could occur.

Other Managerial Accounting Techniques

There are many managerial accounting systems other than those dealing with control and budgeting. In fact, the only constraints on managerial accounting systems are logic and the usefulness of the information generated. Important managerial accounting techniques are cost analysis, cost-volume-profit analysis, and cash budgeting.

Cost Analysis. Managers constantly face situations in which the knowledge of costs helps them make decisions. Knowing how a particular cost relates to changes in sales volume helps managers compare actual costs and predetermined standard costs. With a knowledge of different types of costs, hospitality managers are able to select the costs relevant to a particular decision.

Cost, considered as an expense, is the reduction of an asset to ultimately increase revenue. Costs include cost of food sold, labor expense, supplies expense, utilities, marketing expense, rent expense, depreciation expense, insurance expense, and many other expenses incurred by a hospitality business as reflected on its income statement. Profitability planning requires that management examine how costs are affected by changes in sales volume (occupancy). In this context, costs can be seen as *fixed, variable,* or *mixed* (partly fixed and partly variable).

Fixed costs are costs that remain constant in the short run, even though occupancy may vary. Common examples of fixed costs are salaries, rent expense, insurance expense, property taxes, depreciation expense, and interest expense. Variable costs are costs that change in relation to changes in the volume of business. When a hotel is full, variable costs are at their maximum; when a hotel is empty (for example, during the off season), these costs are at a minimum or, theoretically, at zero. If variable costs are strictly defined as costs that vary in exact proportion to total sales, few, if any, costs are truly variable. However, several costs come close to this definition and may legitimately be considered variable costs. Examples of such variable costs are: the cost of food sold, the cost of beverages sold, some labor costs, and the cost of supplies used in production and service operations.

Mixed costs are costs made up of both fixed and variable cost elements. These costs are sometimes referred to as *semi-variable* or *semi-fixed* costs. For example, expenses incurred by a resort's telephone, golf course, or tennis operation have a fixed cost portion that is independent of the amount of guest usage. Costs incurred by these operations also contain a variable portion that is assumed to vary with the amount of guest usage. Although in practice the variable element of a mixed cost may not be directly proportional to usage or sales volume, this assumption is generally accepted.

Cost-Volume-Profit (CVP) Analysis. An important tool used to set specific profit objectives is cost-volume-profit (CVP) analysis. CVP analysis expresses (in either graphic or equation form) the relationships between costs, sales volume (occupancy), and profits. This profitability-planning tool enables hotel managers to determine the level of occupancy necessary to achieve a specific amount of profit for operations. CVP analysis can also be used to determine the break-even point for a hotel—the level of occupancy at which total revenue equals total costs. In addition, CVP analysis can be used to determine the amount of profit (or loss) that can be expected at any occupancy level.

Cash Budgeting. Cash budgeting is extremely helpful in managing the property's cash flow. A cash budget helps ensure that the operation has enough cash to pay bills when due and, during periods of excess cash, that the excess is invested wisely. Cash budgeting differs from operational budgeting in that it shows when cash is collected and when expenses are paid. The operating budget shows sales when they are earned (not when cash is received) and expenses when they occur (not when they are paid). It is very possible for a hospitality operation to show a profit in the operating budget and on the income statement, but still not have enough cash to pay bills when due.

Routine Activities of the Accounting Division

The routine work of the hotel or restaurant accounting division falls into three categories: revenue, expenses, and salary and wage or payroll. Accounting functions in hotels are more complicated than those in restaurants, so this discussion will focus primarily on hotels. Keep in mind, however, that many of the principles discussed apply to restaurants as well as hotels.

Revenue Accounting

When charges for a hotel guest are incurred, these charges must be entered into the guest folio. These transactions must usually be authorized by a source document—a guest check from a restaurant, for example. In a manual system, the guest check is hand-carried to the front desk, where the charge is posted to the guest folio. Computerized point-of-sale (POS) systems electronically transmit charges from their point of origin (in this case, the restaurant) to the front desk.

All charges sent to the front office cashier, either manually or by computer, must also be posted in the guest ledger (containing all the accounts of people staying at the hotel) or the city ledger (the accounts of local businesspeople, credit card accounts of people not residing in the hotel, and unpaid accounts of departed guests). As with folio entries, posting in the ledger may be done by hand or by computers that accomplish this work in a fraction of the time.

At the close of each day, the night auditor recaps the type and amount of business done by each department. Sources of information include cashier reports from each department producing revenue, and data from the city and guest ledgers.

The night auditor starts with the food and beverage recap. Working with cashiers' reports from the hotel's restaurant(s) and with register readings, the night auditor compiles a complete record of food and beverage sales for the day.

The next step is to complete the rooms revenue. The night auditor posts all room charges to the guest accounts while working in conjunction with the night front desk agent (who must prepare a report). The night auditor also posts any late charges that come in after the front office cashier has left duty. Once all room and late charges are posted, the night auditor compares machine totals with individual reports. Any discrepancies must be checked and corrected.

Having compiled and audited the day's revenue from each department of the hotel, the night auditor turns over all data to the auditor. Once the auditor has compiled, checked, and certified all revenue data from the previous day, he or she completes a daily occupancy and gross revenue report. This report informs the manager of the day's activities. It is a vital tool, since it provides a complete picture of the operation. The manager will discuss data from this report with department heads and other members of the staff. The exact form of the report depends upon the individual manager or the chain.

With the morning reports out of the way, the accounting division turns its attention to recording the revenue figures in the books. The net revenue figures for each department, taken from the daily revenue report, are posted in the sales journal. At the end of the month, the departmental totals of the sales journal are posted to the ledger. The remaining step is to transfer figures from the ledger to the monthly financial statements.

Today, virtually all hotels utilize an integrated computerized property management system that performs revenue accounting automatically. While the night audit function used to require hours of tedious postings and balancing, today the computer completes the task in minutes. In addition, daily management reports are generated by the system in minutes and forwarded to the management team for analysis.

Expense Accounting

The second category of accounting work involves handling expenses. All purchases by the property must be certified, recorded, and paid. Large hotels have a purchasing agent, and all purchases are made through this office; however, most properties are not large enough to justify such a position. For these properties, purchases are made by individual department heads with the approval of the manager. In the case of most small orders, the manager's approval is merely a formality, since the goods have already arrived and may be in use. Ideally, the manager trusts the integrity of department managers and knows they will always obtain approval before entering large orders. In properties using a purchase-order system, the manager approves every expenditure before it is made. A purchase-order system provides close control over expenses, but it also involves much more paperwork than other systems. Which system is used depends entirely on the management policy of each property.

A simple purchase might move through the accounting channels like this: A department head places an order and an invoice arrives in the accounting office. It is stamped when received and then sent to the appropriate department head, who initials the invoice to signify that the goods have been received, that they are in order, and that the charge is correct. The invoice is then returned to the accounts payable clerk, who posts the invoice to a purchase voucher. The clerk checks additions and extensions, then routes the invoice to the auditor, who charges the purchase to the appropriate expense account. From there, the invoice is sent to the manager for approval, then returned to the accounts payable clerk, who distributes the figures. That is, the clerk checks the proper category and lists the account number and the amount of the purchase. At the end of the month, the amounts are totaled, allowable discounts (if any) are calculated, and the voucher is sent to the auditor, who writes a check that is sent to the purveyor. The voucher is entered in the voucher register and the check in the check register. The check and voucher registers are closed to the ledger. At the end of the month, the ledgers are totaled and the financial statements are prepared.

For food and beverage expenses, this procedure is altered somewhat. The invoice arrives with the food or beverage. The steward and/or receiving clerk check(s) all foods and beverages for quantity, quality, and price before accepting them. The steward signs the invoice and forwards it to the accounting office, which performs the necessary changes, distributions, and postings.

Purchasing is discussed in greater detail later in the chapter.

Salary and Wage Accounting

The third principal area of work in accounting involves the preparation and payment of salaries and wages. The payroll clerk sets up an individual earnings record and fills out a time card for every employee. Federal tax forms must be filed and notation of any deductions (insurance, bonds, charities, and so forth) must be made. During the payroll period, the clerk makes up the payroll recap sheet, which lists all employees by departments. On the 15th of the month, the time cards are pulled and compared with the time books kept by department heads.

Today, computerized time check systems are available that automatically record hours worked, pay, withholding taxes, benefits, and so forth for each employee. These systems can also tally labor cost and related information by position, shift, department, and so forth, so that this information can be used for labor control purposes. Some computer systems will even complete required governmental tax withholding and other forms.

Properties without computerized systems must either complete payroll records manually or send basic information (hours worked and pay data) to outside bookkeeping agencies or banks for machine processing and totaling of payroll information.

Purchasing

As noted previously, a purchasing agent is often part of the accounting staff at large hospitality properties, though each department head is often responsible for his or her own purchases in a small property. The role of the purchaser is to assist the staff members who are to use the products being purchased. For example, the chef and/or food and beverage manager must make the final decision about the need for and quality of food products to be used, although the purchasing department may make suggestions.

Lodging and food service operations must purchase a wide variety of products, supplies, and services in the course of daily operations. The purchasing process is complex and multi-faceted, and its proper functioning is vital to the success of the hotel or restaurant. A property cannot provide the best possible products and services or reach its financial goals unless the purchaser does a good job.

Good purchasing systems will have written procedures that are approved by management and adhered to by all those involved. It is also important to have purchase specifications covering at least the expensive and high-volume purchase items. A testing committee under the direction of management and supervised by the purchasing agent is also useful. Every price or transaction either should be verified in writing through the routine use of a system that secures competitive prices or should be the result of a system of negotiated prices.

Purchasing involves a wide range of activities, such as:

- Assessing the quality and quantity of items that are needed

- Selecting suppliers and arranging deliveries

- Negotiating prices, expediting (following up on late deliveries and other problems), and arranging for payment terms

- Maintaining records, controlling inventories, and inspecting products

- Obtaining information, studying the needs of the property, and estimating trends of future product availability, prices, and so forth

Objectives of Effective Purchasing

The goal of the purchasing process is to obtain the right product from the right supplier at the right price at the right time. Unfortunately, this is easier said than done.

The Right Product. Generally speaking, the right product is the one that represents the greatest value to the property. The term *value* relates to concerns for both the cost and the quality of items being purchased. Quality is the suitability of a product for its intended use. The wise purchaser is able to match the desired quality with the intended use to obtain the best value for the purchase dollar expended.

Purchasers record quality requirements on a purchase specification form. Exhibit 10 shows a sample form that outlines the criteria used to help develop specifications for products. Once developed, the form is given to all suppliers who can provide the product, allowing them to quote prices for comparable products.

The Right Supplier. Some hospitality managers believe that items should be purchased from the supplier with the lowest prices. In fact, there are other important factors to be considered. The supplier must be honest and fair. He or she must know the product and the buyer's needs. Meeting quality and quantity requirements consistently is important, as is providing helpful information about products that the operation now uses or may use in the future.

Suppliers who care about their customers' needs and are willing to address problems with deliveries, invoices, and back orders are most likely to continue a mutually profitable business relationship with clients.

Exhibit 10 Purchase Specification Format

(name of food and beverage operation)

1. Product name: _____

2. Product used for:

> Clearly indicate product use (such as olive garnish for beverage, hamburger patty for grill frying for sandwich, etc.).

3. Product general description:

> Provide general quality information about desired product. For example, "iceberg lettuce; heads to be green, firm without spoilage, excessive dirt or damage. No more than 10 outer leaves; packed 24 heads per case."

4. Detailed description:

> Purchaser should state other factors that help to clearly identify desired product. Examples of specific factors, which vary by product being described, may include:
>
> - Geographic origin
> - Variety
> - Type
> - Style
> - Grade
>
> - Product size
> - Portion size
> - Brand name
> - Density
>
> - Medium of pack
> - Specific gravity
> - Container size
> - Edible yield, trim

5. Product test procedures:

> Test procedures occur at time product is received and as/after product is prepared/used. Thus, for example, products to be at a refrigerated temperature upon delivery can be tested with a thermometer. Portion-cut meat patties can be randomly weighed. Lettuce packed 24 heads per case can be counted.

6. Special instructions and requirements:

> Any additional information needed to clearly indicate quality expectations can be included here. Examples include bidding procedures, if applicable, labeling and/or packaging requirements, and special delivery and service requirements.

Source: Jack D. Ninemeier, *Planning and Control for Food and Beverage Operations,* 8th ed. (Lansing, Mich.: American Hotel & Lodging Educational Institute, 2013), p. 190.

The Right Price. Price is an important consideration in all purchasing decisions. Quality (suitability for intended use) has already been noted and is integral to any discussion about purchase price. An experienced purchaser looks for ways to reduce purchase price without sacrificing minimum quality requirements. For example, the purchaser can:

- Reduce costs involving delivery, scheduling of payment, degree to which services are required, and so forth, through negotiation. The purchaser can also take advantage of a supplier's wish to sell overstocked products, break into new markets, or increase sales during highly competitive times. It may also be possible to take advantage of special promotional discounts.

- Purchase products in larger quantities (with possible lower per-unit costs), pay cash if savings can result, or use competitive bidding procedures.

- Venture into creative price agreements. For example, perhaps selling prices can be based on a specified percentage markup above the wholesale price.

The Right Time. Sometimes prices fluctuate. When possible, wise purchasers buy larger quantities during times when prices are increasing and smaller quantities when prices are decreasing.

Many properties use a minimum-maximum inventory system to determine the number or amount of items that should be kept on hand. Under this system, a **par level** (the quantity of a product required to sustain normal operations) is established. Par level equals the **lead-time quantity** plus the **safety stock level** of any given product. The lead-time quantity is the number (or amount) of items that will be used between the time an order is made and the time it arrives on the property. The safety stock level is the number of purchase units (that is, normal-sized shipping containers such as cases, drums, and so on) needed in case of emergencies, spoilage, or unexpected delays in delivery. When the inventory level of an item reaches the minimum quantity, additional supplies must be ordered.

Maximum quantity is the greatest number of purchase units that should be in stock at any time. The maximum quantity must not exceed available storage space and must not be so high that large amounts of cash are tied up in unnecessary items. The shelf life of an item also affects the maximum quantity of purchase units; some products may deteriorate if stored too long before use.

As the amount of product in inventory decreases to par level, additional quantities must be ordered to rebuild the inventory level to the predetermined maximum. Computers are being used more and more frequently to establish or calculate quantities of products to purchase.

Purchasing Food, Equipment, Supplies, and Services

Hotels and restaurants must make purchasing decisions involving major items such as ovens or computers and relatively minor items such as table napkins or business forms.[5] In other instances, purchasers may be involved in obtaining services from outside contractors for such things as pest control or maintenance of office equipment. Buyers usually deal with a distributor (a go-between who obtains products from the manufacturer) but might occasionally deal directly with the manufacturer.

Purchases can be divided into four major categories—food, capital equipment, supplies, and services.

Food. Although poor preparation may destroy the quality of a good product, the best preparation practices cannot put quality into an inferior product that should not have been purchased in the first place. The control of food costs begins at the time of purchase. No set of controls can bring back lost profits that occur through poor buying or dishonesty in buying.

The cost of food supplies accounts for about a quarter of the food sales dollar. Experience has shown that a good purchasing system can reduce food costs by 5 percent or more without reducing the quality of food supplies that are used.

The open market method of food purchasing is used by at least 90 percent of all restaurant and hotel operations. This method requires purchasers to obtain price quotations based on specifications from one or more purveyors on a daily, weekly, or monthly basis. These quotations can be obtained from weekly market lists, over the phone, or as the result of negotiated prices. The order is then placed with the purveyor submitting the best quotation.

The arrival of large restaurant and hotel chains ushered in changes in the usual open market buying methods. Large operators can make use of their concentrated buying power to make long-term contracts with national food distributors. Large multi-unit operators also take advantage of *cost-plus* arrangements (that is, supplies are purchased at cost plus a negotiated percentage). They buy directly from packers or at public produce auctions. They may also have their own private label merchandise, which is rather risky unless the volume is large and the buyer knows how to operate financially with the packers.

An effective food buyer:

- Understands how a kitchen works and what happens during food production

- Knows about market buying techniques and food distribution systems, and where to look for market trends

- Is alert to new markets and products and realizes that weather and politics can affect food supplies and prices

- Works effectively with the food service staff to develop product specifications and perform butchering and yield tests to support the purchase specifications

- Maintains good working relations with chefs, purveyors, and department heads

- Knows about accounting controls and systems and understands the mechanics of purchase orders, invoices, receiving sheets, and credit memoranda

All food purchases should be based on the food service operation's actual need, which is determined by menus, parties actually booked or expected to be booked, and records showing the number/amount of items normally consumed by the operation. As noted previously, most good operations establish a minimum and a maximum stock level. Generally, no more than a ninety-day supply of anything is purchased without the approval of the general manager.

The operation should have a good internal control system run by an alert controller and an involved manager. When the purchasers and suppliers know that they are being checked, they will do a better job than if there were no internal controls in place.

Capital Equipment. Capital equipment purchases are, simply put, "big ticket items." They are usually items that the property expects to use for a year or more. Some examples include walk-in refrigerators, guestroom furniture, and computers.

A buyer's main concern in purchasing capital equipment is to determine how well the item fulfills the function for which it is intended. For example, suppose the front office wants to buy a computer system to help staff keep records. The purchaser must not only find an affordable system, but one that does what the front office staff wants it to do and one that will be easy to learn to use. In addition, purchasers must consider the expected life span of the equipment and the projected downtime needed for routine maintenance or repair.

Suppliers generally offer warranties and provisions for servicing the equipment they sell. A good buyer will include these items in the cost considerations for capital equipment. Also, discounts are frequently offered for large or expensive orders, prompt payment, and other related factors. Buyers should ask suppliers about these discounts when they discuss purchases.

Supplies. Supplies can be defined as consumable or disposable products such as paper cups, soap, and business forms. Purchasers will typically deal with a number of distributors to keep these many small items in stock. For example, a restaurant or food and beverage division in a hotel may have different suppliers for table linens, china, flatware, dishwashing soap, and guest check forms. In addition, each of these suppliers will generally offer the same kind of product at a variety of price ranges and levels of quality. The purchaser must determine an acceptable cost and quality level for the operation and then compare items of similar quality to find the needed item at the right price.

The level of quality needed in supplies is determined by how the product will be used. Items used in front-of-the-house areas where guests will see them may be purchased largely for their appearance. For example, pink linen table napkins might be chosen because they match the dining room's china and create a pleasing effect for guests. By the same token, back-of-the-house items are generally chosen on the basis of their utility. The kitchen staff probably will not care what color the garbage bags are as long as the bags are strong enough to hold the garbage securely.

Services. Hospitality operations are increasingly using outside contractors to supply some services. Examples include pest control, office machine maintenance, and bank deposit pick-up. As a result, purchasers are often required to find companies that will provide these services at a satisfactory price.

When negotiating with service contractors, purchasers need to consider such questions as these:

- Will the contractor consider the property's individual needs?

- What equipment or supplies will the contractor use? Smelly chemicals or noisy, disruptive equipment will probably not be acceptable to guests.

- How will services be scheduled? Will the contractor offer services only at specified times, or will he or she be on call to handle problems that may arise at any time?

- How will the effectiveness of the contractor's services be monitored?

Miscellaneous Purchases. Buyers frequently must handle a number of other purchases not included in the three main categories just discussed. Vending machines, candy and tobacco, periodicals, and electronic games are all items that a hospitality operation may provide and that would involve the purchasing staff.

E-Commerce and Central Purchasing

The tremendous growth of the Internet and e-commerce in recent years has had a profound effect on the hospitality industry. It is estimated that hotels spend some $50 billion annually on supplies. Major suppliers look enviably at this market and see the strong potential for e-commerce partnerships with the six largest lodging companies (InterContinental Hotels, Wyndham, Marriott, Hilton, Accor, and Choice Hotels International). Hotel companies have long sought a way to control purchases. Creating a central Internet purchasing website where vendors are compelled to compete for business can generate considerable cost savings for hotels. Limiting purchasing decisions at the property level to vendors approved by chain headquarters also brings much-desired purchasing discipline to hotel groups that make centralized purchasing decisions. In addition, this practice can create much-wanted product consistency among a chain's diverse group of franchisees. Limiting the quantities that can be purchased by a local manager can also vastly improve controls and, again, save money.

Marriott, Hyatt, InterContinental Hotels, Fairmont, and Club Corporation USA have combined purchasing efforts through the creation of their jointly owned procurement company, Avendra. Starwood formed a partnership with Zoho, an independent third-party purchasing agency. The creation of similar purchasing consortia can be expected as e-commerce becomes more prevalent as a means of doing business in the hospitality industry.

Ethics and Supplier Relationships

Purchasers should make buying decisions based on what is best for the property. A system of ethics ensures that other factors do not enter into the decision. Many operations regulate such things as acceptance of gifts and meals, purchasing for personal use, and showing favoritism to a specific supplier. Successful purchasers must be very knowledgeable as well as honest, fair, and protective of the interests and resources of the hospitality operation.

Both the purchaser and supplier need to win in the business relationship. This cannot occur if, for example, the purchaser does not honor appointments, makes suppliers wait for meetings, shares prices with other suppliers in the hopes that costs can be reduced, and so forth. The buyer must be able to interact effectively with salespeople and recognize that they are partners rather than adversaries in the food service operation. It is always best for the purchaser to think about how he or she would like to be treated if the purchaser/salesperson roles were reversed.

Endnotes

1. This section is adapted from Raymond Cote's *Hotel and Restaurant Accounting*, 7th ed. (Lansing, Mich.: American Hotel & Lodging Educational Institute, 2012).

2. *Uniform System of Accounts for the Lodging Industry,* 10th rev. ed. (Lansing, Mich.: American Hotel & Lodging Educational Institute, 2006). The eleventh revised edition is scheduled for release in 2014.

3. *Uniform System of Accounts for Restaurants*, 8th ed. (Washington, D.C.: National Restaurant Association, 2012).

4. For a more complete discussion of managerial accounting tools and techniques, see Raymond S. Schmidgall's *Hospitality Industry Managerial Accounting*, 7th ed. (Lansing, Mich.: American Hotel & Lodging Educational Institute, 2011).

5. This discussion is taken from William B. Virts, *Purchasing for Hospitality Operations* (Lansing, Mich.: American Hotel & Lodging Educational Institute, 1987), Chapter 17.

 # Key Terms

accrual accounting—In contrast to cash accounting, a method of accounting in which balance sheet adjustments are made to reflect expenses incurred during one accounting period but paid for during a different accounting period.

bookkeeper—A staff member at a small property who records and classifies business transactions.

cash accounting—A method of accounting in which the results of business transactions are recorded only when cash is received or paid out. Compare to accrual accounting.

controller—The head of an accounting division at a large property; accounts for and summarizes the results of business transactions.

generally accepted accounting principles (GAAP)—Guidelines and rules to ensure that members of the accounting profession carry out their responsibilities according to accepted standards.

journal—An accounting document used to record business transactions.

lead-time quantity—The number (or amount) of items that will be used between the time an order is made and the time it arrives on the property.

line items—Specific categories of sales or expenses tracked on an accounting statement or budget.

par level—The quantity of a product required to sustain normal operations.

safety stock level—The number of purchase units (that is, normal-size shipping containers such as cases, drums, and so on) needed in case of emergencies, spoilage, or unexpected delays in delivery.

Review Questions ───────────────────────

1. What functional differences exist between a hotel bookkeeper and a controller?

2. What is accrual accounting?

3. What is a uniform system of accounts? Explain its value in a hotel operation.

4. Is it necessary for all department managers to be familiar with financial information? Why or why not?

5. What does "budgets are a hotel's road map" mean?

6. How does the balance sheet differ from the income statement?

7. What are the distinctions between fixed and variable costs? Give several examples of each.

8. Would you advocate institution of a purchase order system in all hotels and restaurants? Why or why not?

9. What does the term "managerial accounting" mean?

10. If you were writing the job specification for food buyer, what specific knowledge and qualities would you include?

 Internet Sites ──────────────────────────────

For more information, visit the following Internet sites. Remember that Internet addresses can change without notice. If the site is no longer there, you can use a search engine to look for additional sites.

Associations

AH&LA Educational Institute
www.ahlei.org

American Hotel & Lodging Association
www.ahla.com

Hospitality Financial & Technology
  Professionals
www.hftp.org

International Federation for IT and
  Travel & Tourism
www.ifitt.org

International Hotel & Restaurant
  Association
www.ih-ra.com

National Restaurant Association
www.restaurant.org

Chapter 13 Outline

The Mission of the Human Resources
   Division
Hiring the Best Employees
   Recruitment
   Selection
   Wages, Salaries, and Benefits
Retaining Employees
   The Turnover Problem
   Orientation
   Training and Development
   Career Development
   Employee Relations
   Relocation
   The Role of Discipline
Creating the Climate for Productivity
   Evaluating Employee Performance
Recordkeeping
Quality Assurance Programs
Human Resources Globally

Competencies

1. Describe the mission of the human resources division and how the division contributes to management functions within a hospitality organization. (pp. 283–284)

2. Describe the human resources division's responsibilities in relation to recruiting and selection processes. (pp. 285–290)

3. Describe the human resources division's responsibilities in relation to wage, salary, and benefits administration. (pp. 290–292)

4. Describe the problem of and costs associated with turnover. (pp. 292–294)

5. Identify components of a well-designed orientation program for newly hired employees. (pp. 294–295)

6. Describe the human resources division's responsibilities in relation to training and career development programs. (pp. 295–298)

7. Explain the role of the human resources division in employee relations, relocation, discipline, termination, and evaluation, and in recordkeeping and quality assurance. (pp. 298–301)

8. Identify issues and challenges facing the human resources divisions of global hospitality companies. (pp. 301–302)

13

The Human Resources Division

THE HUMAN RESOURCES FUNCTION is handled in a number of ways throughout the industry, often depending on the size of the property. Large operations and multi-unit companies, for example, may have a human resources division that coordinates recruitment, hiring, training, career development, and so forth. At other, smaller properties, the human resources division may have fewer staff members—sometimes only a human resources director—and more limited duties. At very small properties, the general manager or his or her designee typically undertakes all or most of the human resources functions.

Whether human resources activities are conducted by a single manager or an entire staff, most people would agree that the key to successful management in any hospitality operation—no matter how large or small—is the quality of its human resources. All of the activities discussed in this chapter, whether they are performed by a human resources division or by a variety of staff members in a number of departments, must be addressed if the operation is to succeed.

The human resources division must be aware of the important role it plays in the major management functions:

- Planning—Managers set the organization's long-range goals through planning. Planning procedures may include long-range strategic planning, regular operating procedures planning, and daily activities planning. The human resources division plays an advisory role in all phases of operations planning.

- Organizing—Organizing establishes the flow of authority and communication among employees. The human resources division helps maintain this flow. Organizing dictates the number of jobs and the tasks involved in those jobs needed to accomplish goals. The human resources division must be thoroughly familiar with the property's job needs in order to fill slots as they become available and to suggest new positions as the company expands.

- Coordinating—Coordinating brings individual and group goals together to meet the organization's objectives. The human resources division helps managers coordinate the type and the number of employees necessary to attain organizational goals.

- Directing—Directing involves a wide array of activities: motivating, training, overseeing, evaluating, and disciplining subordinates. The human resources division may handle all or some of these duties.

- Controlling—Controlling helps ensure that procedures are aligned with organizational objectives. Controlling requires performance standards, performance assessment, and a comparison between performance standards and actual performance to determine whether or not any corrective action is needed. All of these tasks are human resources functions.

- Evaluating—Evaluating determines whether the property's goals established in the planning process are met. Evaluation measures employee performance and training effectiveness and helps to establish new or revised organizational objectives. While employees are evaluated by their supervisors, the human resources division helps develop evaluation criteria and keeps records of employee evaluations.

In spite of its key role in the organization, however, the human resources division has only recently received the recognition and support from ownership and management it so richly deserves. Several developments have helped underscore the importance of the human resources division in recent years. These developments include the growth of individual properties and chain companies, the heightened importance and complexity of benefit-related issues, and the expansion of workers' compensation issues and costs. In the United States, issues involving illegal immigration and validity of employment have skyrocketed in importance in recent years. Establishing proof of legal residency for all employees is now an important function of the human resources department.

The Mission of the Human Resources Division

The mission of the human resources division, or those staff members involved in human resources functions, should be to:

- Attract, develop, train, and maintain qualified management and staff for the hospitality property.

- Minimize losses by reducing labor charges, liability, and employee turnover.

- Monitor the entire property to ensure that property policy and standards are met by each department head.

- Make sure the property complies with state and federal laws governing employment.

- Administer all aspects of employee benefit programs.

The old saying that "people make the difference" has never been truer than in today's competitive market. If a property wishes to employ the best possible staff, it must identify, screen, and select the best possible applicants. Staff planning and career management programs must be implemented. The property must constantly look to the future and, in so doing, show a continuing concern for employees, even though positions may be eliminated, combined, or otherwise changed as internal and external conditions warrant. The human resources division provides advice about these vital matters to help managers make the best decisions possible for the property.

Hiring the Best Employees

The success or failure of any operation relies on two basic factors: the operation's products and the people providing them. In the hospitality business, these elements are often one and the same. Without staff members who are skilled in serving guests, the hotel or restaurant can never succeed. Human resources management helps ensure quality control.

Recruitment

Hospitality executives agree that two of their toughest challenges are finding good property locations and recruiting good employees. Even during economic downturns and periods of high unemployment, recruitment remains a high priority in the industry.

Employers are finally showing some genuine creativity in developing new and improved means of finding people, hiring them, and keeping them on the payroll. To attract management and staff to the property, the human resources division continues traditional recruiting efforts such as advertising in newspapers and magazines, working with colleges and their placement offices, and using external employment agencies and/or in-house job-posting systems. New recruiting tools include brochures, tray liners, bag stuffers, table tents, signs, and banners, all detailing opportunities with the property and designed to attract good employees. Properties may also offer financial rewards to employees for referring people for jobs if the people are hired and stay with the property for a stipulated period of time. One program offers up to $500 to any non-profit organization that refers an employee who stays on the job for one year. Some properties methodically contact former employees who left voluntarily, in an attempt to attract some of them back to the property. Many hotels and restaurants have discovered that a location that is excellent for attracting guests is a very poor location for finding employees. As a result, some companies bus employees to work, at company expense, for distances of up to sixty miles. A few very innovative properties use their marketing departments in the recruitment process.

Enlightened properties are meeting the worker shortage challenge by providing improved working conditions, better training programs, and more appealing advancement opportunities. Indeed, the hospitality industry is truly selling careers, not just jobs. AH&LA's Educational Institute, for example, has a variety of programs outlining career opportunities in the lodging industry.

These approaches may not, in and of themselves, solve the industry's employee recruitment problem. Charles Bernstein, former editor of *Nation's Restaurant News*, advises managers that they can help alleviate the employment crisis by recognizing employee achievement.

Non-Traditional Employees. Entry-level positions in the hospitality industry have traditionally been filled by high school students seeking their first jobs and college students looking for a way to defray their educational expenses.[1] However, the pool of eighteen- to twenty-four-year-olds has been shrinking for years. To supplement this dwindling labor source, hospitality managers are now considering so-called non-traditional employees—older people, immigrants, disabled people, and others.

Recently, McDonald's devoted at least one national television commercial to the recruitment of older workers. Part-time employment may appeal to retirees for a number of reasons; relief from boredom or the need to augment Social Security or a pension are chief among these. Older workers forced into early retirement or laid off as a result of plant closings may also be willing to enter the work force again, providing they are taught the necessary new skills. Homemakers seeking part-time employment after raising families may also be attracted to jobs that used to be filled by younger people.

While U.S. immigration laws place certain restrictions on hiring immigrants, many are eligible and eager for work. Immigrants may have good job skills but little facility in speaking English. An entry-level position allows them a chance to gradually enter mainstream American life and to improve both language and employment skills on the job.

Physically disabled people have made great progress in the workplace in recent years. Entry-level employees who use wheelchairs have proven that they can handle clerical and desk jobs, answer telephones, and offer information to guests quite efficiently. Many hotels and restaurants already accommodate disabled guests with specially designed entrances and exits that could also be used by disabled workers.

Mentally disabled people have often found work in back-of-the-house areas in the hospitality industry, and they typically perform repetitive tasks more willingly and with lower turnover rates than average workers. As the labor pool of traditional workers dwindles, some properties are discovering that mentally disabled workers can perform front-of-the-house duties as well.

Selection

While department or division heads typically make the final selection of a potential employee, human resources staff must screen candidates to be sure they have the required job skills, knowledge, and attitude for serving guests. Without a human resources staff to help screen candidates, quick hiring—and quick firing—may occur, increasing turnover rates and hindering operational efficiency.

The best candidates are those who enjoy hospitality work because they will be more reliable, capable, and willing to make a long-term commitment to the property. To select the best employees, the human resources division must conduct interviews, administer tests, and ensure that laws affecting hiring procedures are followed.

Staffing Tools: Job Descriptions and Job Breakdowns. Before anyone can be hired to fill a position, the human resources division must know what skills and training the position requires.[2] Job descriptions and breakdowns thus become important tools for human resources staff.

A job description outlines specific information about the job, such as the duties, materials, and equipment necessary to perform those duties; how the job relates to other positions within the property; and working conditions. A sample job description for a barperson is shown in Exhibit 1.

A job breakdown is developed from a job list (see Exhibit 2). The job list enumerates the tasks involved in a particular job, and the job breakdown—too

Exhibit 1   Sample Job Description—Barperson

Job Summary:

Keeps bar supplied, maintains clean linens, and assists bartenders as much as possible.

Work Performed:

1. Carries supplies and equipment, such as liquors, fruit, ice, glasses, linen, and silverware from storeroom to the bar.
2. Slices and pits fruit.
3. Fills ice bins and crushes ice for frappés.
4. Washes fixtures, mops floors, and sweeps carpet in the bar area.
5. Washes and dries bar glasses and utensils.
6. Replaces empty beer kegs with full ones.
7. Helps in setting up service bar and portable bars for catered parties.
8. Carries debris to waste containers.
9. May mix simple drinks under the supervision of the bartender.

Equipment Used:

Hand truck	Furniture polish	Polishing cloths
Glass washer	Broom	Vacuum cleaner
Soap solution	Mop	Metal polish
Bar polish	Ice buckets	

Relation to Other Jobs:

Promotion from: Dishwasher, Yardperson
Promotion to: Cellarperson, Bartender, Server, Assistant Bartender
Transfer from and to: Busperson

Job Combination:

The duties of this job may be combined or included with those of Porter, Dishwasher, Bartender, Cellarperson.

Special Qualifications:

This is usually a beginning job in a club for which experience is not required.

long and involved to include here—outlines how each of those tasks should be performed.

Job descriptions and breakdowns usually include a summary of the employee's duties and responsibilities. They help the human resources staff explain to potential employees what the job entails, provide a basis for developing job performance standards, and play an important role in training later on.

Usually, job descriptions and breakdowns are generated in the department or division in which the job is performed. For example, the housekeeping department would write the job descriptions and breakdowns for its personnel. It is up to the human resources division to find candidates suitable for those positions.

Interviewing and Testing. Interviews are the core of the employee selection process. Human resources staff members may interview prospective employees initially.

Exhibit 2   Sample Job List—Morning Shift Room Attendant

Date: xx/xx/xx

JOB LIST

Position: Housekeeping Room Attendant

Tasks: Employee must be able to:

1. PARK in designated area.
2. WEAR proper uniform.
3. PUNCH in.
4. PICK up clipboard and keys.
5. MEET with supervisor.
6. OBTAIN supplies.
7. PLAN your work.
8. ENTER the room.
9. PREPARE the room.
10. MAKE the beds.
11. GATHER cleaning supplies.
12. CLEAN the bathroom.
13. DUST the room.
14. CHECK/REPLACE paper supplies and amenities.
15. CLEAN windows.
16. INSPECT your work.
17. VACUUM the room.
18. LOCK the door and mark your report.
19. TAKE breaks at designated times.
20. RETURN and restock cart.
21. RETURN to housekeeping with clipboard and keys.
22. PUNCH out.

A second, follow-up interview, again with a human resources staff member or a division or department manager, may also be conducted. In other instances, the division manager or general manager may do all the interviewing.

Generally, the interview should focus on work attitudes, skills, and employment history. In addition, interviewers should look for important personal qualities that mark the successful hospitality employee: an ability to get along with others, an ability to handle oneself with people, an interest in the property, and a desire to learn. Personal appearance and grooming are also important, especially for employees who will work in front-of-the-house areas.

It has often been stated that a smaller, well-trained, well-chosen staff will be more productive and efficient than a larger, less qualified group of employees. The hospitality industry is fast becoming the proving ground for that theory. Properties are becoming much more selective in their hiring procedures even as the labor pool shrinks. More and more job candidates are being tested before or during the interviewing process. It would appear that properties know their new employees will have to be thoroughly trained and so are seeking employees who can absorb the training and achieve a high level of performance quickly.

In addition to skills examinations, such tests as the Human Factors Personnel Selection Inventory and the Employee Attitude Inventory can help screen out candidates with undesirable traits such as dishonesty, violence, and drug abuse. These tests can also be used to measure burnout and dissatisfaction levels.

Some hospitality operations also use computers to help interviewers screen candidates. Prospective employees are asked to respond to computer-generated questions before being interviewed, and the responses help human resources personnel screen candidates.

Employment Laws. Federal and state legislation such as affirmative action programs and fair labor laws have changed the way staff are recruited and selected.

The Civil Rights Act of 1964 as amended in 1972 has done much to increase the importance of the human resources division in the hospitality industry. Among many things, this law requires employers to make judgments about a job candidate or employee based only on business necessity. To begin with, the human resources division needs to make sure that all actions affecting employees are based on business necessity or **bona fide occupational qualifications (BFOQ)**. The human resources division must make line managers aware of their responsibilities to obey all applicable federal and state laws affecting training, promotion, and transfer. If an employee files charges alleging discrimination, the human resources division investigates each allegation, determines its merit, informs managers whether there is just cause for the claim, and provides necessary documentation.

The Immigration Reform and Control Act of 1986 requires employers to make certain that no undocumented workers are hired and provides stiff penalties for violation of the law.

One of the most comprehensive employment laws is the Americans with Disabilities Act (the ADA), which went into full effect in 1992 and was amended and expanded in 2008. Title I of the ADA deals with the employee, while Title III deals with physical facilities.

Title I makes it illegal to discriminate against a qualified disabled person in the job application process and in the hiring, promoting, and discharging of employees. The ADA does not require employers to hire unqualified disabled people, but does require the employer to make some reasonable changes to accommodate an otherwise qualified disabled person in the workplace. The definition of "disabled" is broad and includes people with dyslexia, the AIDS virus, head trauma, and arthritis. Also included are recovering alcoholics, although employees can be disciplined or fired if drinking affects their job performance. People with disabilities can now sue businesses for job discrimination. Basically, the ADA is designed to encourage employers to consider qualified disabled people for jobs.

Title III details the requirements for physical access to the workplace and to public accommodations. Hotels and restaurants are directly affected, and many existing operations have been required to make "reasonable physical changes" to comply with the law. All new construction must comply 100 percent. Some of the areas of concern are the number of parking spaces, accessibility of ramps, the widening of doors to accommodate wheelchairs, special provisions in bathrooms, the change from doorknobs to levers, and the size of bathrooms.

Other laws that affect the hospitality industry include various antidiscrimination statutes, the Fair Labor Standards Act, the National Labor Relations Act, the Equal Pay Act, and more. All of these laws regulate what can and cannot be done to and with an employee. The human resources division helps to keep the property from violating these laws.

Exhibit 3 offers a fifteen-point quiz about the Equal Employment Opportunities Act and indicates some of the matters human resources staff must consider when hiring new employees.

Wages, Salaries, and Benefits

Wages, salaries, and benefits concern everyone. The human resources division must help provide consistency and continuity in wage and salary administration programs, not only because state and federal laws require it, but also because it makes good business sense. In addition, the human resources division must ensure that pay complies with the federal Fair Labor Standards Act, which identifies exempt and non-exempt employees. If employees are eligible for raises on their employment anniversary date, the human resources division identifies those employees and makes recommendations to the proper managers.

As a result of the shrinking labor pool, properties are emphasizing the need to develop new, high-profile compensation and benefit programs designed to make jobs more attractive and to keep employees on the payroll.

Employees in many hospitality operations are not unionized. Human resources staff in a non-union property must help ensure that property pay rates and benefits are comparable to those in unionized operations. The property must make sure it complies with federal law, that no one is paid less than the applicable minimum wage, and that eligible individuals receive overtime. Human resources staff members are expected to conduct periodic wage and benefit competition surveys to ensure that wages for each position match up. Miscellaneous concerns such as meals, lodging, and uniforms are often addressed by the human resources division.

Employees are very concerned about the **fringe benefits** offered by their property. Human resources staff members also monitor the benefits program to see that it is competitive within the local industry and that it meets the needs of employees. Today, benefits range from medical, dental, and disability insurance to leaves of absence and wage-related benefits such as holidays, sick leave, and vacation leave.

Another addition to the list of benefits provided by some hospitality industry properties is the 401(k) retirement benefit vehicle. It wasn't so many years ago that retirement benefits were rare at the executive/managerial level and just about non-existent at other employment levels. The 401(k), widely used in other industries, has gained ground in the hospitality industry as a means of providing retirement benefits. Today most management companies and even a number of independent hotels offer 401(k) plans.

Exhibit 3   Equal Employment Opportunities Act Test

Instructions: Circle "T" for "True" or "F" for "False." For either true or false, depending on the circumstances, draw a circle between the "T" and the "F."

1. Administering general aptitude tests prior to hiring is an acceptable procedure.   T F

2. Requesting an arrest record on an application form is not permitted.   T F

3. An employer may refuse to hire an individual on the grounds that he or she is not a U.S. citizen.   T F

4. An employer must accommodate the religious needs of his or her employees with regard to the Sabbath.   T F

5. An employer may refuse to hire a woman because the job is "too strenuous" for her.   T F

6. A restaurant operator may refuse to hire waitresses because management assumes that customers prefer waiters.   T F

7. If supervisory training is made available to members of one sex, it must be made available to members of the other.   T F

8. If a job requires lifting of more than sixty pounds, it is safe to confine recruiting to men only.   T F

9. It is legal to have a policy to require a woman to start maternity leave two months before delivery.   T F

10. If a group of men paid $5.00 an hour is performing the same work as a group of women whose pay rate is $4.50, the men's pay must be reduced to $4.50.   T F

11. A pay differential between older (40–65) workers and younger ones is permitted on the assumption that older workers as a group are less productive.   T F

12. Help-wanted ads may be placed in classified columns headed "Male" and "Female."   T F

13. Asking for photographs from job applicants before employment does not in itself violate the law.   T F

14. A company may have a policy of not hiring females with pre-school children. T F

15. It is unlawful to mention race or religion on an application form.   T F

KEY: 1-T or F. (The answer is generally false; however, it may be true if the test is validated.) 2-T. 3-F. 4-T or F. (This answer is generally true; it is false, however, if the employee's work cannot be done by another employee of substantially similar qualifications during his or her absence on the Sabbath. The employer has the burden of proving that undue hardship would result from accommodating the employee's religious needs.) 5-F. 6-F. 7-T. 8-F. 9-F. 10-F. (The women's pay must be raised to $5.00 if they perform with equal skill, effort, and responsibility and the jobs are performed under the same working conditions.) 11-F. 12-T or F. (The answer is generally false; it is true, however, if sex is a BFOQ [bona fide occupational qualification].) 13-F. 14-F. 15-T.

Compensation and Benefits Laws. All phases of the benefits program must be controlled by the human resources division to ensure that employees are eligible for the benefits they receive, that laws are obeyed, and that accurate records are maintained. Unemployment compensation is provided in most states to protect individuals who have lost their jobs through no fault of their own. State laws provide for a percentage of salary to be paid to these individuals while they are unemployed. The human resources division plays an integral twofold role in this system: (a) it provides the state with background information required to establish the candidate's eligibility for compensation, and (b) it protects the property against erroneous claims.

Workers' compensation programs may also be available to provide an income for employees who are injured on the job. The human resources division monitors this program both to benefit the employee and to help protect the property from fraudulent or erroneous claims. The condition of the employee should be monitored to permit him or her to return to work as soon as possible and to reduce the amount of lost productivity due to a work-related injury. Human resources officials in some properties are responsible for or share responsibility with security personnel for providing periodic reviews of the property in order to maintain a safe environment for guests and employees.

Compensation and benefits laws greatly affect lodging and food service operations. Most important are the Consolidated Omnibus Budget Reconciliation Act (COBRA), the Tax Reform Act of 1986 (TRA 86), and the Family and Medical Leave Act of 1993 (FMLA). COBRA legislation requires that employers allow employees to stay in the medical coverage program (at the employee's expense) for up to thirty-six months after termination. TRA 86 establishes very stringent nondiscrimination rules that regulate eligibility for medical and life insurance.

The FMLA covers any private-sector employer of fifty or more employees during each working day of twenty or more workweeks in either the current or previous calendar year.[3] An employee is eligible for leave and related benefits if he or she has been employed by a covered employer for at least one year and worked 1,250 hours for that employer in the previous year. Not eligible for coverage in some cases are employees who earn among the highest 10 percent of salaries paid by the company.

Covered employers must let eligible employees take unpaid leaves of absence or a series of leaves totaling twelve weeks to care for a newborn, newly adopted, or newly placed foster child or because of a serious health condition of the employee or the employee's spouse, child, or parent. These leaves can be taken in any twelve-month period. Employers may require employees to use their paid vacation, personal, or sick leave as part of the twelve-week period.

During a leave, the employer must maintain an employee's health insurance coverage. When the leave ends, the employee is entitled to return to his or her old job or to a similar one, without losing any benefits accrued before the leave began. The FMLA does not require accrual of benefits during the leave.

Retaining Employees

Reducing turnover by retaining good employees has been one of the major concerns of the hospitality industry for years and will continue to be important as the labor pool of traditional employees shrinks. Good orientation, training, and career development programs and effective employee relations can help keep good employees at the property. In addition, the human resources division can help smooth relocation of employees and ensure that the property has a fair and equitable disciplinary procedure.

The Turnover Problem

The philosophy of many managers has been: high employee turnover is characteristic of the food service and lodging industry, so accept it and learn to live with it. Fortunately, times and attitudes are changing. The new, more positive approach stresses that turnover can be reduced and that the potential savings in this area could represent big profits. Exhibit 4 indicates some of the cost considerations in hiring and training.

Exhibit 4   Cost Factors in Hiring and Training

Selection and Placement:

Advertising for new employees
Employment agency fees
Brochures, booklets, exhibits
Prizes and awards to employees for encouraging their friends and neighbors to apply for resort jobs
Public relations activities that aid recruiting
Application blanks, printing and processing
Interviewing, screening, and final interview
Medical exams
Reference checking
Testing
Travel expenses of candidates for interviews

On-the-Job Costs:

Setting up payroll records, completing forms, etc.
Identification badges
Orientation
Job training
Increased cost of productivity
Increased cost of supervision
Increased frequency of accidents
Higher cost of damage to equipment, spoilage, errors, etc.

Separation Costs:

Exit interviews
Severance pay
Additional Social Security and unemployment insurance costs
Clerical costs of separation forms

Source: Chuck Yim Gee, *World of Resorts: From Development to Management*, 3d ed. (Lansing, Mich.: American Hotel & Lodging Educational Institute, 2010), p. 251.

As noted previously, human resources staff must provide turnover information to managers and advise them about the extent and potential causes of the
problem. Exit interviews provide an excellent means of identifying problems that
may contribute to high turnover rates. Progressive management also relies on the
human resources staff for advice on developing policies and practices that will
enhance employee morale and productivity while reducing turnover.

Turnover figures for the industry are not entirely reliable, but they provide a
reasonably clear picture of the size of the problem. It is not unusual to find turnover rates above 200 percent and as high as 400 percent for some job categories.
One company in the fast-food industry experienced these turnover rates recently:

- Hourly restaurant personnel—190 percent

- Hourly office/clerical personnel—63 percent

- Restaurant management personnel—32 percent

This company is one of the most progressive in the industry and strongly emphasizes the human resources function.

If only mediocre or below-average workers created all the statistics, turnover
would be easier to accept. However, such is not the case. Good workers also quit,
and when they do so, they most often attribute their decision to limited opportunities for advancement. They also cite lack of recognition from management, dislike
of management, boredom, and inadequate salary and benefits.

While some degree of turnover is unavoidable and probably desirable, it is
nevertheless expensive. Using only actual out-of-pocket expenses to recruit, hire,
and train new employees, industry executives estimate that turnover costs $250
per person at the hourly level and $5,000–$6,000 per person at the managerial level.

While this turnover cost may not seem too high at first glance, its yearly drain
on a large food chain's profits can be dramatic. For example, suppose a chain with
900 units averages fifteen hourly workers and one manager per unit. According to
the turnover rates listed previously (190 percent for hourly workers and 32 percent
for managers), each unit would have to budget training for 28.5 hourly employees
and .32 managers each year. That amounts to $4,845 (28.5 × $170) for hourly workers and $1,280 (.32 × $4,000) for managers. These are not huge sums, of course, but
multiply those costs by 900 units (the total number in the chain), and they add up
to an expense of over $5.5 million.

During periods of economic stagnation and recession, turnover rates tend to
drop considerably because of the scarcity of good alternative jobs. In such times,
human resources departments must not put too much credence in low turnover
rates in assessing work performance and job satisfaction.

Orientation

First impressions are often lasting impressions. The property's orientation program
(or lack of one) is one of the first impressions that employees receive of the property. All too often, employees begin work without being introduced to the property's goals or its complexities. It may be weeks or months before they learn this
information on their own. Such a situation should be avoided. New employees feel

a strong need for security and social acceptance. The human resources division can and should play a major role in welcoming new employees to the organization.

A properly developed orientation program will help foster motivation, promote early success, and prevent employee problems initially and in the future. The program may last one day or several and should be tailored to the property's needs. It may be conducted by human resources staff, the division or department manager, or the general manager—or all of these. Employees generally receive an employee handbook during their orientation. An orientation program might address such topics as:

- An introduction to the job and property including the history, organization, and goals of the property
- Wage concerns, including paydays, shift differentials, deductions, and frequency of pay reviews
- Benefits
- Working conditions, including hours, uniforms and identification cards (if required), parking, meals, and procedures for reporting absences
- Human relations on the job
- A tour of the property including introduction to all staff, location of smoking and break areas, staff restrooms, and cafeterias
- A review of fire and safety procedures, conduct regulations, and grievance procedures
- A question and answer period

Exhibit 5 shows a sample orientation activities checklist.

Essentially, an orientation program opens lines of communication among employees, their fellow workers, and managers. Often the human resources division will help keep those lines of communication open through in-house newsletters, bulletin boards, memos, and so forth.

Training and Development

Training and development takes many forms in the hospitality industry and is becoming increasingly sophisticated. Examples include career development programs, management training activities, training seminars for hourly employees, orientation programs at all organizational levels, career counseling, and miscellaneous workshops. The American Hotel & Lodging Educational Institute, for example, provides college and university textbooks, videos, and computer software covering every subject of importance to the hospitality industry. Other professional associations also provide training programs.

In spite of these efforts, training is probably the most misunderstood function within the industry. Until recently, employees were trained by following an experienced staff member and learning required knowledge and skills on the job. Today, training is much more complex; there are almost as many different ideas on management training as there are properties. Some properties rely solely on

Exhibit 5   Sample Orientation Activities Checklist

New Employee Orientation Checklist

Name of New Employee: _____   Position: _____

Department: _____   Supervisor: _____

Date Hired: _____

Instructions—Initial and date when each of the following is completed.

Part I—Introduction

- ☐ _____ Welcome to new position (give your name, find out what name the employee prefers to be called, etc.)
- ☐ _____ Tour of resort
- ☐ _____ Tour of department work area
- ☐ _____ Introduction to fellow employees
- ☐ _____ Introduction to trainer
- ☐ _____ Explanation of training program
- ☐ _____ Review of job description
- ☐ _____ Explanation of department

Part II—Discussion of Daily Procedures

- ☐ _____ Beginning/ending time of workshift
- ☐ _____ Break and meal periods
- ☐ _____ Uniforms (responsibilities for, cleanliness of, etc.)
- ☐ _____ Assignment of locker
- ☐ _____ Employee meals (if any)
- ☐ _____ Parking requirements
- ☐ _____ First aid and accident reporting procedures
- ☐ _____ Time clock or "sign-in log" requirements
- ☐ _____ Other (specify)
- ☐ _____

Part III—Information About Salary/Wages

- ☐ _____ Rate of pay
- ☐ _____ Deductions
- ☐ _____ Pay periods
- ☐ _____ Overtime policies
- ☐ _____ Complete all payroll withholding, insurance, and related forms
- ☐ _____ Other (specify)

Part IV—Review of Policies and Rules

- ☐ _____ Safety, fires, accidents
- ☐ _____ Maintenance and use of equipment
- ☐ _____ Punctuality
- ☐ _____ Absenteeism
- ☐ _____ Illness
- ☐ _____ Emergencies
- ☐ _____ Use of telephone
- ☐ _____ Leaving work station
- ☐ _____ Smoking/eating/drinking
- ☐ _____ Packages
- ☐ _____ Vacations
- ☐ _____ Other (specify)
- ☐ _____

on-the-job training (OJT) approaches and do not allow trainees any other time to develop or test their knowledge and skills. Other properties require individuals to complete a comprehensive training program before they are allowed to assume management functions. The best method probably lies somewhere between these extremes.

The influx of many more non-traditional workers requires that both skills and attitude training be more intense than in the past. Video is playing a major role in both training and development. Even the chains, with all their resources, are finding this new training a real challenge.

Management trainees are an investment in a property's future. Most large companies have management trainee programs. But it is risky to promote a trainee into a responsible position without properly monitoring his or her success during the training program. The human resources division monitors trainees to ensure that they are not just used as ready labor to fill staffing vacancies.

Skills training has always been important for hospitality employees, but in today's world it is doubly important. Throughout the hospitality industry, the buzzword is *service*. Advertising focuses on it, books are written about it, guests are demanding it, and property after property promises it. If the goal of providing superior service is to be achieved, the industry will need excellent personnel who are well trained. Providing these employees is the greatest challenge the human resources division faces.

One way to promote quality service is to use job breakdowns to develop performance standards. Job breakdowns, as noted previously, list all job tasks and how they should be performed. Once a list of tasks is completed, the department or division personnel can then develop *job performance standards* (a certain level of quality) for each of those tasks.

To be most effective, performance standards must be observable and measurable. For example, telling employees to be pleasant when greeting guests is too general a performance standard. A more measurable and observable standard would be to require that employees smile pleasantly when they greet guests. Once job performance standards are in place, they provide a basis and focus for employee training, which may be conducted by human resources staff or by division or department personnel. Exhibit 6 illustrates how training of new employees and retraining of experienced employees hinges on job breakdowns and performance standards. Job performance standards also become the basis of employee job performance evaluations, which will be discussed later in this chapter.

The human resources department must monitor all training to ensure that employees are capable and understand the job, and that the department has taken the time and effort to train them properly. Most hotels and restaurants realize that their success lies, in part, in making certain that all employees understand their roles in the organization. Therefore, they are investing in programs to train employees not only on what to do, but also on why to do it.

As the workforce of the hospitality industry includes increasing numbers of employees who are first- or second-generation immigrants—especially in the housekeeping and food and beverage departments, where often employees hail from a dozen or more countries—the importance of ensuring that all employees understand the cultural and religious differences of their fellow workers

Exhibit 6   Training with Job Breakdowns

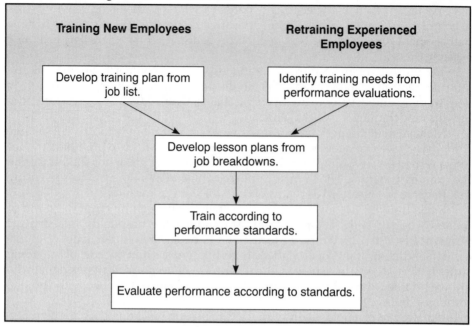

has become very important. The human resources department should conduct diversity training classes for all employees and their managers in order to ensure harmony and cooperation in the workplace.

Career Development

Properties realize that if they wish to attract and retain high-caliber employees, they must provide more than just paychecks and benefits. They must provide advancement and/or skills development programs that will enable employees to advance within the company. Career development programs are becoming more popular within the industry, and the human resources division helps develop and monitor these programs.

There are so many opportunities for success in the hospitality industry that choosing the best course of action is often confusing to both management and employees. The human resources staff can help by counseling employees and providing them with information that will enable them to make decisions about their future.

Employee Relations

Employee relations is a very broad subject, covering everything from employee contests to proper disciplinary action to assisting an employee who has had a tragedy in the family. Staff members in the human resources division interact with and represent all levels of management and non-management staff. Employees must have ready access to the human resources division and feel free to voice their concerns and opinions. Frequently, there is a direct correlation between the success of the hotel or restaurant and the attitude of the employees toward the property. If the human resources director understands the property's goals, the division will be a key element in the success of the hospitality operation. The human resources division can help foster mutual respect between employees and managers, which allows everyone to be proud of his or her association with the organization.

It has been said that 80 percent of one's problems lie in 20 percent of one's misunderstandings, and this is very true in the hospitality industry. The human resources division must represent management to the employees, but it must also communicate information upward to management and laterally to all other divisions. At unionized properties, the **grievance process** is a vital area of communications. It is extremely important to settle a grievance as quickly as possible and at the lowest level in the organization. To accomplish this, the property needs an efficient, well-understood grievance procedure; the human resources director often creates, monitors, and supervises it. It should be noted that, while grievance procedures are emphasized in union operations, a good grievance procedure is also a great asset in non-union operations.

Relocation

During the last thirty years, more and more hospitality managers in the United States have been relocated. Relocation is on the rise for two reasons. First, the tremendous growth of the hospitality industry is forcing the recruitment of managers from all possible sources (including other properties). Second, internal growth has created the need to transfer and relocate management personnel within company operations. The human resources division has become largely responsible for relocating and transferring employees once the decision to do so has been made. Human resources staff members help develop relocation policies and explain those policies to individuals facing relocation. The human resources director should be able to handle problems caused by relocation, such as those concerning the timing of the move and the starting date of the affected employee. Many human resources divisions supply new managers and their families with detailed information about the company, property, and geographical area to which they are being assigned.

The Role of Discipline

Disciplinary action, although negative in its connotation, can have a very positive effect on an employee's performance if used properly. Disciplinary action should be used to modify inappropriate behavior. Under no circumstances should it be used merely as revenge against an employee. The human resources division itself does not discipline employees. It can, however, act as the conscience of the property, to ensure that all employees are disciplined equally and fairly. This concern has become even more important in recent years. Employers who use disciplinary action unequally may be subject to grievances or even to a charge of unfair labor practices. All disciplinary procedures should be submitted in writing and a progressive disciplinary program followed.

Termination. When disciplinary action fails to correct undesirable behavior, it may become necessary to terminate employment. Recent labor laws have focused on termination of employees because, over the years, many businesses (including some hotels and restaurants) fired employees indiscriminately based on personality, background, and appearance, but not necessarily on business necessity. In today's labor market, a property can lose a great deal of money because of lawsuits, attorney's fees, and/or lost time spent in dealing with improperly handled termination matters. An effective human resources division can save the property thousands of dollars by helping to ensure that employees leave the property voluntarily or are terminated with just cause.

Creating the Climate for Productivity

Management has addressed the 1990s decline in productivity, and positive results have been achieved. Now, early in the twenty-first century, industry breakeven points have become easier to achieve. The human resources division must continue to nurture a climate that maintains the current productivity figures and even encourages additional increases.

Evaluating Employee Performance

Employee performance evaluations or performance reviews, as they are sometimes called, can help increase productivity by drawing out the untapped potential of all employees. To be most effective in realizing that potential, however, the evaluation must help motivate the employee to do better. One way to do so is by offering employees information about which tasks they perform well and which tasks they need to work on.

Job breakdowns and performance standards, as discussed previously, can provide this kind of specific information during employee performance evaluations. Using a point system—for example, three points for excellent work, two points for adequate performance, and one point for those areas that need improvement—managers can rate employees on each task they perform. The job performance standards will provide the criteria for determining how well the employee performs any given task.

This kind of evaluation system allows an employee to identify which tasks he or she needs to do better and, more important, indicates *how* to do those tasks more efficiently. By identifying tasks that the employee does well, the system also prevents the evaluation from becoming wholly negative, which might discourage the employee.

Recordkeeping

In addition to all of a human resources division's other duties, recordkeeping is an extremely important function. State laws require employers to maintain accurate and timely personnel records regarding, among other things, participation in benefit programs, amount of reported tips, accident/safety matters, grievances, withholding taxes, and more. Computerized recordkeeping systems are being used more frequently, requiring human resources staff to develop ways to use the computer's capabilities to full advantage. One way is to store data from candidates and employees. This allows quick recall of information as needed. Labor turnover analysis is another prime concern for most properties, and the computer immediately makes available information that may help reveal why people are leaving an organization.

Quality Assurance Programs

One of the most significant management trends dating from the mid-1980s has been to introduce some form of quality assurance into the operation of hospitality properties. A major premise is to instill a sense of responsibility for job performance in every employee. Quality assurance seeks the maximum commitment of every employee to "take care of the customer" and empowers the employee to make decisions for the benefit of his or her customer. In simple terms, each employee understands exactly who his or her customer is. Employees who deal directly with guests know that the guests are their customers. But behind-the-scenes employees also learn that they have "customers." For example, the cook in the kitchen works for the server (the cook's customer), who in turn works for the restaurant guest. The houseperson delivering clean linens and supplies to guest-room floors has customers, too; the room attendants are his or her customers. Once employees understand these worker-customer relationships, they can then discuss how to best serve the customer.

Quality assurance programs simplify the organizational structure and eliminate layers of supervisory staff by taking decision-making to the lowest possible organizational level. Supervisors can concentrate on providing training and other resources to employees, thus ensuring that employees have the right tools to work effectively and serve customers. When employees feel direct responsibility for their efforts, job satisfaction increases.

Responsibility for administering the quality assurance program usually falls to the human resources division. As with many of the hotel's programs, the human resources division must receive full commitment to the program from all departments and all levels of the organization if the program is to succeed. Once assured of complete management commitment, employees can become decision-makers, and the program will more likely achieve the desired results.

Human Resources Globally

Hotel chains and companies are becoming international entities as they expand beyond their own national borders. Concurrently, the world's work force has become increasingly mobile. People from developing countries seek work in the industrialized areas of the world. In Europe, hotels have never employed as many people of different nationalities at one time as they do today. People from other continents have moved to Europe in record numbers. This influx has provoked profound changes socially, politically, and in the workplace. Multiculturalism is increasingly becoming the rule, not the exception. This presents new challenges to the human resources division, which is responsible for molding employees from a wide range of backgrounds into a cohesive and productive staff with a talent for service.

International chains face special problems in the human resources area. Each country into which an international chain expands has a different set of laws and regulations concerning work permits, health programs, wages, job security, and so on. The human resources division at chain headquarters bears the main burden during such periods of expansion, since it must be completely familiar with the laws and regulations of each new country. The director of human resources in each hotel will administer the human resources program, but will depend heavily on the region or chain headquarters for updates and new rules, regulations, and policies.

Earlier in the chapter, the duties and responsibilities of the human resources division in an American hotel were covered in considerable detail. Internationally, the duties and responsibilities are generally the same. Activities related to recruitment, selection, interviewing, wage and salary administration, compensation and benefits laws, training, quality assurance, turnover analysis and reduction, and employee relations are performed in hotels around the world. Techniques, laws, and wages and salaries will vary from region to region, but hotels the world over still strive to increase productivity and provide quality and service to their guests. Regardless of country, the importance of the human resources division is at an all-time high in the hospitality industry.

Endnotes

1. Parts of the discussion in this section are taken from Chuck Yim Gee, *World of Resorts: From Development to Management*, 3d ed. (Lansing, Mich.: American Hotel & Lodging Educational Institute, 2010), pp. 251–252.

2. Parts of the discussion in this section are taken from Stephen J. Shriver, *Managing Quality Services* (Lansing, Mich.: American Hotel & Lodging Educational Institute, 1988), pp. 277–278.

3. This discussion is based on Sean A. Mulloy and Mary C. Crotty, "Making Sense of Family Leave," *Lodging*, March 1993, pp. 13–16.

 ## Key Terms

bona fide occupational qualification (BFOQ)—A provision of the Civil Rights Act that requires employers to use business necessity as the standard in making judgments about job candidates.

fringe benefits—Employment benefits such as medical, dental, and disability insurance; holidays; sick leave; and vacation leave.

grievance process—Formal procedure that employees follow to voice complaints about job conditions or treatment by supervisors and/or co-workers.

? Review Questions

1. What is the mission of the human resources division?

2. What factors and events have led to the greatly increased importance of the human resources division?

3. Can hotels and restaurants hire non-traditional employees? If yes, in which departments? If no, why not?

4. What tools are used in the selection process? Describe them.

5. What effect has government legislation had on the recruitment and selection of employees?

6. What role does human resources play in the area of wages, salaries, and benefits?

7. In what ways does a safety program have both humanitarian and economic aspects?

8. Why is turnover so expensive? What approaches can hospitality employers take to reduce turnover?

9. What employment and benefits laws affect the hospitality industry? What effects do these laws have?

10. What role does the human resources division play in creating a climate conducive to productivity?

 ## Internet Sites

For more information, visit the following Internet sites. Remember that Internet addresses can change without notice. If the site is no longer there, you can use a search engine to look for additional sites.

Associations

AH&LA Educational Institute
www.ahlei.org

American Hotel & Lodging
  Association
www.ahla.com

Hospitality Financial & Technology
  Professionals
www.hftp.org

International Federation for IT and
  Travel & Tourism
www.ifitt.org

International Hotel & Restaurant
  Association
www.ih-ra.com

National Restaurant Association
www.restaurant.org

National Restaurant Association
  Educational Foundation
www.nraef.org

Society for Human Resource
  Management
www.shrm.org

Employment Laws and Applications

Americans with Disabilities Act
www.ada.gov

Job Accommodation Network
askjan.org/

Occupational Safety and Health
  Administration
www.osha.gov

Sexual Harassment Issues and Policy
www.eeoc.gov/policy/docs/
harassment.html

U.S. Department of Labor
www.dol.gov

Chapter 14 Outline

Security: A Constant Concern
Physical Security
    External Security
    Internal Security
Employee Practices and Procedures
    The Accounting Division
    The Human Resources Division
    The Engineering and Maintenance
        Division
    The Rooms Division
    The Food and Beverage Division
    The Marketing and Sales Division
The Guest's Role
Administrative Controls
    Inventory Control
    Key Control
    Other Control Considerations
Safety
    The Safety Committee
    Emergency Plans and Drills

Competencies

1. Identify the responsibilities of a security manager and the components of an effective security system. (pp. 307–308)

2. Describe external and internal components of physical security at hospitality operations. (pp. 308–311)

3. Identify special security responsibilities of major divisions within a hotel, and discuss the guest's role in security. (pp. 311–317)

4. Explain the use of such administrative controls as inventory, key, and other control measures. (pp. 317–319)

5. Describe the importance of safety, the role of a safety committee, and emergency plans and drills. (pp. 319–320)

14

The Security Division

IN THE HOSPITALITY INDUSTRY, change is the name of the game, and security is a prime illustration of that statement. For many years, the security function received little respect, attention, or funding. However, various events in the 1980s and 1990s, and especially the terrorist attacks of 9/11, changed this perception drastically.[1] Most hotel and restaurant executives today rank security with sales, profits, and service in its value to the property.

Even before 9/11, a number of changes on the American scene were causing hospitality managers to rethink the importance of the security division. A rising urban crime rate did not bypass the hospitality industry. As violent crime increased everywhere, incidents occurred in hotels and restaurants, receiving plenty of media play and affecting business as a result. Fire disasters in hotels in Las Vegas, Houston, Puerto Rico, and Westchester, Connecticut, received national attention and heightened guests' concerns about fire safety. An increasing number of court cases held bars liable for crimes committed by intoxicated patrons. White-collar and employee theft increased—not only in the hospitality industry, but in many other businesses as well. International terrorism both at home and abroad led to concerns about whether it was safe to travel.

As these and other security-related incidents occurred more frequently, Americans responded by becoming more security-conscious and demanding to know what hotels and restaurants were doing to protect their guests. More single women traveling alone demanded heightened protection of their accommodations. People became more likely to sue as a result of injuries—either real or imagined.

The *S* in security began to loom like a huge dollar sign in the minds of hotel and restaurant managers. Today, for example, meeting planners will not simply ask about alarms, systems, and procedures; they will expect to have the alarm system demonstrated and the emergency procedure manual reviewed before booking rooms. Several large companies even supply portable smoke detectors to their executives when they travel.

In the broadest sense, the aims of the security division are to protect the property's assets, and to protect guests, employees, and any personal property that is lawfully on the premises. Obviously, the protection of people is the division's highest priority.

Security: A Constant Concern

For the hospitality industry, maintaining security is an all-encompassing endeavor, not limited to the security division. Matters relating to the physical plant, staff,

307

and operations in general affect the protection of the property's assets and its guests and employees. Anything less than a property-wide view of security and the prompt resolution and disposition of security problems leads to inefficiency, needless expense, and great potential for harm to employer and guests.

The security division is an integral part of an operation. The security division should help prevent loss through patrols, parcel inspections, spot-checks of departing delivery trucks, security system monitoring, fire safety inspections, and so forth. Security staff should assist other departments in investigation, detection, and apprehension when such action is warranted by the circumstances.

The security manager is a full-fledged member of the management team and maintains close contact with all management staff. In addition to knowing about protection measures, the security manager should understand property operations, be profit-oriented, and use modern supervisory techniques. He or she should be familiar with all ordinances governing security, know how to deal with law-enforcement personnel, and be diplomatic and tactful in dealing with guests and employees.

The security manager should be watchful of fire safety, the threat of terrorism, the potential for prowlers and burglaries of guestrooms, prostitutes and confidence men operating on the premises, drunken or disruptive guests, and guests who steal or from whom things are stolen. Security personnel also investigate accidents for which the property may be liable. This important task helps determine the legitimacy of any accident claims. It also allows the division to take corrective action so similar accidents do not occur in the future.

The hospitality industry recognizes that good security not only protects the guest and the property; it also helps increase profits and improve operating efficiency for both hotels and restaurants. A sound, properly conceived security program concentrates on four interrelated areas to achieve the best security possible: (1) physical security, (2) employee practices and procedures, (3) administrative controls, and (4) safety. All security measures should be operationally and economically feasible. They must not harm good labor relations nor keep employees from performing their work efficiently. The number-one goal must be *preventing* security problems rather than detecting, apprehending, and prosecuting those responsible for them.

Physical Security

Physical security literally begins at the property line. It involves the protection of the building and grounds and the building's contents. It covers such diverse aspects as layout and design, lighting, alarms, closed-circuit television, and storage facilities.

External Security

A property located on a landscaped plot must consider installing **perimeter protection** and exterior lighting. The grounds must be protected against trespassers and vandals. If parking facilities are provided for guests, automobiles must be safe from theft and burglary. Outdoor swimming pools must be protected to prevent both vandalism and accidents.

The principal means of perimeter protection are fences, shrubbery, and alarms. As a practical matter, fences or shrubs of sufficient height and thickness are best suited to hotels and can even enhance the property's appearance. Swimming pools are best protected by fences with gates that are locked when the pools are closed. Both the grounds in general and parking areas in particular need to be well-lighted at night.

A property that occupies all or part of a city block is confronted with problems different from a property on a landscaped plot. The city, not the property, has control over after-hours exterior lighting. The doors leading from the sidewalk to the property constitute the property's perimeter protection. Local safety statutes or ordinances may require that a certain number of safety exits be available. Nonetheless, the fact that a door must be available does not mean that it cannot be locked and fitted with an alarm to prevent unwanted entry and exit.

Internal Security

Layout and Design. Inside the property, layout and design have important security implications. The locations of work areas—the front office cashier, the head cashier, the human resources office, the controller's office, the receiving dock, the various storerooms, lockers, and refrigerators, the employees' locker rooms, the timekeeper's office (where the employee time clock is kept), the executive offices, housekeeping, and the laundry—all will affect security efforts. In hotels, the design of the lobby, the front desk, the space in which safe deposit boxes are located, and the timekeeper's office all affect physical security. So does the basic design of the guest floors in relation to the hotel's restaurants and bars.

Alarms are part of security. Until relatively recently, a large number of hotels and restaurants had no robbery or burglar alarms. Consequently, areas in which substantial sums of money were handled or in which guests' valuables were kept were extremely vulnerable. In motels, a large number of television sets were stolen because alarms were not used.

Virtually all properties today have fire alarms, but not all alarms are audible throughout the building. Even with the finest alarm system available, the property needs various emergency plans and a staff trained to carry them out. These plans should cover such things as fires, riots, terrorist attacks, and natural disasters such as hurricanes and tornadoes. If the alarm sounds, guests need instructions and reassurance to prevent panic. Management should disseminate the emergency plans to all staff members and periodically conduct emergency drills. The safety, even the survival, of both guests and employees depends greatly on how well the staff carries out the emergency plan.

Communications Systems. Effective security often requires quick action. Alarms indicate that some emergency—a fire, for example—is in progress. Many properties, however, augment their alarms with communications systems. These may be pagers, beepers, two-way radios, and so forth. Such devices allow personnel in any area of the property to contact security staff quickly.

Closed-Circuit Television and Cameras. Hotels and restaurants are considered private property but are open to the public. Because of the property's public nature,

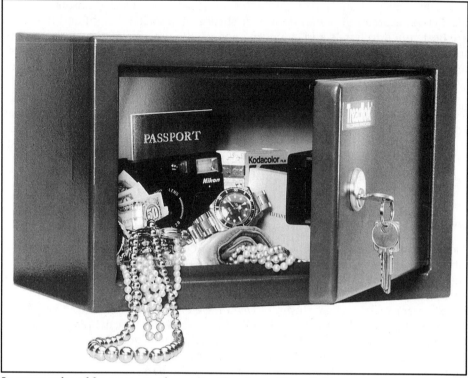

In-room safes add a measure of security. (Courtesy of Treadlok)

unwanted visitors—prostitutes, burglars, vagrants, muggers, and so forth—may be able to enter public areas rather freely. However, the property has a right and a duty to protect guests from unwanted visitors, especially in guestrooms and adjacent corridors. These areas are not considered public areas.

Closed-circuit television and time-lapse cameras can discourage undesirables from entering the hotel and can be particularly effective as protection for the front office cashier. The most effective deterrent, however, is a staff well-trained by security personnel to spot suspicious people or activities and to report them immediately.

Storage Facilities. The storage facilities for negotiables, valuables, and important records are a part of physical security. The mere presence of a lock does not necessarily mean that adequate protection is being provided. Safes and file cabinets provide varying degrees of protection against burglary, vandalism, and fire.

Many properties have safe deposit boxes or even in-room safes in which guests' valuables may be stored. Individual state laws determine the property's liability for the loss of valuables stored in such containers; usually this liability is limited, but managers should be aware of statutes in their own areas.

Managers should develop and monitor safe deposit procedures for their property and carefully train employees to comply with the procedures. Managers should require an immediate report of unusual incidents, and maintain accurate, up-to-date records.

Employee Practices and Procedures

The best security systems will not work without employee cooperation. Security tips that involve many different divisions of the property are listed in Exhibit 1. Each individual division, however, has special security responsibilities. The responsibilities of individual divisions in security functions are outlined in the following sections.

The Accounting Division

The accounting division plays an important role in a property's security program. The division's internal control program is extremely important. The purchasing function constitutes another key element.

Internal control begins with an organization plan that clearly establishes lines of communication and levels of authority and responsibility throughout the operation. A good organization plan separates recordkeeping of assets from the actual control of assets. Additionally, the responsibility for related transactions should be separated so the work of one person can verify that of another. Related transactions

Exhibit 1   Checklist of Procedures to Help Protect Hotel Guests

Using all or any combination of these procedures may be effective in protecting hotel guests:

- The front office clerk can provide information to guests about checking valuables in the hotel safe at time of registration. The clerk might tactfully say, "The hotel accepts responsibility only for guest valuables deposited in its office safe; please let us serve you in this way," or give the guest a card with a similar message printed on it.

- Bellpersons can give guests a card with applicable security information when luggage is taken to the room. They can also ensure that the lock and deadbolt system is working correctly (including those on connecting doors, if any).

- A tent card displaying a security message can be placed in a conspicuous location in the room.

- Hotels with turn-down service can use cards placed on pillows that read, "Please bolt your door before retiring to ensure your privacy and security."

- A decal can be placed on each room's hall door at eye level to remind guests about security concerns.

- Guests placing requests for wake-up calls can be reminded to bolt the door.

- Peepholes can be installed on room doors to allow guests to view visitors before opening the door.

should be separated so that one person receives the payments and another person posts the records.

Internal controls require forms and procedures that measure the efficiency and effectiveness of employees and provide accounting information that, when analyzed, will help identify problem areas. These controls must also be cost-effective.

Another element in a sound system of internal control is the effective selection, training, and supervision of personnel. The hospitality operation must have policies that define employee skill levels, education, and job responsibilities.

In addition to the checks and balances inherent in a well-designed system of paperwork controls (such as pre-numbered guest checks and sales tickets) and the correct use of cash registers, internal control includes the following areas:

- Comparative statistical analysis

- Planning and forecasting sales and the cost of goods sold

- Departmental budgeting controls

- Predetermined standards and evaluation reports

- Properly designed and secured storage areas

- A system for the continuous review and evaluation of the entire internal control system

Good purchasing systems have written procedures that are approved by management and adhered to by all those involved. It is also important to have purchase specifications covering at least the expensive and high-volume purchase items. A testing committee under the direction of management and supervised by the purchasing agent is another useful safeguard. Every price or transaction either should be verified in writing through the routine use of a system that secures competitive prices or should be the result of a system of negotiated prices.

All food purchases should be based on the food service operation's actual need, which is determined by menus, parties actually booked or expected, and records showing the number/amount of items normally consumed. Most good operations establish a minimum and a maximum stock level. Generally, no more than a ninety-day supply of anything is purchased without the approval of the general manager.

The operation should have a good internal control system run by an alert controller and an involved manager. When purchasers and suppliers know that they are being checked, they will do a better job than if there were no internal controls in place.

The Human Resources Division

Properly screened and oriented employees play an important role in maintaining a safe and secure property. The human resources staff usually has the first contact with potential employees and therefore plays a large role in the screening and orienting process.

State and federal privacy laws restrict the kinds of questions that interviewers can ask job candidates and the kind of screening checks they can conduct. It is important, then, that the human resources division develop hiring procedures with an attorney to avoid violations of these laws. Where lawful, the human resources division may consider such measures as:

- Criminal conviction checks

- Background checks through private investigators

- Submitting fingerprints to law enforcement agencies for checks

- Polygraph (lie detector) tests

- Honesty exams

- Credit checks

- **Bonding**

- Department of Motor Vehicles checks

In addition, employers sometimes (again, where lawful) state on the job application that falsifying information will result in immediate dismissal. They may also ask for the job candidate's authorization to review job performance records from former employers. In some regions, the state gambling commission or local unions set standards for job applicants and provide applicant certification.

While smaller properties may not be able to conduct extensive screening checks, operations of all sizes should have an application form. Information on the form should be verified. The form also provides the basis for the interview with potential employees. Human resources staff should note discrepancies between information obtained on the form and that gathered during the interview. Staff should also note unexplained gaps in an applicant's work record and try to have those gaps explained during the interview. Finally, staff should document the reason for rejecting a job candidate. Comments, however, should not be derogatory.

When applicants are hired, human resources personnel often ask for identification proving that employees are who they say they are. Such identification should be requested *only* after the employee has been hired, to avoid charges of age discrimination. The importance of only hiring carefully documented employees has been magnified in the post-9/11 world. It is now absolutely mandatory that employers use the strictest forms of verification and that prospective employees prove they are legally authorized to work in the United States. Hiring undocumented workers is a serious violation of current immigration laws and can result in serious penalties to the employer.

Human resources staff who train employees have an opportunity to stress the importance of everyone's security responsibility. New employees should be made thoroughly familiar with all security communications systems and emergency procedures.

The human resources division may be responsible for making sure that keys, uniforms, or any other property issued to employees are returned when the employees leave the property.

In recent years, employers in virtually all industries across the nation have been concerned about the possibility of employee alcohol and drug abuse. State and federal laws may restrict or prohibit certain procedures designed to uncover substance abuse (locker searches, for example). However, all properties should have a written policy regarding abuse and may consider obtaining legal counsel when such abuse is discovered.

The Engineering and Maintenance Division

The engineering and maintenance division should give high priority to maintaining and repairing security devices and systems. Specially colored work orders or "security priority" stamps can be used to highlight security-related maintenance and repairs. Copies of these work orders should be sent to the security division.

At some properties, engineering personnel may be called on in emergencies. In such cases, a radio system that can dispatch emergency messages to engineering staff right away is useful.

Engineering personnel also play an important part in **key control**. The division should develop and maintain good control procedures for guarding key blanks and key-making machines. Only those with proper authorization should have access to blanks and machines. Inventories of keys and blanks should be conducted periodically. Requests for new keys should come only from authorized personnel in writing. These requests should be kept on file.

Tools and other engineering equipment with home use or resale value should be issued only through a check-out procedure. Conducting occasional, unscheduled inventories of tools and equipment may help uncover problems.

The Rooms Division

Personnel in the rooms division play an important and varied role in security. For example, front desk personnel should never give room keys out on request without asking for identification and ensuring that the person making the request is the guest registered to that room. Front desk personnel are often the first to spot suspicious circumstances or guest activities and should be encouraged to report these situations to the security staff. In some cases, the front desk controls night-time access to the property. The front desk may become a command center in the event of an emergency such as a fire or flood, with the PBX operator facilitating emergency communications. The front desk also plays an important role in asset protection. Regular procedures for handling checks and credit cards should be developed to help the property reduce payment loss.

Uniformed service personnel are also involved in security. They may advise guests to lock valuables in the trunks of their cars when they check in. Car valets should make sure keys are protected. Door attendants should attach receipts to and move luggage and other articles to a secure area where guests can retrieve items. Bellpersons may instruct guests about security devices, fire escapes, emergency phone numbers, and so forth when they show guests to their rooms.

Housekeepers should work closely with security personnel to define their role in maintaining property security. For example, a procedure should be developed for housekeepers to report suspicious circumstances or guests to security personnel. The housekeeping department should maintain good key control. Housekeepers should be instructed never to leave keys on top of cleaning carts or in other places where they could be easily stolen. All properties should require that master keys be signed in and out and that all keys be locked up when not in use. Housekeepers should collect any keys left in guestrooms, secure them, and turn them in in a timely manner.

Housekeepers should not allow anyone to enter a room without showing his or her room key. Often properties require that housekeepers refer anyone requesting entrance to a room to the front desk, where proper identification can be verified.

Checking in-room security devices is another important job of housekeepers. Faulty deadbolt locks, window latches, fire alarms, and the like should be reported immediately.

Housekeeping staff also need to protect the property's supplies and cleaning equipment. Linens and other supplies should be kept in locked storage areas. Keys to these areas should be strictly controlled. A good inventory system that includes unannounced checks can help deter theft.

The Food and Beverage Division

The food and beverage division often implements procedures to guard against theft of food, beverages, and division equipment. Host bars for special functions, for example, pose special problems. The amount of alcohol must be measured exactly so that the guest's bill is accurate. For **cash bars**, some properties sell tickets that can be exchanged for drinks in order to verify the amount of alcohol consumed. Periodic checks by supervisors may also help ensure that alcohol consumption is properly monitored. A procedure for moving the alcohol from storage areas to the bar and back to storage should also be in place.

Food preparation can be monitored by numbered guest checks. Only food listed on the guest checks should be prepared. When checks are voided, they should be retained and the reason for voiding stated on the check. Using duplicate guest checks allows checks in the preparation area to be compared with checks collected at the cashier's area. Discrepancies can be noted and investigated.

A precheck register can also monitor food sales and preparation. Servers use the precheck register (which is like a cash register without a cash drawer) to identify their own orders by pressing a certain key. They then enter items guests wish to order. For example, if a guest orders spaghetti, a key labeled *spaghetti* is pushed and that item and its price automatically appears on the check. The precheck register tallies the total food sales made by a particular server, and this total can be compared with the totals on that server's guest checks. Discrepancies then become the server's responsibility.

Another security measure used in some food and beverage divisions is garbage raking. Garbage is stored in an area or container that can be raked. Raking can uncover utensils and equipment thrown away accidentally or intentionally placed in the garbage to be retrieved later.

The Marketing and Sales Division

The marketing and sales division keeps a close eye on guest concerns, including security and safety issues. Personnel in this division can pass along concerns to appropriate staff members so that the property can address them.

In addition, the public relations staff in the marketing and sales division plays an important role in maintaining the property's image in the event of an emergency or accident. Some properties develop a public relations manual. This manual, developed with legal counsel, offers guidelines for dealing with the media in case of a major incident.

The Guest's Role

Now that the employees' role in security has been outlined, a closer look at guest security considerations is in order. Guests may be victims or perpetrators of accidents or crimes. Whatever the case, the results can work against the property's best interest.

In addition to keeping guests safe for moral, ethical, and humane reasons, there is an economic reason: juries today often make huge awards to guests who are the victims of crimes or accidents. As a result, property liability insurance rates have skyrocketed.

Property owners and managers must be certain that every protective security device is in perfect working order and that staff has exercised reasonable care in protecting guests from any hazards to their safety and well-being. In the well-publicized Connie Francis case, for example, a faulty lock on a sliding glass door led to an award of nearly $1.5 million for the harm Ms. Francis suffered. Guests have been accidentally burned by flaming dishes at tableside; some of these guests have sued and won huge damages. As a result, many dining rooms have eliminated tableside flaming, and many lawyers strongly advise restaurants and hotels against the practice. Guests have also sued restaurants because they found some foreign substance in the food. Swimming pool diving boards are another potential source of costly lawsuits. As a result, most hotels have banned diving boards in all swimming pools on the advice of legal counsel.

Liability suits resulting from liquor sales are increasing and are among the most costly in the hospitality industry. States control the sale and consumption of alcoholic beverages, and laws therefore vary across the nation. However, there has been increased national concern over alcohol abuse. Accidents and deaths involving drunken drivers, and the efforts of Mothers Against Drunk Driving (MADD) and other organizations, have caused a majority of states to pass dram shop acts. These laws place liability for a drunken driver's actions on the establishment where the driver consumed the alcohol. As a result of awards in these cases, insurance has become either unobtainable or unaffordable for many restaurants and hotels. To promote the security of guests, a number of hospitality establishments ban happy hours, conduct alcohol awareness programs for staff, and support community campaigns urging responsible drinking.

Theft by hotel guests is a very serious problem. Guests steal for several reasons. Some consider themselves souvenir hunters, but they do not restrict stealing to keys or ashtrays. Others take things as a matter of convenience (for instance, a bath towel in which to wrap a wet bathing suit). Some steal for home use or for the purpose of resale and profit. Yet others, called *skips*, simply leave the property without paying. Hotels are particularly vulnerable to thefts because virtually everything found on the premises can be used in a private home. Many people are neither deterred nor embarrassed by a name on a towel or a logo on china, glass, or silverware. As a result, except for the professional thief who seeks a buyer for stolen wares, third parties are not involved, and detection and apprehension of thieves virtually never happens.

While some items in guestrooms may have to be written off as expendable, such measures as providing hangers that are not readily adaptable to home use, as well as plastic bags for wet bathing suits and dirty laundry, will help reduce losses at least partially chargeable to convenience. Proper orientation, alertness, and cooperation among front desk personnel, bellpersons, housekeepers, and security personnel can help reduce losses generated by professional thieves. Mechanically securing pictures and wall hangings and using electronic devices (such as alarms that indicate unauthorized unplugging) to protect televisions and radios are additional precautions.

Administrative Controls

Security control systems also play a role in a comprehensive security program. However, they must be viewed in their proper context. Controls will not necessarily prevent employee thefts; they will discourage some and make it easier to fix responsibility when losses do occur. Controls are necessary, but they cannot be so restrictive that, in monetary terms, the loss of efficiency exceeds the loss of assets.

Employee theft in retail business establishments in this country is considerably greater than most people realize and is a serious drain on a business's profitability. Employees need to clearly understand that a variety of activities can constitute stealing. For example, unauthorized use of washers and dryers for personal laundry is a form of stealing. So is punching a time card for a friend who arrives late, leaves early, or is absent. The housekeeper who removes hotel property from the premises and the worker who eats hotel restaurant food on the job in violation of property rules are guilty of theft. The reception agent who accepts a "gratuity" for making a room available is working against a hotel's best interests as surely as the purchasing agent or buyer who accepts kickbacks from vendors. Directly or indirectly, all of these factors will eventually show up as a reduction of profits.

Reliable estimates place the amount of employee theft at 2 percent of retail sales. Specific figures for the hospitality industry are not available, but applying the 2 percent figure to the industry overall results in an annual cost of billions of dollars. This figure may be exaggerated, but the point is clear: security measures to guard against employee theft need to be improved drastically.

The fast-food segment of the industry is especially vulnerable to employee theft because most sales are handled in cash, and, usually, more than one employee accepts cash and operates the register(s). Because of this cash on hand, late hours of operation, and a sometimes isolated location, fast-food corporations have established elaborate security procedures that have been fairly successful in reducing robbery losses. Every major fast-food corporation has a security department plus an internal audit department that devotes a portion of its time to security throughout the corporation.

Full-service restaurants and hotels have much less cash around than fast-food operations because of the widespread use of credit cards and traveler's checks, but they are not immune to the theft of cash by employees. Both restaurants and hotels face the problem of credit card fraud by guests or employees.

Inventory Control

One obvious form of control is the inventory, which should be taken regularly. When inventories are taken, they should be supervised by a representative of the controller's office. It is possible, though, that merely taking frequent inventories offers a false sense of security. Food and beverages provide an excellent illustration. Many operations take these inventories on a monthly basis. If a shortage occurs, management learns of it within a relatively short time; however, management does not necessarily learn the source of the problem—whether it is, for example, the result of collusion between the vendor's driver and the receiving clerk or an in-house theft.

Key Control

Inventories are not the only important controls. Sometimes, controls over hotel keys are lax—grand masters (keys that open all doors in the hotel) are issued to people on the basis of status rather than need; floor masters are made available where section masters would suffice; and far too many people can simply walk up to the reception desk, ask for a room key, and get it without question.

While these situations may be typical of some operations, many hotels now use electronic and other card key systems that provide greatly increased security for guests. Under one method, the guest registers and is given a plastic card the size of a credit card. Only one duplicate of the plastic card is made, which is kept by the front desk agent who inserts it into a master console. When the console receives the duplicate card, it "instructs" the lock on the guestroom door to accept only the identical card issued to the guest.

If a guestroom card is inserted into a guestroom slot for which it is not intended, a signal flashes in the control center to alert security personnel. The door will not unlock, and security personnel will be on the way to investigate. When the guest checks out, the lock combination is changed by memory circuit and new plastic cards with new combinations are issued to the next guest.

Electronic card key systems are among the fastest-growing technology-related amenities in the lodging industry. A number of companies manufacture these systems, and they are becoming more sophisticated each year. With the newer systems, an entire hotel can re-key its rooms in a couple of hours. Compared with manual re-keying, this system saves thousands of dollars in labor and materials costs annually, while providing greater guest security.

Other Control Considerations

The protection of front office, restaurant, and bar cash banks when not in use between shifts is important; it is equally important to fix responsibility when shortages occur. The control of cash register tapes is important to the hotel's security, since the tapes may provide evidence of fund tampering if any occurs. And beware of the cashier whose bank invariably balances to the penny.

Controls must be exercised over procedures as well as over assets. Bar stock should not be replenished on the basis of anything less than a written requisition submitted by the bar manager, and there should be a valid reason behind every food requisition signed by the executive chef. Controls must be considered for the protection of linens, housekeeping supplies, china, glassware, silverware, laundry supplies, tools, furniture and furnishings, office equipment, and even executive office telephones when direct long-distance dialing is available.

The hotelier and restaurateur must recognize the importance of preventive control. Catching the cook who steals food products is commendable. From a profit and loss point of view, however, it is more important to prevent the theft in the first place. If the key to a liquor storeroom has been misplaced or stolen, it is far better to have the engineering staff change the lock cylinder than to leave it alone in the hope of detecting and apprehending a thief.

Safety

Safety, as it affects the well-being of employees and guests, is an important part of security. Like other security considerations, safety is the responsibility of all employees. Many properties may want to encourage a team approach to safety by:

- Developing a system for instructing each new employee on the details of the job
- Fostering employee pride in performing jobs the right—and safe—way
- Discouraging employees from taking shortcuts that may shave time off certain jobs but result in safety risks
- Relating accidents and injuries to human error
- Instructing employees to ask questions to ascertain safe work procedures
- Encouraging employees to report safety hazards and to suggest safety innovations
- Stressing the importance of reporting all injuries, no matter how minor
- Checking from time to time to see that employees are working safely

The Safety Committee

Even small properties can involve employees more fully in safety concerns by forming a safety committee. The committee might consist only of managers and supervisors to begin with. Meetings (every month is usually sufficient) to discuss safety concerns should be well planned, and minutes should be taken. The committee may consider such things as accidents and hazards, unsafe work practices, and solutions to safety problems. Outside experts—insurance company safety engineers, local inspectors, fire department representatives, and so forth—may be called in to provide safety information. Committee members may also want to review films, posters, or other materials to help heighten employee safety awareness, or plan a property safety campaign. A safety self-inspection program could also be developed.

Emergency Plans and Drills

The specter of terrorism has changed the way many businesses throughout the world conduct their affairs. Prudent hotels for years have conducted periodic fire drills to teach employees (and guests, in some cases) the correct procedures to follow in the event of fire and related emergencies. Since the 9/11 terrorist attacks, many hotels have also established procedures for dealing with bomb threats and actual acts of sabotage and terrorism. Key employees in every department must know the exact procedures to follow to ensure the safety of all employees and guests. Hotels often stage emergency safety and fire drills in conjunction with local police and/or fire departments. In addition, specific written information should be provided in all guestrooms to tell guests what to do in various emergencies.

Endnote

1. Some of the material in this chapter is adapted from *Security and Loss Prevention Management*, 2nd ed., by Raymond C. Ellis, Jr., and David M. Stipanuk (Lansing, Mich.: American Hotel & Lodging Educational Institute, 1999). For a more detailed discussion of security issues and the law, readers may consult Jack P. Jefferies and Banks Brown, *Understanding Hospitality Law*, 5th ed. (Lansing, Mich.: American Hotel & Lodging Educational Institute, 2010).

Key Terms

bonding—An insurance agreement in which an agency guarantees payment to an employer in the event of a financial loss due to the actions of an employee.

cash bar—A beverage setup at a special function (such as a banquet) where guests pay for their own beverages.

key control—A security system involving procedures that restrict keys to guestrooms, work areas, and storage areas to authorized personnel and/or guests.

perimeter protection—Fences, shrubbery, alarms, lighting, and other particulars that help guard a property surrounded by a landscaped area. For a property that occupies all or part of a city block, the doors leading from the sidewalk to the property constitute the property's perimeter protection.

Review Questions

1. What are some of the factors that led to the greatly increased importance of the hotel security division?

2. What measures can a hotel take to help ensure its internal security?

3. How can the human resources division assist the security division?

4. In what ways does the engineering division need to cooperate with the security division?

5. Why, in addition to moral, ethical, and humane reasons, is there a vital economic reason to keep guests safe?

6. Why is key control so vital in today's hotels? Describe methods used to control keys.

7. Is employee theft a problem in the hospitality industry? If so, what areas of the industry are most vulnerable?

8. In what ways does the food and beverage division assist in the security function?

9. In what ways is guest theft a problem in hotels and motels?

10. How do security concerns for a suburban hotel differ from those of a center-city hotel?

Internet Sites

For more information, visit the following Internet sites. Remember that Internet addresses can change without notice. If the site is no longer there, you can use a search engine to look for additional sites.

Associations

AH&LA Educational Institute
www.ahlei.org

American Hotel & Lodging Association
www.ahla.com

Hospitality Financial & Technology
  Professionals
www.hftp.org

International Federation for IT and
  Travel & Tourism
www.ifitt.org

International Hotel & Restaurant
  Association
www.ih-ra.com

National Restaurant Association
www.restaurant.org

Society for Human Resource
  Management
www.shrm.org

Appendix I

Periodicals

Lodging and food service trade journals offer the latest information and advice about the hospitality industry. Professionals in the hospitality field rely, in part, on trade publications to help them stay current in this fast-paced industry. These publications also make important reading for hospitality industry students who want to keep up with the latest trends and changes, especially in the job market. Most schools offering hospitality management courses subscribe to some or all of the following publications (many are available online as well). Students should ask the librarian at their school for a list of current periodicals. The following list is merely a sampling of the resources available:

Annals of Tourism Research (quarterly)
Beverage World (monthly)
Bon Appétit (monthly)
Club Management (six times a year)
Cornell Hotel and Restaurant Administration Quarterly
Food Management (monthly)
Food Technology (monthly)
Foodservice and Hospitality (monthly)
Hospitality Review (twice a year)
    Florida International University
Hotel Management (fifteen times a year)
Hotelier (eight times a year)
Hotels (monthly)
International Journal of Hospitality Management (quarterly)
Journal of Hospitality & Tourism Research (quarterly)
    Council on Hotel, Restaurant, and Institutional Education
Journal of Travel Research (quarterly)
    University of Colorado
Lodging (monthly)
Nation's Restaurant News (twenty-six times a year)
Restaurant Business (monthly)
Restaurant Hospitality (monthly)
Sales & Marketing Management (six times a year)
Travel Weekly

Appendix II

Major Hotel Chains with Their Brands

Accor

Adiago Access
Adiago
Grand Mercure
Hotel F1
Hotel Formule 1
Ibis
Ibis Budget
Ibis Styles
Mercure
MGallery
Novotel
Pullman
Sofitel
Suite Novotel
Thalassa Sea & Spa

Carlson Hotels Worldwide

Country Inns & Suites By Carlson
Hotel Missoni
Park Inn by Radisson
Park Plaza
Radisson
Radisson Blu

Choice Hotels International

Ascend Hotel Collection
Cambria Suites
Clarion
Comfort Inn
Comfort Suites
Econo Lodge
MainStay Suites
Quality
Rodeway Inn
Sleep Inn
Suburban Extended Stay Hotel

Global Hyatt Corporation

Andaz
Grand Hyatt
Hyatt

Hyatt House
Hyatt Place
Hyatt Regency
Hyatt Residence Club
Park Hyatt

Hilton Hospitality, Inc.

Conrad Hotels and Suites
DoubleTree
Embassy Suites Hotels
Hampton
Hilton Garden Inn
Hilton Grand Vacations
Hilton Hotels & Resorts
Homewood Suites
Home 2 Suites
Waldorf Astoria

InterContinental Hotels Group

Candlewood Suites
Crowne Plaza Hotels & Resorts
Holiday Inn Express
Holiday Inn Hotels & Resorts
Hotel Indigo
InterContinental Hotels and Resorts
Staybridge Suites

Marriott International

AC Hotels
Autograph Collection
Bulgari Hotels and Resorts
Courtyard by Marriott
Edition
Execustay
Fairfield Inn & Suites
Gaylord Hotels
Grand Residences by Marriott
J.W. Marriott Hotels & Resorts
Marriott Conference Centers
Marriott Executive Apartments
Marriott Vacation Club
Residence Inn by Marriott
The Ritz-Carlton

(continued)

Major Hotel Chains with Their Brands *(continued)*

The Ritz-Carlton Destination Suites
SpringHill Suites by Marriott
TownePlace Suites by Marriott

Starwood Hotels & Resorts Worldwide
aloft Hotels
element by Westin
Four Points by Sheraton
The Luxury Collection
Le Méridien
St. Regis
Sheraton Hotels & Resorts
Starwood Vacation Ownership
W Hotels Worldwide
Westin Hotels & Resorts

Wyndham International
AmeriHost Inn
Baymont Inn & Suites
Cuendet by Wyndham

Days Inn
English Country Cottages
Hawthorn Suites
Howard Johnson
Knights Inn
Landal GreenParks
Microtel Inns & Suites
Novasol
Ramada Worldwide
Super 8
Travelodge
The Registry Collection
Wingate by Wyndham
WorldMark by Wyndham
Wyndham Hotels and Resorts
Wyndham Vacation Resorts

Source: Chain websites

Index